Documents in the History of
American Philosophy

DOCUMENTS IN THE HISTORY OF AMERICAN PHILOSOPHY

From Jonathan Edwards to John Dewey

EDITED WITH COMMENTARY
BY
MORTON WHITE

New York
OXFORD UNIVERSITY PRESS
London 1972 Toronto

PREFACE

The documents gathered together in this volume form a useful companion to my *Science and Sentiment in America: Philosophical Thought from Jonathan Edwards to John Dewey*, but they may be read profitably by those who have not examined that work. Although my selections have been governed in great measure by my interest in American philosophical views of the nature of science and scientific method, the present volume will, I believe, provide the reader with an introduction to the general history of American philosophy from Edwards to Dewey if only because preoccupation with the nature of knowledge, and in particular with scientific knowledge, has been as central in American philosophical thought as it has been in all of Western philosophy. Because American thinkers have shared this concern with their European masters and contemporaries, I have found it useful to include selections from foreign writers like Locke, Coleridge, and Spencer, who have exerted a profound influence on American thought. And because I have been mainly interested in showing how conceptions of and attitudes toward science have affected American views of other aspects of civilization, I have included passages in which American philosophers discuss the impact of science on matters like religion, morals, law, and politics. For this reason I hope that this volume, like its companion, will be of use to philosophers and to historians of American life as a whole.

Because my *Science and Sentiment in America* is available to those readers who may wish to familiarize themselves with the details of my philosophical and historical views, I shall do no more here than present a brief account of how I regard the development from Edwards to Dewey while focusing on the impact that conceptions of scientific knowledge have had on American philosophical thought.

The first philosopher represented by selected writings is John Locke, who probably exerted more influence on early American thought than any other single man. I try to illustrate two opposing strains in his philosophy, his empiricism and his rationalism, especially as they affect his views of science, religion, morals, and law—the areas of most concern to the practically oriented American philosophers of the eighteenth century. Jonathan Edwards and James Wilson here represent that century—the former being its most distinguished philosopher of religion and the latter its most systematic philosopher of law. Edwards developed a Calvinistic philosophy of religion in which he tried to circumvent Locke's empiricism of the five senses by asserting the existence of a mystical Sense of the Heart; and Wilson revised Locke's doctrine of Natural Law so as to give greater importance to moral sentiment than the rationalistic Locke did.

After Part 1 on Locke and Part 2 on the eighteenth century, the next part is on Transcendentalism, which continues the revolt against Locke in a more idealistic manner. Here the main figures represented are the Kantian Coleridge, whose distinction between Reason and Understanding exerted so much influence on Emerson; George Ripley, the clear-headed exponent of moral intuitionism and religious mysticism, who helps us understand the more oblique Emerson; Emerson himself, the chief philosopher of Transcendentalism; and Theodore Parker, probably its most popular expositor.

Part 4 concerns the period immediately after the Civil War, when American philosophy turned from the more literary preoccupations of the Transcendentalists to those of men who had a much greater familiarity with nineteenth-century science. This period was profoundly affected by the evolutionary philosophy of Herbert Spencer and the evolutionary biology of Charles Darwin. The influence of Spencer is most clearly revealed in the writings of his disciple John Fiske; whereas Spencer's capacity to goad thinkers into criticism of him is strikingly illustrated in the work of Chauncey Wright, a follower of Darwin and John Stuart Mill. This period also saw the appearance of J. B. Stallo's reflections on some of the leading doctrines of nineteenth-century physics. Wright and Stallo both helped make the logic of science a respectable philosophical concern, but because they presented no new general philosophical doctrines, they remained relatively minor figures in the story of American philosophy from Edwards to Dewey.

The central figures of that story did not appear until Charles Peirce and William James came upon the scene and offered their different versions of America's one distinctive philosophy, pragmatism. Although they were both trained in the sciences—Peirce in mathematics and physics, and James in physiology and psychology—they were as anxious as some of their more idealistic predecessors to defend certain traditional metaphysical and theological doctrines—often by appealing to the heart. Peirce and James are therefore the two most ambivalent of American philosophers to appear in this volume. They looked backward to certain attitudes and doctrines of Transcendentalism even though pragmatism helped inaugurate a great rebellion against the idealistic tradition of which Transcendentalism was a part.

That idealistic tradition was revived at the end of the

nineteenth century by Josiah Royce, who appropriately stands alone in Part 6. More than any American philosopher of the nineteenth century, he used the techniques of logic, science, and philosophy to defend the existence of an all-knowing Absolute Spirit. Royce was a tough spokesman for what James called a tender-minded philosophy, and his relationship to the idealistic Emerson resembled that of a scholastic to St. Francis. More than any other American philosopher, Royce saw science as *demanding* absolute idealism, not merely as tolerating it. He identified his Absolute with the Christian God.

It was against a scientifically and logically militant idealism like Royce's that Santayana and Dewey reacted. Whatever their differences—and they were great—these two philosophers joined in opposition to the tradition of idealism, though it should be added that critics of Dewey have said that he was more of an idealist than he realized. Still, neither Santayana nor Dewey believed in the existence of anything like Royce's Absolute; and they spent a good deal of their energy in attacking German philosophy of the nineteenth century. With the emergence of Dewey and Santayana as America's two most distinguished philosophers, there began a period that may be called the era of Naturalism. For the first time in the history of American philosophy, the existence of a supernatural being was not defended by its chief thinkers, and for the first time the dominant ethical view was naturalistic. Dewey went even further than Santayana in abandoning the dualism which had dominated American philosophy from the beginning. Dewey rejected Locke's belief in an Intuitive Reason, Edwards' belief in a Sense of the Heart, Emerson's distinction between the Reason and the Understanding, James' Will To Believe, and Peirce's idea that the heart is an organ whereby we can perceive God.

Yet, in spite of abandoning many traditional views in metaphysics and ethics, and in spite of challenging many traditional views about nature and the limits of science, Dewey and Santayana were in their *manner* of philosophizing closely linked with the tradition before them. They perpetuated the idea that a philosopher should discourse about all of civilization even though they rejected the absolute idealism that underlay such a concern in Hegel and Royce. Dewey and Santayana were interested in esthetics, ethics, politics, and the history of philosophy; and both of them were as interested as Emerson and James had been in the state of American culture and society. Santayana viewed America with detachment after he expatriated himself in 1912, but still with considerable interest; and Dewey became the great symbol of philosophical participation in America's political and social affairs. After the death in 1952 of Dewey, born in 1859, and of Santayana, born in 1863, American philosophy's preoccupation with the nature and scope of science continued, but it was no longer primarily motivated by an interest in how science affected such matters as religion, politics, art, and education. With the death of Dewey and Santayana, an era of American philosophy closed.

This volume fulfills a commitment, made while I was a member of the faculty of Harvard University, to prepare an anthology for use in courses in American Philosophy. I have included passages which are longer than those commonly included in anthologies because I believe that a student is better served by reading the extended reflections of a comparatively small number of philosophers than by reading snippets culled from the writings of many. I should say, however, that neither the sizes of individual selections nor the sizes of my introductions are correlated with my evaluations of the achievements of different philosophers. Sometimes I excerpt a longish passage from the writings of a lesser philosopher because I think he has been excessively neglected; and sometimes I preface a selection from the writings of a greater philosopher with a comparatively brief introduction because the selection does not require extended explanation.

Once again I thank my wife, Lucia White, for reading a manuscript of mine and for giving me the benefit of her excellent critical judgment. I also wish to express my gratitude to those who have given permission to reprint material over which they hold copyright. Finally, I must thank Mrs. Patricia J. Fenner for typing my introductions to selections and for carefully including in the manuscript photocopied pages of original material in order to ensure greater accuracy of reproduction.

Princeton, N. J.   M.W.
February 1971

CONTENTS

Part 1: *The Father of American Philosophy*   *1*

   JOHN LOCKE   3

   Empiricism
   Reason: Intuitive and Discursive
   Innate Principles *versus* Self-evident Principles
   Rationalism
   The Light of Reason and the Light of Enthusiasm

Part 2: *The Eighteenth Century: Philosophy in the*
      Service of Religion and Law   37

   JONATHAN EDWARDS   39

   The Sense of the Heart
   Freedom of the Will

   JAMES WILSON   78

   The Law of Nature

Part 3: *Transcendentalism: The Triumph of*
      Sentiment   95

   SAMUEL TAYLOR COLERIDGE   97

   The Reason *versus* The Understanding

GEORGE RIPLEY   106

Against the Argument from Miracles
The Connection between Virtue and Utility

RALPH WALDO EMERSON   141

The Reason *versus* the Understanding
Retrospection
Religion and the Moral Sentiment
The American Scholar
Self-Reliance

THEODORE PARKER   178

Transcendentalism and Sensationalism

*Part 4: The Impact of Nineteenth-Century
        Science*   191

HERBERT SPENCER   193

The Aim of Synthetic Philosophy
The Achievement of Synthetic Philosophy

JOHN FISKE   212

Scientific Axioms
Spencer *versus* Comte

CHAUNCEY WRIGHT   226

Against Spencer
In Defense of Darwin

J. B. STALLO   252

Scientific Hypotheses
The Relation of Thoughts to Things—the Formation of
    Concepts—Metaphysical Theories

*Part 5: Pragmatism: A Tough and Tender
        Philosophy*   285

CHARLES PEIRCE   287

How To Make Our Ideas Clear
Pragmatism and Scholastic Realism

Contents xiii

WILLIAM JAMES 330

The Nature of Metaphysical Axioms
Against Determinism
Pragmatism: "A Happy Harmonizer"

Part 6: *Absolute Idealism* 369

JOSIAH ROYCE 371

God and Science

Part 7: *Naturalism: The Revolt against Gentility and Dualism* 401

GEORGE SANTAYANA 403

The Genteel Tradition
The Poetry of Christian Dogma

JOHN DEWEY 443

Logic and Science
Reconstruction in Philosophy

Part 1: The Father of American Philosophy

JOHN LOCKE

The opening selections in this volume are from writings by the great English philosopher John Locke, who was born in 1632 and who died in 1704. His *Essay Concerning Human Understanding*, from which most of the selections are made, was published in 1690, as was his *Two Treatises of Civil Government*, from which a brief passage is selected. Although Locke may be studied from many different points of view, I have chosen to focus on his conception of the role of reason in science, morals, and religion, in order to illuminate certain features of American philosophy from Edwards to Dewey.

Locke is usually identified as the first of a British trio of empiricists which also included Berkeley and Hume; and when he is classified by historians as an empiricist, he is associated with the view that all of our ideas arise from experience. For Locke, some arise from sense experience of the external world—for example, ideas like redness and whiteness—others from reflection upon our interior mental activities. Yet Locke also held that once we learn the ideas redness and whiteness, we can—by using what he called, according to tradition, "intuitive reason"—immediately see the truth of the statement "No red thing is white". He also calls this a self-evident principle, because it is seen to be true as soon as we understand its component terms, without reasoning, without deducing it from something else.

The principles so established are contrasted by Locke with a number of other kinds. First of all he distinguishes them from principles which are certain but which are not self-evident. These, he maintains, are deduced from self-evident principles by the use of what is traditionally called "discursive reason". He held, for example, that whereas "Things equal to the same thing are equal to each other" is self-evident, the statement "The sum of the angles of a triangle add up to 180 degrees" is not, even though it is certain. It is seen to be true, not immediately, but only after we have gone through a process of deductive reasoning. In the first selection below, Locke's distinction between the two kinds or branches of reason appears.

A second important distinction is that between self-evident principles and what he called innate principles, important if only because he vehemently denied the existence of the latter while he stoutly affirmed that there are, and, indeed, must be, self-evident principles.

A third distinction—as traditional as Locke's distinction between intuitive and discursive reason—is his distinction between what he called speculative and practical principles. This is illustrated by the difference between "It is impossible for the same thing to be and not to be" on the one hand, and moral principles like "One should do as he would be done unto" on the other. In some places Locke seems to hold that there are no self-evident moral principles; in other places that there are. However, the view that there are such principles is fundamental to his political theory, according to which there are self-evident principles of Natural Law which formulate the rights and liberties that underlay the Revolution of 1688. His dominant view is that there are self-evident moral principles even though he diverges from it at times.

Once the reader is familiar with Locke's conception of

self-evident principles, he can see how Locke, in spite of being classified as an empiricist, was led to what is called a rationalistic view of moral, physical, and theological knowledge. He attempted a deductive proof of the existence of God which began with allegedly self-evident premises; he asserted that by devoting enough effort man could make ethics as demonstrative a science as pure mathematics is; and while he was not sanguine about the likelihood of constructing a demonstrative science of physics because of his ignorance of the invisible constituents of gross material bodies, he asserted: "I doubt not but if we could discover the figure, size, texture, and motion of the minute constituent parts of any two bodies, we should know without trial several of the operations one upon another; as we know the properties of a square or a triangle". Sometimes Locke says that the light of reason which reveals to us the axioms of mathematics can, under favorable circumstances, establish moral knowledge and physical knowledge. But Locke doubts that it will in physics and sometimes denies that it can in morals.

Mentioning the light of reason leads to the last Lockeian distinction of importance for us—his distinction between the light of reason to which mathematicians appealed and the bogus light of Enthusiasm to which religious fanatics appealed when they claimed to have seen the truth of certain theological propositions.

By studying the passages below, therefore, the reader may get some idea of Locke's empiricism; his distinction between self-evident principles, which he says exist, and innate principles, of which he says there are none; his vacillations about whether ethics and physics are demonstrative sciences like pure mathematics; and his attack on religious Enthusiasm. All of these views figure prominently in the history of American philosophy, especially in the earlier period from Edwards through the Transcendentalists. They are couched in a vocabulary which formed a good part of American philosophical literature down to the days of William James.

Empiricism [1]

Every man being conscious to himself that he thinks; and that which his mind is applied about whilst thinking being the *ideas* that are there, it is past doubt that men have in their minds several ideas,—such as are those expressed by the words *whiteness, hardness, sweetness, thinking, motion, man, elephant, army, drunkenness,* and others: it is in the first place then to be inquired, *How he comes by them?* . . .

Let us then suppose the mind to be, as we say, white paper, void of all characters, without any ideas:—How comes it to be furnished? Whence comes it by that vast store which the busy and boundless fancy of man has painted on it with an almost endless variety? Whence has it all the *materials* of reason and knowledge? To this I answer, in one word, from EXPERIENCE. In that all our knowledge is founded; and from that it ultimately derives itself. Our observation employed either, about external sensible objects, or about the internal operations of our minds perceived and reflected on by ourselves, is that which supplies our understandings with all the *materials* of thinking. These two are the fountains of knowledge, from whence all the ideas we have, or can naturally have, do spring.

First, our Senses, conversant about particular sensible objects, do convey into the mind several distinct perceptions of things, according to those various ways wherein those objects do affect them. And thus we come by those *ideas* we have of *yellow, white, heat, cold, soft, hard, bitter, sweet,* and all those which we call sensible qualities; which when I say the senses convey into the mind, I mean, they from external ob-

---

[1] This selection comes from Locke's *An Essay Concerning Human Understanding,* Book II, Chapter I, Sections 1–8. Hereafter this work will be referred to as *"Essay"*. I have omitted Locke's numerals and titles throughout these selections, and I have added my own headings.

jects convey into the mind what produces there those perceptions. This great source of most of the ideas we have, depending wholly upon our senses, and derived by them to the
understanding, I call SENSATION.

Secondly, the other fountain from which experience fur-
nisheth the understanding with ideas is,—the perception of
the operations of our own mind within us, as it is employed
about the ideas it has got;—which operations, when the soul
comes to reflect on and consider, do furnish the understanding with another set of ideas, which could not be had from
things without. And such are *perception, thinking, doubting,
believing, reasoning, knowing, willing,* and all the different
actings of our own minds;—which we being conscious of, and
observing in ourselves, do from these receive into our understandings as distinct ideas as we do from bodies affecting our
senses. This source of ideas every man has wholly in himself;
and though it be not sense, as having nothing to do with external objects, yet it is very like it, and might properly
enough be called *internal sense.* But as I call the other Sensation, so I call this REFLECTION, the ideas it affords being such
only as the mind gets by reflecting on its own operations
within itself. By reflection then, in the following part of this
discourse, I would be understood to mean, that notice which
the mind takes of its own operations, and the manner of
them, by reason whereof there come to be ideas of these operations in the understanding. These two, I say, viz. external
material things, as the objects of SENSATION, and the operations of our own minds within, as the objects of REFLECTION,
are to me the only originals from whence all our ideas take
their beginnings. The term *operations* here I use in a large
sense, as comprehending not barely the actions of the mind
about its ideas, but some sort of passions arising sometimes
from them, such as is the satisfaction or uneasiness arising
from any thought.

The understanding seems to me not to have the least glim-
mering of any ideas which it doth not receive from one of

these two. *External objects* furnish the mind with the ideas of sensible qualities, which are all those different perceptions they produce in us; and *the mind* furnishes the understanding with ideas of its own operations.

These, when we have taken a full survey of them, and their several modes, combinations, and relations, we shall find to contain all our whole stock of ideas; and that we have nothing in our minds which did not come in one of these two ways. Let any one examine his own thoughts, and thoroughly search into his understanding; and then let him tell me, whether all the original ideas he has there, are any other than of the objects of his senses, or of the operations of his mind, considered as objects of his reflection. And how great a mass of knowledge soever he imagines to be lodged there, he will, upon taking a strict view, see that he has not any idea in his mind but what one of these two have imprinted;—though perhaps, with infinite variety compounded and enlarged by the understanding, as we shall see hereafter.

He that attentively considers the state of a child, at his first coming into the world, will have little reason to think him stored with plenty of ideas, that are to be the matter of his future knowledge. It is *by degrees* he comes to be furnished with them. And though the ideas of obvious and familiar qualities imprint themselves before the memory begins to keep a register of time or order, yet it is often so late before some unusual qualities come in the way, that there are few men that cannot recollect the beginning of their acquaintance with them. And if it were worth while, no doubt a child might be so ordered as to have but a very few, even of the ordinary ideas, till he were grown up to a man. But all that are born into the world, being surrounded with bodies that perpetually and diversely affect them, variety of ideas, whether care be taken of it or not, are imprinted on the minds of children. Light and colours are busy at hand everywhere, when the eye is but open; sounds and some tangible qualities fail not to solicit their proper senses, and force an entrance to the mind;—but yet, I think, it will be granted easily, that if a child were kept in a place where he never saw any other but black and white till he were a man, he would have no more ideas of scarlet or green, than he that from his childhood never tasted an oyster, or a pine-apple, has of those particular relishes.

Men then come to be furnished with fewer or more simple ideas from without, according as the objects they converse with afford greater or less variety; and from the operations of their minds within, according as they more or less reflect on them. For, though he that contemplates the operations of his mind, cannot but have plain and clear ideas of them; yet, unless he turn his thoughts that way, and considers them *attentively*, he will no more have clear and distinct ideas of all the operations of his mind, and all that may be observed therein, than he will have all the particular ideas of any landscape, or of the parts and motions of a clock, who will not turn his eyes to it, and with attention heed all the parts of it. The picture, or clock may be so placed, that they may come in his way every day; but yet he will have but a confused idea of all the parts they are made up of, till he applies himself with attention, to consider them each in particular.

And hence we see the reason why it is pretty late before most children get ideas of the operations of their own minds; and some have not any very clear or perfect ideas of the greatest part of them all their lives. Because, though they pass there continually, yet, like floating visions, they make not deep impressions enough to leave in their mind clear, distinct, lasting ideas, till the understanding turns inward upon itself, reflects on its own operations, and makes them the objects of its own contemplation. Children when they come first into it, are surrounded with a world of new things, which, by a constant solicitation of their senses, draw the mind constantly to them; forward to take notice of new, and apt to be delighted with the variety of changing objects. Thus the first years are usually employed and diverted in looking abroad.

Men's business in them is to acquaint themselves with what is to be found without; and so growing up in a constant attention to outward sensations, seldom make any considerable reflection on what passes within them, till they come to be of riper years; and some scarce ever at all.

Reason: Intuitive and Discursive [2]

Since the mind, in all its thoughts and reasonings, hath no other immediate object but its own ideas, which it alone does or can contemplate, it is evident that our knowledge is only conversant about them.

Knowledge then seems to me to be nothing but *the perception of the connexion of and agreement, or disagreement and repugnancy of any of our ideas.* In this alone it consists. Where this perception is, there is knowledge, and where it is not, there, though we may fancy, guess, or believe, yet we always come short of knowledge. For when we know that white is not black, what do we else but perceive, that these two ideas do not agree? When we possess ourselves with the utmost security of the demonstration, that the three angles of a triangle are equal to two right ones, what do we more but perceive, that equality to two right ones does necessarily agree to, and is inseparable from, the three angles of a triangle? . . .

All our knowledge consisting, as I have said, in the view the mind has of its own ideas, which is the utmost light and greatest certainty we, with our faculties, and in our way of knowledge, are capable of, it may not be amiss to consider a little the degrees of its evidence. The different clearness of our knowledge seems to me to lie in the different way of per-

[2] The first two paragraphs of this selection are from Locke's *Essay*, Book IV, Chapter I, Sections 1–2, and the remainder from Book IV, Chapter II, Sections 1–7.

ception the mind has of the agreement or disagreement of any of its ideas. For if we will reflect on our own ways of thinking, we will find, that sometimes the mind perceives the agreement or disagreement of two ideas *immediately by themselves*, without the intervention of any other: and this I think we may call *intuitive knowledge*. For in this the mind is at no pains of proving or examining, but perceives the truth as the eye doth light, only by being directed towards it. Thus the mind perceives that *white* is not *black*, that a *circle* is not a *triangle*, that *three* are more than *two* and equal to *one and two*. Such kinds of truths the mind perceives at the first sight of the ideas together, by bare intuition; without the intervention of any other idea: and this kind of knowledge is the clearest and most certain that human frailty is capable of. This part of knowledge is irresistible, and, like bright sunshine, forces itself immediately to be perceived, as soon as ever the mind turns its view that way; and leaves no room for hesitation, doubt, or examination, but the mind is presently filled with the clear light of it. *It is on this intuition that depends all the certainty and evidence of all our knowledge;* which certainty every one finds to be so great, that he cannot imagine, and therefore not require a greater: for a man cannot conceive himself capable of a greater certainty than to know that any idea in his mind is such as he perceives it to be; and that two ideas, wherein he perceives a difference, are different and not precisely the same. He that demands a greater certainty than this, demands he knows not what, and shows only that he has a mind to be a sceptic, without being able to be so. Certainty depends so wholly on this intuition, that, in the next degree of knowledge which I call demonstrative, this intuition is necessary in all the connexions of the intermediate ideas, without which we cannot attain knowledge and certainty.

The next degree of knowledge is, where the mind perceives the agreement or disagreement of any ideas, but not immediately. Though wherever the mind perceives the agreement or disagreement of any of its ideas, there be certain knowledge; yet it does not always happen, that the mind sees that agreement or disagreement, which there is between them, even where it is discoverable; and in that case remains in ignorance, and at most gets no further than a probable conjecture. The reason why the mind cannot always perceive presently the agreement or disagreement of two ideas, is, because those ideas, concerning whose agreement or disagreement the inquiry is made, cannot by the mind be so put together as to show it. In this case then, when the mind cannot so bring its ideas together as by their immediate comparison, and as it were juxta-position or application one to another, to perceive their agreement or disagreement, it is fain, *by the intervention of other ideas* (one or more, as it happens) to discover the agreement or disagreement which it searches; and this is that which we call *reasoning*. Thus, the mind being willing to know the agreement or disagreement in bigness between the three angles of a triangle and two right ones, cannot by an immediate view and comparing them do it: because the three angles of a triangle cannot be brought at once, and be compared with any other one, or two, angles; and so of this the mind has no immediate, no intuitive knowledge. In this case the mind is fain to find out some other angles, to which the three angles of a triangle have an equality; and, finding those equal to two right ones, comes to know their equality to two right ones.

Those intervening ideas, which serve to show the agreement of any two others, are called *proofs;* and where the agreement and disagreement is by this means plainly and clearly perceived, it is called *demonstration;* it being *shown* to the understanding, and the mind made to see that it is so. A quickness in the mind to find out these intermediate ideas, (that shall discover the agreement or disagreement of any other,) and to apply them right, is, I suppose, that which is called *sagacity.*

This knowledge, by intervening proofs, though it be certain, yet the evidence of it is not altogether so clear and bright, nor the assent so ready, as in intuitive knowledge. For, though in demonstration the mind does at last perceive the agreement or disagreement of the ideas it considers; yet it is not without pains and attention: there must be more than one transient view to find it. A steady application and pursuit are required to this discovery: and there must be a progression by steps and degrees, before the mind can in this way arrive at certainty, and come to perceive the agreement or repugnancy between two ideas that need proofs and the use of reason to show it.

Another difference between intuitive and demonstrative knowledge is, that, though in the latter all doubt be removed when, by the intervention of the intermediate ideas, the agreement or disagreement is perceived, yet before the demonstration there was a doubt; which in intuitive knowledge cannot happen to the mind that has its faculty of perception left to a degree capable of distinct ideas; no more than it can be a doubt to the eye (that can distinctly see white and black), Whether this ink and this paper be all of a colour. If there be sight in the eyes, it will, at first glimpse, without hesitation, perceive the words printed on this paper different from the colour of the paper: and so if the mind have the faculty of distinct perception, it will perceive the agreement or disagreement of those ideas that produce intuitive knowledge. If the eyes have lost the faculty of seeing, or the mind of perceiving, we in vain inquire after the quickness of sight in one, or clearness of perception in the other.

It is true, the perception produced by demonstration is also very clear; yet it is often with a great abatement of that evident lustre and full assurance that always accompany that which I call intuitive: like a face reflected by several mirrors one to another, where, as long as it retains the similitude and agreement with the object, it produces a knowledge; but it is still, in every successive reflection, with a lessening of that perfect clearness and distinctness which is in the first; till at last, after many removes, it has a great mixture of dimness, and is not at first sight so knowable, especially to weak eyes.

Thus it is with knowledge made out by a long train of proof.

Now, in every step reason makes in demonstrative knowledge, there is an intuitive knowledge of that agreement or disagreement it seeks with the next intermediate idea which it uses as a proof: for if it were not so, that yet would need a proof; since without the perception of such agreement or disagreement, there is no knowledge produced: if it be perceived by itself, it is intuitive knowledge: if it cannot be perceived by itself, there is need of some intervening idea, as a common measure, to show their agreement or disagreement. By which it is plain, that every step in reasoning that produces knowledge, has intuitive certainty; which when the mind perceives, there is no more required but to remember it, to make the agreement or disagreement of the ideas concerning which we inquire visible and certain. So that to make anything a demonstration, it is necessary to perceive the immediate agreement of the intervening ideas, whereby the agreement or disagreement of the two ideas under examination (whereof the one is always the first, and the other the last in the account) is found. This intuitive perception of the agreement or disagreement of the intermediate ideas, in each step and progression of the demonstration, must also be carried exactly in the mind, and a man must be sure that no part is left out: which, because in long deductions, and the use of many proofs, the memory does not always so readily and exactly retain; therefore it comes to pass, that this is more imperfect than intuitive knowledge, and men embrace often falsehood for demonstrations.

Innate Principles versus *Self-evident Principles*

LOCKE DENIES THAT THERE ARE INNATE PRINCIPLES [3]

It is an established opinion amongst some men, that there are in the understanding certain *innate principles;* some pri-

---

[3] *Essay,* Book I, Chapter I, Sections 1–4, and part of Section 5.

mary notions, . . . characters, as it were stamped upon the mind of man; which the soul receives in its very first being, and brings into the world with it. It would be sufficient to convince unprejudiced readers of the falseness of this supposition, if I should only show (as I hope I shall in the following parts of this Discourse) how men, barely by the use of their natural faculties, may attain to all the knowledge they have, without the help of any innate impressions; and may arrive at certainty, without any such original notions or principles. For I imagine any one will easily grant that it would be impertinent to suppose the ideas of colours innate in a creature to whom God hath given sight, and a power to receive them by the eyes from external objects: and no less unreasonable would it be to attribute several truths to the impressions of nature, and innate characters, when we may observe in ourselves faculties fit to attain as easy and certain knowledge of them as if they were originally imprinted on the mind.

But because a man is not permitted without censure to follow his own thoughts in the search of truth, when they lead him ever so little out of the common road, I shall set down the reasons that made me doubt of the truth of that opinion, as an excuse for my mistake, if I be in one; which I leave to be considered by those who, with me, dispose themselves to embrace truth wherever they find it.

There is nothing more commonly taken for granted than that there are certain *principles,* both *speculative* and *practical,* (for they speak of both), universally agreed upon by all mankind: which therefore, they argue, must needs be the constant impressions which the souls of men receive in their first beings, and which they bring into the world with them, as necessarily and really as they do any of their inherent faculties.

This argument, drawn from universal consent, has this misfortune in it, that if it were true in matter of fact, that there were certain truths wherein all mankind agreed, it would not prove them innate, if there can be any other way shown how men may come to that universal agreement, in the things they do consent in, which I presume may be done.

But, which is worse, this argument of universal consent, which is made use of to prove innate principles, seems to me a demonstration that there are none such: because there are none to which all mankind give an universal assent. I shall begin with the speculative, and instance in those magnified principles of demonstration, 'Whatsoever is, is,' and 'It is impossible for the same thing to be and not to be'; which, of all others, I think have the most allowed title to innate. These have so settled a reputation of maxims universally received, that it will no doubt be thought strange if any one should seem to question it. But yet I take liberty to say, that these propositions are so far from having an universal assent, that there are a great part of mankind to whom they are not so much as known.

For, first, it is evident, that all children and idiots have not the least apprehension or thought of them. And the want of that is enough to destroy that universal assent which must needs be the necessary concomitant of all innate truths: it seeming to me near a contradiction to say, that there are truths imprinted on the soul, which it perceives or understands not: imprinting, if it signify anything, being nothing else but the making certain truths to be perceived. For to imprint anything on the mind without the mind's perceiving it, seems to me hardly intelligible. If therefore children and idiots have souls, have minds, with those impressions upon them, *they* must unavoidably perceive them, and necessarily know and assent to these truths; which since they do not, it is evident that there are no such impressions. For if they are not notions naturally imprinted, how can they be innate? and if they are notions imprinted, how can they be unknown? To say a notion is imprinted on the mind, and yet at the same time to say, that the mind is ignorant of it, and never yet took notice of it, is to make this impression nothing. No proposition can be said to be in the mind which it never yet knew, which it was never yet conscious of. . . .

SPECULATIVE PRINCIPLES MAY BE SELF-EVIDENT
BUT NOT PRACTICAL OR MORAL PRINCIPLES [4]

If those speculative Maxims, whereof we discoursed . . . have not an actual universal assent from all mankind, as we there proved, it is much more visible concerning *practical* Principles, that they come short of an universal reception: and I think it will be hard to instance any one moral rule which can pretend to so general and ready an assent as, 'What is, is'; or to be so manifest a truth as this, that 'It is impossible for the same thing to be and not to be.' Whereby it is evident that they are further removed from a title to be innate; and the doubt of their being native impressions on the mind is stronger against those moral principles than the other. Not that it brings their truth at all in question. They are equally true, though not equally evident. Those speculative maxims carry their own evidence with them: but moral principles require reasoning and discourse, and some exercise of the mind, to discover the certainty of their truth. They lie not open as natural characters engraven on the mind; which, if any such were, they must needs be visible by themselves, and by their own light be certain and known to everybody. But this is no derogation to their truth and certainty; no more than it is to the truth or certainty of the three angles of a triangle being equal to two right ones: because it is not so evident as 'the whole is bigger than a part,' nor so apt to be assented to at first hearing. It may suffice that these moral rules are capable of demonstration: and therefore it is our own faults if we come not to a certain knowledge of them. But the ignorance wherein many men are of them, and the slowness of assent wherewith others receive them, are manifest proofs that they are not innate, and such as offer themselves to their view without searching.

Whether there be any such moral principles, wherein all

[4] *Essay*, Book I, Chapter II, Sections 1–2; 4.

men do agree, I appeal to any who have been but moderately conversant in the history of mankind, and looked abroad beyond the smoke of their own chimneys. Where is that practical truth that is universally received, without doubt or question, as it must be if innate? *Justice*, and keeping of contracts, is that which most men seem to agree in. This is a principle which is thought to extend itself to the dens of thieves, and the confederacies of the greatest villains; and they who have gone furthest towards the putting off of humanity itself, keep faith and rules of justice one with another. I grant that outlaws themselves do this one amongst another: but it is without receiving these as the innate laws of nature. They practise them as rules of convenience within their own communities: but it is impossible to conceive that he embraces justice as a practical principle, who acts fairly with his fellow-highwayman, and at the same time plunders or kills the next honest man he meets with. Justice and truth are the common ties of society; and therefore even outlaws and robbers, who break with all the world besides, must keep faith and rules of equity amongst themselves; or else they cannot hold together. But will any one say, that those that live by fraud or rapine have innate principles of truth and justice which they allow and assent to? . . .

Another reason that makes me doubt of any innate practical principles is, that I think *there cannot any one moral rule be proposed whereof a man may not justly demand a reason:* which would be perfectly ridiculous and absurd if they were innate; or so much as self-evident, which every innate principle must needs be, and not need any proof to ascertain its truth, nor want any reason to gain it approbation. He would be thought void of common sense who asked on the one side, or on the other side went to give a reason *why* 'it is impossible for the same thing to be and not to be.' It carries its own light and evidence with it, and needs no other proof: he that understands the terms assents to it for its own sake or else nothing will ever be able to prevail with him to do it. But should that most unshaken rule of morality and foundation of all social virtue, 'That one should do as he would be done unto,' be proposed to one who never heard of it before, but yet is of capacity to understand its meaning; might he not without any absurdity ask a reason why? And were not he that proposed it bound to make out the truth and reasonableness of it to him? Which plainly shows it not to be innate; for if it were it could neither want nor receive any proof; but must needs (at least as soon as heard and understood) be received and assented to as an unquestionable truth, which a man can by no means doubt of. So that the truth of all these moral rules plainly depends upon some other antecedent to them, and from which they must be *deduced;* which could not be if either they were innate or so much as self-evident.

Rationalism

MORALITY MAY BE A DEMONSTRATIVE SCIENCE [5]

The idea of a supreme Being, infinite in power, goodness, and wisdom, whose workmanship we are, and on whom we depend; and the idea of ourselves, as understanding, rational creatures, being such as are clear in us, would, I suppose, if duly considered and pursued, afford such foundations of our duty and rules of action as might place *morality* amongst the *sciences capable of demonstration:* wherein I doubt not but from self-evident propositions, by necessary consequences, as incontestible as those in mathematics, the measures of right and wrong might be made out, to any one that will apply himself with the same indifferency and attention to the one as he does to the other of these sciences. . . . 'Where there is no property there is no injustice,' is a proposition as certain as any demonstration in Euclid: for the idea of property being a right to anything, and the idea to which the name 'injustice' is given being the invasion or violation of that

[5] *Essay*, Book IV, Chapter III, Section 18.

right, it is evident that these ideas, being thus established, and these names annexed to them, I can as certainly know this proposition to be true, as that a triangle has three angles equal to two right ones. Again: 'No government allows absolute liberty.' The idea of government being the establishment of society upon certain rules or laws which require conformity to them; and the idea of absolute liberty being for any one to do whatever he pleases; I am as capable of being certain of the truth of this proposition as of any in the mathematics.

MORAL PRINCIPLES OF NATURAL LAW
ARE SELF-EVIDENT [6]

To understand political power right and derive it from its original, we must consider what state all men are naturally in, and that is a state of perfect freedom to order their actions and dispose of their possessions and persons as they think fit, within the bounds of the law of nature, without asking leave or depending upon the will of any other man.

A state also of equality, wherein all the power and jurisdiction is reciprocal, no one having more than another; there being nothing more evident than that creatures of the same species and rank, promiscuously born to all the same advantages of nature and the use of the same faculties, should also be equal one amongst another without subordination or subjection; unless the lord and master of them all should, by any manifest declaration of his will, set one above another, and confer on him by an evident and clear appointment an undoubted right to dominion and sovereignty.

This equality of men by nature the judicious Hooker looks upon as so evident in itself and beyond all question that he makes it the foundation of that obligation to mutual love amongst men on which he builds the duties we owe one an-

[6] Locke, *The Second Treatise of Government,* Chapter II, Sections 4–6.

other, and from whence he derives the great maxims of justice and charity. His words are:

> The like natural inducement hath brought men to know that it is no less their duty to love others than themselves; for seeing those things which are equal must needs all have one measure; if I cannot but wish to receive good, even as much at every man's hands as any man can wish unto his own soul, how should I look to have any part of my desire herein satisfied unless myself be careful to satisfy the like desire, which is undoubtedly in other men, being of one and the same nature? To have anything offered them repugnant to this desire must needs in all respects grieve them as much as me; so that, if I do harm, I must look to suffer, there being no reason that others should show greater measure of love to me than they have by me showed unto them; my desire therefore to be loved of my equals in nature, as much as possibly may be, imposeth upon me a natural duty of bearing to them-ward fully the like affection; from which relation of equality between ourselves and them that are as ourselves, what several rules and canons natural reason hath drawn, for direction of life, no man is ignorant.

But though this be a state of liberty, yet it is not a state of license; though man in that state have an uncontrollable liberty to dispose of his person or possessions, yet he has not liberty to destroy himself, or so much as any creature in his possession, but where some nobler use than its bare preservation calls for it. The state of nature has a law of nature to govern it, which obliges every one; and reason, which is that law, teaches all mankind who will but consult it that, being all equal and independent, no one ought to harm another in his life, health, liberty, or possessions; for men being all the workmanship of one omnipotent and infinitely wise Maker—all the servants of one sovereign master, sent into the world by his order, and about his business—they are his property whose workmanship they are, made to last during his, not one another's, pleasure; and being furnished with like faculties, sharing all in one community of nature, there cannot be supposed any such subordination among us that may authorize us to destroy another, as if we were made for one another's uses as the inferior ranks of creatures are for ours. Every one, as he is bound to preserve himself and not to quit his station wilfully, so by the like reason, when his own preservation comes not in competition, ought he, as much as he can, to preserve the rest of mankind, and may not, unless it be to do justice to an offender, take away or impair the life, or what tends to the preservation of the life, the liberty, health, limb, or goods of another.

ON THE FOUNDATIONS OF PHYSICS [7]

Another great cause of ignorance is the want of ideas we are capable of. As the want of ideas which our faculties are not able to give us shuts us wholly from those views of things which it is reasonable to think other beings, perfecter than we, have, of which we know nothing; so the want of ideas I now speak of keeps us in ignorance of things we conceive capable of being known to us. Bulk, figure, and motion we have ideas of. But though we are not without ideas of these primary qualities of bodies in general, yet not knowing what is the particular bulk, figure, and motion, of the greatest part of the bodies of the universe, we are ignorant of the several powers, efficacies, and ways of operation, whereby the effects which we daily see are produced. These are hid from us, in some things by being too remote, and in others by being too minute. When we consider the vast distance of the known and visible parts of the world, and the reasons we have to think that what lies within our ken is but a small part of the universe, we shall then discover a huge abyss of ignorance. What are the particular fabrics of the great masses of matter which make up the whole stupendous frame of corporeal beings; how far they are extended; what is their motion, and how continued or communicated; and what influence they

[7] *Essay*, Book IV, Chapter III, Sections 24–26.

have one upon another, are contemplations that at first glimpse our thoughts lose themselves in. If we narrow our contemplations, and confine our thoughts to this little canton —I mean this system of our sun, and the grosser masses of matter that visibly move about it, What several sorts of vegetables, animals, and intellectual corporeal beings, infinitely different from those of our little spot of earth, may there probably be in the other planets, to the knowledge of which, even of their outward figures and parts, we can no way attain whilst we are confined to this earth; there being no natural means, either by sensation or reflection, to convey their certain ideas into our minds? They are out of the reach of those inlets of all our knowledge: and what sorts of furniture and inhabitants those mansions contain in them we cannot so much as guess, much less have clear and distinct ideas of them.

If a great, nay, far the greatest part of the several ranks of bodies in the universe escape our notice by their remoteness, there are others that are no less concealed from us by their minuteness. These *insensible corpuscles,* being the active parts of matter, and the great instruments of nature, on which depend not only all their secondary qualities, but also most of their natural operations, our want of precise distinct ideas of their primary qualities keeps us in an incurable ignorance of what we desire to know about them. I doubt not but if we could discover the figure, size, texture, and motion of the minute constituent parts of any two bodies, we should know without trial several of their operations one upon another; as we do now the properties of a square or a triangle. Did we know the mechanical affections of the particles of rhubarb, hemlock, opium, and a man, as a watchmaker does those of a watch, whereby it performs its operations; and of a file, which by rubbing on them will alter the figure of any of the wheels; we should be able to tell beforehand that rhubarb will purge, hemlock kill, and opium make a man sleep: as well as a watchmaker can, that a little piece of paper laid

on the balance will keep the watch from going till it be removed; or that, some small part of it being rubbed by a file,
the machine would quite lose its motion, and the watch go no
more. The dissolving of silver in *aqua fortis,* and gold in *aqua
regia,* and not *vice versâ,* would be then perhaps no more difficult to know than it is to a smith to understand why the
turning of one key will open a lock, and not the turning of
another. But whilst we are destitute of senses acute enough to
discover the minute particles of bodies, and to give us ideas
of their mechanical affections, we must be content to be ignorant of their properties and ways of operation; nor can we be
assured about them any further than some few trials we make
are able to reach. But whether they will succeed again another time, we cannot be certain. This hinders our certain
knowledge of universal truths concerning natural bodies: and
our reason carries us herein very little beyond particular matter of fact.

And therefore I am apt to doubt that, how far soever
human industry may advance useful and experimental philosophy in physical things, *scientifical* will still be out of our
reach: because we want perfect and adequate ideas of those
very bodies which are nearest to us, and most under our
command. Those which we have ranked into classes under
names, and we think ourselves best acquainted with, we have
but very imperfect and incomplete ideas of. Distinct ideas of
the several sorts of bodies that fall under the examination of
our senses perhaps we may have: but adequate ideas, I suspect, we have not of any one amongst them. And though the
former of these will serve us for common use and discourse,
yet whilst we want the latter, we are not capable of scientifical knowledge; nor shall ever be able to discover general, instructive, unquestionable truths concerning them. *Certainty*
and *demonstration* are things we must not, in these matters,
pretend to. By the colour, figure, taste, and smell, and other
sensible qualities, we have as clear and distinct ideas of sage
and hemlock, as we have of a circle and a triangle: but hav-

ing no ideas of the particular primary qualities of the minute parts of either of these plants, nor of other bodies which we would apply them to, we cannot tell what effects they will produce; nor when we see those effects can we so much as guess, much less know, their manner of production. Thus, having no ideas of the particular mechanical affections of the minute parts of bodies that are within our view and reach, we are ignorant of their constitutions, powers, and operations: and of bodies more remote we are yet more ignorant, not knowing so much as their very outward shapes, or the sensible and grosser parts of their constitutions.

AN A PRIORI ARGUMENT FOR THE EXISTENCE OF GOD [8]

Though God has given us no innate ideas of himself; though he has stamped no original characters on our minds, wherein we may read his being; yet having furnished us with those faculties our minds are endowed with, he hath not left himself without witness: since we have sense, perception, and reason, and cannot want a clear proof of him, as long as we carry *ourselves* about us. Nor can we justly complain of our ignorance in this great point; since he has so plentifully provided us with the means to discover and know him; so far as is necessary to the end of our being, and the great concernment of our happiness. But, though this be the most obvious truth that reason discovers, and though its evidence be (if I mistake not) equal to mathematical certainty: yet it requires thought and attention; and the mind must apply itself to a regular deduction of it from some part of our intuitive knowledge, or else we shall be as uncertain and ignorant of this as of other propositions, which are in themselves capable of clear demonstration. To show, therefore, that we are capable of *knowing*, i.e. *being certain* that there is a God, and *how*

[8] *Essay,* Book IV, Chapter X, Sections 1–5, and the beginning of Section 6.

we may come by this certainty, I think we need go no further than *ourselves,* and that undoubted knowledge we have of our own existence.

I think it is beyond question, that man has a clear idea of his own being; he knows certainly he exists, and that he is something. He that can doubt whether he be anything or no, I speak not to; no more than I would argue with pure nothing, or endeavour to convince nonentity that it were something. If any one pretends to be so sceptical as to deny his own existence, (for really to doubt of it is manifestly impossible,) let him for me enjoy his beloved happiness of being nothing, until hunger or some other pain convince him of the contrary. This, then, I think I may take for a truth, which every one's certain knowledge assures him of, beyond the liberty of doubting, viz. that he is *something that actually exists.*

In the next place, man knows, by an intuitive certainty, that bare *nothing can no more produce any real being, than it can be equal to two right angles.* If a man knows not that nonentity, or the absence of all being, cannot be equal to two right angles, it is impossible he should know any demonstration in Euclid. If, therefore, we know there is some real being, and that nonentity cannot produce any real being, it is an evident demonstration, that *from eternity there has been something;* since what was not from eternity had a beginning; and what had a beginning must be produced by something else.

Next, it is evident, that what had its being and beginning from another, must also have all that which is in and belongs to its being from another too. All the powers it has must be owing to and received from the same source. This eternal source, then, of all being must also be the source and original of all power; and so *this eternal Being must be also the most powerful.*

Again, a man finds in *himself* perception and knowledge. We have then got one step further; and we are certain now that there is not only some being, but some knowing, intelligent being in the world. There was a time, then, when there was no knowing being, and when knowledge began to be; or else there has been also *a knowing being from eternity.* If it be said, there was a time when no being had any knowledge, when that eternal being was void of all understanding; I reply, that then it was impossible there should ever have been any knowledge: it being as impossible that things wholly void of knowledge, and operating blindly, and without any perception, should produce a knowing being, as it is impossible that a triangle should make itself three angles bigger than two right ones. For it is as repugnant to the idea of senseless matter, that it should put into itself sense, perception, and knowledge, as it is repugnant to the idea of a triangle, that it should put into itself greater angles than two right ones.

Thus, from the consideration of ourselves, and what we infallibly find in our own constitutions, our reason leads us to the knowledge of this certain and evident truth,—*That there is an eternal, most powerful, and most knowing Being;* which whether any one will please to call God, it matters not.

The Light of Reason and the Light of Enthusiasm [9]

Immediate revelation being a much easier way for men to establish their opinions and regulate their conduct, than the tedious and not always successful labour of strict reasoning, it is no wonder that some have been very apt to pretend to revelation, and to persuade themselves that they are under the peculiar guidance of heaven in their actions and opinions, especially in those of them which they cannot account for by the ordinary methods of knowledge and principles of reason. Hence we see, that, in all ages, men in whom melancholy has mixed with devotion, or whose conceit of themselves has raised them into an opinion of a greater familiarity with God,

[9] *Essay,* Book IV, Chapter XIX, Sections 5–16.

and a nearer admittance to his favour than is afforded to others, have often flattered themselves with a persuasion of an
immediate intercourse with the Deity, and frequent commu-
nications from the Divine Spirit. God, I own, cannot be denied to be able to enlighten the understanding by a ray
darted into the mind immediately from the fountain of light:
this they understand he has promised to do, and who then
has so good a title to expect it as those who are his peculiar
people, chosen by him, and depending on him?

Their minds being thus prepared, whatever groundless
opinion comes to settle itself strongly upon their fancies, is an
illumination from the Spirit of God, and presently of divine
authority: and whatsoever odd action they find in themselves
a strong inclination to do, that impulse is concluded to be a
call or direction from heaven, and must be obeyed: it is a
commission from above, and they cannot err in executing it.

This I take to be properly *enthusiasm,* which, though
founded neither on reason nor divine revelation, but rising
from the conceits of a warmed or overweening brain, works
yet, where it once gets footing, more powerfully on the persuasions and actions of men than either of those two, or both
together: men being most forwardly obedient to the impulses
they receive from themselves; and the whole man is sure to
act more vigorously where the whole man is carried by a natural motion. For strong conceit, like a new principle, carries
all easily with it, when got above common sense, and freed
from all restraint of reason and check of reflection, it is
heightened into a divine authority, in concurrence with our
own temper and inclination.

Though the odd opinions and extravagant actions enthusiasm has run men into were enough to warn them against this
wrong principle, so apt to misguide them both in their belief
and conduct: yet the love of something extraordinary, the
ease and glory it is to be inspired, and be above the common
and natural ways of knowledge, so flatters many men's lazi-
ness, ignorance, and vanity, that, when once they are got into

this way of immediate revelation, of illumination without search, and of certainty without proof and without examination, it is a hard matter to get them out of it. Reason is lost upon them, they are above it: they see the light infused into their understandings, and cannot be mistaken; it is clear and visible there, like the light of bright sunshine; shows itself, and needs no other proof but its own evidence: they feel the hand of God moving them within, and the impulses of the Spirit, and cannot be mistaken in what they feel. Thus they support themselves, and are sure reasoning hath nothing to do with what they see and feel in themselves: what they have a sensible experience of admits no doubt, needs no probation. Would he not be ridiculous, who should require to have it proved to him that the light shines, and that he sees it? It is its own proof, and can have no other. When the Spirit brings light into our minds, it dispels darkness. We see it as we do that of the sun at noon, and need not the twilight of reason to show it us. This light from heaven is strong, clear, and pure; carries its own demonstration with it: and we may as naturally take a glow-worm to assist us to discover the sun, as to examine the celestial ray by our dim candle, reason.

This is the way of talking of these men: they are sure, because they are sure: and their persuasions are right, because they are strong in them. For, when what they say is stripped of the metaphor of seeing and feeling, this is all it amounts to: and yet these similes so impose on them, that they serve them for certainty in themselves, and demonstration to others.

But to examine a little soberly this internal light, and this feeling on which they build so much. These men have, they say, clear light, and they see; they have awakened sense, and they feel: this cannot, they are sure, be disputed them. For when a man says he sees or feels, nobody can deny him that he does so. But here let me ask: This seeing, is it the perception of the truth of the proposition, or of this, that it is a revelation from God? This feeling, is it a perception of an inclina-

tion or fancy to do something, or of the Spirit of God moving
that inclination? These are two very different perceptions,
and must be carefully distinguished, if we would not impose
upon ourselves. I may perceive the truth of a proposition,
and yet not perceive that it is an immediate revelation from
God. I may perceive the truth of a proposition in Euclid,
without its being, or my perceiving it to be, a revelation: nay,
I may perceive I came not by this knowledge in a natural
way, and so may conclude it revealed, without perceiving
that it is a revelation of God. Because there be spirits which,
without being divinely commissioned, may excite those ideas
in me, and lay them in such order before my mind, that I
may perceive their connexion. So that the knowledge of any
proposition coming into my mind, I know not how, is not a
perception that it is from God. Much less is a strong persuasion that it is true, a perception that it· is from God, or so
much as true. But however it be called light and seeing, I
suppose it is at most but belief and assurance: and the proposition taken for a revelation, is not such as they *know* to be
true, but *take* to be true. For where a proposition is known to
be true, revelation is needless: and it is hard to conceive how
there can be a revelation to any one of what he knows already. If therefore it be a proposition which they are persuaded, but do not know, to be true, whatever they may call
it, it is not seeing, but believing. For these are two ways
whereby truth comes into the mind, wholly distinct, so that
one is not the other. What I see, I know to be so, by the evidence of the thing itself: what I believe, I take to be so upon
the testimony of another. But this testimony I must know to
be given, or else what ground have I of believing? I must see
that it is God that reveals this to me, or else I see nothing.
The question then here is: How do I know that God is the revealer of this to me; that this impression is made upon my
mind by his Holy Spirit; and that therefore I ought to obey
it? If I know not this, how great soever the assurance is that I
am possessed with, it is groundless; whatever light I pretend

to, it is but *enthusiasm.* For, whether the proposition supposed to be revealed be in itself evidently true, or visibly
probable, or, by the natural ways of knowledge, uncertain,
the proposition that must be well grounded and manifested
to be true, is this, That God is the revealer of it, and that
what I take to be a revelation is certainly put into my mind
by Him, and is not an illusion dropped in by some other
spirit, or raised by my own fancy. For, if I mistake not, these
men receive it for true, because they presume God revealed
it. Does it not, then, stand them upon to examine upon what
grounds they presume it to be a revelation from God? or else
all their confidence is mere presumption: and this light they
are so dazzled with is nothing but an *ignis fatuus,* that leads
them constantly round in this circle; *It is a revelation, because they firmly believe it;* and *they believe it, because it is
a revelation.*

In all that is of divine revelation, there is need of no other
proof but that it is an inspiration from God: for he can neither deceive nor be deceived. But how shall it be known that
any proposition in our minds is a truth infused by God; a
truth that is revealed to us by him, which he declares to us,
and therefore we ought to believe? Here it is that enthusiasm
fails of the evidence it pretends to. For men thus possessed,
boast of a light whereby they say they are enlightened, and
brought into the knowledge of this or that truth. But if they
know it to be a truth, they must know it to be so, either by its
own self-evidence to natural reason, or by the rational proofs
that make it out to be so. If they see and know it to be a
truth, either of these two ways they in vain suppose it to be a
revelation. For they know it to be true the same way that any
other man naturally may know that it is so, without the help
of revelation. For thus, all the truths, of what kind soever,
that men uninspired are enlightened with, came into their
minds, and are established there. If they say they know it to
be true, because it is a revelation from God, the reason is
good: but then it will be demanded how they know it to be a

revelation from God. If they say, by the light it brings with it, which shines bright in their minds, and they cannot resist: I beseech them to consider whether this be any more than what we have taken notice of already, viz. that it is a revelation, because they strongly believe it to be true. For all the light they speak of is but a strong, though ungrounded persuasion of their own minds, that it is a truth. For rational grounds from proofs that it is a truth, they must acknowledge to have none; for then it is not received as a revelation, but upon the ordinary grounds that other truths are received: and if they believe it to be true because it is a revelation, and have no other reason for its being a revelation, but because they are fully persuaded, without any other reason, that it is true, then they believe it to be a revelation only because they strongly believe it to be a revelation; which is a very unsafe ground to proceed on, either in our tenets or actions. And what readier way can there be to run ourselves into the most extravagant errors and miscarriages, than thus to set up fancy for our supreme and sole guide, and to believe any proposition to be true, any action to be right, only because we believe it to be so? The strength of our persuasions is no evidence at all of their own rectitude: crooked things may be as stiff and inflexible as straight: and men may be as positive and peremptory in error as in truth. How come else the untractable zealots in different and opposite parties? For if the light, which every one thinks he has in his mind, which in this case is nothing but the strength of his own persuasion, be an evidence that it is from God, contrary opinions have the same title to be inspirations; and God will be not only the Father of lights, but of opposite and contradictory lights, leading men contrary ways; and contradictory propositions will be divine truths, if an ungrounded strength of assurance be an evidence that any proposition is a Divine Revelation.

This cannot be otherwise, whilst firmness of persuasion is made the cause of believing, and confidence of being in the right is made an argument of truth. St. Paul himself believed he did well, and that he had a call to it, when he persecuted the Christians, whom he confidently thought in the wrong: but yet it was he, and not they, who were mistaken. Good men are men still liable to mistakes, and are sometimes warmly engaged in errors, which they take for divine truths, shining in their minds with the clearest light.

Light, true light, in the mind is, or can be, nothing else but the evidence of the truth of any proposition; and if it be not a self-evident proposition, all the light it has, or can have, is from the clearness and validity of those proofs upon which it is received. To talk of any other light in the understanding is to put ourselves in the dark, or in the power of the Prince of Darkness, and, by our own consent, to give ourselves up to delusion to believe a lie. For, if strength of persuasion be the light which must guide us; I ask how shall any one distinguish between the delusions of Satan, and the inspirations of the Holy Ghost? He can transform himself into an angel of light. And they who are led by this Son of the Morning are as fully satisfied of the illumination, i.e. are as strongly persuaded that they are enlightened by the Spirit of God as any one who is so: they acquiesce and rejoice in it, are actuated by it: and nobody can be more sure, nor more in the right (if their own strong belief may be judge) than they.

He, therefore, that will not give himself up to all the extravagances of delusion and error must bring this guide of his *light within* to the trial. God when he makes the prophet does not unmake the man. He leaves all his faculties in the natural state, to enable him to judge of his inspirations, whether they be of *divine* original or no. When he illuminates the mind with supernatural light, he does not extinguish that which is natural. If he would have us assent to the truth of any proposition, he either evidences that truth by the usual methods of natural reason, or else makes it known to be a truth which he would have us assent to by his authority, and convinces us that it is from him, by some marks which reason cannot be mistaken in. *Reason must be our last judge and guide in everything.*[10] I do not mean that we must consult reason, and examine whether a proposition revealed from God can be made out by natural principles, and if it cannot, that then we may reject it: but consult it we must, and by it examine whether it be a revelation from God or no: and if reason finds it to be revealed from God, reason then declares for it as much as for any other truth, and makes it one of her dictates. Every conceit that thoroughly warms our fancies must pass for an inspiration, if there be nothing but the strength of our persuasions, whereby to judge of our persuasions: if reason must not examine their truth by something extrinsical to the persuasions themselves, inspirations and delusions, truth and falsehood, will have the same measure, and will not be possible to be distinguished.

If this internal light, or any proposition which under that title we take for inspired, be conformable to the principles of reason, or to the word of God, which is attested revelation, reason warrants it, and we may safely receive it for true, and be guided by it in our belief and actions: if it receive no testimony nor evidence from either of these rules, we cannot take it for a revelation, or so much as for true, till we have some other mark that it is a revelation, besides our believing that it is so. Thus we see the holy men of old, who had revelations from God, had something else besides that internal light of assurance in their own minds, to testify to them that it was from God. They were not left to their own persuasions alone, that those persuasions were from God, but had *outward signs* to convince them of the Author of those revelations. And when they were to convince others, they had a power given them to justify the truth of their commission from heaven,

---

[10] Although Locke usually identifies reason with intuition and deduction, he sometimes extends it to include what is frequently called "probable reasoning". See, for example, *Essay*, Book IV, Chapter XVII, Section 2. Many of his observations about the role of reason in religion require him to use the word "reason" in this extended sense. [M.W.]

and by visible signs to assert the divine authority of a message they were sent with. Moses saw the bush burn without being consumed, and heard a voice out of it: this was something besides finding an impulse upon his mind to go to Pharaoh, that he might bring his brethren out of Egypt: and yet he thought not this enough to authorize him to go with that message, till God, by another miracle of his rod turned into a serpent, had assured him of a power to testify his mission, by the same miracle repeated before them whom he was sent to. Gideon was sent by an angel to deliver Israel from the Midianites, and yet he desired a sign to convince him that this commission was from God. These, and several the like instances to be found among the prophets of old, are enough to show that they thought not an inward seeing or persuasion of their own minds, without any other proof, a sufficient evidence that it was from God; though the Scripture does not everywhere mention their demanding or having such proofs.

In what I have said I am far from denying, that God can, or doth sometimes enlighten men's minds in the apprehending of certain truths or excite them to good actions, by the immediate influence and assistance of the Holy Spirit, *without any extraordinary signs accompanying it.* But in such cases too we have reason and Scripture; unerring rules to know whether it be from God or no. Where the truth embraced is consonant to the revelation in the written word of God, or the action conformable to the dictates of right reason or holy writ, we may be assured that we run no risk in entertaining it as such: because, though perhaps it be not an immediate revelation from God, extraordinarily operating on our minds, yet we are sure it is warranted by that revelation which he has given us of truth. But it is not the strength of our private persuasion within ourselves, that can warrant it to be a light or motion from heaven: nothing can do that but the written Word of God without us, or that standard of reason which is common to us with all men. Where reason or Scripture is express for any opinion or action, we may receive it as of divine authority: but it is not the strength of our own persuasions which can by itself give it that stamp. The bent of our own minds may favour it as much as we please: that may show it to be a fondling of our own, but will by no means prove it to be an offspring of heaven, and of divine original.

Part 2: The Eighteenth Century: Philosophy in the Service of Religion and Law

JONATHAN EDWARDS

The first American philosopher of distinction, Jonathan Edwards (1703–1758), was as acute a reasoner as any American philosopher to follow him, though it would be difficult to credit him with any profoundly original philosophical idea because he worked mainly within the confines set by Locke's philosophy and Calvinist theology. Nevertheless, he was able to pen some very interesting and extremely influential philosophical works, which are especially remarkable because he produced them while serving as a minister in eighteenth-century western Massachusetts, deprived of serious philosophical society. His *Treatise Concerning Religious Affections* (1746) was primarily an effort to establish the foundations of what he called "heart religion", by arguing that the Protestant elect have a "Sense of the Heart" which transcends the normal, Lockeian five; in his *Freedom of the Will* (1754), Edwards used great ingenuity in trying to show that a man's actions may be morally judged even when they are in accordance with choices necessitated by his having been born in original sin. According to Edwards, some men may mystically see the loveliness of a God who permits other men to remain in the state of sinfulness which leads to their destruction.

In his effort to steer a course between the excessively rational religion of those he called formalists and the ravings of those whom Locke called Enthusiasts, Edwards maintained that religious affections or emotions are brought about by the presence of the idea of God's loveliness in the understanding of one who has received grace. As a disciple of Locke, Edwards was bound to suppose that all ideas arise from experience, either through sensation or reflection; but since Edwards did not think that the idea of God's loveliness could enter a saint's understanding through reflection or through the ordinary senses, Edwards concluded that it must enter through an extraordinary sense which he called the Sense of the Heart.

Like St. Augustine, Edwards was a mystic who could argue, and this is most evident in his writings on free will. Edwards held, in company with many thinkers before him, that all we need establish in order to judge an action is that it was performed in accordance with the agent's choice. If the moral agent did as he chose, then he had freedom enough for Edwards, who undertook two dialectical tasks in defense of this view. One was primarily negative and the other primarily positive. The negative one consisted of an attack on those whom he called Arminians after the Dutch theologian, Jacobus Arminius (1560–1609). According to one Arminian view, an action may be judged morally only if: (*a*) it has been performed in accordance with the agent's choice and (*b*) the choice has been determined by the agent's will. The addition of condition (*b*) drew Edwards' most effective polemical fire. Edwards also attacked other versions of Arminianism, notably the idea that the moral agent's choice is not determined at all—which he easily showed to be inconsistent with the idea that it was determined by the will—and the idea that the choice is made while the agent is in a state where no motive is "preponderant".

The most important positive part of Edwards' defense of Calvinism was his effort to show that an action performed in accordance with the agent's choice may be judged even though the choice itself had been caused, determined, or necessary. This was required of Edwards not only because he accepted the principle of universal causation, according to which all events, and therefore all choices, are caused; but also because he subscribed to the Calvinist view that a man who was born in original sin and who therefore necessarily acted wrongly can nevertheless be blamed for his action if that action had been performed in accordance with his choice. In this part of his argument Edwards appealed to a distinction between two uses of the word "necessary", one ordinary, the other technically philosophical. In ordinary language, Edwards argued, a man who does as he chooses, acts freely and therefore not of necessity even though his choice is *philosophically* or, as Edwards sometimes says, *morally* necessary. The man who steals by his own choice is said in ordinary language to *act* freely even though a philosopher would say that he *chose* to do so necessarily because his choice was caused. Edwards tried to rebut the argument that the philosophical necessity of the thief's choice excuses his action. Edwards' main argument here was that the only exculpatory necessity is that which we attribute when we say of an *action* that even if the agent had chosen not to perform the action, he still would have performed it. But, Edwards continued, if we try to attribute this kind of necessity to the thief's *choice* in an effort to excuse him, we lapse into nonsense. Edwards held that we cannot significantly say, "Even though the thief had chosen not to choose to steal, he nevertheless chose to steal", because the first clause of this sentence is meaningless. It refers to an inconceivable state of affairs. Edwards granted the meaningfulness of supposing that on Monday a thief chose not to choose on Tuesday to steal the crown jewels, or of supposing that a habitual drunkard resolved on Monday not to choose on Tuesday to take a drink at a forthcoming party. But Edwards asserted the meaninglessness of the supposition that at 9 a.m. on Monday the drunkard chose not to choose at 9 a.m. on Monday to take a drink then. It follows, Edwards argued, that we cannot significantly make the one kind of statement we would have to make in order to excuse a choice; and therefore the Calvinist who maintains that the philosophical necessity of the sinner's choice is compatible with condemning him is not refutable by any appeal to the ordinary conception of necessity.

The selections below are divided into two main sections, one on the Sense of the Heart and the other on free will; and the latter has been further divided by the use of headings which are my own. In the second main section, selections are not arranged in the order in which they appear in Edwards' *Freedom of the Will.* The first presents his view of the ordinary meaning of the phrase "free action"; the second conveys his view that choices are caused or determined, a view which he holds even though he maintains that we can define "free action" without reference to the cause of the agent's choice; the third contains his general reflections on necessity, most notably his idea that choices are necessary in the philosophical but not in the ordinary sense; the fourth deals with his notion of moral necessity, which is for him a species of consequential necessity, which in turn is a species of philosophical necessity; the fifth contains his attack on one of three Arminian views he opposes; and the sixth reveals the connection between his Calvinism and his views on free will.

The Sense of the Heart [1]

There is such a thing, if the Scriptures are of any use to teach us anything, as a spiritual, supernatural understanding of divine things, that is peculiar to the saints, and which those who are not saints have nothing of. 'Tis certainly

[1] This passage comes from Jonathan Edwards, *Religious Affections,* edited by J. E. Smith. Copyright 1959 by Yale University Press, pp. 270–75. Reprinted by permission.

a kind of understanding, apprehending or discerning of divine things, that natural men have nothing of, which the Apostle speaks of, "But the natural man receiveth not the things of the Spirit of God; for they are foolishness unto him; neither can he know them, because they are spiritually discerned" (I Cor. 2:14). 'Tis certainly a kind of seeing or discerning spiritual things, peculiar to the saints, which is spoken of, "Whosoever sinneth hath not seen him, neither known him" (I John 3:6). "He that doeth evil hath not seen God" (III John 11). And "This is the will of him that sent me, that every one that seeth the Son, and believeth on him, may have everlasting life" (John 6:40). "The world seeth me no more; but ye see me" (ch. 14:19). "This is eternal life, that they might know thee the only true God, and Jesus Christ whom thou has sent" (ch. 17:3). "No man knoweth the Son, but the Father; neither knoweth any man the Father, but the Son, and he to whomsoever the Son will reveal him" (Matt. 11:27). "He that seeth me, seeth him that sent me" (John 12:45). "They that know thy name, will put their trust in thee" (Ps. 9:10). "I count all things but loss, for the excellency of the knowledge of Christ Jesus my Lord" (Phil. 3:8). "That I may know him" (ver. 10). And innumerable other places there are, all over the Bible, which show the same. And that there is such a thing as an understanding of divine things, which in its nature and kind is wholly different from all knowledge that natural men have, is evident from this, that there is an understanding of divine things, which the Scripture calls spiritual understanding; "We do not cease to pray for you, and to desire that you may be filled with the knowledge of his will, in all wisdom, and spiritual understanding" (Col. 1:9). It has been already shown, that that which is spiritual, in the ordinary use of the word in the New Testament, is entirely different in nature and kind, from all which natural men are, or can be the subjects of.

From hence it may be surely inferred, wherein spiritual understanding consists. For if there be in the saints a kind of apprehension or perception, which is in its nature, perfectly diverse from all that natural men have, or that it is possible they should have, till they have a new nature; it must consist in their having a certain kind of ideas or sensations of mind, which are simply diverse from all that is or can be in the minds of natural men. And that is the same thing as to say, that it consists in the sensations of a new spiritual sense, which the souls of natural men have not; as is evident by what has been before, once and again observed. But I have already shown what that new spiritual sense is, which the saints have given them in regeneration, and what is the object of it. I have shown that the immediate object of it is the supreme beauty and excellency of the nature of divine things, as they are in themselves. And this is agreeable to the Scripture: the Apostle very plainly teaches that the great thing discovered by spiritual light, and understood by spiritual knowledge, is the glory of divine things, "But if our gospel be hid, it is hid to them that are lost; in whom the God of this world hath blinded the minds of them that believe not, lest the light of the glorious gospel of Christ, who is the image of God, should shine unto them" (II Cor. 4:3–4), together with: "For God who commanded the light to shine out of darkness, hath shined in our hearts, to give the light of the knowledge of the glory of God in the face of Jesus Christ" (ver. 6): and ch. 3:18 preceding: "But we all, with open face, beholding as in a glass, the glory of the Lord, are changed into the same image, from glory to glory, even as by the Spirit of the Lord." And it must needs be so, for as has been before observed, the Scripture often teaches that all true religion summarily consists in the love of divine things. And therefore that kind of understanding or knowledge, which is the proper foundation of true religion, must be the knowledge of the loveliness of divine things. For doubtless, that knowledge which is the proper foundation of love, is the knowledge of loveliness. What that beauty or loveliness of divine things is, which is the proper and immediate object of a spiritual sense of mind, was showed under the last head insisted on, viz. that it is the beauty of their moral perfection. Therefore it is in the view or sense of this, that Spiritual understanding does more immediately and primarily consist. And indeed it is plain it can be nothing else; for (as has been shown) there is nothing pertaining to divine things besides the beauty of their moral excellency, and those properties and qualities of divine things which this beauty is the foundation of, but what natural men and devils can see and know, and will know fully and clearly to all eternity.

From what has been said, therefore, we come necessarily to this conclusion, concerning that wherein spiritual understanding consists; viz. that it consists in a sense of the heart, of the supreme beauty and sweetness of the holiness or moral perfection of divine things, together with all that discerning and knowledge of things of religion, that depends upon, and flows from such a sense.

Spiritual understanding consists primarily in a sense of heart of that spiritual beauty. I say, a sense of heart; for it is not speculation merely that is concerned in this kind of understanding: nor can there be a clear distinction made between the two faculties of understanding and will, as acting distinctly and separately, in this matter. When the mind is sensible of the sweet beauty and amiableness of a thing, that implies a sensibleness of sweetness and delight in the presence of the idea of it: and this sensibleness of the amiableness or delightfulness of beauty, carries in the very nature of it, the sense of the heart; or an effect and impression the soul is the subject of, as a substance possessed of taste, inclination and will.

There is a distinction to be made between a mere notional understanding, wherein the mind only beholds things in the exercise of a speculative faculty; and the sense of the heart, wherein the mind don't only speculate and behold, but relishes and feels. That sort of knowledge, by which a man has a sensible perception of amiableness and loathsomeness, or of sweetness and nauseousness, is not just the same sort of knowledge with that, by which he knows what a triangle is, and what a square is. The one is mere speculative knowledge; the other sensible knowledge, in which more than the mere intellect is concerned; the heart is the proper subject of it, or the soul as a being that not only beholds, but has inclination, and is pleased or displeased. And yet there is the nature of instruction in it; as he that has perceived the sweet taste of honey, knows much more about it; than he who has only looked upon and felt of it.

The Apostle seems to make a distinction between mere speculative knowledge of the things of religion, and spiritual knowledge, in calling that the form of knowledge, and of the truth; "which has the form of knowledge, and of the truth in the law" (Rom. 2:20). The latter is often represented by relishing, smelling, or tasting; "Now thanks be to God, which always causeth us to triumph in Christ Jesus, and maketh manifest the savor of his knowledge, in every place" (II Cor. 2:14). "Thou savorest not the things that be of God, but those things that be of man" (Matt. 16:23). "As newborn babes, desire the sincere milk of the word, that ye may grow thereby; if so be ye have tasted that the Lord is gracious" (I Pet. 2:2–3). "Because of the savor of thy good ointment, thy name is as ointment poured forth; therefore do the virgins love thee" (Cant. 1:3); compared with: "But ye have an unction from the holy One, and ye know all things" (I John 2:20).

Spiritual understanding primarily consists in this sense, or taste of the moral beauty of divine things; so that no knowledge can be called spiritual, any further than it arises from this, and has this in it. But secondarily, it includes all that discerning and knowledge of things of religion, which depends upon, and flows from such a sense.

When the true beauty and amiableness of the holiness or true moral good that is in divine things, is discovered to the soul, it as it were opens a new world to its view. This shows the glory of all the perfections of God, and of everything appertaining to the divine being: for, as was observed before, the beauty of all arises from God's moral perfection. This shows the glory of all God's works, both of creation and providence: for 'tis the special glory of them, that God's holiness, righteousness, faithfulness and goodness are so manifested in them; and without these moral perfections, there would be no glory in that power and skill with which they are wrought. The glorifying of God's moral perfections, is the special end of all the works of God's hands. By this sense of the moral beauty of divine things, is understood the sufficiency of Christ as a mediator: for 'tis only by the discovery of the beauty of the moral perfection of Christ, that the believer is let into the knowledge of the excellency of his person, so as to know anything more of it than the devils do: and 'tis only by the knowledge of the excellency of Christ's person, that any know his sufficiency as a mediator; for the latter depends upon, and arises from the former. 'Tis by seeing the excellency of Christ's person, that the saints are made sensible of the preciousness of his blood, and its sufficiency to atone for sin: for therein consists the preciousness of Christ's blood, that 'tis the blood of so excellent and amiable a person. And on this depends the meritoriousness of his obedience, and sufficiency and prevalence of his intercession. By this sight of the moral beauty of divine things, is seen the beauty of the way of salvation by Christ: for that consists in the beauty of the moral perfections of God, which wonderfully shines forth in every step of this method of salvation, from beginning to end. By this is seen the fitness and suitableness of this way: for this wholly consists in its tendency to deliver us from sin and hell, and to bring us to the happiness which consists in the possession and enjoyment of moral good, in a way sweetly agreeing with God's moral perfections. And in the way's being contrived so as to attain these ends, consists the excellent wisdom of that way. By this is seen the excellency of the Word of God: take away all the moral beauty and sweetness in the Word, and the Bible is left

wholly a dead letter, a dry, lifeless, tasteless thing. By this is
seen the true foundation of our duty; the worthiness of God
to be so esteemed, honored, loved, submitted to, and served,
as he requires of us, and the amiableness of the duties themselves that are required of us. And by this is seen the true
evil of sin: for he who sees the beauty of holiness, must necessarily see the hatefulness of sin, its contrary. By this men understand the true glory of heaven, which consists in the
beauty and happiness that is in holiness. By this is seen the
amiableness and happiness of both saints and angels. He that
sees the beauty of holiness, or true moral good, sees the
greatest and most important thing in the world, which is the
fullness of all things, without which all the world is empty,
no better than nothing, yea, worse than nothing. Unless this
is seen, nothing is seen, that is worth the seeing: for there is
no other true excellency or beauty. Unless this be understood, nothing is understood, that is worthy of the exercise of
the noble faculty of understanding. This is the beauty of the
Godhead, and the divinity of Divinity (if I may so speak), the
good of the infinite Fountain of Good; without which God
himself (if that were possible to be) would be an infinite evil:
without which, we ourselves had better never have been; and
without which there had better have been no being. He
therefore in effect knows nothing, that knows not this: his
knowledge is but the shadow of knowledge, or the form of
knowledge, as the Apostle calls it. Well therefore may the
Scripture represent those who are destitute of that spiritual
sense, by which is perceived the beauty of holiness, as totally
blind, deaf and senseless, yea dead. And well may regeneration, in which this divine sense is given to the soul by its Creator, be represented as opening the blind eyes, and raising
the dead, and bringing a person into a new world. For if
what has been said be considered, it will be manifest, that
when a person has this sense and knowledge given him, he
will view nothing as he did before; though before he knew all
things after the flesh, yet henceforth he will know them so no

more; and he is become "a new creature, old things are passed away, behold all things are become new"; agreeable to II Cor. 5:16–17.

And besides the things that have been already mentioned, there arises from this sense of spiritual beauty, all true experimental knowledge of religion; which is of itself, as it were a new world of knowledge. He that sees not the beauty of holiness, knows not what one of the graces of God's Spirit is; he is destitute of any idea or conception of all gracious exercises of soul, and all holy comforts and delights, and all effects of the saving influences of the Spirit of God on the heart: and so is ignorant of the greatest works of God, the most important and glorious effects of his power upon the creature: and also is wholly ignorant of the saints as saints; he knows not what they are: and in effect is ignorant of the whole spiritual world.

Things being thus, it plainly appears, that God's implanting that spiritual supernatural sense which has been spoken of, makes a great change in a man. And were it not for the very imperfect degree, in which this sense is commonly given at first, or the small degree of this glorious light that first dawns upon the soul; the change made by this spiritual opening of the eyes in conversion, would be much greater, and more remarkable, every way, than if a man, who had been born blind, and with only the other four senses, should continue so for a long time, and then at once should have the sense of seeing imparted to him, in the midst of the clear light of the sun, discovering a world of visible objects. For though sight be more noble than any of the other external senses; yet this spiritual sense which has been spoken of, is infinitely more noble than that, or any other principle of discerning that a man naturally has, and the object of this sense infinitely greater and more important.

This sort of understanding or knowledge is that knowledge of divine things from whence all truly gracious affections do proceed: by which therefore all affections are to be tried.

Those affections that arise wholly from any other kind of knowledge, or do result from any other kind of apprehensions of mind, are vain.

Freedom of the Will
THE ORDINARY MEANING OF "FREE ACTION" [2]

The plain and obvious meaning of the words "freedom" and "liberty," in common speech, is power, opportunity, or advantage, that anyone has, to do as he pleases. Or in other words, his being free from hindrance or impediment in the way of doing, or conducting in any respect, as he wills.[3] And the contrary to liberty, whatever name we call that by, is a person's being hindered or unable to conduct as he will, or being necessitated to do otherwise.

If this which I have mentioned be the meaning of the word "liberty," in the ordinary use of language; as I trust that none that has ever learned to talk, and is unprejudiced, will deny; then it will follow, that in propriety of speech, neither liberty, nor its contrary, can properly be ascribed to any being or thing, but that which has such a faculty, power or property, as is called "will." For that which is possessed of no such thing as will, can't have any power or opportunity of doing according to its will, nor be necessitated to act contrary to its will, nor be restrained from acting agreeably to it. And therefore to talk of liberty, or the contrary, as belonging to the very will itself, is not to speak good sense; if we judge of sense, and nonsense, by the original and proper signification of words. For the will itself is not an agent that has a will: the power of choosing, itself, has not a power of choosing.

[2] From Jonathan Edwards, *Freedom of the Will*, edited by Paul Ramsey. Copyright 1957 by Yale University Press, pp. 163–64. Reprinted by permission.
[3] Here Edwards adds the following note: "I say not only 'doing,' but 'conducting'; because a voluntary forbearing to do, sitting still, keeping silence, etc. are instances of persons' conduct, about which liberty is exercised; though they are not properly called 'doing' ". [M.W.]

That which has the power of volition or choice is the man or
the soul, and not the power of volition itself. And he that has
the liberty of doing according to his will, is the agent or doer
who is possessed of the will; and not the will which he is possessed of. We say with propriety, that a bird let loose has
power and liberty to fly; but not that the bird's power of
flying has a power and liberty of flying. To be free is the
property of an agent, who is possessed of powers and faculties, as much as to be cunning, valiant, bountiful, or zealous.
But these qualities are the properties of men or persons; and
not the properties of properties.

There are two things that are contrary to this which is
called liberty in common speech. One is *constraint;* the same
is otherwise called force, compulsion, and coaction; which is
a person's being necessitated to do a thing *contrary* to his
will. The other is *restraint;* which is his being hindered, and
not having power to do *according* to his will. But that which
has no will, can't be the subject of these things.—I need say
the less on this head, Mr. Locke having set the same thing
forth, with so great clearness, in his *Essay on the Human Understanding.*

But one thing more I would observe concerning what is
vulgarly called liberty; namely, that power and opportunity
for one to do and conduct as he will, or according to his
choice, is all that is meant by it; without taking into the
meaning of the word, anything of the cause or original of that
choice; or at all considering how the person came to have
such a volition; whether it was caused by some external motive, or internal habitual bias; whether it was determined by
some internal antecedent volition, or whether it happened
without a cause; whether it was necessarily connected with
something foregoing, or not connected. Let the person come
by his volition or choice how he will, yet, if he is able, and
there is nothing in the way to hinder his pursuing and executing his will, the man is fully and perfectly free, according
to the primary and common notion of freedom.

THE DETERMINATION OF THE WILL [4]

By "determining the will," if the phrase be used with any meaning, must be intended, causing that the act of the will or choice should be thus, and not otherwise: and the will is said to be determined, when, in consequence of some action, or influence, its choice is directed to, and fixed upon a particular object. As when we speak of the determination of motion, we mean causing the motion of the body to be such a way, or in such a direction, rather than another.

To talk of the determination of the will, supposes an effect, which must have a cause. If the will be determined, there is a determiner. This must be supposed to be intended even by them that say, the will determines itself. If it be so, the will is both determiner and determined; it is a cause that acts and produces effects upon itself, and is the object of its own influence and action.

With respect to that grand inquiry, what determines the will, it would be very tedious and unnecessary at present to enumerate and examine all the various opinions, which have been advanced concerning this mattter; nor is it needful that I should enter into a particular disquisition of all points debated in disputes on that question, whether the will always follows the last dictate of the understanding. It is sufficient to my present purpose to say, it is that motive, which, as it stands in the view of the mind, is the strongest, that determines the will.—But it may be necessary that I should a little explain my meaning in this.

By "motive," I mean the whole of that which moves, excites or invites the mind to volition, whether that be one thing singly, or many things conjunctly. Many particular things may concur and unite their strength to induce the mind; and when it is so, all together are as it were one com-

[4] Edwards, *Freedom of the Will*, pp. 141–42; p. 185.

plex motive. And when I speak of the "strongest motive," I have respect to the strength of the whole that operates to induce to a particular act of volition, whether that be the strength of one thing alone, or of many together.

Whatever is a motive, in this sense, must be something that is extant in the view or apprehension of the understanding, or perceiving faculty. Nothing can induce or invite the mind to will or act anything, any further than it is perceived, or is some way or other in the mind's view; for what is wholly unperceived, and perfectly out of the mind's view, can't affect the mind at all. 'Tis most evident, that nothing is in the mind, or reaches it, or takes any hold of it, any otherwise than as it is perceived or thought of.

And I think it must also be allowed by all, that everything that is properly called a motive, excitement or inducement to a perceiving willing agent, has some sort and degree of tendency, or advantage to move or excite the will, previous to the effect, or to the act of the will excited. This previous tendency of the motive is what I call the "strength" of the motive. That motive which has a less degree of previous advantage or tendency to move the will, or that appears less inviting, as it stands in the view of the mind, is what I call a "weaker motive." On the contrary, that which appears most inviting, and has, by what appears concerning it to the understanding or apprehension, the greatest degree of previous tendency to excite and induce the choice, is what I call the "strongest motive." And in this sense, I suppose the will is always determined by the strongest motive.

Things that exist in the view of the mind, have their strength, tendency or advantage to move or excite its will, from many things appertaining to the nature and circumstances of the thing viewed, the nature and circumstances of the mind that views, and the degree and manner of its view; which it would perhaps be hard to make a perfect enumeration of. But so much I think may be determined in general, without room for controversy, that whatever is perceived or apprehended by an intelligent and voluntary agent, which has the nature and influence of a motive to volition or choice, is considered or viewed *as good;* nor has it any tendency to invite or engage the election of the soul in any further degree than it appears such. For to say otherwise, would be to say, that things that appear have a tendency by the appearance they make, to engage the mind to elect them, some other way than by their appearing eligible to it; which is absurd. And therefore it must be true, in some sense, that the will always is as the greatest apparent good is.

. . . [I]t is indeed as repugnant to reason, to suppose that an act of the will should come into existence without a cause, as to suppose the human soul, or an angel, or the globe of the earth, or the whole universe, should come into existence without a cause. And if once we allow, that such a sort of effect as a volition may come to pass without a cause, how do we know but that many other sorts of effects may do so too?

THE MEANING OF "NECESSARY" [5]

The words "necessary," "impossible," etc. are abundantly used in controversies about free will and moral agency; and therefore the sense in which they are used, should be clearly understood.

Here I might say, that a thing is then said to be necessary, when it must be, and cannot be otherwise. But this would not properly be a definition of necessity, or an explanation of the word, any more than if I explained the word "must" by there being a necessity. The words "must," "can," and "cannot" need explication as much as the words "necessary" and "impossible"; excepting that the former are words that children commonly use, and know something of the meaning of earlier than the latter.

The word "necessary," as used in common speech, is a rela-

[5] *Ibid.*, pp. 149–54.

tive term; and relates to some supposed opposition made to the existence of the thing spoken of, which is overcome, or proves in vain to hinder or alter it. That is necessary, in the original and proper sense of the word, which is, or will be, notwithstanding all supposable opposition. To say; that a thing is necessary, is the same thing as to say, that it is impossible [it] should not be: but the word "impossible" is manifestly a relative term, and has reference to supposed power exerted to bring a thing to pass, which is insufficient for the effect; as the word "unable" is relative, and has relation to ability or endeavor which is insufficient; and as the word "irresistible" is relative, and has always reference to resistance which is made, or may be made to some force or power tending to an effect, and is insufficient to withstand the power, or hinder the effect. The common notion of necessity and impossibility implies something that frustrates endeavor or desire.

Here several things are to be noted.

1. Things are said to be necessary *in general*, which are or will be notwithstanding any supposable opposition from us or others, or from whatever quarter. But things are said to be necessary *to us*, which are or will be notwithstanding all opposition supposable in the case *from us*. The same may be observed of the word "impossible" and other suchlike terms.

2. These terms "necessary," "impossible," "irresistible," etc. do especially belong to the controversy about liberty and moral agency, as used in the latter of the two senses now mentioned, viz. as necessary or impossible *to us*, and with relation to any supposable opposition or endeavor *of ours*.

3. As the word "necessity," in its vulgar and common use, is relative, and has always reference to some supposable insufficient opposition; so when we speak of anything as necessary *to us*, it is with relation to some supposable opposition of our wills, or some voluntary exertion or effort of ours to the contrary. For we don't properly make opposition to an event, any otherwise than as we voluntarily oppose it. Things are

said to be what must be, or necessarily are, *as to us,* when they are, or will be, though we desire or endeavor the contrary, or try to prevent or remove their existence: but such opposition of ours always either consists in, or implies opposition of our wills.

'Tis manifest that all suchlike words and phrases, as vulgarly used, are used and accepted in this manner. A thing is said to be necessary, when we can't help it, let us do what we will. So anything is said to be impossible to us, when we would do it, or would have it brought to pass, and endeavor it; or at least may be supposed to desire and seek it; but all our desires and endeavors are, or would be vain. And that is said to be irresistible, which overcomes all our opposition, resistance, and endeavor to the contrary. And we are to be said unable to do a thing, when our supposable desires and endeavors to do it are insufficient.

We are accustomed, in the common use of language, to apply and understand these phrases in this sense: we grow up with such a habit; which by the daily use of these terms, in such a sense, from our childhood, becomes fixed and settled; so that the idea of a relation to a supposed will, desire and endeavor of ours, is strongly connected with these terms, and naturally excited in our minds, whenever we hear the words used. Such ideas, and these words, are so united and associated, that they unavoidably go together; one suggests the other, and carries the other with it, and never can be separated as long as we live. And if we use the words, as terms of art, in another sense, yet, unless we are exceeding circumspect and wary, we shall insensibly slide into the vulgar use of them, and so apply the words in a very inconsistent manner: this habitual connection of ideas will deceive and confound us in our reasonings and discourses, wherein we pretend to use these terms in that manner, as terms of art.

4. It follows from what has been observed, that when these terms "necessary," "impossible," "irresistible," "unable," etc. are used in cases wherein no opposition, or insufficient will or

endeavor, is supposed, or can be supposed, but the very nature of the supposed case itself excludes and denies any such opposition, will or endeavor; these terms are then not used in their proper signification, but quite beside their use in common speech. The reason is manifest; namely, that in such cases, we can't use the words with reference to a supposable opposition, will or endeavor. And therefore if any man uses these terms in such cases, he either uses them nonsensically, or in some new sense, diverse from their original and proper meaning. As for instance; if a man should affirm after this manner, that it is necessary for a man, and what must be, that a man should choose virtue rather than vice, during the time that he prefers virtue to vice; and that it is a thing impossible and irresistible, that it should be otherwise than that he should have this choice, so long as this choice continues; such a man would use these terms "must," "irresistible," etc. with perfect insignificance and nonsense, or in some new sense, diverse from their common use; which is with reference, as has been observed, to supposable opposition, unwillingness and resistance; whereas, here, the very supposition excludes and denies any such thing: for the case supposed is that of being willing, and choosing.

5. It appears from what has been said, that these terms "necessary," "impossible," etc. are often used by philosophers and metaphysicians in a sense quite diverse from their common use and original signification: for they apply them to many cases in which no opposition is supposed or supposable. Thus they use them with respect to God's existence before the creation of the world, when there was no other being but he: so with regard to many of the dispositions and acts of the divine Being, such as his loving himself, his loving righteousness, hating sin, etc. So they apply these terms to many cases of the inclinations and actions of created intelligent beings, angels and men; wherein all opposition of the will is shut out and denied, in the very supposition of the case.

Metaphysical or philosophical necessity is nothing different from certainty.[6] I speak not now of the certainty of knowledge, but the certainty that is in things themselves, which is the foundation of the certainty of the knowledge of them; or that wherein lies the ground of the infallibility of the proposition which affirms them.

What is sometimes given as the definition of philosophical necessity, namely, that by which a thing cannot but be, or whereby it cannot be otherwise, fails of being a proper explanation of it, on two accounts: first, the words "can" or "cannot" need explanation as much as the word "necessity"; and the former may as well be explained by the latter, as the latter by the former. Thus, if anyone asked us what we mean, when we say, a thing cannot but be, we might explain ourselves by saying, we mean, it must necessarily be so; as well as explain necessity, by saying, it is that by which a thing cannot but be. And secondly, this definition is liable to the forementioned great inconvenience: the words "cannot" or "unable" are properly relative, and have relation to power exerted, or that may be exerted, in order to the thing spoken of; to which, as I have now observed, the word "necessity," as used by philosophers, has no reference.

Philosophical necessity is really nothing else than the full and fixed connection between the things signified by the subject and predicate of a proposition, which affirms something to be true. When there is such a connection, then the thing affirmed in the proposition is necessary, in a philosophical sense; whether any opposition, or contrary effort be supposed, or supposable in the case, or no. When the subject and predicate of the proposition, which affirms the existence of anything, either substance, quality, act or circumstance, have a full and certain connection, then the existence or being of

---

[6] Here Edwards' editor, Paul Ramsey, writes: "The 1754 ed. reads *their* certainty.' Here I follow JE, Jr., in correcting the text. See the list of errata added to the printed list in his copy of his father's book, Rare Book Room, Sterling Memorial Library, Yale University". [M.W.]

that thing is said to be necessary in a metaphysical sense. And in this sense I use the word "necessity," in the following discourse, when I endeavor to prove that necessity is not inconsistent with liberty.

The subject and predicate of a proposition, which affirms existence of something, may have a full, fixed, and certain connection several ways.

(1) They may have a full and perfect connection *in and of themselves;* because it may imply a contradiction, or gross absurdity, to suppose them not connected. Thus many things are necessary in their own nature. So the eternal existence of being generally considered, is necessary in itself: because it would be in itself the greatest absurdity, to deny the existence of being in general, or to say there was absolute and universal nothing; and is as it were the sum of all contradictions; as might be shewn, if this were a proper place for it. So God's infinity, and other attributes are necessary. So it is necessary in its own nature, that two and two should be four; and it is necessary, that all right lines drawn from the center of a circle to the circumference should be equal. It is necessary, fit and suitable, that men should do to others, as they would that they should do to them. So innumerable metaphysical and mathematical truths are necessary in themselves; the subject and predicate of the proposition which affirms them, are perfectly connected of themselves.

(2) The connection of the subject and predicate of a proposition, which affirms the existence of something, may be fixed and made certain, because the existence of that thing is already come to pass; and either now is, or has been; and so has as it were made sure of existence. And therefore, the proposition which affirms present and past existence of it, may by this means be made certain, and necessarily and unalterably true; the past event has fixed and decided the matter, as to its existence; and has made it impossible but that existence should be truly predicated of it. Thus the existence of whatever is already come to pass, is now become neces-

sary; 'tis become impossible it should be otherwise than true, that such a thing has been.

(3) The subject and predicate of a proposition which affirms something to be, may have a real and certain connection *consequentially;* and so the existence of the thing may be consequentially necessary; as it may be surely and firmly connected with something else, that is necessary in one of the former respects: as [7] it is either fully and thoroughly connected with that which is absolutely necessary in its own nature, or with something which has already received and made sure of existence. This necessity lies in, or may be explained by the connection of two or more propositions one with another. Things which are perfectly connected with other things that are necessary, are necessary themselves, by a necessity of consequence.

And here it may be observed, that all things which are future, or which will hereafter begin to be, which can be said to be necessary, are necessary only in this last way. Their existence is not necessary in itself; for if so, they always would have existed. Nor is their existence become necessary by being made sure, by being already come to pass. Therefore, the only way that anything that is to come to pass hereafter, is or can be necessary, is by a connection with something that is necessary in its own nature, or something that already is, or has been; so that the one being supposed, the other certainly follows. And this also is the only way that all things past, excepting those which were from eternity, could be necessary before they came to pass, or could come to pass necessarily; and therefore the only way in which any effect or event, or anything whatsoever that ever has had, or will have a beginning, has come into being necessarily, or will hereafter necessarily exist. And therefore this is the necessity which especially belongs to controversies about the acts of the will.

[7] Here Edwards' editor notes: "The 1754 ed. begins a new incomplete sentence". [M.W.]

MORAL NECESSITY AND INABILITY [8]

That necessity which has been explained, consisting in an infallible connection of the things signified by the subject and predicate of a proposition, as intelligent beings are the subjects of it, is distinguished into moral and natural necessity.

I shall not now stand to inquire whether this distinction be a proper and perfect distinction; but shall only explain how these two sorts of necessity are understood, as the terms are sometimes used, and as they are used in the following discourse.

The phrase "moral necessity" is used variously: sometimes 'tis used for a necessity of moral obligation. So we say, a man is under necessity, when he is under bonds of duty and conscience, which he can't be discharged from. So the word "necessity" is often used for great obligation in point of interest. Sometimes by "moral necessity" is meant that apparent connection of things, which is the ground of moral evidence; and so is distinguished from absolute necessity, or that sure connection of things, that is a foundation for infallible certainty. In this sense, "moral necessity" signifies much the same as that high degree of probability, which is ordinarily sufficient to satisfy, and be relied upon by mankind, in their conduct and behavior in the world, as they would consult their own safety and interest, and treat others properly as members of society. And sometimes by "moral necessity" is meant that necessity of connection and consequence, which arises from such *moral causes,* as the strength of inclination, or motives, and the connection which there is in many cases between these, and such certain volitions and actions. And it is in this sense, that I use the phrase "moral necessity" in the following discourse.

[8] Edwards, *Freedom of the Will,* pp. 156–62.

By "natural necessity," as applied to men, I mean such necessity as men are under through the force of natural causes; as distinguished from what are called moral causes, such as habits and dispositions of the heart, and moral motives and inducements. Thus men placed in certain circumstances, are the subjects of particular sensations by necessity: they feel pain when their bodies are wounded; they see the objects presented before them in a clear light, when their eyes are opened: so they assent to the truth of certain propositions, as soon as the terms are understood; as that two and two make four, that black is not white, that two parallel lines can never cross one another: so by a natural necessity men's bodies move downwards, when there is nothing to support them.

But here several things may be noted concerning these two kinds of necessity.

1. Moral necessity may be as absolute, as natural necessity. That is, the effect may be as perfectly connected with its moral cause, as a naturally necessary effect is with its natural cause. Whether the will in every case is necessarily determined by the strongest motive, or whether the will ever makes any resistance to such a motive, or can ever oppose the strongest present inclination, or not; if that matter should be controverted, yet I suppose none will deny, but that, in some cases, a previous bias and inclination, or the motive presented, may be so powerful, that the act of the will may be certainly and indissolubly connected therewith. When motives or previous bias are very strong, all will allow that there is some difficulty in going against them. And if they were yet stronger, the difficulty would be still greater. And therefore, if more were still added to their strength, to a certain degree, it would make the difficulty so great, that it would be wholly impossible to surmount it; for this plain reason, because whatever power men may be supposed to have to surmount difficulties, yet that power is not infinite; and so goes not beyond certain limits. If a man can surmount ten degrees of difficulty of this kind, with twenty degrees of strength, because

the degrees of strength are beyond the degrees of difficulty; yet if the difficulty be increased to thirty, or an hundred, or a thousand degrees, and his strength not also increased, his strength will be wholly insufficient to surmount the difficulty. As therefore it must be allowed, that there may be such a thing as a sure and perfect connection between moral causes and effects; so this only is what I call by the name of "moral necessity."

2. When I use this distinction of moral and natural necessity, I would not be understood to suppose, that if anything comes to pass by the former kind of necessity, the nature of things is not concerned in it, as well as in the latter. I don't mean to determine, that when a moral habit or motive is so strong, that the act of the will infallibly follows, this is not owing to the nature of things. But these are the names that these two kinds of necessity have usually been called by; and they must be distinguished by some names or other; for there is a distinction or difference between them, that is very important in its consequences: which [9] difference does not lie so much in the nature of the connection, as in the two terms connected. The cause with which the effect is connected, is of a particular kind; viz. that which is of a moral nature; either some previous habitual disposition, or some motive exhibited to the understanding. And the effect is also of a particular kind; being likewise of a moral nature; consisting in some inclination or volition of the soul, or voluntary action.

I suppose, that necessity which is called natural, in distinction from moral necessity, is so called, because "mere nature," as the word is vulgarly used, is concerned, without anything of choice. The word "nature" is often used in opposition to "choice"; not because nature has indeed never any hand in

[9] Here Ramsey writes: "The 1754 ed. begins a new incomplete sentence. A correction seems to be needed at this point, although I ordinarily retain JE's longer incomplete sentences characteristically beginning with 'Which' ". [M.W.]

our choice; but this probably comes to pass by means that we first get our notion of nature from that discernible and obvious course of events, which we observe in many things that our choice has no concern in; and especially in the material world; which, in very many parts of it, we easily perceive to be in a settled course; the stated order and manner of succession being very apparent. But where we don't readily discern the rule and connection (though there be a connection, according to an established law, truly taking place), we signify the manner of event by some other name. Even in many things which are seen in the material and inanimate world, which don't discernibly and obviously come to pass according to any settled course, men don't call the manner of the event by the name of nature, but by such names as "accident," "chance," "contingence," etc. So men make a distinction between "nature" and "choice"; as though they were completely and universally distinct. Whereas, I suppose none will deny but that choice, in many cases, arises from nature, as truly as other events. But the dependence and connection between acts of volition or choice, and their causes, according to established laws, is not so sensible and obvious. And we observe that choice is as it were a new principle of motion and action, different from that established law and order of things which is most obvious, that is seen especially in corporeal and sensible things; and also that choice often interposes, interrupts and alters the chain of events in these external objects, and causes 'em to proceed otherwise than they would do, if let alone, and left to go on according to the laws of motion among themselves. Hence it is spoken of, as if it were a principle of motion entirely distinct from nature, and properly set in opposition to it—names [10] being commonly given to things, according to what is most obvious, and is suggested

[10] Here Ramsey writes: "The 1754 ed. begins a new incomplete sentence". [M.W.]

by what appears to the senses without reflection and research.

3. It must be observed, that in what has been explained, as
signified by the name of "moral necessity," the word "necessity" is not used according to the original design and meaning of the word: for, as was observed before, such terms
"necessary," "impossible," "irresistible," etc. in common
speech, and their most proper sense, are always relative; having reference to some supposable voluntary opposition or endeavor, that is insufficient. But no such opposition, or contrary will and endeavor, is supposable in the case of moral
necessity; which is a certainty of the inclination and will itself; which does not admit of the supposition of a will to oppose and resist it. For 'tis absurd, to suppose the same individual will to oppose itself, in its present act; or the present
choice to be opposite to, and resisting present choice: as absurd as it is to talk of two contrary motions, in the same moving body, at the same time. And therefore the very case supposed never admits of any trial, whether an opposing or
resisting will can overcome this necessity.

What has been said of natural and moral necessity, may
serve to explain what is intended by natural and moral *inability*. We are said to be *naturally* unable to do a thing,
when we can't do it if we will, because what is most commonly called nature don't allow of it, or because of some
impeding defect or obstacle that is extrinsic to the will; either
in the faculty of understanding, constitution of body, or external objects. *Moral* inability consists not in any of these
things; but either in the want of inclination; or the strength
of a contrary inclination; or the want of sufficient motives in
view, to induce and excite the act of the will, or the strength
of apparent motives to the contrary. Or both these may be resolved into one; and it may be said in one word, that moral
inability consists in the opposition or want of inclination. For
when a person is unable to will or choose such a thing,

through a defect of motives, or prevalence of contrary motives, 'tis the same thing as his being unable through the
want of an inclination, or the prevalence of a contrary inclination, in such circumstances, and under the influence of
such views.

To give some instances of this moral inability: A woman of
great honor and chastity may have a moral inability to prosti-
tute herself to her slave. A child of great love and duty to his
parents, may be unable to be willing to kill his father. A very
lascivious man, in case of certain opportunities and tempta-
tions, and in the absence of such and such restraints, may be
unable to forbear gratifying his lust. A drunkard, under such
and such circumstances, may be unable to forbear taking of
strong drink. A very malicious man may be unable to exert
benevolent acts to an enemy, or to desire his prosperity: yea,
some may be so under the power of a vile disposition, that they
may be unable to love those who are most worthy of their esteem and affection. A strong habit of virtue and great degree
of holiness may cause a moral inability to love wickedness in
general, may render a man unable to take complacence in
wicked persons or things; or to choose a wicked life, and prefer it to a virtuous life. And on the other hand, a great degree
of habitual wickedness may lay a man under an inability to
love and choose holiness; and render him utterly unable to
love an infinitely holy Being, or to choose and cleave to him
as his chief good.

Here it may be of use to observe this distinction of moral
inability, viz. of that which is general and habitual, and that
which is particular and occasional. By a *general and habitual*
moral inability, I mean an inability in the heart to all exercises or acts of will of that nature or kind, through a fixed
and habitual inclination, or an habitual and stated defect, or
want of a certain kind of inclination. Thus a very ill-natured
man may be unable to exert such acts of benevolence, as another, who is full of good nature, commonly exerts; and a
man, whose heart is habitually void of gratitude, may be un-

able to exert such and such grateful acts, through that stated defect of a grateful inclination. By *particular and occasional* moral inability, I mean an inability of the will or heart to a particular act, through the strength or defect of present motives, or of inducements presented to the view of the understanding, on this occasion. If it be so, that the will is always determined by the strongest motive, then it must always have an inability, in this latter sense, to act otherwise than it does; it not being possible, in any case, that the will should, at present, go against the motive which has now, all things considered, the greatest strength and advantage to excite and induce it. The former of these kinds of moral inability, consisting in that which is stated habitual and general, is most commonly called by the name of "inability"; because the word "inability," in its most proper and original signification, has respect to some stated defect. And this especially obtains the name of "inability" also upon another account: I before observed, that the word "inability" in its original and most common use, is a relative term; and has respect to will and endeavor, as supposable in the case, and as insufficient to bring to pass the thing desired and endeavored. Now there may be more of an appearance and shadow of this, with respect to the acts which arise from a fixed and strong habit, than others that arise only from transient occasions and causes. Indeed will and endeavor against, or diverse from present acts of the will, are in no case supposable, whether those acts be occasional or habitual; for that would be to suppose the will, at present, to be otherwise than, at present, it is. But yet there may be will and endeavor against future acts of the will, or volitions that are likely to take place, as viewed at a distance. 'Tis no contradiction, to suppose that the acts of the will at one time, may be against the acts of the will at another time; and there may be desires and endeavors to prevent or excite future acts of the will; but such desires and endeavors are, in many cases, rendered insufficient and vain, through fixedness of habit: when the occasion returns, the strength of habit overcomes, and baffles all such opposition. In this respect, a man may be in miserable slavery and bondage to a strong habit. But it may be comparatively easy to make an alteration with respect to such future acts, as are only occasional and transient; because the occasion or transient cause, if foreseen, may often easily be prevented or avoided. On this account, the moral inability that attends fixed habits, especially obtains the name of "inability." And then, as the will may remotely and indirectly resist itself, and do it in vain, in the case of strong habits; so reason may resist present acts of the will, and its resistance be insufficient; and this is more commonly the case also, when the acts arise from strong habit.

But it must be observed concerning [11] moral inability, in each kind of it, that the word "inability" is used in a sense very diverse from its original import. The word signifies only a natural inability, in the proper use of it; and is applied to such cases only wherein a present will or inclination to the thing, with respect to which a person is said to be unable, is supposable. It can't be truly said, according to the ordinary use of language, that a malicious man, let him be never so malicious, can't hold his hand from striking, or that he is not able to shew his neighbor kindness; or that a drunkard, let his appetite be never so strong, can't keep the cup from his mouth. In the strictest propriety of speech, a man has a thing in his power, if he has it in his choice, or at his election: and a man can't be truly said to be unable to do a thing, when he can do it if he will. 'Tis improperly said, that a person can't perform those external actions, which are dependent on the act of the will, and which would be easily performed, if the act of the will were present. And if it be improperly said, that he cannot perform those external voluntary actions, which depend on the will, 'tis in some respect more improperly said, that he is unable to exert the acts of the will themselves; be-

---

[11] Here Ramsey notes that the 1754 ed. reads "concerned". [M.W.]

cause it is more evidently false, with respect to these, that he
can't if he will: for to say so, is a downright contradiction: it
is to say, he *can't* will, if he *does* will. And in this case, not
only is it true, that it is easy for a man to do the thing if he
will, but the very willing is the doing; when once he has
willed, the thing is performed; and nothing else remains to be
done. Therefore, in these things to ascribe a nonperformance
to the want of power or ability, is not just; because the thing
wanting is not a being *able*, but a being *willing*. There are
faculties of mind, and capacity of nature, and everything else,
sufficient, but a disposition: nothing is wanting but a will.

AGAINST THE ARMINIANS [12]

What has been said may be sufficient to shew what is
meant by liberty, according to the common notions of mankind, and in the usual and primary acceptation of the word:
but the word, as used by Arminians, Pelagians and others,
who oppose the Calvinists, has an entirely different signification. These several things belong to their notion of liberty:
1. That it consists in a self-determining power in the will, or
a certain sovereignty the will has over itself, and its own acts,
whereby it determines its own volitions; so as not to be dependent in its determinations, on any cause without itself, nor
determined by anything prior to its own acts. 2. Indifference
belongs to liberty in their notion of it, or that the mind, previous to the act of volition be, *in equilibrio*. 3. Contingence is
another thing that belongs and is essential to it; . . . as opposed to all necessity, or any fixed and certain connection
with some previous ground or reason of its existence. They
suppose the essence of liberty so much to consist in these
things, that unless the will of man be free in this sense, he has

[12] Edwards, *Freedom of the Will*, pp. 164–65; pp. 171–74. In this excerpt only Arminian views on self-determination are attacked by Edwards in detail.

no real freedom, how much soever he may be at liberty to act according to his will. . . .

Having taken notice of those things which may be necessary to be observed, concerning the meaning of the principal terms and phrases made use of in controversies concerning human liberty, and particularly observed what liberty is, according to the common language, and general apprehension of mankind, and what it is as understood and maintained by Arminians; I proceed to consider the Arminian notion of the freedom of the will, and the supposed necessity of it in order to moral agency, or in order to anyone's being capable of virtue or vice, and properly the subject of command or counsel, praise or blame, promises or threatenings, rewards or punishments; or whether that which has been described, as the thing meant by liberty in common speech, be not sufficient, and the only liberty, which makes, or can make anyone a moral agent, and so properly the subject of these things. In this part, I shall consider whether any such thing be possible or conceivable, as that freedom of will which Arminians insist on; and shall inquire whether any such sort of liberty be necessary to moral agency, etc. in the next part.

And first of all, I shall consider the notion of a self-determining power in the will: wherein, according to the Arminians, does most essentially consist the will's freedom; and shall particularly inquire, whether it be not plainly absurd, and a manifest inconsistence, to suppose that the will itself determines all the free acts of the will.

Here I shall not insist on the great impropriety of such phrases, and ways of speaking, as "the will's determining itself"; because actions are to be ascribed to agents, and not properly to the powers of agents; which improper way of speaking leads to many mistakes, and much confusion, as Mr. Locke observes. But I shall suppose that the Arminians, when they speak of the will's determining itself, do by the will mean "the soul willing." I shall take it for granted, that when they speak of the will, as the determiner, they mean the soul in the exercise of a power of willing, or acting voluntarily. I shall suppose this to be their meaning, because nothing else can be meant, without the grossest and plainest absurdity. In all cases, when we speak of the powers or principles of acting, as doing such things, we mean that the agents which have these powers of acting, do them, in the exercise of those powers. So when we say, valor fights courageously, we mean, the man who is under the influence of valor fights courageously. When we say, love seeks the object loved, we mean, the person loving seeks that object. When we say, the understanding discerns, we mean the soul in the exercise of that faculty. So when it is said, the will decides or determines, the meaning must be, that the person in the exercise of a power of willing and choosing, or the soul acting voluntarily, determines.

Therefore, if the will determines all its own free acts, the soul determines all the free acts of the will in the exercise of a power of willing and choosing; or, which is the same thing, it determines them of choice; it determines its own acts by choosing its own acts. If the will determines the will, then choice orders and determines the choice: and acts of choice are subject to the decision, and follow the conduct of other acts of choice. And therefore if the will determines all its own free acts, then every free act of choice is determined by a preceding act of choice, choosing that act. And if that preceding act of the will or choice be also a free act, then by these principles, in this act too, the will is self-determined; that is, this, in like manner, is an act that the soul voluntarily chooses; or which is the same thing, it is an act determined still by a preceding act of the will, choosing that. And the like may again be observed of the last mentioned act. Which brings us directly to a contradiction: for it supposes an act of the will preceding the first act in the whole train, directing and determining the rest; or a free act of the will, before the first free act of the will. Or else we must come at last to an act of the will, determining the consequent acts, wherein the will is not self-determined, and so is not a free act, in this notion of freedom: but if the first act in the train, determining and fixing the rest, be not free, none of them all can be free; as is manifest at first view, but shall be demonstrated presently.

If the will, which we find governs the members of the body, and determines and commands their motions and actions, does also govern itself, and determine its own motions and acts, it doubtless determines them the same way, even by antecedent volitions. The will determines which way the hands and feet shall move, by an act of volition or choice: and there is no other way of the will's determining, directing or commanding anything at all. Whatsoever the will commands, it commands by an act of the will. And if it has itself under its command, and determines itself in its own actions, it doubtless does it the same way that it determines other things which are under its command. So that if the freedom of the will consists in this, that it has itself and its own actions under its command and direction, and its own volitions are determined by itself, it will follow, that every free volition arises from another antecedent volition, directing and commanding that: and if that *directing* volition be also free, in that also the will is self-determined; that is to say, that directing volition is determined by another going before that; and so on, till we come to the first volition in the whole series: and if that first volition be free, and the will self-determined in it, then that is determined by another volition preceding that. Which is a contradiction; because by the supposition, it can have none before it, to direct or determine it, being the first in the train. But if that first volition is not determined by any preceding act of the will, then that act is not determined by the will, and so is not free, in the Arminian notion of freedom, which consists in the will's self-determination. And if that first act of the will, which determines and fixes the subsequent acts, be not free, none of the following acts, which are determined by it, can be free. If we suppose there are five acts in the train, the fifth and last determined by the fourth, and the fourth by the third, the third by the second, and the second by the first; if the first is not determined by the will, and so not free, then none of them are truly determined by the will: that is, that each of them are as they are, and not otherwise, is not first owing to the will, but to the determination of the first in the series, which is not dependent on the will, and is that which the will has no hand in the determination of. And this being that which decides what the rest shall be, and determines their existence; therefore the first determination of their existence is not from the will. The case is just the same, if instead of a chain of five acts of the will, we should suppose a succession of ten, or an hundred, or ten thousand. If the first act be not free, being determined by something out of the will, and this determines the next to be agreeable to itself, and that the next, and so on; they are none of them free, but all originally depend on, and are determined by some cause out of the will: and so all freedom in the case is excluded, and no act of the will can be free, according to this notion of freedom. If we should suppose a long chain, of ten thousand links, so connected, that if the first link moves, it will move the next, and that the next; and so the whole chain must be determined to motion, and in the direction of its motion, by the motion of the first link; and that is moved by something else: in this case, though all the links, but one, are moved by other parts of the same chain; yet it appears that the motion of no one, nor the direction of its motion, is from any self-moving or self-determining power in the chain, any more than if every link were immediately moved by something that did not belong to the chain. If the will be not free in the first act, which causes the next, then neither is it free in the next, which is caused by that first act: for though indeed the will caused it, yet it did not cause it freely; because the preceding act, by which it was caused, was not free. And again, if the will ben't free in the second act, so neither can it be in the third, which is caused by that; because, in like manner, that third was determined by an act of the will that was not free. And so we may go on to the next act, and from that to the next; and how long soever the succession of acts is, it is all one; if the first on which the whole chain depends, and which determines all the rest, ben't a free act, the will is not free in causing or determining any one of those acts; because the act by which it determines them all, is not a free act; and therefore the will is no more free in determining them, than if it did not cause them at all. Thus, this Arminian notion of liberty of the will, consisting in the will's self-determination, is repugnant to itself, and shuts itself wholly out of the world.

IN DEFENSE OF CALVINISM [13]

'Tis easy to see how the decision of most of the points in controversy, between Calvinists and Arminians, depends on the determination of this grand article concerning *the freedom of the will requisite to moral agency;* and that by clearing and establishing the Calvinistic doctrine in this point, the chief arguments are obviated, by which Arminian doctrines in general are supported, and the contrary doctrines demonstratively confirmed. Hereby it becomes manifest, that God's moral government over mankind, his treating them as moral agents, making them the objects of his commands, counsels, calls, warnings, expostulations, promises, threatenings, rewards and punishments, is not inconsistent with a determining disposal of all events, of every kind, throughout the universe, in his providence; either by positive efficiency, or permission. Indeed such an *universal, determining providence,* infers some kind of necessity of all events; such a necessity as implies an infallible previous fixedness of the futurity of the event: but no other necessity of moral events, or voli-

[13] *Ibid.*, pp. 431–33.

tions of intelligent agents, is needful in order to this, than *moral* necessity; which does as much ascertain the futurity of the event, as any other necessity. But, as has been demonstrated, such a necessity is not at all repugnant to moral agency, and the reasonable use of commands, calls, rewards, punishments, etc. Yea, not only are objections of this kind against the doctrine of an universal determining providence, removed by what has been said; but the truth of such a doctrine is demonstrated. As it has been demonstrated, that the futurity of all future events is established by previous necessity, either natural or moral; so 'tis manifest, that the sovereign Creator and Disposer of the world has ordered this necessity, by ordering his own conduct, either in designedly acting, or forbearing to act. For, as the being of the world is from God, so the circumstances in which it had its being at first, both negative and positive, must be ordered by him, in one of these ways; and all the necessary consequences of these circumstances, must be ordered by him. And God's active and positive interpositions, after the world was created, and the consequences of these interpositions; also every instance of his forbearing to interpose, and the sure consequences of this forbearance, must all be determined according to his pleasure. And therefore every event which is the consequence of anything whatsoever, or that is connected with any foregoing thing or circumstance, either positive or negative, as the ground or reason of its existence, must be ordered of God; either by a designed efficiency and interposition, or a designed forbearing to operate or interpose. But, as has been proved, all events whatsoever are necessarily connected with something foregoing, either positive or negative, which is the ground of its existence. It follows therefore, that the whole series of events is thus connected with something in the state of things, either positive or negative, which is original in the series; i.e. something which is connected with nothing preceding that, but God's own immediate conduct, either his acting or forbearing to act. From whence it follows,

that as God designedly orders his own conduct, and its connected consequences, it must necessarily be, that he designedly orders all things.

The things which have been said, obviate some of the chief
objections of Arminians against the Calvinistic doctrine of the
total depravity and corruption of man's nature, whereby his
heart is wholly under the power of sin, and he is utterly unable, without the interposition of sovereign grace, savingly to
love God, believe in Christ, or do anything that is truly good
and acceptable in God's sight. For the main objection against
this doctrine is, that it is inconsistent with the freedom of
man's will, consisting in indifference and self-determining
power; because it supposes man to be under a necessity of
sinning, and that God requires things of him, in order to his
avoiding eternal damnation, which he is unable to do; and
that this doctrine is wholly inconsistent with the sincerity of
counsels, invitations, etc. Now this doctrine supposes *no
other necessity* of sinning, than a moral necessity; which, as
has been shewn, don't at all excuse sin; and supposes *no
other inability* to obey any command, or perform any duty,
even the most spiritual and exalted, but a moral inability,
which, as has been proved, don't excuse persons in the nonperformance of any good thing, or make 'em not to be the
proper objects of commands, counsels and invitations. And
moreover, it has been shewn, that there is not, and never can
be, either in existence, or so much as in idea, any such freedom of will, consisting in indifference and self-determination,
for the sake of which, this doctrine of original sin is cast out;
and that no such freedom is necessary, in order to the nature
of sin, and a just desert of punishment.

The things which have been observed, do also take off the
main objections of Arminians against the doctrine of *efficacious grace;* and at the same time, prove the grace of God in
a sinner's conversion (if there be any grace or divine influence in the affair) to be efficacious, yea, and *irresistible* too, if
by irresistible is meant, that which is attended with a moral

necessity, which it is impossible should ever be violated by any resistance. The main objection of Arminians against this doctrine is, that it is inconsistent with their self-determining freedom of will; and that it is repugnant to the nature of virtue, that it should be wrought in the heart by the determining efficacy and power of another, instead of its being owing to a self-moving power; that in that case, the good which is wrought, would not be *our* virtue, but rather *God's* virtue; because it is not the person in whom it is wrought, that is the determining author of it, but God that wrought it in him. But the things which are the foundation of these objections, have been considered; and it has been demonstrated, that the liberty of moral agents does not consist in self-determining power; and that there is no need of any such liberty, in order to the nature of virtue; nor does it at all hinder, but that the state or act of the will may be the virtue of the subject, though it be not from self-determination, but the determination of an extrinsic cause; even so as to cause the event to be morally necessary to the subject of it. And as it has been proved, that nothing in the state or acts of the will of man is contingent; but that on the contrary, every event of this kind is necessary, by a moral necessity; and has also been now demonstrated, that the doctrine of an universal determining providence, follows from that doctrine of necessity, which was proved before: and so, that God does decisively, in his providence, order all the volitions of moral agents, either by positive influence or permission. . . .

JAMES WILSON

American philosophy has always had a tendency to be practical and to be directly concerned with the fundamental institutions of civilized life. This has been true of it from the very beginning, and especially true of it in the period before the Civil War. Edwards was primarily a philosopher of religion; Emerson was a social critic and a man of letters; and between the death of the former and the birth of the latter, the most interesting philosophical writing of the Revolutionary era was concerned with the foundations of law and politics. One of the most articulate legal philosophers among the practical Revolutionary lawyers was James Wilson. He was one of the six signers of both the Declaration of Independence and the Constitution; and his views on fundamental legal concepts show his considerable familiarity with eighteenth-century epistemology and ethics. Therefore Wilson was, in spite of being one of the less famous figures in this volume, a writer of considerable interest to the historian of American philosophical thought. He was born in Scotland in 1742, came to America in 1765, and died in 1798. He produced revolutionary pamphlets of great influence; was one of the first set of justices of the Supreme Court; and in 1790–91 delivered an important series of *Lectures on Law*, from which the passage below is taken.

That work is of interest to us mainly because of its doctrine of Natural Law, so fundamental a concept in the Declaration of Independence; and it is of particular interest because it shows how a very influential Revolutionary thinker explicitly transformed Locke's view of Natural Law by allowing sentiment to play a part in the establishment of fundamental moral principles. In this respect, Wilson followed the so-called Moral Sense theorists, Shaftesbury, Hutcheson, and Hume. He also followed Thomas Reid in abandoning the Lockeian idea that morality can be a demonstrative science like mathematics. With Thomas Jefferson, Wilson insisted that the axioms of morality may be perceived as easily by a ploughman as by a professor—to use Jefferson's words—and that in ethics the need for deduction is minimal. Just as Edwards transformed the Lockeian empiricist theory of perception for religious purposes by introducing the "Sense of the Heart," so Wilson abandoned Locke's rationalistic theory of Natural Law by giving sentiment a central place in ethics; and both of these eighteenth-century developments prefigured some of the doctrines and attitudes of the Transcendentalists, as we shall see later.

Before reproducing parts of Wilson's *Lectures on Law*, I should point out that when he says that reason plays a part in moral argumentation, he usually does not have in mind what Locke meant by "intuitive reason", which discerns the truth of mathematical axioms. Wilson is thinking of empirical investigations whereby matters of fact are discovered.[1] Following Hume—whom he never mentions when he is repeating his views but only when he is attacking him—Wilson holds that reason may tell us how to achieve an ultimate end, but

---

[1] Here Wilson is using "reason" in a sense licensed by Locke when Locke used that word broadly. See note 10 in the section on Locke above, p. 34.

that we arrive at a moral evaluation of such an end by appealing to our feelings or to sentiment. Wilson's idea that beliefs about ultimate moral ends are established by sentiment is in opposition to the Lockeian idea that they are established by intuitive reason, and this should not be obscured by the fact that Wilson often calls such beliefs "self-evident". The fact that he speaks of them as self-evident shows only that he continues to use Lockeian terminology even though he has abandoned a Lockeian conception of the principles of Natural Law.

The Law of Nature [2]

Of law there are different kinds. All, however, may be arranged in two different classes. 1. Divine. 2. Human laws. The descriptive epithets employed denote, that the former have God, the latter, man, for their author.

The laws of God may be divided into the following species.

I. That law, the book of which we are neither able nor worthy to open. Of this law, the author and observer is God. He is a law to himself, as well as to all created things. This law we may name the "law eternal."

II. That law, which is made for angels and the spirits of the just made perfect. This may be called the "law celestial." This law, and the glorious state for which it is adapted, we see, at present, but darkly and as through a glass: but hereafter we shall see even as we are seen; and shall know even as we are known. From the wisdom and the goodness of the adorable Author and Preserver of the universe, we are justified in concluding, that the celestial and perfect state is governed, as all other things are, by his established laws. What those laws are, it is not yet given us to know; but on one

[2] The following passages appear in *The Works of James Wilson*, edited by Robert Green McCloskey (Cambridge, Mass.: The Belknap Press of Harvard University Press), Volume I, pp. 123–25; p. 126; pp. 132–39; p. 141; pp. 142–43. Copyright 1967 by the President and Fellows of Harvard College. Reprinted by permission.

truth we may rely with sure and certain confidence—those laws are wise and good. For another truth we have infallible authority—those laws are strictly obeyed: "In heaven his will is done."

III. That law, by which the irrational and inanimate parts of the creation are governed. The great Creator of all things has established general and fixed rules, according to which all the phenomena of the material universe are produced and regulated. These rules are usually denominated laws of nature. The science, which has those laws for its object, is distinguished by the name of natural philosophy. It is sometimes called, the philosophy of body. Of this science, there are numerous branches.

IV. That law, which God has made for man in his present state; that law, which is communicated to us by reason and conscience, the divine monitors within us, and by the sacred oracles, the divine monitors without us. This law has undergone several subdivisions, and has been known by distinct appellations, according to the different ways in which it has been promulgated, and the different objects which it respects.

As promulgated by reason and the moral sense, it has been called natural; as promulgated by the holy scriptures, it has been called revealed law.

As addressed to men, it has been denominated the law of nature; as addressed to political societies, it has been denominated the law of nations.

But it should always be remembered, that this law, natural or revealed, made for men or for nations, flows from the same divine source: it is the law of God.

Nature, or, to speak more properly, the Author of nature, has done much for us; but it is his gracious appointment and will, that we should also do much for ourselves. What we do, indeed, must be founded on what he has done; and the deficiencies of our laws must be supplied by the perfections of his. Human law must rest its authority, ultimately, upon the authority of that law, which is divine.

Of that law, the following are maxims—that no injury should be done—that a lawful engagement, voluntarily made, should be faithfully fulfilled. We now see the deep and the solid foundations of human law.

It is of two species. 1. That which a political society makes for itself. This is municipal law. 2. That which two or more political societies make for themselves. This is the voluntary law of nations.

In all these species of law—the law eternal—the law celestial—the law natural—the divine law, as it respects men and nations—the human law, as it also respects men and nations—man is deeply and intimately concerned. Of all these species of law, therefore, the knowledge must be most important to man.

Those parts of natural philosophy, which more immediately relate to the human body, are appropriated to the profession of physick.

The law eternal, the law celestial, and the law divine, as they are disclosed by that revelation, which has brought life and immortality to light, are the more peculiar objects of the profession of divinity.

The law of nature, the law of nations, and the municipal law form the objects of the profession of law.

From this short, but plain and, I hope, just statement of things, we perceive a principle of connexion between all the learned professions; but especially between the two last mentioned. Far from being rivals or enemies, religion and law are twin sisters, friends, and mutual assistants. Indeed, these two sciences run into each other. The divine law, as discovered by reason and the moral sense, forms an essential part of both.

From this statement of things, we also perceive how important and dignified the profession of the law is, when traced to its sources, and viewed in its just extent. . . .

In every period of our existence, in every situation, in which we can be placed, much is to be known, much is to be done, much is to be enjoyed. But all that is to be known, all that is to be done, all that is to be enjoyed, depends upon the proper exertion and direction of our numerous powers. In this immense ocean of intelligence and action, are we left without a compass and without a chart? Is there no pole star, by which we may regulate our course? Has the all-gracious and all-wise Author of our existence formed us for such great and such good ends; and has he left us without a conductor to lead us in the way, by which those ends may be attained? Has he made us capable of observing a rule, and has he furnished us with no rule, which we ought to observe? Let us examine these questions—for they are important ones—with patience and with attention. Our labours will, in all probability, be amply repaid. We shall probably find that, to direct the more important parts of our conduct, the bountiful Governour of the universe has been graciously pleased to provide us with a law; and that, to direct the less important parts of it, he has made us capable of providing a law for ourselves.

That our Creator has a supreme right to prescribe a law for our conduct, and that we are under the most perfect obligation to obey that law, are truths established on the clearest and most solid principles. . . .

Having thus stated the question—what is the efficient cause of moral obligation?—I give it this answer—the will of God. This is the supreme law. His just and full right of imposing laws, and our duty in obeying them, are the sources of our moral obligations. If I am asked—why do you obey the will of God? I answer—because it is my duty so to do. If I am asked again—how do you know this to be your duty? I answer again—because I am told so by my moral sense or conscience. If I am asked a third time—how do you know that you ought to do that, of which your conscience enjoins the performance? I can only say, I *feel* that such is my duty. Here investigation must stop; reasoning can go no farther. The science of morals, as well as other sciences, is founded on truths, that cannot be discovered or proved by reasoning.

Reason is confined to the investigation of unknown truths by the means of such as are known. We cannot, therefore, begin to reason, till we are furnished, otherwise than by reason, with some truths, on which we can found our arguments. Even in mathematicks, we must be provided with axioms perceived intuitively to be true, before our demonstrations can commence. Morality, like mathematicks, has its intuitive truths, without which we cannot make a single step in our reasonings upon the subject. Such an intuitive truth is that, with which we just now closed our investigation. If a person was not possessed of the feeling before mentioned; it would not be in the power of arguments, to give him any conception of the distinction between right and wrong. These terms would be to him equally unintelligible, as the term *colour* to one who was born and has continued blind. But that there is, in human nature, such a moral principle, has been felt and acknowledged in all ages and nations.

Now that we have stated and answered the first question; let us proceed to the consideration of the second—how shall we, in particular instances, learn the dictates of our duty, and make, with accuracy, the proper distinction between right and wrong; in other words, how shall we, in particular cases, discover the will of God? We discover it by our conscience, by our reason, and by the Holy Scriptures. The law of nature and the law of revelation are both divine: they flow, though in different channels, from the same adorable source. It is, indeed, preposterous to separate them from each other. The object of both is—to discover the will of God—and both are necessary for the accomplishment of that end.

I. The power of moral perception is, indeed, a most important part of our constitution. It is an original power—a power of its own kind; and totally distinct from the ideas of utility and agreeableness. By that power, we have conceptions of merit and demerit, of duty and moral obligation. By that power, we perceive some things in human conduct to be right, and others to be wrong. We have the same reason to rely on the dictates of this faculty, as upon the determinations of our senses, or of our other natural powers. When an action is represented to us, flowing from love, humanity, gratitude, an ultimate desire of the good of others; though it happened in a country far distant, or in an age long past, we admire the lovely exhibition, and praise its author. The contrary conduct, when represented to us, raises our abhorrence and aversion. But whence this secret chain betwixt each person and mankind? If there is no moral sense, which makes benevolence appear beautiful; if all approbation be from the interest of the approver; "What's Hecuba to us, or we to Hecuba?"

The mind, which reflects on itself, and is a spectator of other minds, sees and feels the soft and the harsh, the agreeable and the disagreeable, the foul and the fair, the harmonious and the dissonant, as really and truly in the affections and actions, as in any musical numbers, or the outward forms or representations of sensible things. It cannot withhold its approbation or aversion in what relates to the former, any more than in what relates to the latter, of those subjects. To deny the sense of a sublime and beautiful and of their contraries in actions and things, will appear an affectation merely to one who duly considers and traces the subject. Even he who indulges this affectation cannot avoid the discovery of those very sentiments, which he pretends not to feel. A Lucretius or a Hobbes cannot discard the sentiments of praise and admiration respecting some moral forms, nor the sentiments of censure and detestation concerning others. Has a man gratitude, or resentment, or pride, or shame? If he has and avows it; he must have and acknowledge a sense of something benevolent, of something unjust, of something worthy, and of something mean. Thus, so long as we find men pleased or angry, proud or ashamed; we may appeal to the reality of the moral sense. A right and a wrong, an honourable and a dishonourable is plainly conceived. About these there may be mistakes; but this destroys not the infer-

ence, that the things are, and are universally acknowledged
—that they are of nature's impression, and by no art can be
obliterated.

This sense or apprehension of right and wrong appears
early, and exists in different degrees. The qualities of love,
gratitude, sympathy unfold themselves, in the first stages of
life, and the approbation of those qualities accompanies the
first dawn of reflection. Young people, who think the least
about the distant influences of actions, are, more than others,
moved with moral forms. Hence that strong inclination in
children to hear such stories as paint the characters and fortunes of men. Hence that joy in the prosperity of the kind
and faithful, and that sorrow upon the success of the treach-
erous and cruel, with which we often see infant minds
strongly agitated.

There is a natural beauty in figures; and is there not a
beauty as natural in actions? When the eye opens upon
forms, and the ear to sounds; the beautiful is seen, and harmony is heard and acknowledged. When actions are viewed
and affections are discerned, the inward eye distinguishes the
beautiful, the amiable, the admirable, from the despicable,
the odious, and the deformed. How is it possible not to own,
that as these distinctions have their foundation in nature, so
this power of discerning them is natural also?

The universality of an opinion or sentiment may be
evinced by the structure of languages. Languages were not
invented by philosophers, to countenance or support any artificial system. They were contrived by men in general, to express common sentiments and perceptions. The inference is
satisfactory, that where all languages make a distinction,
there must be a similar distinction in universal opinion or
sentiment. For language is the picture of human thoughts;
and, from this faithful picture, we may draw certain conclusions concerning the original. Now, a universal effect must
have a universal cause. No universal cause can, with pro-

priety, be assigned for this universal opinion, except that intuitive perception of things, which is distinguished by the name of common sense.

All languages speak of a beautiful and a deformed, a right and a wrong, an agreeable and disagreeable, a good and ill, in actions, affections, and characters. All languages, therefore, suppose a moral sense, by which those qualities are perceived and distinguished.

The whole circle of the arts of imitation proves the reality of the moral sense. They suppose, in human conduct, a sublimity, a beauty, a greatness, an excellence, independent of advantage or disadvantage, profit or loss. On him, whose heart is indelicate or hard; on him, who has no admiration of what is truly noble; on him, who has no sympathetick sense of what is melting and tender, the highest beauty of the mimick arts must make indeed, but a very faint and transient impression. If we were void of a relish for moral excellence, how frigid and uninteresting would the finest descriptions of life and manners appear! How indifferent are the finest strains of harmony, to him who has not a musical ear!

The force of the moral sense is diffused through every part of life. The luxury of the table derives its principal charms from some mixture of moral enjoyments, from communicating pleasures, and from sentiments honourable and just as well as elegant—"The feast of reason, and the flow of soul."

The chief pleasures of history, and poetry, and eloquence, and musick, and sculpture, and painting are derived from the same source. Beside the pleasures they afford by imitation, they receive a stronger charm from something moral insinuated into the performances. The principal beauties of behaviour, and even of countenance, arise from the indication of affections or qualities morally estimable.

Never was there any of the human species above the condition of an idiot, to whom all actions appeared indifferent. All feel that a certain temper, certain affections, and certain

actions produce a sentiment of approbation; and that a sentiment of disapprobation is produced by the contrary temper,
affections, and actions.

This power is capable of culture and improvement by
habit, and by frequent and extensive exercise. A high sense of
moral excellence is approved above all other intellectual talents. This high sense of excellence is accompanied with a
strong desire after it, and a keen relish for it. This desire and
this relish are approved as the most amiable affections, and
the highest virtues.

This moral sense, from its very nature, is intended to regulate and control all our other powers. It governs our passions
as well as our actions. Other principles may solicit and allure;
but the conscience assumes authority, it must be obeyed. Of
this dignity and commanding nature we are immediately
conscious, as we are of the power itself. It estimates what it
enjoins, not merely as superiour in degree, but as superiour
likewise in kind, to what is recommended by our other perceptive powers. Without this controlling faculty, endowed as
we are with such a variety of senses and interfering desires,
we should appear a fabrick destitute of order: but possessed
of it, all our powers may be harmonious and consistent; they
may all combine in one uniform and regular direction.

In short; if we had not the faculty of perceiving certain
things in conduct to be right, and others to be wrong; and of
perceiving our obligation to do what is right, and not to do
what is wrong; we should not be moral and accountable
beings.

If we be, as, I hope, I have shown we are, endowed with
this faculty; there must be some things, which are immediately discerned by it to be right, and others to be wrong.
There must, consequently, be in morals, as in other sciences,
first principles, which derive not their evidence from any antecedent principles, but which may be said to be intuitively
discerned.

Moral truths may be divided into two classes; such as are

selfevident, and such as, from the selfevident ones, are deduced by reasoning. If the first be not discerned without reasoning, reasoning can never discern the last. The cases that require reasoning are few, compared with those that require none; and a man may be very honest and virtuous, who cannot reason, and who knows not what demonstration means.

If the rules of virtue were left to be discovered by reasoning, even by demonstrative reasoning, unhappy would be the condition of the far greater part of men, who have not the means of cultivating the power of reasoning to any high degree. As virtue is the business of all men, the first principles of it are written on their hearts, in characters so legible, that no man can pretend ignorance of them, or of his obligation to practise them. Reason, even with experience, is too often overpowered by passion; to restrain whose impetuosity, nothing less is requisite than the vigorous and commanding principle of duty.

II. The first principles of morals, into which all moral argumentation may be resolved, are discovered in a manner more analogous to the perceptions of sense than to the conclusions of reasoning. In morality, however, as well as in other sciences, reason is usefully introduced, and performs many important services. In many instances she regulates our belief; and in many instances she regulates our conduct. She determines the proper means to any end; and she decides the preference of one end over another. She may exhibit an object to the mind, though the perception which the mind has, when once the object is exhibited, may properly belong to a sense. She may be necessary to ascertain the circumstances and determine the motives to an action; though it be the moral sense that perceives the action to be either virtuous or vicious, after its motive and its circumstances have been discovered. She discerns the tendencies of the several senses, affections, and actions, and the comparative value of objects and gratifications. She judges concerning subordinate ends; but concerning ultimate ends she is not employed. These we prosecute by some immediate determination of the mind, which, in the order of action, is prior to all reasoning; for no opinion or judgment can move to action, where there is not a previous desire of some end.—This power of comparing the several enjoyments, of which our nature is susceptible, in order to discover which are most important to our happiness, is of the highest consequence and necessity to corroborate our moral faculty, and to preserve our affections in just rank and regular order.

A magistrate knows that it is his duty to promote the good of the commonwealth, which has intrusted him with authority. But whether one particular plan or another particular plan of conduct in office, may best promote the good of the commonwealth, may, in many cases, be doubtful. His conscience or moral sense determines the end, which he ought to pursue; and he has intuitive evidence that his end is good: but the means of attaining this end must be determined by reason. To select and ascertain those means, is often a matter of very considerable difficulty. Doubts may arise; opposite interests may occur; and a preference must be given to one side from a small over-balance, and from very nice views. This is particularly the case in questions with regard to justice. If every single instance of justice, like every single instance of benevolence, were pleasing and useful to society, the case would be more simple, and would be seldom liable to great controversy. But as single instances of justice are often pernicious in their first and immediate tendency; and as the advantage to society results only from the observance of the general rule, and from the concurrence and combination of several persons in the same equitable conduct; the case here becomes more intricate and involved. The various circumstances of society, the various consequences of any practice, the various interests which may be proposed, are all, on many occasions, doubtful, and subject to much discussion and inquiry. The design of municipal law (for let us still, from every direction, open a view to our principal object) the design of municipal law is to fix all the questions which regard justice. A very accurate reason or judgment is often requisite, to give the true determination amidst intricate doubts, arising from obscure or opposite utilities.

Thus, though good and ill, right and wrong are ultimately perceived by the moral sense, yet reason assists its operations, and, in many instances, strengthens and extends its influence. We may argue concerning propriety of conduct: just reasonings on the subject will establish principles for judging of what deserves praise: but, at the same time, these reasonings must always, in the last resort, appeal to the moral sense.

Farther; reason serves to illustrate, to prove, to extend, to apply what our moral sense has already suggested to us, concerning just and unjust, proper and improper, right and wrong. A father feels that paternal tenderness is refined and confirmed, by reflecting how consonant that feeling is to the relation between a parent and his child; how conducive it is to the happiness, not only of a single family, but, in its extension, to that of all mankind. We feel the beauty and excellence of virtue; but this sense is strengthened and improved by the lessons, which reason gives us concerning the foundations, the motives, the relations, the particular and the universal advantages flowing from this virtue, which, at first sight, appeared so beautiful.

Taste is a faculty, common, in some degree, to all men. But study, attention, comparison operate most powerfully towards its refinement. In the same manner, reason contributes to ascertain the exactness, and to discover and correct the mistakes, of the moral sense. A prejudice of education may be misapprehended for a determination of morality. 'Tis reason's province to compare and discriminate.

Reason performs an excellent service to the moral sense in another respect. It considers the relations of actions, and traces them to the remotest consequences. We often see men, with the most honest hearts and most pure intentions, embarrassed and puzzled, when a case, delicate and complicated,

comes before them. They feel what is right; they are unshaken in their general principles; but they are unaccus-
tomed to pursue them through their different ramifications,
to make the necessary distinctions and exceptions, or to modify them according to the circumstances of time and place.
'Tis the business of reason to discharge this duty; and it will
discharge it the better in proportion to the care which has
been employed in exercising and improving it. . . .

It is with much reluctance, that the power of our instinctive or intuitive faculties is acknowledged by some philosophers. That the brutes are governed by instinct, but that man
is governed by reason, is their favourite position. But fortunately for man, this position is not founded on truth. Our
instincts, as well as our rational powers, are far superiour,
both in number and in dignity, to those, which the brutes
enjoy; and it were well for us, on many occasions, if we laid
our reasoning systems aside, and were more attentive in observing the genuine impulses of nature. In this enlarged and
elevated meaning, the sentiment of Pope receives a double
portion of force and sublimity.

> And reason raise o'er instinct as you can,
> In this, 'tis God directs, in that, 'tis man.

This sentiment is not dictated merely in the fervid glow of
enraptured poetry; it is affirmed by the deliberate judgment
of calm, sedate philosophy. Our instincts are no other than
the oracles of eternal wisdom; our conscience, in particular, is
the voice of God within us: it teaches, it commands, it pun-
ishes, it rewards. The testimony of a good conscience is the
purest and the noblest of human enjoyments.

It will be proper to examine a little more minutely the
opinions of those, who allege reason to be the sole directress
of human conduct. Reason may, indeed, instruct us in the
pernicious or useful tendency of qualities and actions: but
reason alone is not sufficient to produce any moral approbation or blame. Utility is only a tendency to a certain end; and

if the end be totally indifferent to us, we shall feel the same indifference towards the means. It is requisite that *sentiment* should intervene, in order to give a preference to the useful above the pernicious tendencies. . . .

The *ultimate* ends of human actions, can never, in any case, be accounted for by reason. They recommend themselves entirely to the sentiments and affections of men, without dependence on the intellectual faculties. Why do you take exercise? Because you desire health. Why do you desire health? Because sickness is painful. Why do you hate pain? No answer is heard. Can one be given? No. This is an ultimate end, and is not referred to any farther object.

To the second question, you may, perhaps, answer, that you desire health, because it is necessary for your improvement in your profession. Why are you anxious to make this improvement? You may, perhaps, answer again, because you wish to get money by it. Why do you wish to get money? Because, among other reasons, it is the instrument of pleasure. But why do you love pleasure? Can a reason be given for loving pleasure, any more than for hating pain? They are both ultimate objects. 'Tis impossible there can be a progress *in infinitum;* and that one thing can always be a reason, why another is hated or desired. Something must be hateful or desirable on its own account, and because of its immediate agreement or disagreement with human sentiment and affection.

Virtue and vice are ends; and are hateful or desirable on their own account. It is requisite, therefore, that there should be some sentiment, which they touch—some internal taste or sense, which distinguishes moral good and evil, and which embraces one, and rejects the other. Thus are the offices of reason and of the moral sense at last ascertained. The former conveys the knowledge of truth and falsehood: the latter, the sentiment of beauty and deformity, of vice and virtue. The standard of one, founded on the nature of things, is eternal and inflexible. The standard of the other is ultimately derived from that supreme will, which bestowed on us our peculiar nature, and arranged the several classes and orders of existence. In this manner, we return to the great principle, from which we set out. It is necessary that reason should be fortified by the moral sense: without the moral sense, a man may be prudent, but he cannot be virtuous.

Philosophers have degraded our senses below their real importance. They represent them as powers, by which we have sensations and ideas only. But this is not the whole of their office; they judge as well as inform. Not confined to the mere office of conveying impressions, they are exalted to the function of judging of the nature and evidence of the impressions they convey. If this be admitted, our moral faculty may, without impropriety, be called the *moral sense*. Its testimony, like that of the external senses, is the immediate testimony of nature, and on it we have the same reason to rely. In its dignity, it is, without doubt, far superiour to every other power of the mind.

The moral sense, like all our other powers, comes to maturity by insensible degrees. It is peculiar to human nature. It is both intellectual and active. It is evidently intended, by nature, to be the immediate guide and director of our conduct, after we arrive at the years of understanding.

Part 3: Transcendentalism: The Triumph of Sentiment

SAMUEL TAYLOR COLERIDGE

In keeping with the idea that philosophy in America is not merely philosophy written by Americans, I append below a selection from the writings of Samuel Taylor Coleridge (1772–1834), the English poet and philosopher who expounded a very popular version of the philosophy of Kant. The selection is mainly concerned with the contrast between the Reason and the Understanding, so important in the writings of the Transcendentalists. A letter of Emerson's which is included later in the section on him is clear testimony to Coleridge's influence on the Concord sage, an influence made clearer if one has already read Coleridge himself. Of special note in this passage from Coleridge is the way in which he distinguishes not only the Understanding and the Reason but also the Pure and the Practical Reason. It is also instructive to see how he links the Understanding as "the faculty of judging according to sense" with understanding as the process of grasping the meanings of words, and also with the idea that the Understanding is a *discursive* faculty.

Coleridge's view that this discursive faculty is not a branch of Reason represents a departure from the terminology of Locke; and when Coleridge treats the Understanding as the faculty of judging according to *sense,* he seems to remove from its purview the activity of deduction, which Locke had assigned to it. It is also worth remarking that according to Coleridge, Ptolemy's achievement in stellar mechanics was the highest boast of the Understanding, whereas Newton's achievement was the offspring of the Pure Reason. This influenced Emerson's denigration of "empirical science", by which he meant something like Ptolemy's science, and not Newton's; something which could not rise to necessary truth.

In the practical sphere, the Understanding is for Coleridge merely the faculty of selecting means, whereas the Practical Reason—which, he says in one place, is "reason in the full and substantive sense"—perceives the highest moral principles. Moreover, when a person subjects his will to the Practical Reason, Coleridge says he is regenerate and is capable "of a quickening inter-communion with the Divine Spirit". By contrast to Edwards, who endowed his saints with a Lockeian Understanding possessing a *sixth sense,* Coleridge thought of the redeemed man as one who had subjected his will to Reason. Here Coleridge was followed by Transcendentalists, who regarded Edwards' terminology as much too Lockeian even when they admired a great deal of what their distinguished colonial predecessor had said about religious matters.

The Reason versus *The Understanding* [1]

My remarks . . . cannot be better introduced, or their purport more distinctly announced, than by the following sentence from Harrington,[2] with no other change than is necessary to make the words express, without aid of the context, what from the context it is evident was the writer's meaning.

---

[1] These passages appear in Samuel Taylor Coleridge, *Aids to Reflection,* ed. H. N. Coleridge (London, 1839), p. 151; pp. 154–60; pp. 162–64; pp. 167–72. I have omitted Coleridge's footnotes. [M.W.]

[2] Probably James Harrington (1611–1677). [M.W.]

"The definition and proper character of man—that, namely, which should contra-distinguish him from the animals—is to be taken from his reason rather than from his understanding: in regard that in other creatures there may be something of understanding, but there is nothing of reason." . . . [T]here is no want of authorities ancient and modern for the distinction of the faculties, and the distinct appropriation of the terms, yet our best writers too often confound the one with the other. Even Lord Bacon himself, who in his *Novum Organum* has so incomparably set forth the nature of the difference, and the unfitness of the latter faculty for the objects of the former, does nevertheless in sundry places use the term reason where he means the understanding, and sometimes, though less frequently, understanding for reason. In consequence of thus confounding the two terms, or rather of wasting both words for the expression of one and the same faculty, he left himself no appropriate term for the other and higher gift of reason, and was thus under the necessity of adopting fantastical and mystical phrases, for example, the dry light (*lumen siccum*) the lucific vision, and the like, meaning thereby nothing more than reason in contra-distinction from the understanding. . . .

ON THE DIFFERENCE IN KIND OF REASON

AND THE UNDERSTANDING

SCHEME OF THE ARGUMENT

. . . [R]eason is the power of universal and necessary convictions, the source and substance of truths above sense, and having their evidence in themselves. Its presence is always marked by the necessity of the position affirmed: this necessity being conditional, when a truth of reason is applied to facts of experience, or to the rules and maxims of the understanding; but absolute, when the subject matter is itself the growth or offspring of reason. Hence arises a distinction in reason itself, derived from the different mode of applying it, and from the objects to which it is directed: accordingly as we consider one and the same gift, now as the ground of formal principles, and now as the origin of ideas. Contemplated distinctively in reference to formal (or abstract) truth, it is the speculative reason; but in reference to actual (or moral) truth, as the fountain of ideas and the light of the conscience, we name it the practical reason. Whenever by self-subjection to this universal light, the will of the individual, the particular will, has become a will of reason, the man is regenerate: and reason is then the spirit of the regenerated man, whereby the person is capable of a quickening inter-communion with the Divine Spirit.[3] And herein consists the mystery of Redemption, that this has been rendered possible for us. *And so it is written; the first man Adam was made a living soul, the last Adam a quickening Spirit.* (I Cor. xv. 45.) We need only compare the passages in the writings of the Apostles Paul and John, concerning the Spirit and spiritual gifts, with those in the Proverbs and in the Wisdom of Solomon respecting reason, to be convinced that the terms are synonymous. In this at once most comprehensive and most appropriate acceptation of the word, reason is pre-eminently spiritual, and a spirit, even our spirit, through an effluence of the same grace by which we are privileged to say Our Father!

On the other hand, the judgments of the understanding are binding only in relation to the objects of our senses, which

---

[3] It is of some interest to readers of Emerson, who, as we shall see, put so much stress on the role of Reason in morals, that his mentor Coleridge wrote in the very last section of *Aids to Reflection:* "The practical reason alone is reason in the full and substantive sense. It is reason in its own sphere of perfect freedom; as the source of ideas, which ideas, in their conversion to the responsible will, become ultimate ends. On the other hand, theoretic reason, as the ground of the universal and absolute in all logical conclusion, is rather the light of reason in the understanding, and known to be such by its contrast with the contingency and particularity which characterize all the proper and indigenous growths of the understanding", *Aids to Reflection,* p. 314, note. [M.W.]

we reflect under the forms of the understanding. It is, as Leighton [4] rightly defines it, "the faculty judging according to sense." Hence we add the epithet human without tautology: and speak of the human understanding in disjunction from that of beings higher or lower than man. . . . Beasts, we have said, partake of understanding. If any man deny this, . . . [l]et him give a careful perusal to Huber's two small volumes on bees and ants.[5] . . .

Huber put a dozen bumble-bees under a bell-glass along with a comb of about ten silken cocoons so unequal in height as not to be capable of standing steadily. To remedy this two or three of the bumble-bees got upon the comb, stretched themselves over its edge, and with their heads downwards fixed their forefeet on the table on which the comb stood, and so with their hind feet kept the comb from falling. When these were weary others took their places. In this constrained and painful posture, fresh bees relieving their comrades at intervals, and each working in its turn, did these affectionate little insects support the comb for nearly three days: at the end of which they had prepared sufficient wax to build pillars with. But these pillars having accidentally got displaced, the bees had recourse again to the same manoeuvre, till Huber pitying their hard case, &c. . . .

Now I assert, that the faculty manifested in the acts here narrated does not differ *in kind* from understanding, and that it *does* so differ from reason. What I conceive the former to be, physiologically considered, will be shown hereafter. In this place I take the understanding as it exists in men,

---

[4] Archbishop Robert Leighton (1611–1684). [M.W.]
[5] Coleridge seems to be confusing François Huber's (1705–1831) *Nouvelles Observations sur les abeilles* (1792; Eng. tr. 1806) and Pierre Huber's (1777–1840) *Recherches sur les moeurs des fourmis indigènes* (1810). The Hubers were father and son. Emerson also seems to have confused them, *The Journals of Ralph Waldo Emerson*, eds. W. H. Gilman and A. R. Ferguson (Cambridge, Mass., 1963), Volume III, p. 342, note. [M.W.]

and in exclusive reference to its *intelligential* functions; and it is in this sense of the word that I am to prove the necessity of contra-distinguishing it from reason.

Premising then, that two or more subjects having the same essential characters are said to fall under the same general definition, I lay it down, as a self-evident truth,—(it is, in fact, an identical proposition)—that whatever subjects fall under one and the same general definition are of one and the same kind: consequently, that which does *not* fall under this definition, must differ in kind from each and all of those that *do*. Difference in degree does indeed suppose sameness in kind; and difference in kind precludes distinction from difference of degree. . . .

To apply these remarks for our present purpose, we have only to describe Understanding and Reason, each by its characteristic qualities. The comparison will show the difference.

UNDERSTANDING	REASON
1. Understanding is discursive.	1. Reason is fixed.
2. The understanding in all its judgments refers to some other faculty as its ultimate authority.	2. The reason in all its decisions appeals to itself as the ground and *substance* of their truth. (Heb. vi. 13.)
3. Understanding is the faculty of reflection.	3. Reason of contemplation. Reason indeed is much nearer to Sense than to Understanding: for Reason (says our great Hooker) is a direct aspect of truth, an inward beholding, having a similar relation to the intelligible or spiritual, as sense has to the material or phenomenal.

The result is: that neither falls under the definition of the other. They differ *in kind:* and had my object been confined to the establishment of this fact, the preceding columns would have superseded all further disquisition. But I have ever in view the especial interest of my youthful readers, whose reflective power is to be cultivated, as well as their particular reflections to be called forth and guided. Now the main chance of their reflecting on religious subjects aright, and of their attaining to the contemplation of spiritual truths at all rests on their insight into the nature of this disparity still more than on their conviction of its existence. I now, therefore, proceed to a brief analysis of the understanding, in elucidation of the definitions already given.

The understanding then (considered exclusively as an organ of human intelligence,) is the faculty by which we reflect and generalize. Take, for instance, any objects consisting of many parts, a house, or a group of houses: and if it be contemplated, as a whole, that is, as many constituting a one, it forms what, in the technical language of psychology, is called a total impression. Among the various component parts of this, we direct our attention especially to such as we recollect to have noticed in other total impressions. Then, by a voluntary act, we withhold our attention from all the rest to reflect exclusively on these; and these we henceforward use as common characters, by virtue of which the several objects are referred to one and the same sort. Thus, the whole process may be reduced to three acts, all depending on and supposing a previous impression on the senses: first, the appropriation of our attention; 2. (and in order to the continuance of the first) abstraction, or the voluntary withholding of the attention; and 3. generalization. And these are the proper functions of the understanding: and the power of so doing, is what we mean, when we say we possess understanding, or are created with the faculty of understanding. . . .

Now when a person speaking to us of any particular object or appearance refers it by means of some common character to a known class (which he does in giving it a name), we say, that we understand him; that is, we understand his words. The name of a thing, in the original sense of the word name, . . . expresses that which is *understood* in an appearance, that which we place (or make to *stand*) *under* it, as the condition of its real existence, and in proof that it is not an accident of the senses, or affection of the individual, not a phantom or apparition, that is, an appearance which is *only* an appearance. . . . In like manner, in a connected succession of names, as the speaker passes from one to the other, we say that we understand his *discourse* (*discursio intellectus, discursus,* his passing rapidly from one thing to another). Thus, in all instances, it is words, names, or, if images, yet images used as words or names, that are the only and exclusive subjects of understanding. In no instance do we understand a thing in itself; but only the name to which it is referred. Sometimes indeed, when several classes are recalled conjointly, we identify the words with the object—though by courtesy of idiom rather than in strict propriety of language. Thus we may say that we *understand* a rainbow, when recalling successively the several names for the several sorts of colours, we know that they are to be applied to one and the same *phenomenon,* at once distinctly and simultaneously; but even in common speech we should not say this of a single colour. No one would say he understands red or blue. He *sees* the colour, and had seen it before in a vast number and variety of objects; and he understands the *word* red, as referring his fancy or memory to this his collective experience.

If this be so, and so it most assuredly is—if the proper functions of the understanding be that of generalizing the notices received from the senses in order to the construction of names: of referring particular notices (that is, impressions or sensations) to their proper names; and, *vice versa,* names to their correspondent class or kind of notices—then it follows of necessity, that the understanding is truly and accurately defined in the words of Leighton and Kant, a faculty judging according to sense.

Now whether in defining the speculative reason (that is, the reason considered abstractedly as an intellective power) we call it "the source of necessary and universal principles, according to which the notices of the senses are either affirmed or denied;" or describe it as "the power by which we are enabled to draw from particular and contingent appearances universal and necessary conclusions:" it is equally evident that the two definitions differ in their essential characters, and consequently the subjects differ in *kind*.

The dependence of the understanding on the representations of the senses, and its consequent posteriority thereto, as contrasted with the independence and antecedency of reason, are strikingly exemplified in the Ptolemic System (that truly wonderful product and highest boast of the faculty, judging according to the senses!) compared with the Newtonian, as the offspring of a yet higher power, arranging, correcting, and annulling the representations of the senses according to its own inherent laws and constitutive ideas.

GEORGE RIPLEY

George Ripley is not a famous American philosopher but, like James Wilson, he is given space in this volume because he represents an important tendency in the history of American philosophical thought. Ripley was born in 1802, a year before his celebrated cousin, Ralph Waldo Emerson; and he died in 1880, two years before Emerson's death. Ripley is better known as the leader of the Brook Farm experiment than he is as a moral and religious philosopher, yet his earliest writing in the eighteen-thirties contains some of the clearest pages of the least clear chapter in the history of American philosophy —Transcendentalism. Ripley's lucidity helps explain why in later life he became one of the most distinguished American newspapermen, and it leads one to regret that he did not continue to apply his considerable analytical power to philosophical problems. The history of American philosophy might have been different if Ripley had not left abstract speculation, first for the frustrations of politics and then for ephemeral journalism.

Ripley was born in Greenfield, Massachusetts, not far from the Connecticut River Valley towns where Edwards had preached a half-century earlier. Like the great Northampton theologian, he was not only an acute dialectician but also a man of deep religious feeling. When Ripley rebelled against Unitarianism, which had done so much to lower the reputation of Edwards in America, Ripley allowed that "with all its defects, the advocacy which Edwards has given to the faculty of spiritual intuition forms an invaluable contribution to a sound religious philosophy." [1] This sympathy with Edwards the mystic is evident in Ripley's attack on the Unitarian theologian, Andrews Norton, sometimes called the "Unitarian pope"; and Ripley's logical skill is strikingly illustrated in his review of Mackintosh's *General View of the Progress of Ethical Philosophy*, a review which has rightly been called "the best piece of moral philosophy by a Transcendentalist". [2] Ripley's attack on Norton and the review of Mackintosh form a very useful introduction to the more famous but much more obscure writings of Emerson on related matters. Like Emerson and other Transcendentalists, Ripley celebrated the importance of sentiment. This was part of their romantic anti-intellectualism, which led them to think that ordinary people who rely more on their hearts and hands than on their heads can reach a more profound truth than is revealed to learned scholars. In this respect, they were part of an American tradition which looked back to Edwards, Wilson, and Jefferson; and forward to William James.

The first passage below is an excerpt from Ripley's attack on Norton, which takes the form of an open letter to him. The second is from Ripley's review of Mackintosh. In the latter we see Ripley trying to sketch an ethical theory which would do justice to the claims of the intellect and of feeling

---

[1] See Volume I, pp. 220–21 of George Ripley, ed., *Philosophical Miscellanies from the French of Cousin, Jouffroy, and Benjamin Constant* (2 volumes, Boston, 1838). These are the first two volumes of Ripley's *Specimens of Foreign Standard Literature* (14 volumes, Boston, 1838–1842). [M.W.]

[2] William Frankena, "Moral Philosophy in America", in *Encyclopedia of Morals*, ed. V. Ferm (New York, 1956).

while rejecting the doctrine of utilitarianism. Neither Emerson nor Thoreau ever achieved the degree of analytical acuity exhibited in Ripley's review of Mackintosh.

Against the Argument from Miracles [3]

The doctrine . . . which I now mean to discuss is that THE MIRACLES RECORDED IN THE NEW TESTAMENT ARE THE ONLY PROOF OF THE DIVINE ORIGIN OF CHRISTIANITY.

You assert, (p. 5.) "that the divine authority of him whom God commissioned to speak to us in his name was attested, in the *only* mode in which it could be, by miraculous displays of his power." Christianity offers, (p. 18.) "in attestation of the truths of the facts, which it reveals, the *only* satisfactory proof, the authority of God, evidenced by miraculous display of his power." (p. 22.) "*No proof* of the divine commission of Christ could be afforded but through miraculous displays of God's power." But I need not multiply quotations to show your advocacy of a doctrine, for which, I presume, you will not disclaim being responsible.

The question at issue, therefore, ought to be distinctly understood. It is not concerning the divine mission of Jesus Christ. The certainty of that will be at the foundation of my reasonings; and it is admitted, as far as I know, in all the controversies to which the subject has given rise in our own country.

Nor is it, whether Jesus Christ performed the miracles ascribed to him in the New Testament. I shall hereafter allude to the doubts which are felt by many excellent Christians on

[3] These passages are from George Ripley, "*The Latest Form of Infidelity*" *Examined: A Letter to Mr. Andrews Norton* (Boston, 1839), pp. 31–33; p. 55; pp. 61–63; pp. 85–89; p. 99; pp. 101–9. The *Letter* was occasioned by Norton's *A Discourse on the Latest Form of Infidelity* (Cambridge, Mass., 1839). The "You" in Ripley's *Letter* refers of course to Norton, and the numerals in parentheses are page-references to Norton's pamphlet. [M.W.]

this point; but for my own part, I cannot avoid the conclusion, that the miracles related in the Gospels were actually wrought by Jesus. Without being blind to the difficulties of the subject, I receive this view, according to my best knowledge and understanding, on the evidence presented; and in this belief I am joined by a large number of those, against whom your charge of infidelity is alleged among ourselves.

Neither does the question, I am about to consider, relate to any philosophical explanation of the miracles of Christ. I believe that he gave health to the sick, sight to the blind, and life to the dead; and my explanation of these facts is that presented in the New Testament. "No man could do the miracles which he did, except God were with him." [4] "God anointed Jesus of Nazareth with the Holy Ghost and with power; who went about doing good; for God was with him." [5] If you have any different, or any better explanation to offer of these facts, it would furnish an interesting object of examination, but can form no part of the present discussion.

Nor, finally, does the question relate to the validity of miracles as the credentials of a divine messenger. That question, it is true, forms an important topic of theological science; much vague and superficial thought is exercised concerning it; it is often presented in a manner, adapted to awaken the most lively doubts; and it demands a wise and thorough revision, before, in the present state of opinion, it can receive an answer that will satisfy the earnest and reflecting Christian inquirer. But this is, by no means, the question at issue on the present occasion.

The point now to be considered is simply this, Are miracles the only evidence of the divine origin of Christianity? . . .

Time would fail me, if I were to attempt to quote a thousandth part of what has been written in opposition to your principle. I might indeed transcribe nearly the whole of mod-

[4] John iii. 2.
[5] Acts x. 38.

ern English Theology, with the exception of a few writers, who were led by the philosophy of Locke to attach an extravagant value to external evidence. It everywhere recognises the fact, that miracles are not the only proof of Christianity, and strongly insists on other arguments which furnish a valid defence of its divine origin. . . .

The exclusive doctrine of your Discourse presents a striking contrast to the views of the leading writers, whom, as liberal Christians, we are accustomed to venerate. No class of men have dwelt more earnestly or more successfully on the proof of the divine origin of Christianity, from considerations independent of miracles, than the honored theologians whose names are identified with mental freedom and religious progress in this country.

I commence with Buckminster.[6] . . . The character of Christ was the ground on which he loved to rest his faith in the Gospel; like the Apostle, he saw the divine glory in the face of Jesus. He did not believe, according to the representation of your Discourse, that we can have no "perception," or "intuition" of the truth of Christianity; that outward prodigies are essential to a living faith within the soul; though fond of historical research, and attached to the evidence of miracles, so far from deeming them the only proof of the divinity of the Gospel, he declares that there is much evidence beside them, and superior to them; that a constant study of Christianity furnishes a constant increase of its proofs; and that having satisfied himself, as far as possible, concerning the historical testimony to its truth, the learner should direct his attention to the internal evidence, the character of Christ, the nature of his instructions, and the spirit of the Gospel. . . .

[6] Joseph Stevens Buckminster (1784–1812), an eloquent preacher, much admired by Ripley and Emerson. For a brief statement about him and his impact, see Perry Miller, ed., *The Transcendentalists: An Anthology* (Cambridge, Mass., 1950), pp. 16–17. [M.W.]

This appears to me to be the soundest theology . . . ; and it involves more than is obvious on a hasty perusal. It comprises almost every thing, on the present subject, which I should be disposed to contend for. According to this statement, the relics of doubt, which are left, after the historical testimony has produced all the conviction of which it is capable, are removed by an intuitive perception of the divinity of the Gospel. External evidence alone can never completely satisfy the mind; but the inherent character of Christianity shows the ingenuous inquirer, that it is the word of God.

Mr. Buckminster proceeds to illustrate the superiority of the evidence of a divine interposition, taken from the character of Christ, over that derived from the record of miracles. "There is something in the character of Christ, which, to an attentive reader of his history, is of more force than ALL THE WEIGHT of EXTERNAL evidence to prove him DIVINE." [7] After a masterly portraiture of the character of the Redeemer, showing the fulness of Divinity with which it was pervaded, proving that Christ himself was the great moral miracle, far transcending the outward works which he performed, the Discourse concludes with an express recognition of the power in human nature, to discover the manifestations of God, in the presence of moral sublimity and loveliness. . . .

I will conclude the discussion of this topic with a brief reference to the manner in which the Apostle Paul presents the evidence of the religion, of which he was so powerful an advocate. He did not limit himself to the proof from miracles. He allowed every important consideration in favor of Christianity its due place. Now he spoke of the resurrection of Christ; now of the fulfilment of prophecy; now of the external signs which had been wrought by him; and now of the intrinsic divinity of the Gospel itself. While the Jews demanded a new miracle; while the Greeks sought after wisdom; while the sages of the schools, and the disputers of the world, saw

[7] Buckminster's *Sermons* (Third Edition), p. 19.

nothing but foolishness in the doctrine of Christ; Paul persisted in preaching it; he knew that it was filled with a divine
life; and that they who were called to its enjoyment, they
whose souls were in unison with its spirit, would intuitively
perceive that it was the wisdom of God, and the power of
God.[8] . . .

The Apostle continues to speak of the light which had been
granted, enabling him to see the glory of God in the face of
Jesus Christ.[9] His meaning cannot be better illustrated, than
by the following admirable remarks from the most profound
theologian, whom this country has produced. "If a sight of
Christ's outward glory might give a rational assurance of his
divinity, why may not an apprehension of his spiritual glory
do so too? Doubtless Christ's spiritual glory is in itself as distinguishing, and as plainly showing his divinity, as his outward glory, and a great deal more. For his spiritual glory is
that wherein his divinity consists; and the outward glory of
his transfiguration showed him to be divine, only as it was a
remarkable image or representation of that spiritual glory.
Doubtless, therefore, he that has had a clear sight of the
spiritual glory of Christ may say, 'I have not followed cun-
ningly devised fables, but have been an eye witness of his
majesty,' upon as good grounds as the Apostle, when he had
respect to the outward glory of Christ that he had seen. A
true sense of the divine excellency of the things of God's
word doth more directly and immediately convince of the
truth of them; and that because the excellency of these things
is so superlative. There is a beauty in them that is so divine
and Godlike, that is greatly and evidently distinguishing of
them from things merely human, or that men are the inventors and authors of; a glory, that is so high and great, that
when clearly seen, commands assent to their divinity and
reality. The evidence, which they who are spiritually enlight-

[8] I Cor. i. 20–24.
[9] II Cor. iv. 6.

ened have of the truth of the things of religion, is a kind of intuition and immediate evidence. They believe the doctrines of God's word to be divine, because they see divinity in them. That is, they see a divine and transcendent and most evidently distinguishing glory in them; such a glory, as, if clearly seen, does not leave room to doubt of their being of God, and not of men." [10] . . .

I object again to your exclusive principle, on account of its injurious bearing on the character of a large portion of the most sincere believers in Christ. . . . Pressed to its logical consequences, it denies the Christian name to all who do not receive Christianity in the method which you prescribe. For it is clear, that if Christianity be founded ONLY on its historical evidence, he, who does not receive it on that evidence, cannot strictly be said to receive it at all. . . .

I know not a few individuals,—neither very wise, nor very unwise, compared with the average of men,—certainly not persons qualified by the "knowledge of which extensive learning commonly makes a part," to express an opinion on the subject, who still venture, with a modest confidence, to assume the name of Christians. They inform me that they obtain no satisfaction from such works as Paley's "Evidences of Christianity," or Lardner's "Credibility of the Gospel History." Books of this character do not speak to their condition; their minds are so constructed as to be little affected by such reasonings; but yet the truth of Christianity commends itself to their souls; and they believe in Christ, because they behold his glory. They do not even question the divine origin of

[10] Ripley's citation from *The Works of President Edwards*, Volume 8 (Worcester, 1809), is simply to "pp. 300, 305, 306"; but Ripley does not indicate that the first part of the quotation—up to "that he had seen"—appears on pp. 305–6, whereas the remainder, from "A true sense," is on p. 300. Both passages come from Edwards' sermon, "A Divine and Supernatural Light, Immediately Imparted to the Soul by the Spirit of God, Shown To Be Both a Scriptural and Rational Doctrine." [M.W.]

Christianity; they would as soon think of asking whether the sun shines at noon; and cheerful and contented in their faith, they leave the problems, which require curious historical research, to scholars, whose business it is to deal with them.

I have known many persons of this description; indeed, if I am not greatly deceived, they are to be found in all our congregations; I have witnessed their unobtrusive piety in the daily walks of life; I have visited them in scenes of deepest sorrow; I have stood at the side of their death-beds; and I could no more doubt their genuine Christian faith, because it was not the product of historical evidence, than I could deny the skill of one of our native artists, because it did not grow up from the study of classic models.

This experience is confirmed by the testimony of an eminent man, already quoted, who, whatever portion of truth he might have failed to perceive, it would be extreme folly to doubt, was conversant with the workings of the soul, in the affairs of religion, as few have ever been, in our country, or in any other. "If the evidence of the Gospel depended only on history, and such reasonings as learned men only are capable of, it would be above the reach of far the greatest part of mankind. But persons with but an ordinary degree of knowledge are capable, without a long and subtile train of reasoning, to see the divine excellency of the things of religion. They are capable of being taught by the Spirit of God, as well as learned men. The evidence, that is this way obtained, is vastly better and more satisfying, than all that can be obtained by the arguings of those that are the most learned, and the greatest masters of reason. And babes are as capable of knowing these things, as the wise and prudent; and they are often hid from these when they are revealed to those." [11]

The preceding views suggest another fatal objection to the doctrine of your Discourse. It removes Christianity from its strong hold in the common mind, and puts it into the keeping

[11] *Ibid.*, pp. 310–11.

of scholars and antiquaries. I have already hinted at this objection, but it deserves a more particular consideration. It follows, as the necessary consequence of your exclusive hypothesis. For if the truth of Christianity rests entirely on the foundation of historical evidence; if there be nothing in its intrinsic character to commend it to the soul, as the revelation of God; if the uneducated inquirer must make up his mind, either from his own investigations or from the testimony of others, in regard to the subtlest questions of literary criticism, before he can cherish a vital faith in the doctrines of Christ, of course, he resigns his opinions to the guidance of the learned. He must give up his birth-right as a man, before he can establish his faith as a Christian. For he cannot enter into such investigations himself; he has neither the ability, the leisure, nor the apparatus, that is requisite; he must sue at the feet of the scholar for the light which he needs for the salvation of the soul. . . .

It may appear incredible to many, that you should fully admit this consequence, although it is the inevitable result of your reasonings. There are few minds, at the present day, however wedded to prescription and form, however great their distrust of the mass of the people, that would not shrink from the distinct avowal of such an opinion, even though it were privately cherished. I honor the frankness with which you express it,—. . . a more ingenious defence of the principle, perhaps, cannot be made, than that contained in the Note which you devote to the subject. At all events, we shall look in vain for a clearer statement of the opinion objected to, than the following words. "The full comprehension of the character and evidence of Christianity is the result of *studies which are pursued only by few,* and the *many want capacity* or opportunity to satisfy themselves on the subject by their independent, unassisted exertions." (p. 57.) "It is said, that a *great majority of men are not capable* of investigating for themselves the evidences and character of Christianity, and therefore can have no reasonable foundation for their belief in Christianity. The direct answer is, that TRUST *in the infor-mation, judgment, and integrity of others,* to a greater or less extent, as it is a universal and necessary, is also a rational principle of belief." (p. 63.)

The great majority of people, accordingly, having no power to perceive the intrinsic divinity of Christian truth, to behold the glory of God in the character of Christ, are doomed, by the very nature of the case, to dependence on the learned class, for the foundation of their faith.

The first astonishing circumstance connected with this dec-laration is, that it was addressed to a body of Christians, whose prominent characteristic is the defence of freedom of mind,—of not only the right, but the duty, and of course, the power of private judgment, to the most unlimited extent. We have claimed to be the very Protestants of the Protestants; our watchword has been, "The people, and not the priests;" we have taken our stand on the broad foundation of the uni-versal mind; we have fought for the inherent privileges of hu-manity; and if we have, in any degree, secured a hold on the affections of the community; if the term "liberal Christian" is sacred and dear to any hearts among the breathing multi-tudes around us; it is because we have discarded the lifeless formulas of the schools; because we have sought to make Christianity a vital sentiment, instead of a barren tradition; because we have endeavored to bring the Bible out of the "dusty corners" in which learned speculations had placed it; and boldly appealed to the sense of truth in every man, to SEE and JUDGE for himself what is right.

Again, I cannot but be surprised at the remarkable confu-sion of the statement, in which you recognise no distinction between the evidence of the truth of physical science and that of moral and religious truth. You assert that "religious knowledge has the character common to all our higher knowledge, that it requires labor, thought, and learning to at-tain it." (p. 54.) The truth of Christianity is to be received on the same ground, on which we admit, that "all the motions of the bodies of the solar system in relation to each other are to be referred to the one law of gravity." (p. 58.) The spiritual truths of Christianity are to be ascertained by the same method as the physical truths of astronomy. The growth in the "knowledge of our Lord Jesus Christ," which is demanded of the most unlearned believer, is made to depend on the same conditions as the increase of our knowledge of "all subjects, lying beyond the sphere of personal experience." (p. 59.) Our faith no longer proceeds from the "demonstration of the Spirit;" it stands not "in the power of God," but "in the wisdom of men."

But if this theory be true, it not only makes a large proportion of unlettered Christians dependent on scholars for their knowledge of Christ, but actually deprives them of all religious knowledge whatever. They have not the requisite culture even to understand the results of critical investigation; they do not feel sufficient interest in the subject to make any inquiries concerning them; still, they "know" in whom they believe; they have a faith, no less rational, no less enlightened, no less fervent, than that of the most profound antiquary; for they have the witness in their own hearts; the truths of the Gospels are the very life of their souls; they have seen, and tasted, and been nourished by the bread of God, which came down out of Heaven; and it is in vain to tell them, that they are ignorant of the truth of Christianity, that they have no solid foundation for their faith, because they have not besieged the libraries of the learned, to ask them whether they might believe in Christ or no. . . .

Nor is it merely those whom we speak of in our pride, as the less favored classes, to whom the supply of their daily wants seems like a daily miracle, that are obliged to found their convictions of the truth of Christianity on more direct evidence, than is furnished by the investigations of science for the truths of astronomy. The learned themselves are often so absorbed in their favorite studies, that they can give little attention to the critical researches of the theologian. Yet, if they are religious men, they feel that their faith is built on stronger evidence than he could supply them with. They do not need to solicit his advice before they can believe in Christianity. They have settled their faith for themselves; and seen, from the intrinsic divinity of the Gospel, that it is the gift of God. They know that different branches of inquiry demand different kinds of evidence; a scholastic logic, with them, is not the only organ of truth; they have confidence in the inward eye, which penetrates where the telescope cannot reach; they do not confound the truths of religion with the discoveries of astronomy, in regard to their manner of proof; and, . . . while they establish the facts of physical science by learned research and subtle calculations, they perceive the truths of the Gospel by the intuitions of the soul.

The Connection between Virtue and Utility [12]

. . . The attention of Sir James Mackintosh has . . . been directed, with strong interest, to the celebrated question respecting the relation of Utility to Virtue. Some of his most important suggestions are in elucidation of this topic, but, after all that he has said, we do not perceive that he has exhausted the subject, or, indeed, that he has presented it in the most satisfactory lights of which it is susceptible. He must be entitled to the credit of noticing certain distinctions, the neglect of which has introduced great confusion into the discussion of this question; but whether they satisfactorily explain the difficulties which have attended it, we must confess that we are entirely in doubt. Thus, he clearly perceives and states the distinction between the Theory of Moral Sentiments and the Criterion of Moral Actions. He maintains that

[12] This is from Ripley's very long review of Mackintosh's *General View of the Progress of Ethical Philosophy* in *The Christian Examiner*, Volume XIII (New Series, Volume VIII) (January 1833), pp. 311–32. [M.W.]

we may have a perception of moral qualities, independent of the Utility of the actions to which they belong; this is one thing; but the actions which give us such perceptions, agree in conducing to the welfare of mankind, or in their utility; this is another thing; and the two facts are neither to be confounded, nor placed in opposition to each other. The first relates to the nature of the feelings, with which right and wrong are contemplated by human beings; and the second to the nature of the distinction between right and wrong in human conduct. So that he admits, that we may have the emotion of moral approbation, without reference to the perception of utility; while we are taught by experience that all actions which excite this emotion, have the common element of utility. By this admission, he escapes the odious and absurd consequences which are charged upon those moralists who make the essence of utility and of virtue one and the same thing; but he does not make out, to our conviction, the grounds upon which that identity can be avoided. Again, Sir James very justly argues, that the perception of utility is unfit to be an immediate incentive and guide to right action, and is adapted only to be the general test of virtuous dispositions and sentiments; that it is a legitimate criterion of these last, he confidently maintains; but, as we think, he fails in pointing out why it is a suitable standard for the one and not for the other.

After all the ingenuity which he has exercised upon the subject, we cannot see that he has extricated it from the difficulty in which he found it, and the reason is, that he was misled by an imperfect conception of the true relation between virtue and utility. Indeed, we do not know any writer who appears to have viewed this point in all its bearings, and thence arrived at satisfactory conclusions. It is with great diffidence, then, that we approach it; and begging the patience of our readers, we proceed to offer such remarks as have been suggested by our own reflections.

The first point which it is necessary to consider in this discussion, is the nature of the feelings, with which we regard the distinctions of Right and Wrong in human conduct. It is a question of pure psychology, and is to be determined by an appeal to our own consciousness, as much as the nature of any mental pleasure or pain whatever. Is, then, the mental feeling consequent upon the perception of Right and Wrong, the same as that which arises upon the perception of utility, or the want of it? Is our perception of the Useful and the Right, one and the same thing? If so, then the essence of virtue and utility are identical. We have only to ask whether an action is Useful, and the true answer to the question will determine whether or not it is Right. But on the other hand, is not the perception of the Right essentially distinct from that of the Useful, as distinct as the perception of beauty in the starry heavens is from that of the sphericity of the orbs, which compose them? We maintain that it is. We are conscious, that when we contemplate a virtuous action, we experience a different emotion from that which arises upon the sight of a useful one. The two emotions may be,—indeed they usually are,—excited by the same object, since a virtuous action is almost always useful, but they can be resolved into different feelings with as much certainty, as the red and violet rays are divided in the prismatic spectrum. We might safely leave this point, if it had not been so much disputed, with the consciousness of each of our readers, assured that he would no more confound the two emotions produced respectively by the Useful and the Right, than he would the heat of a fire with the sensation of burning, or the form and color of a rose, with the perception of its fragrance. But we beg leave to look a little further at it together. Do not the Useful and the Right differ in the kind of impression, which they produce upon the mind, inasmuch as the one is addressed principally to the understanding, and the other always terminates upon the feelings? The perception of utility in an action or object is related to the intellect. The powers of discrimination are exercised to ascertain its existence. We compare, reflect, and judge, whether the act is useful or not, and the result is the conviction of the understanding. And there, generally, so far as utility is concerned, the mental operation terminates. In some cases, it is true, the perception of utility is succeeded by the sentiment of admiration,—for instance, when we view a useful work of art of extraordinary ingenuity,—but here, it is the skill of the artificer, which we admire, not the usefulness of the machine. In some cases, also, the perception of utility is followed by the sentiment of moral approbation,—for instance, when we contemplate the labors of a Howard or an Oberlin,—but here it is the character of the men that we approve, not the utility of their actions, as is evident from the fact, that if we knew the actions to have been prompted by motives of envy, malignity, or revenge, our approbation would be withdrawn. But regarding the perception of utility by itself, it is clear, that we determine whether or not an action is useful, by an exercise of judgment, just as much as we determine the properties of a triangle or circle by the same power. The perception itself is not an emotion, and does not necessarily involve one. The perception of Right, on the contrary, always involves the sentiment of moral approbation, so much so, indeed, that the perception and the sentiment have been confounded by many eminent philosophers. The quality which excites it, though in our opinion perceived by the understanding, touches the feelings, creates a vivid sentiment, which possesses a character of its own, unlike any other, and is evidently altogether and absolutely distinct from the calm conclusions of the intellect, which determine whether or not an action is Useful.

This is one psychological distinction between the perception of the Right and the Useful. But this is not all. Are there not many objects, which give the perception of utility, but excite no emotion of moral approbation? If there are such, of course, the essence of the Useful and of the Right are not the same thing, since we know nothing of essences, but from their effects. The effects being different, the qualities cannot be the same. But it is very certain, that we pronounce many objects useful, which we never call virtuous. We often perceive the utility of actions, to which it would be absurd to ascribe virtue. No inanimate object, however useful, excites the emotion of moral approbation. The very supposition of its being virtuous is ludicrous. But why should it be? If utility and virtue, as perceived by the mind, are identical, it follows, with the clearness of demonstration, that wherever we perceive the one, we must attribute the other. But, who ever thought of asking a question concerning the virtue of the most valuable machine? But why not? If the power of doing good, if the actual amount of benefit produced, excite in our minds the same emotion with a virtuous deed, why not ask the same questions concerning a machine as concerning a man? Indeed, in point of utility, the machine, in many instances, has incomparably the advantage over the best man. A spinning-mill, which saves the labor of many hands, and puts bread into many mouths, has been of more real use to mankind, than the decision of Aristides, in refusing to burn the enemy's fleet. But is there the same emotion, in thinking of the two cases? If there be no distinction between the Useful and the Right, why do we praise the patriot martyr, more than we do the sword and the cannon, with which he defended his country's rights? Why do we extol the philanthropist, who went down into the depths of dungeons to relieve the misery of the prisoner, more than we do the vessel that bore him over the waters, in his "grand circumnavigation of charity?" If the perception of virtue be nothing more than the perception of utility, why do we not fall in with that beautiful form of Eastern superstition, and give the Sun the adoration which we confine to its Intelligent Maker? Certainly, no created intelligence can boast of utility like that of the Sun, but we regard the humblest sacrifice to duty, though in the meanest tenant of the straw-thatched cottage, with an emotion, which that glorious luminary, "walking in the greatness of his strength, and rejoicing as a strong man to run a race," can never excite.

The perception of utility is given to us every day by the actions of the inferior animals. But does any one ever inquire into the merit of those actions? Did any rational mind ever regard them with the emotion of moral approbation? If we behold a flock of sheep grazing in a meadow, it is not improbable that we may engage in a calculation respecting the benefit to the country, we may think of the various uses to which their fleece, their flesh, or their skin may be applied, and perhaps come to the conclusion that they are of far more utility than their benevolent owner, who inhabits the neighboring dwelling; but we suppose no one ever thought of making a comparison between the virtue of the animals and that of the man. It would, however, be a just comparison, if the perception of utility and of virtue were the same. Even in those cases, in which by the force of our habitual associations, we experience an emotion similar to that of moral approbation, when contemplating the actions of certain animals, the emotion is, by no means, in proportion to the utility of the actions by which it is excited. We behold the slow and sluggish ox transporting the yellow treasures of a fruitful harvest to the store-house of the husbandman, and if a thought is suggested, it is that of the utility of the animal to the interests of his owner. No emotion whatever is produced. We behold, on the other hand, a faithful dog refusing his daily sustenance, that he may watch at his master's grave, and although we see no manner of use in the action, we cannot help feeling a strong emotion, sufficiently resembling that of moral approbation, to show us that it does not always correspond to the perception of utility.

But it may be said by those who hold that the Useful and the Right are identical, that our moral sentiments are never called forth, except by the actions of rational and voluntary agents. By this very admission, then, it is conceded, that the perception of the Useful and the Right are not always the same, that an element is necessary to the existence of virtue, in addition to utility. This is the precise point for which we contend. And we may then conclude, that this admission puts an end to the question. But no, it is said, we must believe until further proof, that when we contemplate the actions of rational and voluntary agents, it is the perception of utility that causes the emotion of moral approbation, that the two things are indeed one and the same. Is it then a fact, that our feelings are similar when we witness an instance of utility, and a display of virtue, in a rational agent? Do we not perceive many actions, of which we say they are useful, but of which we can never say, they are virtuous? Do we not, for instance, look into the intention of the agent, before we pronounce upon the moral character of his actions? But their utility is the same whatever be his intentions. The author of a valuable work on astronomy or political economy, may be of far greater service to his country and to the world, than the most patient sufferer, who is supported, by strong Christian principle, under the pangs of sickness or the wretchedness of poverty. But no one hesitates to say, that however useful the former, he is not necessarily a good man, he is not necessarily regarded with moral approbation; while no one can behold the latter, without bearing testimony to his virtue, and experiencing a deep emotion of approbation. One of the most useful men that ever lived, was the inventor of logarithms. That invention, in its remote consequences, has probably saved more lives than the efforts of all the philanthropists, who have sacrificed themselves to a sense of duty. But do we give the reward of moral approbation to the inventor for that act? Never. Why should we not, if the Useful and the Virtuous are the same? Do we think of Sir Isaac Newton, as the discoverer of the law of gravitation and the method of fluxions, when we extol his virtue? Is his utility as a philosopher in our minds, when we praise his excellence as a Christian? But why not? If the perception of utility and the emotion of moral approbation are identical, how can we separate them, as we always do, in the instances that have been named?

But to dwell no longer on this part of the argument, let us proceed to another point. Are there not certain actions which excite the emotion of moral approbation, before we have gained any perception of their utility? Do we not often witness conduct which we pronounce at once to be right, and behold with profound admiration, before we can calculate its consequences? We do not deny that the utility of such actions can be made apparent, after sufficient examination, but we maintain, that we approve of them the moment we understand the circumstances of the case, whether we think of their utility or not. When the youthful Lafayette replied to the American commissioners, who told him that they were too poor to furnish a vessel for his passage to this country, "then I will purchase and fit out one for myself," we are immediately affected by the magnanimity, perseverance, and disinterestedness of the intrepid friend of liberty, and speak of the action with enthusiastic praise, long before we perceive the train of beneficial consequences which it has since put in motion. And suppose the vessel which bore the devoted hero to the great struggle for human rights, had perished at sea, and the generous intentions of its owner been frustrated, should we any the less pronounce his action a right and noble one? . . .

We have thus far proved that there is a state of mind, which we call moral approbation, distinct from that which we call the perception of utility. There are actions to which we apply the epithet Right, belonging to a different order from those to which we apply the epithet Useful. The conception of the Right and the conception of the Useful, then, considered as actual ideas of the human intellect, are by no means one and the same. It is essential to the idea of a right action, one to which we yield our moral approbation, that it be performed by an intelligent Being, and that it be voluntary. A useful action does not require either of these conditions. If it be now asked what we mean by a right action, it may be as difficult to give a general answer, as to the question, what we mean by a true proposition. That there is any single element which can be applied as the criterion of Right,

any more than there is a single criterion of truth, we acknowledge that we have never been convinced. We cannot
say of any proposition, that it is useful, that it is agreeable to
the will of God, or the like, and therefore it is true; its truth
is presupposed, in the assertion of its utility; and its truth
must be ascertained, before we can know it is agreeable to
the will of God. The same reasoning holds, it appears to us,
respecting the Right. We cannot say of any action, that it is
useful, that it is agreeable to the will of God, or the like, and
therefore, it is Right; its being Right is presupposed in the
fact of its utility, and we must ascertain that that is Right, before we can know that it is agreeable to the will of God. We
may say that truth is conformity to our intellectual nature;
and in like manner, that virtue is conformity to our moral nature; but this is very different from stating a single element,
as a criterion, by which either the one or the other may be
tested. We may go still further, and describe the Idea of
truth and of virtue. Truth is in relation to Belief; Virtue to
Practice. A true proposition is one which must be believed; a
right action, one which must be done. This is the simple Idea
of Right. Turn it which way we will, we cannot get rid of it.
We may think we have resolved it into something else, that it
consists in a regard to our own greatest happiness, in the pursuit of the general good, in obedience to the divine will, in
propriety, and so on, but all these expressions only describe
particular right actions; they shed no light on the general and
absolute Idea of Right, which we can carry no further than
this, namely,—that, which *must* be done, which *ought* to be
done, which we are *obliged* to do, which it is *wrong* to omit;
all which are clearly equivalent expressions for the same
thing, differing only in form, as statements of one fundamental Idea. That such an Idea exists in the human mind, we will
not stop to prove at greater length, only premising that if any
one is disposed to question it, we would ask him if he has not
the Idea of Cause and Effect, of Identity, of Duration, of
Space, and of Substance, and if so, whether the Idea of Right,

as we have stated it, is not as distinct and real as either of the former. If he denies this, we have no common ground to stand upon, and cannot make our voices heard across the chasm which separates us.

Admitting, then, the fundamental Idea of Right, in the mature mind, as distinct from every other, the question is still pending, What is the common quality in those actions, by which the idea is suggested? What is the criterion by which we may determine whether or not an action or mental disposition is Right? It is to be determined by utility, say the advocates of the theory, which we oppose. As soon as it is proved to be useful, it is proved to be Right. Let us consider, in the first place, if this criterion will hold in its application to individual actions, for if it will not, its importance as a test is at once diminished, since it is individual actions, of which we have the most frequent occasion to determine the character. Now it is plain, that there are many actions of a moral nature, which we immediately pronounce to be wrong, of which no one hesitates to say that they are wrong, yet the actual effects of which have been beneficial to mankind. If utility were the criterion, such actions would be Right. If the case can be fairly made out that they have done good to the world, and utility be assumed as the only test of their character, of course, we must admit that they ought to have been done,—however repugnant to our natural feelings,—since we have pronounced them useful, we must also pronounce them right. But let us make the attempt. We shall find it impossible. We might as well hope to move the Sun at our bidding, as to make a wrong action, useful though it be, appear to our moral faculty as right. Take as an example, the death of Socrates. The crime against philosophy, which the Athenians committed in his martyrdom, has never been forgiven, from that day to the present. The universal sense of mankind is against it. It is unequivocally and unanimously condemned as wrong. But no one can doubt that the ultimate effects of that atrocious and unjust deed have been eminently useful. It was a matter of small importance for Socrates to leave the world, though by a violent death. He was ripe in years and in virtue. He had exhausted the usual sources of enjoyment which life affords. He could, at best, have been spared but a little while. He was taken from the world, in the full possession of all his faculties, neither his mind nor body impaired by the touch of a loathsome disease, calmly conversing with the troops of friends, who were faithful to the last, and, finally, yielding to the gentle operation of the poison, resigned his breath without a struggle. If we were asked what injury were done to Socrates, we should not know where to look for a reply. Indeed, it is difficult to conceive a more enviable situation than that of the martyred philosopher, when, after blessing his executioner, he tasted the fatal cup and surrendered himself to the pleasing visions of Immortality, which hovered around his last moments. But does all this prove that his condemnation was just? Does it not rather lead us to regard the crime of his accusers, with deeper indignation? Are we in the slightest degree reconciled to them, by the assurance of the good effects which their crime has produced? Of these good effects, there can be doubt. The manner of his death, far more than the spirit of his philosophy, or the beauty of his character, has embalmed the memory of Socrates, in the hearts of every succeeding generation. The remembrance of his name has given a charm to his principles, and the efficacy of his example added strength to virtue. If, then, we judge of the sentence which doomed him to drink hemlock, by the test of utility, how can we avoid pronouncing it virtuous? Why do we not praise the Athenian populace for the incalculable good which they have been the agents in effecting? We hold up the action of Brutus, "who slew his best lover for the good of Rome," as commendable and noble. Yet the death of Julius Caesar has been of far less use to his country and to the world, than the death of Socrates. If utility is the criterion of Right and Wrong, how do we account for the different feelings with which we contemplate the instances that have been mentioned? We might multiply examples of this kind to an unlimited extent. The blood of the martyrs has in every age been the seed of the church; and if the character of actions is determined by their utility, we must approve of those which have erected the scaffold and kindled the fires; since these have been the means of the promotion of truth and the progress of righteousness.

It may be maintained with regard to such actions, that the good which they have accomplished is incidental, while the intention which prompted them is wrong, and that it is the intention and not the consequence of the action, to which the criterion of utility is to be applied. But this admission concedes the very point in question. It allows that the beneficial effects of an action, are not all at which we are to look, in determining its moral character. So that it virtually renounces the theory of utility as the criterion of Right. Besides, the most distinguished advocates of this theory, Dr. Paley and his followers, for instance, expressly limit its application to actions. It has no concern, according to them, with the intentions of the agent. But we have seen that it does not hold good as a test of actions; if we retain the criterion, then, we must in opposition to Paley himself, make use of it as the test of intentions. If we apply the test of utility at all, as the ultimate ground of our decisions, we must so apply it, as to show that the intended production of good is always Right, as well as that the intended production of evil is always wrong. This last proposition, of course, we would not be supposed to deny; but we believe it on other grounds than those taken by the advocates of utility. But to consider the first proposition alluded to above, is the intentional production of good always Right? Is every action, which I mean to be a useful one, therefore Right? We deny that it is. To take a very familiar instance, the persecution of the primitive Christians by Paul, before his conversion. There is no doubt, he thought, that he was doing God service, by this action; and there is as little doubt that the ultimate effects of the persecutions endured

by the infant church, were beneficial to its growth and to its
virtues. But Paul never dreamed of justifying his conduct on
the score of its utility, or of his sincere conviction of its utility. On the contrary, he regarded himself as one of the chief
of sinners, on account of his crimes in persecuting the disciples. But taking utility as the test, we do not perceive that
the Apostle was not fully justified.

Another instance to illustrate our views, may be found in
the case of the assassin, as stated by Dr. Paley, for a different
purpose. Suppose that an old man of worthless character is in
possession of a large fortune, which I can attain by putting
him to death, and employ for my own benefit and that of
mankind. Why should not I knock the rich villain in the
head, and do good with the money, of which he makes no
use? The action, by the very terms of the statement, will be a
beneficial one. My intentions in committing it, are with a single view to the benefit it will produce. If utility is the criterion, the old miser must die. There is no other way. But, says
Dr. Paley, the action is unlawful, because a general rule to
sanction such actions would be injurious. Be it so. But in this
instance, what have I to do with general rules, if utility be
my only guide? I know that the action will be useful, and
that is all I want to know. What consequence is it to me, that
a general rule, taken by others from my conduct, might in
some future, uncertain cases, be injurious? I know not that
such cases will ever occur, and if they do, they are nothing to
me, let them be determined by those who are called to act
upon them. Utility is my only guide, and utility I will follow.
Utility tells me to take this man's life for his money, and utility I will obey. We do not see that such reasoning can be set
aside, allowing that the operation of the general rule in question would be injurious. But, still further, we cannot see how
a general rule, formed from a particular beneficial action can
be injurious. The general rule would comprehend only such
actions as are precisely similar to the one upon which it is
founded. If it be useful in a given case to take the life of an

old man because I can make a better use of his money than
he does himself, it would also be useful to take the lives of
ten, twenty, thirty, or as many as were in similar circumstances. If the utility of one action makes it Right, it is impossible that the utility of ten, twenty, or thirty actions precisely
similar, should not also make them Right. If the particular
case be beneficial, the general rule must be beneficial also.
But, the truth is, in cases of this kind we must have recourse
to some criterion, less flexible, less vague, less uncertain than
that of utility.

We have now seen that there are useful actions, which
have no moral character whatever,—actions, intended to be
useful, which are wrong—and actions, intended to be wrong,
committed with a criminal motive, which are useful. Hence it
follows, that utility cannot be the legitimate criterion of
Right and Wrong. That the dispositions and sentiments
which are universally regarded as virtuous, are generally useful to their possessors and to mankind, we have not a shadow
of doubt. We are certain that this element is common to all
the motives and feelings which the collected sense of the
human race has pronounced to be right; that it would be in-
calculably for the benefit of the world, if the actions which
are agreed to be virtuous, were universally practised. But this
is a very different thing—and it is utterly surprising that the
difference has been so generally overlooked—from making
the actual utility of actions, a criterion of their moral character. It is certainly one thing to say, that the practice of Right
actions would be generally useful; and another, and quite a
different thing to say, that the fact of its utility determines an
action to be Right. Yet this distinction has been usually kept
out of sight, by writers of no mean influence on the philosophy of ethics. It seems scarcely to have been recognized, that
we may ascertain an action to be Right, on grounds independent of its utility, and yet admit, to its fullest extent, the fact
that utility is a quality common to actions of that character.
The distinction between the virtue of an action and its ten-

dency to promote the private happiness of the agent, though denied or disregarded by many respectable moral writers, is far more generally admitted than the one to which we have just alluded. Yet it is no less certain, that the virtue of an action, and its tendency to promote our own happiness, usually coincide, than that the virtue of an action coincides with its tendency to promote the happiness of mankind, or its general utility. We do not make its tendency, in the one case, the test of its character; we determine it by a different order of considerations; it should be the same in the other; as the tendency to promote our own happiness is a quality of virtuous actions, without being their general criterion, so the tendency to promote the happiness of mankind is a quality of virtuous actions, without being their general criterion. Admitting, then, that utility, though usually connected with virtuous actions, is not the ultimate test to which they must be brought, the question is now to be answered, What is the positive relation of utility to virtue? We reply that is the test of those dispositions and actions only, which have immediate reference to our fellow men; and of these, we say that the Useful is Right only when it does not interfere with any prior obligation. We therefore take it for granted that there are grounds of obligation, different from, and superior to those of utility; and of these it is necessary for us to give an explanation.

This leads us to consider the true theory of moral obligation in general. It is evident, that there are many instances, in which the utility of an action convinces us that the action is right, and that we are under a moral obligation to perform it. Now is utility the sole and ultimate ground upon which the obligation rests, or can we discover, after further analysis, a more general element, which constitutes the ground of obligation? We think there is an element more general than utility, and which, in fact, gives to utility its binding power. It is conformity to our moral relations, as intuitively perceived, in the final analysis, by the moral faculty.

From all the relations, which man is called to sustain, proceed a corresponding order of duties, the perception of which is as intuitive to the mature mind, as the perception of the first principles of philosophy, or the axioms of mathematics. These intuitive perceptions are the foundation of moral science, and the ultimate standard by which we settle all questions of practical duty. Thus, among the relations, sustained by man, the most important is that, by which he is connected with his Maker. From this relation, as soon as it is understood, are deduced several duties, the obligation of which we perceive no less intuitively than we do the mathematical truths, deduced from the relations of quantity and magnitude. Let us place, on one side, the idea of a Creator, omnipotent, independent, perfectly wise, benevolent, and just; and, on the other, the idea of creatures, weak, dependent, receiving every thing which they possess from the goodness of God, and capable of understanding, in some degree, the perfections of his character;—we perceive an existing relation, and from this relation, we deduce the duty of the creature to exercise Love, Veneration, Gratitude, and Obedience towards the Creator. If we bring the subject fully and fairly before our minds, we cannot help seeing that such is our duty. We perceive a conformity between it, and the relation we have considered. We recognize a moral obligation to discharge it. We perceive that it is fit, right, and our bounden duty, to love, venerate, worship, and obey the Almighty. We cannot resolve this obligation into any considerations of the utility which may accrue to ourselves or to others, from its faithful fulfilment. We cannot reduce it into any more simple elements. It would be as absurd to ask the reason of this obligation, as to ask the reason why two and two are equal to four. We may ask indeed a reason for our fulfilling this obligation, but that is another, and quite a different question. Since we must make out our obligation, before we can seek reasons for fulfilling it; the contrary would be like trying to build a house in the air.

In like manner, from the relation, which man sustains to himself, considered as a sensitive and intelligent being, capable of happiness and improvement, with the power of election, volition, and action, we deduce several duties, which may perhaps be summed up in the two general principles, that he is under obligation to seek his own greatest perfection, and his own highest happiness;—provided always, that in so doing, he does not interfere with any obligation, which the moral faculty designates as possessing prior claims. Like the duties, growing out of the former relation, these are objects of intuitive perception. As soon as we understand the relation, we understand the duties, just as when we understand the definition of a circle, we understand its primary properties. In either case, when we come to propositions that are intuitively perceived, we have arrived at the end of our line; there is nothing more to be said, and he who does not recognize these fundamental perceptions, cannot of course be convinced by argument; since he denies the very ground on which any argument can be built. Should it be said, that many do not acknowledge the primary perceptions of morality, we reply that many do not understand the relations, from which they proceed; but that any who have attended to the relations, and understand them should not admit the perceptions, we confess seems as inconceivable, as that any should maintain, that, though four times five are twenty, five times four are not twenty, but five hundred. Of course, the consciousness of every individual must determine the question for himself, and to that we cheerfully submit it.

We come now to the considerations, which, in our opinion, clearly settle the relation of utility to virtue. The duties, which we have already noticed, though undoubtedly productive of incalculable benefit to mankind, derive their obligation, not from their utility, but from their conformity to the relations of things, as intuitively perceived by the moral faculty. But the relations, which we sustain to our fellow men are more comprehensive, more obvious, more universal in their application, than any others which we sustain. We are born into the world to be at once dependent on others. We are placed from the first in society. We are hemmed in, and pressed around, by all those responsible and delightful relations, which give life its brightest charms, and make the discharge of our duty no less beautiful than it is binding. They are the element in which we live and move, and have our being. They surround us in their comprehensive grasp as closely as the all-embracing atmosphere. From these relations, a new order of duties is derived. A conformity to these relations, as dictated by the moral faculty, includes a wide circle of dispositions and actions. But they may all be summed up in this general rule, abstain from injury and do good. Here, then, the element of utility comes in. We infer, from our relations with our fellow men, that it is our duty to be as useful to them as we can,—but with the limitation before laid down, that we never sacrifice to utility any higher obligation. Utility is itself an obligation, whenever it is in conformity to all the relations which we sustain to God, to ourselves, and to our fellow men: and this conformity is pointed out by our moral faculty in the same manner as conformity to truth is pointed out, by our intellectual faculties; but, whenever utility comes in competition with any prior obligation, when it calls upon us to violate any duty superior to itself, its own obligation ceases, and our conduct is to be determined by a reference to the unchanging principles, in which the intuitive perceptions of the moral faculty are embodied. Thus, to resort to our former example, though it might be useful to deprive the wealthy miser of the treasures, which were rusting in his coffers, it would violate the rule, which the moral faculty approves, that to destroy life for wealth is forbidden by the relations, which men in a social state sustain to each other. On similar principles, we establish the obligations, by which parents are bound to their children, and children to their parents, and, in general, the members of the same family to each other. There may be cases, in which a child could promote the welfare of the community by an injury inflicted upon his parent, but it would be in contradiction to our clearest intuitive perceptions, of the duties arising from that relation, and we therefore pronounce the action wrong.

Such are the views of moral obligation which appear to us sound and unanswerable. We have a perception of certain duties growing out of our various relations, among which is the duty of utility to our fellow men; but this, so far from being our only duty, or the criterion of other duties, is itself subject to the decisions of a higher tribunal. The whole sum of duties, which result from conformity to all the variety of relations, which we sustain, are expressed in certain general rules, and these are the first principles, the fundamental elements of morality.

If we have settled in our minds the authority of any general principles, which we are to adopt as the foundation of practical morality, we should carefully distinguish between the obligation of those principles, and the motives, by which we may be urged to their observance. We would submit to the reflection of our readers, whether the neglect of this distinction has not introduced great uncertainty and confusion into the reasonings of many eminent writers, who have attempted to set forth a true theory of morals. In our apprehension, the distinction is of vital importance, and goes far to settle some of the most difficult questions, that have been subjects of vehement controversy among the students of moral philosophy. The principal difficulty on this point has arisen from an unphilosophical mode of asking questions. There have been two great errors, namely, asking an absurd question, that is, a question demanding an analysis of a simple element; and asking an irrelevant question, that is, putting a right question in the wrong place. Thus, after having decided that such or such an action is our duty, and stated the ultimate ground upon which it rests, the question is asked, why we are obliged to perform it, or why it is our duty, that is, why are we obliged to do what we are obliged to do, or why is our duty our duty, which is as absurd as to ask, why a triangle has three sides, and not four, or why a three-sided figure is not square. Again, a right question is put in a wrong place. Thus, having decided that such or such an action is our duty, we ask, why we should perform it, meaning what is the obligation which we are under to perform it, which is irrelevant, since in deciding that it was our duty, we decided the obligation: whereas, if we meant, what motive can be urged to induce us to do what we have already determined is our duty, or that which we are obliged to do, the question is legitimate, a right question in a right place, but requiring a very different answer from that given to the same question as put before; and it is the confounding of these questions which has perplexed many of the plainest facts and principles of moral science, and kept out of sight the fundamental and everlasting difference between the Idea of Duty and the Idea of Interest.

A short statement of our mental operations, when deciding a practical moral question, we trust, will remove any difficulties that may occur to our readers, with respect to this topic. We wish to know if we shall or shall not perform a given action. We refer it to a general maxim of conduct, the truth of which is intuitively perceived by the mature reason, and this, we will suppose in the present case, determines the action to be right. We have, then, a perception of its rectitude, and this intellectual perception is always succeeded by an emotion more or less vivid, according to the strength and quickness of our moral feelings, of obligation to perform the action. We view the action, at this moment in the following manner. We approve it; it is morally right; it is fit to be done; we ought to do it; it is our duty to do it; we are obliged to do it; we are bound in conscience to do it; we shall be unworthy if we omit it; we shall merit condemnation if we omit it; we shall despise ourselves, and deserve to be despised by others, if we omit it. All these are equivalent expressions, different modes of stating the primary fundamental idea of rectitude. It will be seen, then, that in the very idea of an action's being right is involved that of obligation to perform it. This, in fact, is the essential element of the idea itself. Do you ask, then, why you are obliged to perform an action, which you admit to be right; your question is a mere tautology; as much so, as if if you asked, why you were obliged to believe a proposition which you admitted to be true, or why, if the whole be greater than a part, you must believe that a part is less than the whole.

If, then, the idea of obligation is involved in the idea of right, when we ask, respecting the action, which we have found to be right, why we should perform it, we do not mean, if we know what we are about, what is our obligation to perform it, but what personal consideration, acting on our wills, can urge us to perform it, what shall we gain by its performance; what interest will it promote; what feeling or sentiment will it gratify; in short, what motive have we for its performance. We come then to the distinction, which has been so generally forgotten, between motive and obligation. This may be expressed, in a brief manner, thus: When I ask, why I should perform an action, the word *why* is used in two different senses. First, when the answer involves any of the ideas, enumerated before as belonging to right, and stops at some self-evident element, in which I find duty. This is obligation. Second, when the answer involves any of the personal considerations enumerated before, and stops at some self-evident element in which I find interest. This is motive. The confounding of the two different senses of the same word *why*, has led to the common confusion between obligation and motive, duty and interest.

If we ask, in the former sense of the term, why we should do such or such an action, we analyze the action, till it can be referred to some general principle of which the obligation is intuitively perceived; if in the latter sense we seek for some motive which may induce us to fulfill our obligations. Thus, if we ask, why we should relieve the distress of a friend, we perceive at once, that it is a duty growing out of the relation of friendship. This is the obligation. If we still ask, why we should perform the duty, we come to the consideration of motives; and to this question, a variety of answers may be given. It may be said, we should do it, because it is right, and this answer is legitimate, because the perception of right is followed by a sense of duty, and this is an active principle of our nature. Again, it may be said that we should do it, because it is demanded by gratitude, and here a motive is addressed to an active principle. Again, it may be said that we should do it, because our friend will do as much for us in return, and here a motive is addressed to self-love, another active principle. Or it may be said, that we should do it because it is agreeable to the will of God, and we shall be rewarded for it in a future state; here the motive is addressed to our religious sentiment, certainly one of the most active principles of human nature. But in all these cases, the ground of obligation, and that of motive, are palpably distinct, and the statement which may explain the one, will be far from explaining the others.

The application of these views to the relation between utility and virtue is obvious, and we shall not dwell upon it. It is plain, that if we are right in the principles which we have advanced, the utility of an action to others or to ourselves may be a strong motive for its performance, while it does not constitute its primary obligation. We must leave it with our readers to follow out the conclusions to which this distinction leads.

We ought, perhaps, to offer an apology for occupying so many of our pages with a subject relating to the abstract philosophy of ethics, which cannot be supposed to possess the same interest for others, which we take in it ourselves. We may be permitted, however, to say, that there is a far more intimate connexion between sound theoretical principles, and the advancement and prosperity of society, than is generally imagined. It has been abundantly verified by experience, that when the primitive and sublime sentiment of Duty, engraved by the finger of God on the heart of man, has been lost sight of, or merged in an inferior order of principles, a slow but fatal poison has preyed upon the vital interests of the community. We cannot but regret, that there is so strong a tendency at the present day, among a great number of benevolent and philanthropic men, who, we are sure, have deeply at heart the welfare of their race, to forget the eternal distinctions of right and wrong, and to substitute in their place, as the criterion of actions, and the motives of conduct, merely empirical considerations, derived from an exaggerated sense of public utility, and connected, as they generally are, with exclusive appeals to private interest. We yield to none, in our earnest desire to see the measures of governments, and the institutions of public policy, brought to the test of utility, so far as that is conformable to the dictates of unchangeable justice; we cherish the deepest conviction, that the performance of duty is the best security for private happiness; but we can never believe, that the interests of states or of individuals are best provided for, when the primitive nature of man is obscured, and the immutable perceptions of his reason, and the noble sentiments of his heart, are commuted for uncertain and selfish calculations, which exercise only a small portion of his faculties, and those of the least exalted and venerable character.

RALPH WALDO EMERSON

Of all the thinkers represented in this volume, Emerson is least in need of biographical identification. It is enough to say here that he was born in 1803; that he died in 1882; and that in between he became America's most honored writer. No American before Emerson had entered the annals of world literature more triumphantly—not Edwards, not Franklin, not Jefferson—and after him no American save William James achieved as much fame in philosophy. It has been doubted whether Emerson was a philosopher, but to argue the point would be to risk logomachy. A Plato, an Aristotle, a Hume, a Kant he was not. He made no contribution to logic, to metaphysics, to epistemology, or even to ethics when that is understood as an effort to analyze fundamental moral concepts. Emerson was a professional moralist, a man who thought deeply and wrote persuasively about the goodness and badness of specific things, and about the rightness and wrongness of specific actions. And if this be philosophy, Emerson made the most of it. Unlike many professional moralists, he sought instruction from those who had more technical philosophical pretensions than he himself had, notably from Coleridge, the self-appointed representative of Kant.

From Coleridge, it seems, Emerson first learned of the distinction between the Reason and the Understanding, which he glows about in a letter reproduced below. This "Germano-Coleridgian" view of Reason—as John Stuart Mill dubbed it —cooperated with a vast number of other philosophical influences—including those more clearly reflected in Ripley's writings—to reinforce Emerson's tendency to reach moral conclusions by trusting his own sentiments.

Once he left the Unitarian ministry and fell under the spell of Germano-Coleridgian Reason, he confidently turned to the major institutions of American civilization and eloquently delivered himself of many thoughtful disquisitions that have become classics in American literature. From the point of view of the history of American philosophy, they are best seen as part of Transcendentalism's continuation of the American tendency to give sentiment more importance than it had in Locke's philosophy; and also as expressions of Emerson's special antipathy to retrospection and the mouldy past. Although he was no technician, Emerson's acute insight into the practical problems of American life led John Dewey to call him America's greatest moralist; and at the age of 89, Justice Holmes, that very practical man, said: "The only fire-brand of my youth that burns to me as brightly as ever is Emerson".[1] William James, focusing on Emerson's antipathy to retrospection, wrote in 1873: "I am sure that an age will come when our present devotion to history, and scrupulous care for what men have done before us merely as fact, will seem incomprehensible; when acquaintance with books will be no duty, but a pleasure for odd individuals; when Emerson's philosophy will be in our bones, not our dramatic imaginations".[2] By contrast to Dewey, Holmes, and James, George Santayana

---

[1] *Holmes-Pollock Letters*, ed. M. DeW. Howe (Cambridge, Mass., 1944), Volume II, p. 264.

[2] R. B. Perry, *The Thought and Character of William James* (Boston, 1935), Volume I, p. 352.

saw Emerson as part of what he called the genteel tradition, removed from the driving forces of American life—science and technology—primarily because of Emerson's idealistic theory of knowledge. Yet Santayana recognized with Matthew Arnold that Emerson's genius did not lie in technical philosophy; and therefore Santayana rightly called him a "Puritan mystic with a poetic fancy and a gift for observation and epigram".[3] No matter what one may think of Emerson's metaphysical effusions in such works as his first book, *Nature* (1836), some of his comments on education, on religion, and on self-reliance will reward all readers who are able to forget about his dubious epistemology and to think of him as a philosopher in the original sense—as a lover of wisdom.

It would seem that the moral wisdom of Emerson needed no highly technical vocabulary for its expression, but the fact is that he conveyed many of his moral attitudes in the philosophical jargon of his day. The invidious distinction between the exalted Reason and the despised Understanding continued to be present in his writing long after he had ceased being an acolyte of Coleridge; and his idea that Reason expresses the ever-to-be-respected moral sentiment often appears in very untechnical essays on religion, education, and politics. In language that might have surprised Kant and Coleridge, Emerson in 1834 was calling Jesus Christ a minister of the *Pure* Reason. He also identified the distinction between the Reason and the Understanding with the opposition between Law and Gospel in Paul and Luther, with Swedenborg's love of self versus love of the Lord, with William Penn's opposition between the world and the spirit, and with the Court of Honor's separation of Gentleman and Knave. "The dualism is ever present", Emerson says.[4]

---

[3] George Santayana, *Interpretations of Poetry and Religion* (New York, 1922; original edition, 1900), p. 230.
[4] Ralph Waldo Emerson, *The Journals and Miscellaneous Notebooks*, ed. A. R. Ferguson (Cambridge, Mass., 1964), Volume IV, p. 348.

This dualism underlies much of Emerson's language in the selections to follow. It helps explain why he identified religion at its best with the use of Reason and the expression of moral sentiment; why he regarded the Argument from Miracles as an appeal to the despised Understanding; why he attacked the emphasis upon personal and ritualistic elements in religion on the ground that they were objects of the Understanding rather than of the Reason; why he complained, in a manner reminiscent of Edwards, that formalists who lacked the power of Reason were usurping pulpits; why he decried the decline of poetic eloquence in the Church; why he said in the letter excerpted below that "Religion Poetry Honor belong to Reason"; why he loved the country, which he thought of as the home of Reason; why he regarded the city as the home of deceit and the Understanding. Well might Emerson have said about the distinction between the Reason and the Understanding that it was "a philosophy itself. & like all truth very practical". If he had been deprived of that distinction, no doubt he would have been *able* to say many of the things he did say about religion, education, and urban life in America, but one wonders whether he *would* have said them.

It is worth adding that whereas in his "Divinity School Address", Emerson emphasized the dualistic contrast between Reason and the Understanding, in "The American Scholar" the emphasis was laid more heavily on the idea that one divine soul animates all men. In the minds of Coleridge's followers—notably James Marsh [5]—this was another way of expressing the ancient doctrine that of all the dwellers on earth only man was created in the image of God, and that the most conspicuous result of this was man's possession of Reason; indeed this defined man's essence. Beasts, as Emerson

[5] James Marsh, the American editor of Coleridge's *Aids to Reflection* (Burlington, Vermont, 1829), was much admired by the Transcendentalists. See his "Preliminary Essay" in that edition. [M.W.]

said in his Coleridgian letter excerpted below, have some Understanding but no Reason. In "The American Scholar", therefore, we can also discern the formulae of technical philosophy, though they lie further beneath the surface. The basic theme of that address is that education must succeed in bringing man to "the right state", which is that of *Man Thinking*. But Man Thinking is man engaged in the exercise of his Reason and *not* in the exercise of the Understanding he shares with the beasts. That is why Emerson's most serious command to the American scholar is delivered in the following words: "Whatsoever oracles the human heart, in all emergencies, in all solemn hours, has uttered as its commentary on the world of actions—these he shall receive and impart. And whatsoever new verdict Reason from her inviolable seat pronounces on the passing men and events of today—this he shall hear and promulgate". The oracles of the heart and the verdicts of Reason, virtually identical for Emerson, contain the basic moral truths; and for Emerson, the heart or the Reason is far higher than the faculties he associated with State Street merchants and utilitarian thinkers like Paley. It also transcended the powers he saw in bookworms and all those who confused the instruments of scholarship with a truly scholarly life. The bookworm of "The American Scholar" is brother to the formalist who usurps the pulpit in "The Divinity School Address". Neither of them receives the oracles of the heart or the verdicts of Reason, and both of them, Emerson hoped, would be replaced by men who, like Edwards' saints, had the power of what Ripley called spiritual intuition.

Unlike Edwards, however, Emerson thought that *all* men are capable of spiritual intuition; and to that extent Emerson was in tune with democratic America of the early nineteenth century. This is most evident in his famous essay, "Self-Reliance", where he urged not only the scholar but every man to trust his own intuition. This created a certain problem for

Emerson's moral philosophy, a problem he never clearly perceived or resolved. While urging the scholar to trust his own judgment, he encouraged him to think that "the deeper he dives into his privatest, secretest presentiment, to his wonder he finds this is the most acceptable, most public, and universally true". How, then, would Emerson arbitrate between two opposing intuitions or impulses which claim to represent public and universal moral truth? This question he fails to answer successfully. There are places where he seems to recognize a problem here, as when he quotes a friend who warns in the spirit of Locke,[6] "But these impulses may be from below, not from above". To this Emerson replied: " 'They do not seem to me to be such; but if I am the Devil's child, I will live then from the Devil.' No law can be sacred to me but that of my nature. Good and bad are but names very readily transferable to that or this; the only right is what is after my constitution; the only wrong what is against it". Here Emerson seems to retreat to a variety of moral relativism and to withdraw the suggestion that one who dives deeply into his privatest sentiment will inevitably arrive at universal moral truth. But this is not the dominant theme in his writing on moral questions. Usually he adopts the optimistic view that one who feels very strongly about the goodness or rightness of something and respects this feeling is bound, somehow, to arrive at a moral conclusion which is objectively right. This view, of course, is not very far from what Locke attacked when he complained of the Enthusiasts' tendency to allow their feelings to dictate their conclusions without making any appeal to reason or experience. And it is fair to say that insofar as Emerson was content to rely exclusively on his own feelings in religion, he represented a return to Enthusiasm.

[6] See above, p. 33.

The Reason versus *the Understanding* [7]
TO EDWARD BLISS EMERSON, NEWTON, MASSACHUSETTS,
MAY 31, 1834

Newton, 31 May, 1834.

My dear brother,

Your last letter to mother postpones to a pretty distance
our prospect of seeing you but as some of our feet were shod
with quicksilver when we came into the world there is still
an even chance that you may slip in upon us in some of these
revolutions of Night & Morn. Here sit Mother & I among the
pine trees still almost as we shall lie by & by under them.
Here we sit always learning & never coming to the knowledge of.—The greatest part of my virtue—that mustard seed-
let that no man wots of—is Hope. I am ever of good cheer &
if the heaven asks no service at my hands am reconciled to
my insignificance yet keeping my eye open upon the brave &
the beautiful. Philosophy affirms that the outward world is
only phenomenal & the whole concern of dinners of tailors of
gigs of balls whereof men make such account is a quite relative & temporary one—an intricate dream—the exhalation of
the present state of the Soul—wherein the Understanding
works incessantly as if it were real but the eternal Reason
when now & then he is allowed to speak declares it is an accident a smoke nowise related to his permanent attributes.
Now that I have used the words, let me ask you do you draw
the distinction of Milton Coleridge & the Germans between

[7] The letter below, in which Emerson praises the distinction we have
already met in Coleridge, is taken from *The Letters of Ralph Waldo
Emerson*, edited by Ralph L. Rusk (New York, 1939), Volume I, pp.
412–14. I have not included the footnotes. Reprinted by permission of
Columbia University Press and the Ralph Waldo Emerson Memorial
Foundation. Emerson's failure to use commas should not lead us to suppose that there is a thinker named "Milton Coleridge".

Reason & Understanding. I think it a philosophy itself. & like all truth very practical. So now lay away the letter & take up the following dissertation on Sunday. Reason is the highest faculty of the soul—what we mean often by the soul itself; it never *reasons*, never proves, it simply perceives; it is vision. The Understanding toils all the time, compares, contrives, adds, argues, near sighted but strong-sighted, dwelling in the present the expedient the customary. Beasts have some understanding but no Reason. Reason is potentially perfect in every man—Understanding in very different degrees of strength. The thoughts of youth, & 'first thoughts,' are the revelations of Reason. the love of the beautiful & of Goodness as the highest beauty the belief in the absolute & universal superiority of the Right & the True But understanding that wrinkled calculator the steward of our house to whom is committed the support of our animal life contradicts evermore these affirmations of Reason & points at Custom & Interest & persuades one man that the declarations of Reason are false & another that they are at least impracticable. Yet by & by after having denied our Master we come back to see at the end of years or of life that he was the Truth. 'Tell him,' was the word sent by Posa to the Spanish prince 'when he is a man to reverence the dreams of his youth.' And it is observed that 'our first & third thoughts usually coincide.' Religion Poetry Honor belong to the Reason; to the real the absolute. These the Understanding sticks to it are chimaeras he can prove it. Can he, dear? The blind men in Rome said the streets were dark. Finally to end my quotations, Fen [elon] said, 'O Reason! Reason! art not thou He whom I seek.'—The manifold applications of the distinction to Literature to the Church to Life will show how good a key it is. So hallelujah to the Reason forevermore.

But glad should I be to hold academical questions with you here at Newton. Whenever you are tired of working at Porto Rico & want a vacation or whenever your strength or your weakness shall commend to you the high countenances of the Muses, come & live with me. The Tucker estate is so far settled that I am made sure of an income of about $1200. wherewith the Reason of Mother & you & I might defy the Understanding upon his own ground, for the rest of the few years in which we shall be subject to his insults. I need not say that what I speak in play I speak in earnest. If you will come we will retreat into Berkshire & make a little world of other stuff. Your brother

Waldo.

Retrospection [8]

Our age is retrospective. It builds the sepulchres of the fathers. It writes biographies, histories, and criticism. The foregoing generations behold God and nature face to face; we, through their eyes. Why should not we also enjoy an original relation to the universe? Why should not we have a poetry and philosophy of insight and not of tradition, and a religion by revelation to us, and not the history of theirs? Embosomed for a season in nature, whose floods of life stream around and through us, and invite us, by the powers they supply, to action proportioned to nature, why should we grope among the dry bones of the past, or put the living generation into masquerade out of its faded wardrobe? The sun shines to-day also. There is more wool and flax in the fields. There are new lands, new men, new thoughts. Let us demand our own works and laws and worship.

Religion and the Moral Sentiment [9]

In this refulgent summer, it has been a luxury to draw the breath of life. The grass grows, the buds burst, the meadow is

---

[8] This is the famous opening paragraph of Emerson's first book, *Nature* (1836). [M.W.]

[9] From Emerson's "Divinity School Address" of 1838.

spotted with fire and gold in the tint of flowers. The air is full
of birds, and sweet with the breath of the pine, the balm-of-
Gilead, and the new hay. Night brings no gloom to the heart
with its welcome shade. Through the transparent darkness
the stars pour their almost spiritual rays. Man under them
seems a young child, and his huge globe a toy. The cool
night bathes the world as with a river, and prepares his eyes
again for the crimson dawn. The mystery of nature was never
displayed more happily. The corn and the wine have been
freely dealt to all creatures, and the never-broken silence
with which the old bounty goes forward has not yielded yet
one word of explanation. One is constrained to respect the
perfection of this world in which our senses converse. How
wide; how rich; what invitation from every property it gives
to every faculty of man! In its fruitful soils; in its navigable
sea; in its mountains of metal and stone; in its forests of all
woods; in its animals; in its chemical ingredients; in the powers and path of light, heat, attraction and life, it is well worth
the pith and heart of great men to subdue and enjoy it. The
planters, the mechanics, the inventors, the astronomers, the
builders of cities, and the captains, history delights to honor.

But when the mind opens and reveals the laws which tra-
verse the universe and make things what they are, then
shrinks the great world at once into a mere illustration and
fable of this mind. What am I? and What is? asks the human spirit with a curiosity new-kindled, but never to be
quenched. Behold these outrunning laws, which our imperfect apprehension can see tend this way and that, but not
come full circle. Behold these infinite relations, so like, so unlike; many, yet one. I would study, I would know, I would
admire forever. These works of thought have been the enter-
tainments of the human spirit in all ages.

A more secret, sweet, and overpowering beauty appears to
man when his heart and mind open to the sentiment of virtue. . . . —The sentiment of virtue is a reverence and delight
in the presence of certain divine laws. It perceives that this

homely game of life we play, covers, under what seem foolish details, principles that astonish. The child amidst his baubles is learning the action of light, motion, gravity, muscular force; and in the game of human life, love, fear, justice, appetite, man, and God, interact. These laws refuse to be adequately stated. They will not be written out on paper, or spoken by the tongue. They elude our persevering thought; yet we read them hourly in each other's faces, in each other's actions, in our own remorse. The moral traits which are all globed into every virtuous act and thought—in speech we must sever, and describe or suggest by painful enumeration of many particulars. Yet, as this sentiment is the essence of all religion, let me guide your eye to the precise objects of the sentiment, by an enumeration of some of those classes of facts in which this element is conspicuous.

The intuition of the moral sentiment is an insight of the perfection of the laws of the soul. These laws execute themselves. They are out of time, out of space, and not subject to circumstance. . . . Thought may work cold and intransitive in things, and find no end or unity; but the dawn of the sentiment of virtue on the heart, gives and is the assurance that Law is sovereign over all natures; and the worlds, time, space, eternity, do seem to break out into joy.

This sentiment is divine and deifying. It is the beatitude of man. It makes him illimitable. Through it, the soul first knows itself. It corrects the capital mistake of the infant man, who seeks to be great by following the great, and hopes to derive advantages *from another*—by showing the fountain of all good to be in himself, and that he, equally with every man, is an inlet into the deeps of Reason. When he says, "I ought;" when love warms him; when he chooses, warned from on high, the good and great deed; then, deep melodies wander through his soul from Supreme Wisdom. Then he can worship, and be enlarged by his worship; for he can never go behind this sentiment. In the sublimest flights of the soul, rectitude is never surmounted, love is never outgrown.

This sentiment lies at the foundation of society, and successively creates all forms of worship. The principle of veneration never dies out. Man fallen into superstition, into sensuality, is never quite without the visions of the moral sentiment. In like manner, all the expressions of this sentiment are sacred and permanent in proportion to their purity. The expressions of this sentiment affect us more than all other compositions. The sentences of the oldest time, which ejaculate this piety, are still fresh and fragrant. This thought dwelled always deepest in the minds of men in the devout and contemplative East; not alone in Palestine, where it reached its purest expression, but in Egypt, in Persia, in India, in China. Europe has always owed to oriental genius its divine impulses. What these holy bards said, all sane men found agreeable and true. And the unique impression of Jesus upon mankind, whose name is not so much written as ploughed into the history of this world, is proof of the subtle virtue of this infusion.

Meantime, whilst the doors of the temple stand open, night and day, before every man, and the oracles of this truth cease never, it is guarded by one stern condition; this, namely, it is an intuition. It cannot be received at second hand. Truly speaking, it is not instruction, but provocation, that I can receive from another soul. What he announces, I must find true in me, or reject; and on his word, or as his second, be he who he may, I can accept nothing. On the contrary, the absence of this primary faith is the presence of degradation. As is the flood, so is the ebb. Let this faith depart, and the very words it spake and the things it made become false and hurtful. Then falls the church, the state, art, letters, life. The doctrine of the divine nature being forgotten, a sickness infects and dwarfs the constitution. Once man was all; now he is an appendage, a nuisance. And because the indwelling Supreme Spirit cannot wholly be got rid of, the doctrine of it suffers this perversion, that the divine nature is attributed to one or two persons, and denied to all the rest, and denied with fury.

The doctrine of inspiration is lost; the base doctrine of the majority of voices usurps the place of the doctrine of the soul. Miracles, prophecy, poetry, the ideal life, the holy life, exist as ancient history merely; they are not in the belief, nor in the aspiration of society; but, when suggested, seem ridiculous. Life is comic or pitiful as soon as the high ends of being fade out of sight, and man becomes near-sighted, and can only attend to what addresses the senses.

These general views, which, whilst they are general, none will contest, find abundant illustration in the history of religion, and especially in the history of the Christian church. In that, all of us have had our birth and nurture. The truth contained in that, you, my young friends, are now setting forth to teach. As the Cultus, or established worship of the civilized world, it has great historical interest for us. Of its blessed words, which have been the consolation of humanity, you need not that I should speak. I shall endeavor to discharge my duty to you on this occasion, by pointing out two errors in its administration, which daily appear more gross from the point of view we have just now taken.

Jesus Christ belonged to the true race of prophets. He saw with open eye the mystery of the soul. Drawn by its severe harmony, ravished with its beauty, he lived in it, and had his being there. Alone in all history he estimated the greatness of man. One man was true to what is in you and me. He saw that God incarnates himself in man, and evermore goes forth anew to take possession of his World. He said, in this jubilee of sublime emotion, 'I am divine. Through me, God acts; through me, speaks. Would you see God, see me; or see thee, when thou also thinkest as I now think.' But what a distortion did his doctrine and memory suffer in the same, in the next, and the following ages! There is no doctrine of the Reason which will bear to be taught by the Understanding. The understanding caught this high chant from the poet's lips, and said, in the next age, 'This was Jehovah come down out of heaven. I will kill you, if you say he was a man.' The idioms of his language and the figures of his rhetoric have usurped the place of his truth; and churches are not built on his principles, but on his tropes. Christianity became a Mythus, as the poetic teaching of Greece and of Egypt, before. He spoke of miracles; for he felt that man's life was a miracle, and all that man doth, and he knew that this daily miracle shines as the character ascends. But the word Miracle, as pronounced by Christian churches, gives a false impression; it is Monster. It is not one with the blowing clover and the falling rain. . . .

1. In this point of view we become sensible of the first defect of historical Christianity. Historical Christianity has fallen into the error that corrupts all attempts to communicate religion. As it appears to us, and as it has appeared for ages, it is not the doctrine of the soul, but an exaggeration of the personal, the positive, the ritual. It has dwelt, it dwells, with noxious exaggeration about the *person* of Jesus. The soul knows no persons. It invites every man to expand to the full circle of the universe, and will have no preferences but those of spontaneous love. But by this eastern monarchy of a Christianity, which indolence and fear have built, the friend of man is made the injurer of man. The manner in which his name is surrounded with expressions which were once sallies of admiration and love, but are now petrified into official titles, kills all generous sympathy and liking. All who hear me, feel that the language that describes Christ to Europe and America is not the style of friendship and enthusiasm to a good and noble heart, but is appropriated and formal—paints a demigod, as the Orientals or the Greeks would describe Osiris or Apollo. . . . To aim to convert a man by miracles is a profanation of the soul. A true conversion, a true Christ, is now, as always, to be made by the reception of beautiful sentiments. . . . The injustice of the vulgar tone of preaching is not less flagrant to Jesus than to the souls which it profanes. The preachers do not see that they make his gospel not glad, and shear him of the locks of beauty and the attributes of

heaven. When I see a majestic Epaminondas, or Washington; when I see among my contemporaries a true orator, an upright judge, a dear friend; when I vibrate to the melody and fancy of a poem; I see beauty that is to be desired. And so lovely, and with yet more entire consent of my human being, sounds in my ear the severe music of the bards that have sung of the true God in all ages. Now do not degrade the life and dialogues of Christ out of the circle of this charm, by insulation and peculiarity. Let them lie as they befell, alive and warm, part of human life and the landscape and the cheerful day.

2. The second defect of the traditionary and limited way of using the mind of Christ is a consequence of the first; this, namely; that the Moral Nature, that Law of laws whose revelations introduce greatness—yea, God himself—into the open soul, is not explored as the fountain of the established teaching in society. Men have come to speak of the revelation as somewhat long ago given and done, as if God were dead. The injury to faith throttles the preacher; and the goodliest of institutions becomes an uncertain and inarticulate voice.

It is very certain that it is the effect of conversation with the beauty of the soul, to beget a desire and need to impart to others the same knowledge and love. If utterance is denied, the thought lies like a burden on the man. Always the seer is a sayer. Somehow his dream is told; somehow he publishes it with solemn joy: sometimes with pencil on canvas, sometimes with chisel on stone, sometimes in towers and aisles of granite, his soul's worship is builded; sometimes in anthems of indefinite music; but clearest and most permanent, in words.

The man enamored of this excellency becomes its priest or poet. The office is coeval with the world. But observe the condition, the spiritual limitation of the office. The spirit only can teach. Not any profane man, not any sensual, not any liar, not any slave can teach, but only he can give, who has; he only can create, who is. The man on whom the soul descends, through whom the soul speaks, alone can teach. Courage, piety, love, wisdom, can teach; and every man can open his door to these angels, and they shall bring him the gift of tongues. But the man who aims to speak as books enable, as synods use, as the fashion guides, and as interest commands, babbles. Let him hush. . . .

Whenever the pulpit is usurped by a formalist, then is the worshipper defrauded and disconsolate. We shrink as soon as the prayers begin, which do not uplift, but smite and offend us. We are fain to wrap our cloaks about us, and secure, as best we can, a solitude that hears not. I once heard a preacher who sorely tempted me to say I would go to church no more. Men go, thought I, where they are wont to go, else had no soul entered the temple in the afternoon. A snow-storm was falling around us. The snow-storm was real, the preacher merely spectral, and the eye felt the sad contrast in looking at him, and then out of the window behind him into the beautiful meteor of the snow. He had lived in vain. He had no one word intimating that he had laughed or wept, was married or in love, had been commended, or cheated, or chagrined. If he had ever lived and acted, we were none the wiser for it. The capital secret of his profession, namely, to convert life into truth, he had not learned. Not one fact in all his experience had he yet imported into his doctrine. This man had ploughed and planted and talked and bought and sold; he had read books; he had eaten and drunken; his head aches, his heart throbs; he smiles and suffers; yet was there not a surmise, a hint, in all the discourse, that he had ever lived at all. . . .

It is still true that tradition characterizes the preaching of this country; that it comes out of the memory, and not out of the soul; that it aims at what is usual, and not at what is necessary and eternal; that thus historical Christianity destroys the power of preaching, by withdrawing it from the exploration of the moral nature of man; where the sublime is, where are the resources of astonishment and power. What a cruel injustice it is to that Law, the joy of the whole earth, which alone can make thought dear and rich; that Law whose fatal sureness the astronomical orbits poorly emulate; that it is travestied and depreciated, that it is behooted and behowled, and not a trait, not a word of it articulated. The pulpit in losing sight of this Law, loses its reason, and gropes after it knows not what. And for want of this culture the soul of the community is sick and faithless. It wants nothing so much as a stern, high, stoical, Christian discipline, to make it know itself and the divinity that speaks through it. Now man is ashamed of himself; he skulks and sneaks through the world, to be tolerated, to be pitied, and scarcely in a thousand years does any man dare to be wise and good, and so draw after him the tears and blessings of his kind.

Certainly there have been periods when, from the inactivity of the intellect on certain truths, a greater faith was possible in names and persons. The Puritans in England and America found in the Christ of the Catholic Church and in the dogmas inherited from Rome, scope for their austere piety and their longings for civil freedom. But their creed is passing away, and none arises in its room. I think no man can go with his thoughts about him into one of our churches, without feeling that what hold the public worship had on men is gone, or going. It has lost its grasp on the affection of the good and the fear of the bad. In the country, neighborhoods, half parishes are *signing off,* to use the local term. It is already beginning to indicate character and religion to withdraw from the religious meetings. . . .

My friends, in these two errors, I think, I find the causes of a decaying church and a wasting unbelief. And what greater calamity can fall upon a nation than the loss of worship? Then all things go to decay. Genius leaves the temple to haunt the senate or the market. Literature becomes frivolous. Science is cold. The eye of youth is not lighted by the hope of other worlds, and age is without honor. Society lives to trifles, and when men die we do not mention them.

And now, my brothers, you will ask, What in these de-
sponding days can be done by us? The remedy is already declared in the ground of our complaint of the Church. We
have contrasted the Church with the Soul. In the soul then
let the redemption be sought. Wherever a man comes, there
comes revolution. The old is for slaves. When a man comes,
all books are legible, all things transparent, all religions are
forms. He is religious. Man is the wonderworker. He is seen
amid miracles. All men bless and curse. He saith yea and nay,
only. The stationariness of religion; the assumption that the
age of inspiration is past, that the Bible is closed; the fear of
degrading the character of Jesus by representing him as a
man; indicate with sufficient clearness the falsehood of our
theology. . . .

Let me admonish you, first of all, to go alone; to refuse the
good models, even those which are sacred in the imagination
of men, and dare to love God without mediator or veil.
Friends enough you shall find who will hold up to your emu-
lation Wesleys and Oberlins, Saints and Prophets. Thank God
for these good men, but say, 'I also am a man.' Imitation cannot go above its model. The imitator dooms himself to hopeless mediocrity. The inventor did it because it was natural to
him, and so in him it has a charm. In the imitator something
else is natural, and he bereaves himself of his own beauty, to
come short of another man's.

Yourself a newborn bard of the Holy Ghost, cast behind
you all conformity, and acquaint men at first hand with
Deity. Look to it first and only, that fashion, custom, authority, pleasure, and money, are nothing to you—are not ban-
dages over your eyes, that you cannot see—but live with the
privilege of the immeasurable mind. Not too anxious to visit
periodically all families and each family in your parish
connection—when you meet one of these men or women, be
to them a divine man; be to them thought and virtue; let
their timid aspirations find in you a friend; let their trampled
instincts be genially tempted out in your atmosphere; let

their doubts know that you have doubted, and their wonder feel that you have wondered. By trusting your own heart, you shall gain more confidence in other men. For all our penny-wisdom, for all our soul-destroying slavery to habit, it is not to be doubted that all men have sublime thoughts; that all men value the few real hours of life; they love to be heard; they love to be caught up into the vision of principles. . . .

And now let us do what we can to rekindle the smouldering, nigh quenched fire on the altar. The evils of the church that now is are manifest. The question returns, What shall we do? I confess, all attempts to project and establish a Cultus with new rites and forms, seem to me vain. Faith makes us, and not we it, and faith makes its own forms. All attempts to contrive a system are as cold as the new worship introduced by the French to the goddess of Reason—to-day, pasteboard and filigree, and ending to-morrow in madness and murder. Rather let the breath of new life be breathed by you through the forms already existing. For if once you are alive, you shall find they shall become plastic and new. The remedy to their deformity is first, soul, and second, soul, and evermore, soul. . . .

The American Scholar [10]

. . . It is one of those fables which out of an unknown antiquity convey an unlooked-for wisdom, that the gods, in the beginning, divided Man into men, that he might be more helpful to himself; just as the hand was divided into fingers, the better to answer its end. The old fable covers a doctrine ever new and sublime; that there is One Man—present to all particular men only partially, or through one faculty; and that you must take the whole society to find the whole man.

[10] From "The American Scholar," Emerson's Phi Beta Kappa address at Harvard in 1837.

Man is not a farmer, or a professor, or an engineer, but he is all. Man is priest, and scholar, and statesman, and producer, and soldier. In the *divided* or social state these functions are parcelled out to individuals, each of whom aims to do his stint of the joint work, whilst each other performs his. The fable implies that the individual, to possess himself, must sometimes return from his own labor to embrace all the other laborers. But, unfortunately, this original unit, this fountain of power, has been so distributed to multitudes, has been so minutely subdivided and peddled out, that it is spilled into drops, and cannot be gathered. The state of society is one in which the members have suffered amputation from the trunk, and strut about so many walking monsters—a good finger, a neck, a stomach, an elbow, but never a man.

Man is thus metamorphosed into a thing, into many things. The planter, who is Man sent out into the field to gather food, is seldom cheered by any idea of the true dignity of his ministry. He sees his bushel and his cart, and nothing beyond, and sinks into the farmer, instead of Man on the farm. The tradesman scarcely ever gives an ideal worth to his work, but is ridden by the routine of his craft, and the soul is subject to dollars. The priest becomes a form; the attorney a statute-book; the mechanic a machine; the sailor a rope of the ship.

In this distribution of functions the scholar is the delegated intellect. In the right state he is *Man Thinking*. In the degenerate state, when the victim of society, he tends to become a mere thinker, or still worse, the parrot of other men's thinking.

In this view of him, as Man Thinking, the theory of his office is contained. Him Nature solicits with all her placid, all her monitory pictures; him the past instructs; him the future invites. . . . Let us see him in his school, and consider him in reference to the main influences he receives.

I. The first in time and the first in importance of the influences upon the mind is that of nature. Every day, the sun;

and, after sunset, Night and her stars. Ever the winds blow; ever the grass grows. Every day, men and women, conversing—beholding and beholden. The scholar is he of all men whom this spectacle most engages. He must settle its value in his mind. What is nature to him?

. . . [T]o him, to this schoolboy under the bending dome of day, is suggested that he and it proceed from one root; one is leaf and one is flower; relation, sympathy, stirring in every vein. And what is that root? Is not that the soul of his soul? A thought too bold; a dream too wild. Yet when this spiritual light shall have revealed the law of more earthly natures— when he has learned to worship the soul, and to see that the natural philosophy that now is, is only the first gropings of its gigantic hand, he shall look forward to an ever expanding knowledge as to a becoming creator. He shall see that nature is the opposite of the soul, answering to it part for part. One is seal and one is print. Its beauty is the beauty of his own mind. Its laws are the laws of his own mind. Nature then becomes to him the measure of his attainments. So much of nature as he is ignorant of, so much of his own mind does he not yet possess. And, in fine, the ancient precept, "Know thyself," and the modern precept, "Study nature," become at last one maxim.

II. The next great influence into the spirit of the scholar is the mind of the Past—in whatever form, whether of literature, of art, of institutions, that mind is inscribed. Books are the best type of the influence of the past, and perhaps we shall get at the truth—learn the amount of this influence more conveniently—by considering their value alone.

The theory of books is noble. The scholar of the first age received into him the world around; brooded thereon; gave it the new arrangement of his own mind, and uttered it again. It came into him life; it went out from him truth. It came to him short-lived actions; it went out from him immortal thoughts. It came to him business; it went from him poetry. It was dead fact; now, it is quick thought. It can stand, and it can go. It now endures, it now flies, it now inspires. Precisely in proportion to the depth of mind from which it issued, so high does it soar, so long does it sing.

Or, I might say, it depends on how far the process had gone, of transmuting life into truth. In proportion to the completeness of the distillation, so will the purity and imperishableness of the product be. But none is quite perfect. As no air-pump can by any means make a perfect vacuum, so neither can any artist entirely exclude the conventional, the local, the perishable from his book, or write a book of pure thought, that shall be as efficient, in all respects, to a remote posterity, as to contemporaries, or rather to the second age. Each age, it is found, must write its own books; or rather, each generation for the next succeeding. The books of an older period will not fit this.

Yet hence arises a grave mischief. The sacredness which attaches to the act of creation, the act of thought, is transferred to the record. The poet chanting was felt to be a divine man: henceforth the chant is divine also. The writer was a just and wise spirit: henceforward it is settled the book is perfect; as love of the hero corrupts into worship of his statue. Instantly the book becomes noxious: the guide is a tyrant. The sluggish and perverted mind of the multitude, slow to open to the incursions of Reason, having once so opened, having once received this book, stands upon it, and makes an outcry if it is disparaged. Colleges are built on it. Books are written on it by thinkers, not by Man Thinking; by men of talent, that is, who start wrong, who set out from accepted dogmas, not from their own sight of principles. Meek young men grow up in libraries, believing it their duty to accept the views which Cicero, which Locke, which Bacon, have given; forgetful that Cicero, Locke, and Bacon were only young men in libraries when they wrote these books.

Hence, instead of Man Thinking, we have the bookworm. Hence the book-learned class, who value books, as such; not as related to nature and the human constitution, but as making a sort of Third Estate with the world and the soul. Hence the restorers of readings, the emendators, the bibliomaniacs of all degrees.

Books are the best of things, well used; abused, among the worst. What is the right use? What is the one end which all means go to effect? They are for nothing but to inspire. I had better never see a book than to be warped by its attraction clean out of my own orbit, and made a satellite instead of a system. The one thing in the world, of value, is the active soul. This every man is entitled to; this every man contains within him, although in almost all men obstructed and as yet unborn. The soul active sees absolute truth and utters truth, or creates. In this action it is genius; not the privilege of here and there a favorite, but the sound estate of every man. In its essence it is progressive. The book, the college, the school of art, the institution of any kind, stop with some past utterance of genius. This is good, say they—let us hold by this. They pin me down. They look backward and not forward. But genius looks forward: the eyes of man are set in his forehead, not in his hindhead: man hopes: genius creates. Whatever talents may be, if the man create not, the pure efflux of the Deity is not his; cinders and smoke there may be, but not yet flame. There are creative manners, there are creative actions, and creative words; manners, actions, words, that is, indicative of no custom or authority, but springing spontaneous from the mind's own sense of good and fair. . . .

Of course there is a portion of reading quite indispensable to a wise man. History and exact science he must learn by laborious reading. Colleges, in like manner, have their indispensable office—to teach elements. But they can only highly serve us when they aim not to drill, but to create; when they gather from far every ray of various genius to their hospitable halls, and by the concentrated fires, set the hearts of their youth on flame. Thought and knowledge are natures in which apparatus and pretension avail nothing. Gowns and pecuniary foundations, though of towns of gold, can never countervail the least sentence or syllable of wit. Forget this, and our American colleges will recede in their public importance, whilst they grow richer every year.

III. There goes in the world a notion that the scholar should be a recluse, a valetudinarian—as unfit for any handiwork or public labor as a penknife for an axe. The so-called "practical men" sneer at speculative men, as if, because they speculate or *see,* they could do nothing. I have heard it said that the clergy—who are always, more universally than any other class, the scholars of their day—are addressed as women; that the rough, spontaneous conversation of men they do not hear, but only a mincing and diluted speech. They are often virtually disfranchised; and indeed there are advocates for their celibacy. As far as this is true of the studious classes, it is not just and wise. Action is with the scholar subordinate, but it is essential. Without it he is not yet man. Without it thought can never ripen into truth. Whilst the world hangs before the eye as a cloud of beauty, we cannot even see its beauty. Inaction is cowardice, but there can be no scholar without the heroic mind. The preamble of thought, the transition through which it passes from the unconscious to the conscious, is action. Only so much do I know, as I have lived. Instantly we know whose words are loaded with life, and whose not. . . .

So much only of life as I know by experience, so much of the wilderness have I vanquished and planted, or so far have I extended my being, my dominion. I do not see how any man can afford, for the sake of his nerves and his nap, to spare any action in which he can partake. It is pearls and rubies to his discourse. Drudgery, calamity, exasperation, want, are instructors in eloquence and wisdom. The true scholar grudges every opportunity of action past by, as a loss of power. It is the raw material out of which the intellect moulds her splendid products. A strange process too, this by which experience is converted into thought, as a mulberry leaf is converted into satin. . . .

If it were only for a vocabulary, the scholar would be covetous of action. Life is our dictionary. Years are well spent in country labors; in town; in the insight into trades and manufactures; in frank intercourse with many men and women; in science; in art; to the one end of mastering in all their facts a language by which to illustrate and embody our perceptions. I learn immediately from any speaker how much he has already lived, through the poverty or the splendor of his speech. Life lies behind us as the quarry from whence we get tiles and copestones for the masonry of to-day. This is the way to learn grammar. Colleges and books only copy the language which the field and the work-yard made. . . .

The mind now thinks, now acts, and each fit reproduces the other. When the artist has exhausted his materials, when the fancy no longer paints, when thoughts are no longer apprehended and books are a weariness—he has always the resources *to live*. Character is higher than intellect. Thinking is the function. Living is the functionary. The stream retreats to its source. A great soul will be strong to live, as well as strong to think. Does he lack organ or medium to impart his truths? He can still fall back on this elemental force of living them. This is a total act. Thinking is a partial act. Let the grandeur of justice shine in his affairs. Let the beauty of affection cheer his lowly roof. . . .

I hear therefore with joy whatever is beginning to be said of the dignity and necessity of labor to every citizen. There is virtue yet in the hoe and the spade, for learned as well as for unlearned hands. And labor is everywhere welcome; always we are invited to work; only be this limitation observed, that a man shall not for the sake of wider activity sacrifice any opinion to the popular judgments and modes of action.

I have now spoken of the education of the scholar by nature, by books, and by action. It remains to say somewhat of his duties.

They are such as become Man Thinking. They may all be comprised in self-trust. The office of the scholar is to cheer, to

raise, and to guide men by showing them facts amidst appearances. He plies the slow, unhonored, and unpaid task of
observation. Flamsteed and Herschel, in their glazed obser-
vatories, may catalogue the stars with the praise of all men,
and the results being splendid and useful, honor is sure. But
he, in his private observatory, cataloguing obscure and nebu-
lous stars of the human mind, which as yet no man has
thought of as such—watching days and months sometimes for
a few facts; correcting still his old records; must relinquish
display and immediate fame. In the long period of his preparation he must betray often an ignorance and shiftlessness in
popular arts, incurring the disdain of the able who shoulder
him aside. Long he must stammer in his speech; often forego
the living for the dead. Worse yet, he must accept—how
often!—poverty and solitude. For the ease and pleasure of
treading the old road, accepting the fashions, the education,
the religion of society, he takes the cross of making his own,
and, of course, the self-accusation, the faint heart, the frequent uncertainty and loss of time, which are the nettles and
tangling vines in the way of the self-relying and self-directed;
and the state of virtual hostility in which he seems to stand to
society, and especially to educated society. For all this loss
and scorn, what offset? He is to find consolation in exercising
the highest functions of human nature. He is one who raises
himself from private considerations and breathes and lives on
public and illustrious thoughts. He is the world's eye. He is
the world's heart. He is to resist the vulgar prosperity that
retrogrades ever to barbarism, by preserving and communicating heroic sentiments, noble biographies, melodious
verse, and the conclusions of history. Whatsoever oracles the
human heart, in all emergencies, in all solemn hours, has uttered as its commentary on the world of actions—these he
shall receive and impart. And whatsoever new verdict Reason from her inviolable seat pronounces on the passing men
and events of to-day—this he shall hear and promulgate.

These being his functions, it becomes him to feel all confidence in himself, and to defer never to the popular cry. He and he only knows the world. The world of any moment is the merest appearance. Some great decorum, some fetish of a government, some ephemeral trade, or war, or man, is cried up by half mankind and cried down by the other half, as if all depended on this particular up or down. The odds are that the whole question is not worth the poorest thought which the scholar has lost in listening to the controversy. Let him not quit his belief that a popgun is a popgun, though the ancient and honorable of the earth affirm it to be the crack of doom. In silence, in steadiness, in severe abstraction, let him hold by himself; add observation to observation, patient of neglect, patient of reproach, and bide his own time—happy enough if he can satisfy himself alone that this day he has seen something truly. Success treads on every right step. For the instinct is sure, that prompts him to tell his brother what he thinks. He then learns that in going down into the secrets of his own mind he has descended into the secrets of all minds. . . .

In self-trust all the virtues are comprehended. Free should the scholar be—free and brave. Free even to the definition of freedom, "without any hindrance that does not arise out of his own constitution." Brave; for fear is a thing which a scholar by his very function puts behind him. Fear always springs from ignorance. It is a shame to him if his tranquillity, amid dangerous times, arise from the presumption that like children and women his is a protected class; or if he seek a temporary peace by the diversion of his thoughts from politics or vexed questions, hiding his head like an ostrich in the flowering bushes, peeping into microscopes, and turning rhymes, as a boy whistles to keep his courage up. So is the danger a danger still; so is the fear worse. Manlike let him turn and face it. Let him look into its eye and search its nature, inspect its origin—see the whelping of this lion—which lies no great way back; he will then find in himself a perfect comprehension of its nature and extent; he will have made his hands meet on the other side, and can henceforth defy it and pass on superior. The world is his who can see through its pretension. What deafness, what stone-blind custom, what overgrown error you behold is there only by sufferance—by your sufferance. See it to be a lie, and you have already dealt it its mortal blow. . . .

For this self-trust, the reason is deeper than can be fathomed—darker than can be enlightened. I might not carry with me the feeling of my audience in stating my own belief. But I have already shown the ground of my hope, in adverting to the doctrine that man is one. I believe man has been wronged; he has wronged himself. He has almost lost the light that can lead him back to his prerogatives. . . . For a man, rightly viewed, comprehendeth the particular natures of all men. Each philosopher, each bard, each actor has only done for me, as by a delegate, what one day I can do for myself. . . . The human mind cannot be enshrined in a person who shall set a barrier on any one side to this unbounded, unboundable empire. It is one central fire, which, flaming now out of the lips of Etna, lightens the capes of Sicily, and now out of the throat of Vesuvius, illuminates the towers and vineyards of Naples. It is one light which beams out of a thousand stars. It is one soul which animates all men.

But I have dwelt perhaps tediously upon this abstraction of the Scholar. I ought not to delay longer to add what I have to say of nearer reference to the time and to this country. . . . Our age is bewailed as the age of Introversion. Must that needs be evil? We, it seems, are critical; we are embarrassed with second thoughts; we cannot enjoy any thing for hankering to know whereof the pleasure consists; we are lined with eyes; we see with our feet; the time is infected with Hamlet's unhappiness—

"Sicklied o'er with the pale cast of thought."

It is so bad then? Sight is the last thing to be pitied. Would we be blind? Do we fear lest we should outsee nature and

God, and drink truth dry? I look upon the discontent of the literary class as a mere announcement of the fact that they find themselves not in the state of mind of their fathers, and regret the coming state as untried; as a boy dreads the water before he has learned that he can swim. If there is any period one would desire to be born in, is it not the age of Revolution; when the old and the new stand side by side and admit of being compared; when the energies of all men are searched by fear and by hope; when the historic glories of the old can be compensated by the rich possibilities of the new era? This time, like all times, is a very good one, if we but know what to do with it.

I read with some joy of the auspicious signs of the coming days, as they glimmer already through poetry and art, through philosophy and science, through church and state.

One of these signs is the fact that the same movement which effected the elevation of what was called the lowest class in the state, assumed in literature a very marked and as benign an aspect. Instead of the sublime and beautiful, the near, the low, the common, was explored and poetized. That which had been negligently trodden under foot by those who were harnessing and provisioning themselves for long journeys into far countries, is suddenly found to be richer than all foreign parts. The literature of the poor, the feelings of the child, the philosophy of the street, the meaning of household life, are the topics of the time. It is a great stride. It is a sign —is it not?—of new vigor when the extremities are made active, when currents of warm life run into the hands and the feet. I ask not for the great, the remote, the romantic; what is doing in Italy or Arabia; what is Greek art, or Provençal minstrelsy; I embrace the common, I explore and sit at the feet of the familiar, the low. Give me insight into to-day, and you may have the antique and future worlds. What would we really know the meaning of? The meal in the firkin; the milk in the pan; the ballad in the street; the news of the boat; the glance of the eye; the form and the gait of the body; show

me the ultimate reason of these matters; show me the sublime presence of the highest spiritual cause lurking, as always
it does lurk, in these suburbs and extremities of nature; let
me see every trifle bristling with the polarity that ranges it
instantly on an eternal law; and the shop, the plough, and the
ledger referred to the like cause by which light undulates
and poets sing; and the world lies no longer a dull miscellany
and lumber-room, but has form and order; there is no trifle,
there is no puzzle, but one design unites and animates the
farthest pinnacle and the lowest trench.

This idea has inspired the genius of Goldsmith, Burns,
Cowper, and, in a newer time, of Goethe, Wordsworth, and
Carlyle. This idea they have differently followed and with
various success. In contrast with their writing, the style of
Pope, of Johnson, of Gibbon, looks cold and pedantic. This
writing is blood-warm. Man is surprised to find that things
near are not less beautiful and wondrous than things remote. The near explains the far. The drop is a small ocean. A
man is related to all nature. This perception of the worth of
the vulgar is fruitful in discoveries. Goethe, in this very thing
the most modern of the moderns, has shown us, as none ever
did, the genius of the ancients.

There is one man of genius who has done much for this
philosophy of life, whose literary value has never yet been
rightly estimated; I mean Emanuel Swedenborg. The most
imaginative of men, yet writing with the precision of a math-
ematician, he endeavored to engraft a purely philosophical
Ethics on the popular Christianity of his time. Such an attempt of course must have difficulty which no genius could
surmount. But he saw and showed the connection between
nature and the affections of the soul. He pierced the emblem-
atic or spiritual character of the visible, audible, tangible
word. Especially did his shade-loving muse hover over and
interpret the lower parts of nature; he showed the mysterious
bond that allies moral evil to the foul material forms, and has
given in epical parables a theory of insanity, of beasts, of un-
clean and fearful things.

Another sign of our times, also marked by an analogous political movement, is the new importance given to the single person. Every thing that tends to insulate the individual—to surround him with barriers of natural respect, so that each man shall feel the world is his, and man shall treat with man as a sovereign state with a sovereign state—tends to true union as well as greatness. . . . Help must come from the bosom alone. The scholar is that man who must take up into himself all the ability of the time, all the contributions of the past, all the hopes of the future. He must be an university of knowledges. If there be one lesson more than another which should pierce his ear, it is, The world is nothing, the man is all; in yourself is the law of all nature, and you know not yet how a globule of sap ascends; in yourself slumbers the whole of Reason; it is for you to know all; it is for you to dare all.

. . . [T]his confidence in the unsearched might of man belongs, by all motives, by all prophecy, by all preparation, to the American Scholar. We have listened too long to the courtly muses of Europe. The spirit of the American freeman is already suspected to be timid, imitative, tame. Public and private avarice make the air we breathe thick and fat. The scholar is decent, indolent, complaisant. See already the tragic consequence. The mind of this country, taught to aim at low objects, eats upon itself. There is no work for any but the decorous and the complaisant. Young men of the fairest promise, who begin life upon our shores, inflated by the mountain winds, shined upon by all the stars of God, find the earth below not in unison with these, but are hindered from action by the disgust which the principles on which business is managed inspire, and turn drudges, or die of disgust, some of them suicides. What is the remedy? They did not yet see, and thousands of young men as hopeful now crowding to the barriers for the career do not yet see, that if the single man plant himself indomitably on his instincts, and there abide, the huge world will come round to him. Patience—patience; with the shades of all the good and great for company; and for solace the perspective of your own infinite life; and for work the study and the communication of priniciples, the making those instincts prevalent, the conversion of the world. Is it not the chief disgrace in the world, not to be an unit; not to be reckoned one character; not to yield that peculiar fruit which each man was created to bear, but to be reckoned in the gross, in the hundred, or the thousand, of the party, the section, to which we belong; and our opinion predicted geographically, as the north, or the south? Not so, brothers and friends—please God, ours shall not be so. We will walk on our own feet; we will work with our own hands; we will speak our own minds. The study of letters shall be no longer a name for pity, for doubt, and for sensual indulgence. The dread of man and the love of man shall be a wall of defence and a wreath of joy around all. A nation of men will for the first time exist, because each believes himself inspired by the Divine Soul which also inspires all men.

Self-Reliance [11]

. . . To believe your own thought, to believe that what is true for you in your private heart is true for all men—that is genius. Speak your latent conviction, and it shall be the universal sense; for the inmost in due time becomes the outmost, and our first thought is rendered back to us by the trumpets of the Last Judgment. Familiar as the voice of the mind is to each, the highest merit we ascribe to Moses, Plato and Milton is that they set at naught books and traditions, and spoke not what men, but what *they* thought. A man should learn to detect and watch that gleam of light which flashes across his mind from within, more than the lustre of the firmament of bards and sages. Yet he dismisses without notice his thought, because it is his. In every work of genius we recognize our own rejected thoughts; they come back to us with a certain alienated majesty. . . .

[11] From "Self-Reliance", one of Emerson's *Essays: First Series* (1841).

Trust thyself: every heart vibrates to that iron string. Accept the place the divine providence has found for you, the society of your contemporaries, the connection of events. Great men have always done so, and confided themselves childlike to the genius of their age, betraying their perception that the absolutely trustworthy was seated at their heart, working through their hands, predominating in all their being. And we are now men, and must accept in the highest mind the same transcendent destiny; and not minors and invalids in a protected corner, not cowards fleeing before a revolution, but guides, redeemers and benefactors, obeying the Almighty effort and advancing on Chaos and the Dark. . . .

Society everywhere is in conspiracy against the manhood of every one of its members. Society is a joint-stock company, in which the members agree, for the better securing of his bread to each shareholder, to surrender the liberty and culture of the eater. The virtue in most request is conformity. Self-reliance is its aversion. It loves not realities and creators, but names and customs.

Whoso would be a man, must be a nonconformist. He who would gather immortal palms must not be hindered by the name of goodness, but must explore if it be goodness. Nothing is at last sacred but the integrity of your own mind. Absolve you to yourself, and you shall have the suffrage of the world. I remember an answer which when quite young I was prompted to make to a valued adviser who was wont to importune me with the dear old doctrines of the church. On my saying, "What have I to do with the sacredness of traditions, if I live wholly from within?" my friend suggested—"But these impulses may be from below, not from above." I replied, "They do not seem to me to be such; but if I am the Devil's child, I will live then from the Devil." No law can be sacred to me but that of my nature. Good and bad are but names very readily transferable to that or this; the only right is what is after my constitution; the only wrong what is against it. A man is to carry himself in the presence of all opposition as if every thing were titular and ephemeral but he. I am ashamed to think how easily we capitulate to badges and names, to large societies and dead institutions. . . .

What I must do is all that concerns me, not what the people think. This rule, equally arduous in actual and in intellectual life, may serve for the whole distinction between greatness and meanness. It is the harder because you will always find those who think they know what is your duty better than you know it. It is easy in the world to live after the world's opinion; it is easy in solitude to live after our own; but the great man is he who in the midst of the crowd keeps with perfect sweetness the independence of solitude.

The objection to conforming to usages that have become dead to you is that it scatters your force. It loses your time and blurs the impression of your character. If you maintain a dead church, contribute to a dead Bible-society, vote with a great party either for the government or against it, spread your table like base housekeepers—under all these screens I have difficulty to detect the precise man you are: and of course so much force is withdrawn from your proper life. But do your work, and I shall know you. Do your work, and you shall reinforce yourself. A man must consider what a blind-man's-buff is this game of conformity. If I know your sect I anticipate your argument. I hear a preacher announce for his text and topic the expediency of one of the institutions of his church. Do I not know beforehand that not possibly can he say a new and spontaneous word? Do I not know that with all this ostentation of examining the grounds of the institution he will do no such thing? Do I not know that he is pledged to himself not to look but at one side, the permitted side, not as a man, but as a parish minister? He is a retained attorney, and these airs of the bench are the emptiest affectation. Well, most men have bound their eyes with one or another handkerchief, and attached themselves to some one of these communities of opinion. This conformity makes them not false in a few particulars, authors of a few lies, but false in all particulars. . . .

The other terror that scares us from self-trust is our consistency; a reverence for our past act or word because the eyes of others have no other data for computing our orbit than our past acts, and we are loth to disappoint them.

But why should you keep your head over your shoulder? Why drag about this corpse of your memory, lest you contradict somewhat you have stated in this or that public place? Suppose you should contradict yourself; what then? It seems to be a rule of wisdom never to rely on your memory alone, scarcely even in acts of pure memory, but to bring the past for judgment into the thousand-eyed present, and live ever in a new day. In your metaphysics you have denied personality to the Deity, yet when the devout motions of the soul come, yield to them heart and life, though they should clothe God with shape and color. Leave your theory, as Joseph his coat in the hand of the harlot, and flee.

A foolish consistency is the hobgoblin of little minds, adored by little statesmen and philosophers and divines. With consistency a great soul has simply nothing to do. He may as well concern himself with his shadow on the wall. Speak what you think now in hard words and to-morrow speak what to-morrow thinks in hard words again, though it contradict every thing you said to-day.—'Ah, so you shall be sure to be misunderstood.'—Is it so bad then to be misunderstood? Pythagoras was misunderstood, and Socrates, and Jesus, and Luther, and Copernicus, and Galileo, and Newton, and every pure and wise spirit that ever took flesh. To be great is to be misunderstood. . . .

The magnetism which all original action exerts is explained when we inquire the reason of self-trust. Who is the Trustee? What is the aboriginal Self, on which a universal reliance may be grounded? What is the nature and power of that science-baffling star, without parallax, without calculable elements, which shoots a ray of beauty even into trivial and impure actions, if the least mark of independence appear? The inquiry leads us to that source, at once the essence of genius, of virtue, and of life, which we call Spontaneity or Instinct.

We denote this primary wisdom as Intuition, whilst all later teachings are tuitions. In that deep force, the last fact behind which analysis cannot go, all things find their common origin. . . . Here is the fountain of action and of thought. Here are the lungs of that inspiration which giveth man wisdom and which cannot be denied without impiety and atheism. We lie in the lap of immense intelligence, which makes us receivers of its truth and organs of its activity. When we discern justice, when we discern truth, we do nothing of ourselves, but allow a passage to its beams. If we ask whence this comes, if we seek to pry into the soul that causes, all philosophy is at fault. Its presence or its absence is all we can affirm. . . .

The relations of the soul to the divine spirit are so pure that it is profane to seek to interpose helps. It must be that when God speaketh he should communicate, not one thing, but all things; should fill the world with his voice; should scatter forth light, nature, time, souls, from the centre of the present thought; and new date and new create the whole. Whenever a mind is simple and receives a divine wisdom, old things pass away—means, teachers, texts, temples fall; it lives now, and absorbs past and future into the present hour. All things are made sacred by relation to it—one as much as another. All things are dissolved to their centre by their cause, and in the universal miracle petty and particular miracles disappear. If therefore a man claims to know and speak of God and carries you backward to the phraseology of some old mouldered nation in another country, in another world, believe him not. Is the acorn better than the oak which is its fulness and completion? Is the parent better than the child into whom he has cast his ripened being? Whence then this worship of the past? The centuries are conspirators against the sanity and authority of the soul. Time and space are but physiological colors which the eye makes, but the soul is light: where it is, is day; where it was, is night; and history is an impertinence and an injury if it be any thing more than a cheerful apologue or parable of my being and becoming. . . .

This should be plain enough. Yet see what strong intellects dare not yet hear God himself unless he speak the phraseology of I know not what David, or Jeremiah, or Paul. We shall not always set so great a price on a few texts, on a few lives. . . . When we have new perception, we shall gladly disburden the memory of its hoarded treasures as old rubbish. When a man lives with God, his voice shall be as sweet as the murmur of the brook and the rustle of the corn.

And now at last the highest truth on this subject remains unsaid; probably cannot be said; for all that we say is the far-off remembering of the intuition. That thought by what I can now nearest approach to say it, is this. When good is near you, when you have life in yourself, it is not by any known or accustomed way; you shall not discern the footprints of any other; you shall not see the face of man; you shall not hear any name; the way, the thought, the good, shall be wholly strange and new. It shall exclude example and experience. . . .

THEODORE PARKER

Theodore Parker (1810–1860), one of the most learned of all the Transcendentalists, has been called the Paul of the movement. The selection below is of interest not only because it shows the depth of the Transcendentalists' antipathy toward Locke's "sensationalism", but also because it reveals the extent to which they identified his philosophy with a worship of established fact and with the idea that whatever is, is right. Sympathetic students of the history of empiricism may well regard this as a caricature of that movement, but caricature or not, it was the picture of empiricism that many Transcendentalists carried about in their heads.

I do not select this passage for any profundity I suppose it to have, so much as for its liveliness and bluntness. George Ripley attained a deep clarity that illuminates Emerson's views, but Parker's intellectual relationship with Emerson is more like John Fiske's relationship with Herbert Spencer in a later generation. Parker said in crudely clear language what Emerson could only adumbrate obscurely. It is therefore no wonder that Emerson called him, not the Paul of Transcendentalism, but its Savonarola.

Transcendentalism and Sensationalism [1]

. . . In metaphysics there are and have long been two schools of philosophers. The first is the sensational school.[2] Its most important metaphysical doctrine is this: There is nothing in the intellect which was not first in the senses. Here "intellect" means the whole intellectual, moral, affectional and religious consciousness of man. The philosophers of this school claim to have reached this conclusion legitimately by the inductive method. It was at first an hypothesis; but after analyzing the facts of consciousness, interrogating all the ideas and sentiments and sensations of man, they say the hypothesis is proved by the most careful induction. They appeal to it as a principle, as a maxim, from which other things are deduced. They say that experience by one or more of the senses is the ultimate appeal in philosophy: all that I know is of sensational origin; the senses are the windows which let in all the light I have; the senses afford a sensation. I reflect upon this, and by reflection transform a sensation into an idea. An idea, therefore, is a transformed sensation.

A school in metaphysics soon becomes a school in physics, in politics, ethics, religion. The sensational school has been long enough in existence to assert itself in each of the four great forms of human action. Let us see what it amounts to.

I. In physics. 1. It does not afford us a certainty of the existence of the outward world. The sensationalist believes it, not on account of his sensational philosophy, but in spite of it; not by his philosophy, but by his common sense: he does not

[1] This is a selection from Parker's lecture, "Transcendentalism", first printed posthumously in 1876. It appears in Theodore Parker, *The World of Matter and The Spirit of Man: Latest Discourses of Religion,* edited by George Willis Cooke (Boston, 1907), pp. 1–38. The passages selected appear in pp. 7–23.

[2] In a part of the essay not reproduced here, Parker summarizes the views of the other school, the Transcendentalists. [M.W.]

philosophically know it. . . . How can I *know* philosophically the existence of the material world? With only the sensational philosophy I cannot! I can only *know* the facts of consciousness. . . .

2. From its hypothetical world sensationalism proceeds to the laws of matter; but it cannot logically get beyond its facts. . . . The sensational philosophy has no idea of cause, except that of empirical connection in time and place; no idea of substance, only of body, or form of substance; no ontology, but phenomenology. It refers all questions—say of the planets about the sun—to an outward force: when they were made, God, standing outside, gave them a push and set them a-going; or else their motion is the result of a fortuitous concourse of atoms, a blind fate. Neither conclusion is a philosophical conclusion, each an hypothesis. Its physics are mere materialism; hence it delights in the atomistic theory of nature and repels the dynamic theory of matter. The sensationalist's physics appear well in a celebrated book, "The Vestiges of the Natural History of Creation." The book has many valuable things in it, but the philosophy of its physics is an unavoidable result of sensationalism. There is nothing but materialism in his world. All is material, effects material, causes material, his God material,—not surpassing the physical universe, but co-extensive therewith. In zoology life is the result of organization, but is an immanent life. In anthropology the mind is the result of organization, but is an immanent mind; in theology God is the result of organization, but is an immanent God. Life does not *transcend* organization, nor does mind, nor God. All is matter.

II. In politics. Sensationalism knows nothing of absolute right, absolute justice; only of historical right, historical justice. "There is nothing in the intellect which was not first in the senses." The senses by which we learn of justice and right are hearing and seeing. Do I reflect, and so get a righter right and juster justice than I have seen or heard of, it does me no good, for "nothing is in the intellect which was not in the

senses." Thus absolute justice is only a whim, a no-thing, a
dream. Men that talk of absolute justice, absolute right, are
visionary men.

In politics, sensationalism knows nothing of ideas, only of
facts; "the only lamp by which its feet are guided is the lamp
of experience." All its facts are truths of observation, not of
necessity. "There is no right but might," is the political philosophy of sensationalism. It may be the might of a king, of
an aristocracy, of a democracy, the might of passions, the
might of intellect, the might of muscle,—it has a right to what
it will. It appeals always to human history, not human
nature. Now human history shows what has been, not what
should be or will be. To reason about war it looks not to the
natural justice, only to the cost and present consequences. To
reason about free trade or protection, it looks not to the natural justice or right of mankind, but only to the present expediency of the thing. Political expediency is the only right or
justice it knows in its politics. So it always looks back, and
says "it worked well at Barcelona or Venice," or "did not
work well." It loves to cite precedents out of history, not laws
out of nature. It claims a thing not as a human right, but as
an historical privilege received by Magna Charta or the Constitution; as if a right were more of a right because time-hon-
ored and written on parchment; or less, because just claimed
and for the first time and by a single man. The sensationalist
has no confidence in ideas, so asks for facts to hold on to and
to guide him in his blindness. Said a governor in America,
"The right of suffrage is universal." "How can that be," said a
sensationalist, "when the Constitution of the state declares
that certain persons shall not vote?" He knew no rights before they became constitutional, no rights but vested rights,
—perhaps none but "*invested*."

The sensationalists in politics divide into two parties, each
with the doctrine that in politics "might makes right." One
party favors the despotism of the few,—is an oligarchy; or of
the one,—is a monarchy. Hence the doctrine is, "The king

can do no wrong." All power is his; he may delegate it to the people as a privilege; it is not theirs by right, by nature, and his as a trust. He has a right to make any laws he will, not merely any just laws. The people must pay passive obedience to the king, he has eminent domain over them. The celebrated Thomas Hobbes is the best representative of this party, and has one great merit,—of telling what he thought.

The other party favors the despotism of the many,—is a democracy. The doctrine is, "The people can do no wrong." The majority of the people have the right to make any laws they will, not merely any just laws; and the minority must obey, right or wrong. You must not censure the measures of the majority, you afford "aid and comfort to the enemy." The state has absolute domain over the citizen, the majority over the minority; this holds good of the voters, and of any political party in the nation. For the majority has power of its own right, for its own behoof; not in trust, and for the good of all and each! The aim of sensational politics is the greatest good of the greatest number; this may be obtained by sacrificing the greatest good of the lesser number,—by sacrificing any individual,—or sacrificing absolute good. In No-man's-land this party prevails: the dark-haired men, over forty million,— the red-haired, only three million five hundred thousand,— the dark-haired enslave the red-haired for the greatest good of the greatest number. But in a hundred years the red-haired men are most numerous, and turn round and enslave the black-haired.

Thomas Paine is a good representative of this party; so is Marat, Robespierre, the author of the "Système de la Nature." In the old French Revolution you see the legitimate consequence of this doctrine, that might makes right, that there is no absolute justice, in the violence, the murder, the wholesale assassination. The nation did to masses, and in the name of democracy, what all kings had done to the nation and in the name of monarchy,—sought the greatest good of the controlling power at the sacrifice of an opponent. It is the same maxim which in cold blood hangs a single culprit, enslaves three million negroes, and butchers thousands of men as in the September massacres. The sensational philosophy established the theory that might makes right,—and the mad passions of a solitary despot, or a million-headed mob, made it a fact. Commonly the two parties unite by a compromise, and then it consults not the greatest good of its king alone, as in a brutal, pure monarchy; not of the greatest number, as in a pure and brutal democracy; but the greatest good of a class,—the nobility and gentry in England, the landed proprietors and rich burghers in Switzerland, the slaveholders in South Carolina. Voltaire is a good representative of this type of sensational politics, not to come nearer home. In peaceful times England shares the defect of the sensational school in politics. Her legislation is empirical; great ideas do not run through her laws; she loves a precedent better than a principle; appeals to an accidental fact of human history, not an essential fact of human nature which is prophetic. Hence legislative politics is not a great science which puts the facts of human consciousness into a state, making natural justice common law; nothing but a poor dealing with precedents, a sort of national housekeeping and not very thrifty housekeeping. In our own nation you see another example of the same, —result of the same sensational philosophy. There is no right, says Mr. Calhoun, but might; the white man has that, so the black man is his political prey. And Mr. Polk tells us that Vermont, under the Constitution, has the same right to establish slavery as Georgia to abolish it.

III. In ethics. Ethics are the morals of the individual; politics of the mass. The sensationalist knows no first truths in morals; the source of maxims in morals is experience; in experience there is no absolute right. Absolute justice, absolute right, were never in the senses, so not in the intellect; only whimsies, words in the mouth. The will is not free, but wholly conditioned, in bondage; character made always for you, not by you. The intellect is a smooth table; the moral power a smooth table; and experience writes there what she will, and what she writes is law of morality. Morality is expediency, nothing more; nothing is good of itself, right of itself, just of itself,—but only because it produces agreeable consequences, which are agreeable sensations. Dr. Paley is a good example of the sensational moralist. I ask him "What is right, just?" He says, "There are no such things; they are the names to stand for what works well in the long run." "How shall I know what to do in a matter of morals? by referring to a moral sense?" "Not at all: only by common sense, by observation, by experience, by learning what works well in the long run; by human history, not human nature. To make a complete code of morals by sensationalism you must take the history of mankind, and find what has worked well, and follow that because it worked well." "But human history only tells what has been and worked well, not what is right. I want what is right!" He answers, "It is pretty much the same thing." "But suppose the first men endowed with faculties perfectly developed, would they know what to do?" "Not at all. Instinct would tell the beast antecedent to experience, but man has no moral instinct, must learn only by actual trial." "Well," say I, "let alone that matter, let us come to details. What is honesty?" "It is the best policy." "Why must I tell the truth, keep my word, be chaste, temperate?" "For the sake of the reward, the respect of your fellows, the happiness of a long life and heaven at last. On the whole God pays well for virtue; though slow pay, he is sure." "But suppose the devil paid the better pay?" "Then serve him, for the end is not the service, but the pay. Virtue, and by virtue I mean all moral excellence, is not a good in itself, but good as producing some other good." "Why should I be virtuous?" "For the sake of the reward." "But vice has its rewards, they are present and not future, immediate and certain, not merely contingent and mediate. I should think them greater than the reward of virtue." Then vice to you is virtue, for it pays best. The sensational philosophy knows no conscience to sound in the man's ears the stern word, Thou oughtest so to do, come what will come!

In politics might makes right, so in morals. Success is the touchstone; the might of obtaining the reward the right of doing the deed. Bentham represents the sensational morals of politics; Paley of ethics. Both are Epicureans. The sensationalist and the Epicurean agree in this,—enjoyment is the touchstone of virtue and determines what is good, what bad, what indifferent: this is the generic agreement. Heathen Epicurus spoke only of enjoyment in this life; Christian Archdeacon Paley—and a very *arch*deacon—spoke of enjoyment also in the next: this is the specific difference. In either case virtue ceases to be virtue, for it is only a bargain.

There is a school of sensationalists who turn off and say, "Oh, you cannot answer the moral questions and tell what is right, just, fair, good. We must settle that by revelation." That, of course, only adjourns the question and puts the decision on men who received the revelation or God who made it. They do not meet the philosopher's question; they assume that the difference between right and wrong is not knowable by human faculties, and, if there be any difference between right and wrong, there is no faculty in man which naturally loves right and abhors wrong, still less any faculty which can find out what *is* right, what wrong. So all moral questions are to be decided by authority, because somebody said so; not by reference to facts of consciousness, but to phenomena of history. Of course the moral law is not a law which is of me, rules in me and by me; only one put on me, which rules over me! Can any lofty virtue grow out of this theory? any heroism? Verily not. Regulus did not ask a reward for his virtue; if so, he made but a bargain, and who would honor him more than a desperate trader who made a good speculation? There is something in man which scoffs at expediency; which will do right, justice, truth, though hell itself should gape and bid him hold his peace; the morality which anticipates history, loves the right for itself. Of this Epicurus knew nothing,

Paley nothing, Bentham nothing, sensationalism nothing. Sensationalism takes its standard of political virtue from the House of Commons; of right from the Constitution and common law; of commercial virtue from the board of brokers at their best, and the old bankrupt law; or virtue in general from the most comfortable classes of society, from human history, not human nature; and knows nothing more. . . .

IV. In religion. Sensationalism must have a philosophy of religion, a theology; let us see what theology. There are two parties; one goes by philosophy, the other mistrusts philosophy.

1. The first thing in theology is to know God. The idea of God is the touchstone of a theologian. Now to know the existence of God is to be certain thereof as of my own existence. "Nothing in the intellect which was not first in the senses," says sensationalism; "all comes by sensational experience and reflection thereon." Sensationalism—does that give us the idea of God? I ask the sensationalist, "Does the sensational eye see God?" "No." "The ear hear him?" "No." "Do the organs of sense touch or taste him?" "No." "How then do you get the idea of God?" "By induction from facts of observation *a posteriori*. The senses deal with finite things; I reflect on them, put them all together I assume that they have *cause;* then by the inductive method I find out the character of that cause: that is God." Then I say, "But the senses deal with only finite things, so you must infer only a finite maker, else the induction is imperfect. So you have but a finite God. Then these finite things, measured only by my experience, are imperfect things. Look at disorders in the frame of nature; the sufferings of animals, the miseries of men; here are seeming imperfections which the sensational philosopher staggers at. But to go on with this induction: from an imperfect work you must infer an imperfect author. So the God of sensationalism is not only finite, but imperfect even at that. But am I certain of the existence of the finite and imperfect God? The existence of the outward world is only an hypothe-

sis, its laws hypothetical; all that depends on that or them is but an hypothesis,—the truth of your faculties, the forms of matter only an hypothesis: so the existence of God is not a certainty; he is but our hypothetical God. But a hypothetical God is no God at all, not the living God: an imperfect God is no God at all, not the true God: a finite God is no God at all, not the absolute God. But this hypothetical, finite, imperfect God, where is he? In matter? No. In spirit? No. Does he act in matter or spirit? No, only now and then he did act by miracle; he is outside of the world of matter and spirit. Then he is a non-resident, an absentee. A non-resident God is no God at all, not the all-present God."

The above is the theory on which Mr. Hume constructs his notion of God with the sensational philosophy, the inductive method; and he arrives at the hypothesis of a God, of a finite God, of an imperfect God, of a non-resident God. Beyond that the sensational philosophy as philosophy cannot go.

But another party comes out of the same school to treat of religious matters; they give their philosophy a vacation, and to prove the existence of God they go back to tradition, and say, "Once God revealed himself to the senses of men; they heard him, they saw him, they felt him; so to them the existence of God was not an induction, but a fact of observation; they told it to others, through whom it comes to us; we can say it is not a fact of observation but a fact of testimony."

"Well," I ask, "are you certain then?" "Yes." "Quite sure? Let me look. The man to whom God revealed himself may have been mistaken; it may have been a dream, or a whim of his own, perhaps a fib; at any rate, he was not philosophically certain of the existence of the outward world in general; how could he be of anything that took place in it? Next, the evidence which relates the transaction is not wholly reliable: how do I know the books which tell of it tell the truth, that they were not fabricated to deceive me? All that rests on testimony is a little uncertain if it took place one or two thousand years ago; especially if I know nothing about the per-

sons who testify or of that whereof they testify; still more so
if it be a thing, as you say, unphilosophical and even supernatural."

So, then, the men who give a vacation to their philosophy
have slurred the philosophical argument for a historical, the
theological for the mythological, and have gained nothing except the tradition of God. By this process we are as far from
the infinite God as before, and have only arrived at the same
point where the philosophy left us.

The English Deists and the Socinians and others have approached religion with the sensational philosophy in their
hands; we are to learn of God philosophically only by induction. And such is their God. They tell us that God is not
knowable; the existence of God is not a certainty to us; it is a
probability, a credibility, a possibility,—a certainty to none.
You ask of sensationalism, the greatest question, "Is there a
God?" Answer: "Probably." "What is his character?" "Finite,
imperfect." "Can I trust him?" "If we consult tradition it is
creditable; if philosophy, possible."

2. The next great question in theology is that of the immortality of the soul. That is a universal hope of mankind;
what does it rest on? Can I know my immortality? Here are
two wings of the sensational school. The first says, "No, you
cannot know it; it is not true. Mind, soul, are two words to
designate the result of organization. Man is not a mind, not a
soul, not a free will. Man is a body, with blood, brains,
nerves—nothing more; the organization gone, all is gone."
Now that is sound, logical, consistent; that was the conclusion of Hume, of many of the English Deists, and of many
French philosophers in the last century; they looked the fact
in the face. But mortality, annihilation, is rather an ugly fact
to look fairly in the face; but Mr. Hume and others have
done it, and died brave with the sensational philosophy.

The other wing of the sensational school gives its philosophy another vacation, rests the matter not on philosophy but

history; not on the theological but the mythological argument; on authority of tradition asserting a phenomenon of human history, they try to establish the immortality of man by a single precedent, a universal law by the tradition of a single, empirical, contingent phenomenon.

But I ask the sensational philosopher, "Is immortality certain?" "No." "Probable?" "No." "Credible?" "No." "Possible?" "Barely." I ask the traditional division, "Is immortality certain?" "No, it is left uncertain to try your faith." "Is it probable?" "Yes, there is one witness in six thousand years, one out of ten million times ten million." "Well, suppose it is probable; is immortality, if it be sure to be a good thing, for me, for mankind?" "Not at all! There is nothing in the nature of man, nothing in the nature of the world, nothing in the nature of God to make you sure immortality will prove a blessing to mankind in general, to yourself in special!"

3. That is not quite all. Sensationalism does not allow freedom of the will; I say not, absolute freedom—that belongs only to God,—but it allows no freedom of the will. See the result: all will is God's, all willing therefore is equally divine, and the worst vice of Pantheism follows. "But what is the will of God, is that free?" "Not at all; man is limited by the organization of his body, God by the organization of the universe." So God is not absolute God, not absolutely free; and as man's will is necessitated by God's, so God's will by the universe of matter; and only a boundless fate and pitiless encircles man and God.

This is the philosophy of sensationalism; such its doctrine in physics, politics, ethics, religion. It leads to boundless uncertainty. Berkeley resolves the universe into subjective ideas; no sensationalist knows a law in physics to be universal. Hobbes and Bentham and Condillac in politics know of no right but might; Priestley denies the spirituality of man, Collins and Edwards his liberty; Dodwell affirms the materiality of the soul, and the mortality of all men not baptized;

Mandeville directly, and others indirectly, deny all natural distinction between virtue and vice; Archdeacon Paley knows no motive but expediency.

The materialist is puzzled with the existence of matter; finds its laws general, not universal. The sensational philosophy meets the politician and tells him through Rousseau and others, "Society has no divine original, only the social compact; there is no natural justice, natural right; no right, but might; no greater good than the greatest good of the greatest number, and for that you may sacrifice all you will; to defend a constitution is better than to defend justice." In morals the sensational philosophy meets the young man and tells him all is uncertain; he had better be content with things as they are, himself as he is; to protest against a popular wrong is foolish, to make money by it, or ease, or power, is a part of wisdom; only the fool is wise above what is written. It meets the young minister with its proposition that the existence of God is not a certainty, nor the immortality of the soul; that religion is only traditions of the elders and the keeping of a form. It says to him, "Look there, Dr. Humdrum has got the tallest pulpit and the quietest pews, the fattest living and the cosiest nook in all the land; how do you think he won it? Why, by letting well-enough alone; he never meddles with sin; it would break his heart to hurt a sinner's feelings,—he might lose a parishioner; he never dreams to make the world better, or better off. Go thou and do likewise." . . .

Part 4: The Impact of Nineteenth-Century Science

HERBERT SPENCER

Among famous foreign thinkers who influenced nineteenth-century American philosophy, Herbert Spencer (1820–1903) was certainly the least distinguished—especially by comparison with Locke, Reid, Kant, and Mill. One might even make a very strong case for the view that Spencer was less distinguished as a philosopher than Coleridge, though that would take a very fine measuring instrument. Nevertheless, it is very likely that no foreign philosopher has ever had a wider influence on American thought. This was especially true of Spencer's impact on sociology and social philosophy; but even in metaphysics, epistemology, and philosophy of science, Spencer was a towering figure on the American scene. No other foreign philosopher has ever had as slavish a follower as Spencer had in John Fiske (1842–1901), whose *Outlines of Cosmic Philosophy* (1874) was for the most part an exposition of Spencer's system. And for more than a half-century after Spencer's *First Principles* appeared in 1862, he was deemed so important as an intellectual force that American philosophers like Chauncey Wright, William James, Josiah Royce, and John Dewey devoted a very large amount of energy to trying to refute him.

Spencer's *First Principles* had two main aims. One was to effect a reconciliation between science and religion by showing that they were both based on a belief in the existence of an ultimate, inscrutable cause of all phenomena, which Spencer called the Unknowable. The other was to argue that in the sphere of the Knowable, the Principle of Conservation of Energy—which Spencer calls the Law of Persistence of Force —is the widest law of philosophy, from which all lesser laws of science may be deduced, including a Spencerian law of universal evolution that went beyond the organic evolution of Darwin. Spencer's *Principles of Psychology*, which first appeared in 1864–67, sought to arbitrate between empiricism and rationalism. He argued that although all knowledge rests on experience, what is commonly called *a priori* knowledge was inherited by today's men from their remote ancestors. According to Spencer, those ancestors of men acquired their knowledge that 2 and 2 make 4 by experience, much as ancestors of today's giraffes are supposed by Lamarckians to have acquired their long necks by stretching to reach food on high trees. Today's men, Spencer held, inherited the knowledge that 2 and 2 make 4 from ancestors who acquired it by efforts analogous to those expended by the ancestors of today's giraffes. Therefore, Spencer argued, today's men do not arrive at the knowledge that 2 and 2 make 4 by appealing to experience.

In the history of post-Spencerian American philosophy, some philosophers concentrated their fire on Spencer's Unknowable; some attacked his conception of the philosopher as a super-scientist; others took aim at his version of the "experience-hypothesis"; and still others attacked his evolutionary ethics. By the time they had all hammered away at the system, little was left of it, yet it is fair to say that no foreign philosopher had ever stimulated as much controversy and conversation as Spencer. For this reason it is hard to understand many writings of Chauncey Wright, William James, or Josiah Royce without some familiarity with the writings of

Herbert Spencer. Because the latter were so voluminous and variegated, however, it is very hard to do them justice in as small a selection as the one to follow. In it Spencer presents his conception of philosophy and tries to show how all of scientific knowledge may be derived from what he was given to calling one "primordial truth".

The Aim of Synthetic Philosophy [1]

Though in the extent of the sphere which they have supposed Philosophy to fill, men have differed and still differ very widely; yet there is a real if unavowed agreement among them in signifying by this title a knowledge which transcends ordinary knowledge. That which remains as the common element in these conceptions of Philosophy, after the elimination of their discordant elements, is—*knowledge of the highest degree of generality.* We see this tacitly asserted by the simultaneous inclusion of God, Nature, and Man, within its scope; or still more distinctly by the division of Philosophy as a whole into Theological, Physical, Ethical, &c. For that which characterizes the genus of which these are species, must be something more general than that which distinguishes any one species.

What must be the shape here given to this conception? Though persistently conscious of a Power manifested to us, we have abandoned as futile the attempt to learn anything respecting that Power, and so have shut out Philosophy from much of the domain supposed to belong to it. The domain left is that occupied by Science. Science concerns itself with the co-existences and sequences among phenomena; grouping these at first into generalizations of a simple or low order, and rising gradually to higher and more extended generali-

[1] This selection comes from Herbert Spencer, *First Principles* (Sixth Edition, New York, 1902), pp. 117–20.

zations. But if so, where remains any subject-matter for Philosophy?

The reply is—Philosophy may still properly be the title retained for knowledge of the highest generality. Science means merely the family of the Sciences—stands for nothing more than the sum of knowledge formed of their contributions; and ignores the knowledge constituted by the *fusion* of these contributions into a whole. As usage has defined it, Science consists of truths existing more or less separated and does not recognize these truths as entirely integrated. An illustration will make the difference clear.

If we ascribe the flow of a river to the same force which causes the fall of a stone, we make a statement that belongs to a certain division of Science. If, to explain how gravitation produces this movement in a direction almost horizontal, we cite the law that fluids subject to mechanical forces exert reactive forces which are equal in all directions, we formulate a wider truth, containing the scientific interpretations of many other phenomena; as those presented by the fountain, the hydraulic press, the steam-engine, the air-pump. And when this proposition, extending only to the dynamics of fluids, is merged in a proposition of general dynamics, comprehending the laws of movement of solids as well as of fluids, there is reached a yet higher truth; but still a truth that comes wholly within the realm of Science. Again looking around at Birds and Mammals, suppose we say that air-breathing animals are hot-blooded; and that then, remembering how Reptiles, which also breathe air, are not much warmer than their media, we say, more truly, that animals (bulks being equal) have temperatures proportionate to the quantities of air they breathe; and that then, calling to mind certain large fish, as the tunny, which maintain a heat considerably above that of the water they swim in, we further correct the generalization by saying that the temperature varies as the rate of oxygenation of the blood; and that then, modifying the statement to meet other criticisms, we finally assert the relation to be between the amount of heat and the amount of molecular change—supposing we do all this, we state scientific truths that are successively wider and more complete, but truths which, to the last, remain purely scientific. Once more if, guided by mercantile experiences, we reach the conclusions that prices rise when the demand exceeds the supply; that commodities flow from places where they are abundant to places where they are scarce; that the industries of different localities are determined in their kinds mainly by the facilities which the localities afford for them; and if, studying these generalizations of political economy, we trace them all to the truth that each man seeks satisfaction for his desires in ways costing the smallest efforts—such social phenomena being *resultants* of individual actions so guided; we are still dealing with the propositions of Science only.

How, then, is Philosophy constituted? It is constituted by carrying a stage further the process indicated. So long as these truths are known only apart and regarded as independent, even the most general of them cannot without laxity of speech be called philosophical. But when, having been severally reduced to a mechanical axiom, a principle of molecular physics, and a law of social action, they are contemplated together as corollaries of some ultimate truth, then we rise to the kind of knowledge which constitutes Philosophy proper.

The truths of Philosophy thus bear the same relation to the highest scientific truths, that each of these bears to lower scientific truths. As each widest generalization of Science comprehends and consolidates the narrower generalizations of its own division; so the generalizations of Philosophy comprehend and consolidate the widest generalizations of Science. It is therefore a knowledge the extreme opposite in kind to that which experience first accumulates. It is the final product of that process which begins with a mere colligation of crude observations, goes on establishing propositions that are broader and more separated from particular cases, and ends in universal propositions. Or to bring the definition to its simplest and clearest form:—Knowledge of the lowest kind is *un-unified* knowledge; Science is *partially-unified* knowledge; Philosophy is *completely-unified* knowledge.

Such, at least, is the meaning we must here give to the word Philosophy, if we employ it at all. In so defining it, we accept that which is common to the various conceptions of it current among both ancients and moderns—rejecting those elements in which these conceptions disagree. In short, we are simply giving precision to that application of the word which has been gradually establishing itself.

Two forms of Philosophy, as thus understood, may be distinguished and dealt with separately. On the one hand, the things contemplated may be the universal truths: all particular truths referred to being used simply for proof or elucidation of these universal truths. On the other hand, setting out with the universal truths, the things contemplated may be the particular truths as interpreted by them. In both cases we deal with the universal truths; but in the one case they are passive and in the other case active—in the one case they form the products of exploration and in the other case the instruments of exploration. These divisions we may appropriately call General Philosophy and Special Philosophy respectively.

The Achievement of Synthetic Philosophy [2]

At the close of a work like this, it is more than usually needful to contemplate as a whole that which the successive chapters have presented in parts. A coherent knowledge implies something more than the establishment of connexions: we must not rest after seeing how each minor group of truths falls into its place within some major group, and how all the major groups fit together. It is requisite that we should retire

[2] This selection comes from Spencer's *First Principles*, pp. 494–508.

a space, and, looking at the entire structure from a distance at which details are lost to view, observe its general character. . . .

When we inquired what constitutes Philosophy—when we compared men's various conceptions of Philosophy, so that, eliminating the elements in which they differed, we might see in what they agreed; we found in them all the tacit implication that Philosophy is completely unified knowledge. Apart from each scheme of unified knowledge, and apart from proposed methods by which unification is to be effected, we traced in every case a belief that unification is possible, and that the end of Philosophy is achievement of it.

After reaching this conclusion we considered the data with which Philosophy must set out. Fundamental propositions, or propositions not deducible from deeper ones, can be established only by showing the complete congruity of all the results reached through the assumption of them; and, premising that they were simply assumed till thus established, we took as our data those components of our intelligence without which there cannot go on the mental processes implied by philosophizing.

From the specification of these we passed to certain primary truths—"The Indestructibility of Matter," "The Continuity of Motion," and "The Persistence of Force;" of which the last is ultimate and the others derivative. Having previously seen that our experiences of Matter and Motion are resolvable into experiences of Force, we further saw the truths that Matter and Motion are unchangeable in quantity, to be implications of the truth that Force is unchangeable in quantity. This we concluded is the truth by derivation from which all other truths are to be proved.

The first of the truths which presented itself to be so proved, is "The Persistence of the Relations among Forces." This, which is ordinarily called Uniformity of Law, we found to be a necessary implication of the truth that Force can neither arise out of nothing nor lapse into nothing.

The next deduction was that forces which seem to be lost are transformed into their equivalents of other forces; or, conversely, that forces which become manifest, do so by disappearance of pre-existing equivalent forces. These truths we found illustrated by the motions of the heavenly bodies, by the changes going on over the Earth's surface, and by all organic and super-organic actions.

It was shown to be the same with the law that everything moves along the line of least resistance, or the line of greatest traction, or their resultant. Among movements of all orders, from those of stars down to those of nervous discharges and commercial currents, it was shown both that this is so, and that, given the Persistence of Force, it must be so.

So, too, we saw it to be with "The Rhythm of Motion." All motion alternates—be it the motion of planets in their orbits or ethereal molecules in their undulations—be it the cadences of speech or the rises and falls of prices; and, as before, it became manifest that Force being persistent, this perpetual reversal of Motion between limits is inevitable.

These truths holding of existences at large, were recognized as of the kind required to constitute what we distinguish as Philosophy. But, on considering them, we perceived that as they stand they do not form a Philosophy; and that a Philosophy cannot be formed by any number of such truths separately known. Each expresses the law of some one factor by which phenomena, as we experience them, are produced; or, at most, expresses the law of co-operation of some two factors. But knowing what are the elements of a process, is not knowing how these elements combine to effect it. That which alone can unify knowledge must be the law of co-operation of the factors—a law expressing simultaneously the complex antecedents and the complex consequents which any phenomenon as a whole presents.

A further inference was that Philosophy, as we understand

it, must not unify the changes displayed in separate concrete phenomena only; and must not stop short with unifying the changes displayed in separate classes of concrete phenomena; but must unify the changes displayed in all concrete phenomena. If the law of operation of each factor holds true throughout the Cosmos, so, too, must the law of their co-operation. And hence in comprehending the Cosmos as conforming to this law of co-operation, must consist that highest unification which Philosophy seeks.

Descending to a more concrete view, we saw that the law sought must be the law of the continuous re-distribution of Matter and Motion. The changes everywhere going on, from those which are slowly altering the structure of our galaxy down to those which constitute a chemical decomposition, are changes in the relative positions of component parts; and everywhere necessarily imply that along with a new arrangement of Matter there has arisen a new arrangement of Motion. Hence it follows that there must be a law of the concomitant re-distribution of Matter and Motion which holds of every change, and which, by thus unifying all changes, must be the basis of a Philosophy.

In commencing our search for this universal law of redistribution, we contemplated from another point of view the problem of Philosophy, and saw that its solution could not but be of the nature indicated. It was shown that an ideally complete Philosophy must formulate the whole series of changes passed through by existences separately and as a whole in passing from the imperceptible to the perceptible and again from the perceptible to the imperceptible. If it begins its explanations with existences that already have concrete forms, or leaves off while they still retain concrete forms, then, manifestly, they had preceding histories, or will have succeeding histories, or both, of which no account is given. Whence we saw it to follow that the formula sought, equally applicable to existences taken singly and in their totality, must be applicable to the whole history of each and to the whole history of all. This must be the ideal form of a Philosophy, however far short of it the reality may fall.

By these considerations we were brought within view of the formula. For if it had to express the entire progress from the imperceptible to the perceptible and from the perceptible to the imperceptible; and if it was also to express the continuous re-distribution of Matter and Motion, then, obviously, it could be no other than one defining the opposite processes of concentration and diffusion in terms of Matter and Motion. And if so, it must be a statement of the truth that the concentration of Matter implies the dissipation of Motion, and that, conversely, the absorption of Motion implies the diffusion of Matter.

Such, in fact, we found to be the law of the entire cycle of changes passed through by every existence. Moreover we saw that besides applying to the whole history of each existence, it applies to each detail of the history. Both processes are going on at every instant; but always there is a differential result in favour of the first or the second. And every change, even though it be only a transposition of parts, inevitably advances the one process or the other.

Evolution and Dissolution, as we name these opposite transformations, though thus truly defined in their most general characters, are but incompletely defined; or rather, while the definition of Dissolution is sufficient, the definition of Evolution is extremely insufficient. Evolution is always an integration of Matter and dissipation of Motion; but it is in nearly all cases much more than this. The primary re-distribution of Matter and Motion is accompanied by secondary re-distributions.

Distinguishing the different kinds of Evolution thus produced as simple and compound, we went on to consider under what conditions the secondary re-distributions which make Evolution compound, take place. We found that a concentrating aggregate which loses its contained motion rapidly, or integrates quickly, exhibits only simple Evolution; but in proportion as its largeness, or the peculiar constitution of its components, hinders the dissipation of its motion, its parts, while undergoing that primary re-distribution which results in integration, undergo secondary re-distributions producing more or less complexity.

From this conception of Evolution and Dissolution as together making up the entire process through which things pass; and from this conception of Evolution as divided into simple and compound; we went on to consider the law of Evolution, as exhibited among all orders of existences, in general and in detail.

The integration of Matter and concomitant dissipation of Motion, was traced not in each whole only, but in the parts into which each whole divides. By the aggregate Solar System, as well as by each planet and satellite, progressive concentration has been, and is still being, exemplified. In each organism that general incorporation of dispersed materials which causes growth, is accompanied by local incorporations, forming what we call organs. Every society, while it displays the aggregative process by its increasing mass of population, displays it also by the rise of dense masses in special parts of its area. And in all cases, along with these direct integrations there go the indirect integrations by which parts are made mutually dependent.

From this primary re-distribution we were led on to consider the secondary re-distributions, by inquiring how there came to be a formation of parts during the formation of a whole. It turned out that there is habitually a passage from homogeneity to heterogeneity, along with the passage from diffusion to concentration. While the matter composing the Solar System has been assuming a denser form, it has changed from unity to variety of distribution. Solidification of the Earth has been accompanied by a progress from comparative uniformity to extreme multiformity. In the course of its advance from a germ to a mass of relatively great bulk, every plant and animal also advances from simplicity to complexity. The increase of a society in numbers and consolidation has for its concomitant an increased heterogeneity both of its political and its industrial organization. And the like holds of all super-organic products—Language, Science, Art, and Literature.

But we saw that these secondary re-distributions are not thus completely expressed. While the parts into which each whole is resolved become more unlike one another, they also become more sharply marked off. The result of the secondary re-distributions is therefore to change an indefinite homogeneity into a definite heterogeneity. This additional trait also we found in evolving aggregates of all orders. Further consideration, however, made it apparent that the increasing definiteness which goes along with increasing heterogeneity is not an independent trait, but that it results from the integration which progresses in each of the differentiating parts, while it progresses in the whole they form.

Further, it was pointed out that in all evolutions, inorganic, organic, and super-organic, this change in the arrangement of Matter is accompanied by a parallel change in the arrangement of contained Motion: every increase in structural complexity involving a corresponding increase in functional complexity. It was shown that along with the integration of molecules into masses, there arises an integration of molecular motion into the motion of masses; and that as fast as there results variety in the sizes and forms of aggregates and their relations to incident forces, there also results variety in their movements.

The transformation thus contemplated under separate aspects, being in itself but one transformation, it became needful to unite these separate aspects into a single conception—to regard the primary and secondary re-distributions as simultaneously working their various effects. Everywhere the change from a confused simplicity to a distinct complexity, in the distribution of both matter and motion, is incidental to the consolidation of the matter and the loss of its internal motion. Hence the re-distribution of the matter and of its retained motion, is from a relatively diffused, uniform, and indeterminate arrangement, to a relatively concentrated, multiform, and determinate arrangement.

We come now to one of the additions that may be made to the general argument while summing it up. Here is the fit occasion for observing a higher degree of unity in the foregoing inductions, than we observed while making them.

The law of Evolution has been thus far contemplated as holding true of each order of existences, considered as a separate order. But the induction as so presented, falls short of that completeness which it gains when we contemplate these several orders of existences as forming together one natural whole. While we think of Evolution as divided into astronomic, geologic, biologic, psychologic, sociologic, &c., it may seem to some extent a coincidence that the same law of metamorphosis holds throughout all its divisions. But when we recognize these divisions as mere conventional groupings, made to facilitate the arrangement and acquisition of knowledge—when we remember that the different existences with which they severally deal are component parts of one Cosmos; we see at once that there are not several kinds of Evolution having certain traits in common, but one Evolution going on everywhere after the same manner. We have repeatedly observed that while any whole is evolving, there is always going on an evolution of the parts into which it divides itself; but we have not observed that this equally holds of the totality of things, which is made up of parts within parts from the greatest down to the smallest. We know that while a physically-cohering aggregate like the human body is getting larger and taking on its general shape, each of its organs is doing the same; that while each organ is growing and becoming unlike others, there is going on a differentiation and integration of its component tissues and vessels; and that even the components of these components are severally increasing and passing into more definitely heterogeneous structures. But we have not duly remarked that while each individual is developing, the society of which he is an insignificant unit is developing too; that while the aggregate mass forming a society is integrating and becoming more definitely heterogeneous, so, too, that total aggregate, the Earth, is continuing to integrate and differentiate; that while the Earth, which in bulk is not a millionth of the Solar System, progresses towards its more concentrated structure, the Solar System similarly progresses.

So understood, Evolution becomes not one in principle only, but one in fact. There are not many metamorphoses similarly carried on, but there is a single metamorphosis universally progressing, wherever the reverse metamorphosis has not set in. In any locality, great or small, where the occupying matter acquires an appreciable individuality or distinguishableness from other matter, there Evolution goes on; or rather, the acquirement of this appreciable individuality is the commencement of Evolution. And this holds regardless of the size of the aggregate, and regardless of its inclusion in other aggregates.

After making them, we saw that the inductions which, taken together, establish the law of Evolution, do not, so long as they remain inductions, form that whole rightly named Philosophy; nor does even the foregoing passage of these inductions from agreement into identity, suffice to produce the unity sought. For, as was pointed out at the time, to unify the truths thus reached with other truths, they must be deduced from the Persistence of Force. Our next step, therefore, was to show why, Force being persistent, the transformation which Evolution shows us necessarily results.

The first conclusion was, that any finite homogeneous aggregate must lose its homogeneity, through the unequal exposures of its parts to incident forces, and that the imperfectly homogeneous must lapse into the decidedly non-homogeneous. It was pointed out that the production of diversities of structure by diverse forces, and forces acting under diverse conditions, has been illustrated in astronomic evolution; and that a like connexion of cause and effect is seen in the large and small modifications undergone by our globe. The early changes of organic germs supplied further evidence that unlikenesses of structure follow unlikenesses of relations to surrounding agencies—evidence enforced by the tendency of the differently-placed members of each species to diverge into varieties. And we found that the contrasts, political and industrial, which arise between the parts of societies, serve to illustrate the same principle. The instability of the relatively homogeneous thus everywhere exemplified, we saw also holds in each of the distinguishable parts into which any whole lapses; and that so the less heterogeneous tends continually to become more heterogeneous.

A further step in the inquiry disclosed a secondary cause of increasing multiformity. Every differentiated part is not simply a seat of further differentiations, but also a parent of further differentiations; since in growing unlike other parts, it becomes a centre of unlike reactions on incident forces, and by so adding to the diversity of forces at work, adds to the diversity of effects produced. This multiplication of effects proved to be similarly traceable throughout all Nature—in the actions and reactions that go on throughout the Solar System, in the never-ceasing geologic complications, in the involved changes produced in organisms by new influences, in the many thoughts and feelings generated by single impressions, and in the ever-ramifying results of each additional agency brought to bear on a society. To which was joined the corollary that the multiplication of effects advances in a geometrical progression along with advancing heterogeneity.

Completely to interpret the structural changes constituting Evolution, there remained to assign a reason for that increasingly-distinct demarcation of parts, which accompanies the production of differences among parts. This reason we discovered to be the segregation of mixed units under the action of forces capable of moving them. We saw that when unlike incident forces have made the parts of an aggregate unlike in the natures of their component units, there necessarily arises a tendency to separation of the dissimilar units from one another, and to a clustering of those units which are similar. This cause of the definiteness of the local integrations which accompany local differentiations, turned out to be likewise exemplified by all kinds of Evolution—by the formation of celestial bodies, by the moulding of the Earth's crust, by organic modifications, by the establishment of mental distinctions, by the genesis of social divisions.

At length, to the query whether these processes have any limit, there came the answer that they must end in equilibrium. That continual division and sub-division of forces which changes the uniform into the multiform and the multiform into the more multiform, is a process by which forces are perpetually dissipated; and dissipation of them, continuing as long as there remain any forces unbalanced by opposing forces, must end in rest. It was shown that when, as happens in aggregates of various orders, many movements go on together, the earlier dispersion of the smaller and more resisted movements, establishes moving equilibria of different kinds: forming transitional stages on the way to complete equilibrium. And further inquiry made it apparent that for the same reason, these moving equilibria have certain self-conserving powers; shown in the neutralization of perturbations, and in the adjustment to new conditions. This general principle of equilibration, like the preceding general principles, was traced throughout all forms of Evolution— astronomic, geologic, biologic, mental, and social. And our concluding inference was, that the penultimate stage of equilibration in the organic world, in which the extremest multiformity and most complex moving equilibrium are established, must be one implying the highest state of humanity.

But the fact which here chiefly concerns us, is that each of these laws of the re-distribution of Matter and Motion, was found to be a derivative law—a law deducible from the fundamental law. The Persistence of Force being granted, there follow as inevitable inferences "The Instability of the Homogeneous" and "The Multiplication of Effects;" while "Segregation" and "Equilibration" also become corollaries. And on thus discovering that the processes of change grouped under these titles are so many different aspects of one transformation, determined by an ultimate necessity, we arrive at a complete unification of them—a synthesis in which Evolution in general and in detail becomes known as an implication of the law that transcends proof. Moreover, in becoming thus unified with one another the complex truths of Evolution become simultaneously unified with those simpler truths shown to have a like origin—the equivalence of transformed forces, the movement of every mass and molecule along its line of least resistance, and the limitation of its motion by rhythm. Which further unification brings us to a conception of the entire plexus of changes presented by each concrete phenomenon, and by the aggregate of concrete phenomena, as a manifestation of one fundamental fact—a fact shown alike in the total change and in all the separate changes composing it.

Finally we turned to contemplate, as exhibited throughout Nature, that process of Dissolution which forms the complement of Evolution, and which, at some time or other, undoes what Evolution has done.

Quickly following the arrest of Evolution in aggregates that are unstable, and following it at periods often long delayed but reached at last in the stable aggregates around us, we saw that even to the vast aggregate of which all these are parts—even to the Earth as a whole—Dissolution must eventually come. Nay we even saw grounds for the belief that local assemblages of those far vaster masses we know as stars will eventually be dissipated: the question remaining unanswered whether our Sidereal System as a whole may not at a time beyond the reach of finite imagination share the same fate. While inferring that in many parts of the visible universe dissolution is following evolution, and that throughout these regions evolution will presently recommence, the question whether there is an alternation of evolution and dissolution in the totality of things is one which must be left unanswered as beyond the reach of human intelligence.

If, however, we lean to the belief that what happens to the parts will eventually happen to the whole, we are led to entertain the conception of Evolutions that have filled an immeasurable past and Evolutions that will fill an immeasurable future. We can no longer contemplate the visible creation as having a definite beginning or end, or as being isolated. It becomes unified with all existence before and after; and the Force which the Universe presents, falls into the same category with its Space and Time, as admitting of no limitation in thought.

This conception is congruous with the conclusion reached in Part I., where we dealt with the relation between the Knowable and the Unknowable.

It was there shown by analysis of both religious and scientific ideas, that while knowledge of the Cause which produces effects on consciousness is impossible, the existence of a Cause for these effects is a datum of consciousness. Belief in a Power which transcends knowledge is that fundamental element in Religion which survives all its changes of form. This inexpugnable belief proved to be likewise that on which all exact Science is based. And this is also the implication to which we are now led back by our completed synthesis. The recognition of a persistent Force, ever changing its manifestations but unchanged in quantity throughout all past time and all future time, is that which we find alone makes possible each concrete interpretation, and at last unifies all concrete interpretations.

Towards some conclusion of this order, inquiry, scientific, metaphysical, and theological, has been, and still is, manifestly advancing. The coalescence of polytheistic conceptions into the monotheistic conception, and the reduction of the monotheistic conception to a more and more general form, in which personal superintendence becomes merged in universal immanence, clearly shows this advance. It is equally shown in the fading away of old theories about "essences," "potentialities," "occult virtues," &c.; in the abandonment of such doctrines as those of "Platonic Ideas," "Pre-established Harmonies," and the like; and in the tendency towards the identification of Being as present in consciousness, with Being as otherwise conditioned beyond consciousness. Still more conspicuous is it in the progress of Science, which, from the beginning, has been grouping isolated facts under laws, uniting special laws under more general laws, and so reaching on to laws of higher and higher generality; until the conception of universal laws has become familiar to it.

Unification being thus the characteristic of developing thought of all kinds, and eventual arrival at unity being fairly inferable, there arises yet a further support to our conclusion. Since, unless there is some other and higher unity, the unity we have reached must be that towards which developing thought tends.

Let no one suppose that any such implied degree of trustworthiness is alleged of the various minor propositions brought in illustration of the general argument. Such an assumption would be so manifestly absurd, that it seems scarcely needful to disclaim it. But the truth of the doctrine as a whole, is unaffected by errors in the details of its presentation. If it can be shown that the Persistence of Force is not a datum of consciousness; or if it can be shown that the several laws of force above specified are not corollaries from it; or if it can be shown that, given these laws, the re-distribution of Matter and Motion does not necessarily proceed as described; then, indeed, it will be shown that the theory of Evolution has not the high warrant claimed for it. But nothing short of this can invalidate the general conclusions arrived at.

JOHN FISKE

If one thinks of Plato, Aristotle, Hume, and Kant as philosophers of the first rank, and of, say, Schelling and Vico as philosophers of the second rank, then it is embarrassing to have to say where John Fiske (1842–1901) belongs. Yet he exerted a great deal of influence in America, chiefly because of his great power as a popularizer. It is true that Fiske's *Outlines of Cosmic Philosophy*, first published in 1874, contains views in sociology which anticipated some that Spencer later came to espouse, and it is true that even in his *Cosmic Philosophy*, Fiske was inclined to shy away from the more materialistic aspects of Spencer's thought.[1] But Fiske's views on the cosmos and on knowledge were Spencer's, and Fiske was at best a clear expositor of those views. He was a disciple of Spencer who added very little to his master's voice.

He was also a very loyal disciple, and in the selections

[1] Josiah Royce was inclined to give Fiske more credit in his *Introduction* to a posthumous reprint of Fiske's *Outlines of Cosmic Philosophy* (Cambridge, Mass., 1902), especially pp. xxxvii–xli. It should be remarked, however, that Royce, as a representative of a philosophy which he did not originate, had something of a stake in distinguishing between "disciples pure and simple" and disciples who add something to their master's doctrine. [M.W.]

below the reader will find Fiske comparing Spencer with Auguste Comte to the latter's detriment, because Comte "merged philosophy in logic" whereas Spencer wisely regarded philosophy as a synthetic discipline. According to Fiske, Comte not only treated philosophy as an Organon rather than as a Synthesis, but also lacked the imagination to appreciate certain scientific discoveries like the cell-doctrine of biology, inquiries into the origin of the human race, and the possibilities of stellar astronomy. Historians of philosophy will find it especially interesting to read Fiske's statements that Comte "did not really apprehend the distinction between metaphysics and science", and that "every hypothesis which went a little way beyond the limited science of his day be wrongly stigmatized as 'metaphysical'". They will also find it interesting to read what Fiske says about Spencer's fundamental principle. That is very reminiscent of Locke's views on the foundations of physics; for it is fair to say that Fiske regarded Spencer's law of the persistence of force as one of those self-evident principles upon which Locke had hoped, without success, to rest all of natural science. To this extent, Fiske was a rationalist in spite of his attachment to what Spencer called the "experience-hypothesis", in spite of insisting that knowledge of first principles is knowledge we have come to as a result of the experiences of numberless generations of our ancestors. It is not surprising, therefore, that Fiske sided with Spencer against John Stuart Mill, who commanded the support of Fiske's Cambridge contemporary and philosophical superior, Chauncey Wright. Wright, as we shall see in the next chapter, was much less respectful of Spencer than Fiske was—a fact which led Fiske to say after Wright's death: "Mr. Wright seems to have been fitted for the work of sceptical criticism or for the discovery of specific truths, rather than for the elaboration of a general system of philosophy".[2]

[2] *The Writings of John Fiske*, Volume XX, *Darwinism and Other Essays* (Cambridge, Mass., 1902), pp. 81–83.

Scientific Axioms [3]

. . . [T]he mental compulsion under which we accept mathematical truths is of precisely the same character as that under which we accept physical or chemical truths. Our conception of parallel lines—a conception which the Kantian admits to have been formed by experience—is a conception of lines which do not enclose space. And just as we found that, in order to imagine nitrogen supporting combustion, we were obliged to suppress the conception of nitrogen altogether and substitute for it some other conception, we also find that, in order to imagine two parallel lines enclosing a space, we must suppress the conception of parallel lines altogether, and substitute for it the conception of bent or converging lines. The two cases are exactly similar. In the one case, as in the other, our conceptions are but the registry of our experience, and can therefore be altered only by being temporarily annihilated. Our minds being that which intercourse with the environment—both their own intercourse and that of ancestral minds, as will be shown hereafter—has made them, it follows that our indestructible beliefs must be the registry of that intercourse, must be necessarily true, not because they are independent of experience, but because they are the only complete unqualified expression of it. . . .

It is indeed a popular misconception,—a misconception which lies at the bottom of that manner of philosophizing which is called Empiricism,—that nothing can be known to be true which cannot be demonstrated. To be convinced that this is a misconception, we need but to recollect what a demonstration is. Every demonstration consists, in the first place,

[3] The following selection is from Fiske's *Outlines of Cosmic Philosophy*, reprinted as Volumes XIII–XVI of *The Writings of John Fiske*. The selection is a combination of passages from Volume XIII, pp. 86–87 and pp. 91–92; and from Volume XIV, pp. 144–48.

of a series of steps in each of which the group of relations expressed in a proposition is included in some other and wider group of relations,—is seen to be like some other group previously constituted. Now if this process of inclusion is not to be carried on forever, we must come at last to some widest group,—to some generalization which cannot be included in any wider generalization, and of which we can only say that the truth which it expresses is so completely abstracted from perturbing conditions that it can be recognized by a simple act of consciousness as self-evident. If, for example, "we ascribe the flow of a river to the same force which causes the fall of a stone," and if, "in further explanation of a movement produced by gravitation in a direction almost horizontal, we cite the law that fluids subject to mechanical forces exert reactive forces which are equal in all directions," we are going through a process of demonstration,—we are including a special fact under a more general fact. If now we seek the warrant for this more general fact, and find it in that most general fact that force persists, we are still going through a process of demonstration. But if lastly we inquire for the warrant of this most general fact, we shall get no reply save that no alternative can be framed in thought. That force persists we are compelled to believe, since the proposition that force can arise out of nothing or can lapse into nothing is a verbal proposition which we can by no amount of effort translate into thought. Thus at the end of every demonstration we must reach an axiom for the truth of which our only test is the inconceivability of its negation. . . .

[T]he assertion that force is persistent is the fundamental axiom of physics: it is the deepest truth which analytic science can disclose. But now what warrant have we for this fundamental axiom? How do we know that force is persistent? If force is not persistent, if a single unit of force can ever be added to or subtracted from the sum total at any moment existing, our entire physical science is, as we have seen, a mere delusion. In such case, it is a delusion to believe that action and reaction are always equal, that the strongest bow, bent by the strongest muscles, will always send its arrow to the greatest distance if otherwise unimpeded—it is a delusion to believe that the pressure of the atmosphere and its temperature must always affect the height of enclosed columns of alcohol or mercury, or that a single molecule of nitrogen will always just suffice to saturate three molecules of chlorine. And this being the case, our concrete sciences also fall to the ground, and our confidence in the stability of nature is shown to be baseless; since for aught we can say to the contrary, the annihilation of a few units of the earth's centrifugal force may cause us to fall upon the sun to-morrow.

But how do we know that all science is not a delusion, since there still exist upon the earth's surface persons who will tell us that it is so? Why do we so obstinately refuse to doubt the constancy of the power manifested in nature? What proof have we that no force is ever created or destroyed?

Logically speaking, we have no proof. An axiom which lies below all framable propositions cannot be deductively demonstrated. Below the world stands the elephant on the back of the tortoise, and if under the tortoise we put the god Vishnu, where is Vishnu to get a foothold? Nor can our axiom be demonstrated inductively, without reasoning in a circle. We cannot adduce the observed equality of action and reaction in proof of the persistence of force, because this persistence is taken for granted in every observation by which the equality of action and reaction is determined. Obviously it is impossible to prove the truth of an axiom by any demonstration in every step of which the truth of the axiom must be assumed.

But these results need not surprise or disturb us. As we saw, when discussing the Test of Truth, the process of demonstration, which consists in continually "merging derivative truths in those wider and wider truths from which they are derived," must eventually reach a widest truth, which cannot be contained in or derived from any other. At the bottom of all demonstration there must lie an indemonstrable axiom. And the truth of this axiom can only be certified by the direct application of the test of inconceivability. We are compelled to believe in the persistence of force, because it is impossible to conceive a variation in the unit by which force is measured. It is impossible to conceive something becoming nothing or nothing becoming something, without establishing in thought an equation between something and nothing; and this cannot be done. That one is equal to zero is a proposition of which the subject and predicate will destroy each other sooner than be made to unite.

Thus the proof of our fundamental axiom is not logical, but psychological. And, as was formerly shown, this is the strongest possible kind of proof. Inasmuch as our capacity for conceiving any proposition is entirely dependent upon the manner in which objective experiences have registered themselves upon our minds, our utter inability to conceive a variation in the sum total of force implies that such variation is negatived by the whole history of the intercourse between the mind and its environment since intelligence first began. The inconceivability test of Kant and the experience test of Hume, when fused in this deeper synthesis, unite in declaring that the most irrefragable of truths is that which survives all possible changes in the conditions under which phenomena are manifested to us. The persistence of force, therefore, being an axiom which survives under all conditions cognizable by our intelligence, being indeed the ultimate test by which we are compelled to estimate the validity of any proposition whatever concerning any imaginable set of phenomena and under any conceivable circumstances, must be an axiom necessitated by the very constitution of the thinking mind, as perennial intercourse with the environment has moulded it. . . .

Spencer versus *Comte* [4]

. . . *Comte merged Philosophy in Logic.* Or, in other words, *from his point of view, Philosophy is not a Synthesis, but an Organon.* Nowhere in that portion of the "Philosophie Positive" which treats of the organization of the sciences, do we catch any glimpse of that Cosmic conception of the scope of philosophy. . . . For according to that conception, . . . philosophy is an all-comprehensive Synthesis of the doctrines and methods of science; a coherent body of theorems concerning the Cosmos, and concerning Man in his relations to the Cosmos of which he is part. Now, though Comte enriched mankind with a new conception of the aim, the methods, and the spirit of philosophy, he never even attempted to construct any such coherent body of theorems. He constructed a classification of the sciences and a general theory of scientific methods; but he did not extract from each science that quota of general doctrines which it might be made to contribute toward a universal doctrine, and then proceed to fuse these general doctrines into such a universal doctrine. From first to last, so far as the integration of science is concerned, his work was logical rather than philosophical. And here we shall do well to note an apparent confusion between these two points of view, which occurs in Mr. Mill's essay on Comte. "The philosophy of science," says Mr. Mill, "consists of two principal parts: the methods of investigation, and the requisites of proof. The one points out the roads by which the human intellect arrives at conclusions; the other, the mode of testing their evidence. The former, if complete, would be an

[4] The following selection is from Fiske's *Writings*, Volume XIV, pp. 88–101. In connection with Fiske's decided preference for Spencer over Comte, it is worth noting that the subtitle of Fiske's *Outlines of Cosmic Philosophy* was "Based on the Doctrine of Evolution, With Criticisms on the Positive Philosophy". [M.W.]

Organon of Discovery; the latter, of Proof." Now I call this an admirable definition; but it is not the definition of Philosophy, it is the definition of Logic. If we were to accept it as a definition of philosophy, we might admit that Comte constructed a philosophy; as it is, we can only admit that he constructed a logic, or general theory of methods. . . . But an Organon of Methods is one thing, and a Synthesis of Doctrines is another thing; and a system of philosophy which is to be regarded as a comprehensive theory of the universe must include both. Yet Comte never attempted any other synthesis than that wretched travesty which, with reference to the method employed in it, is aptly entitled "Synthèse Subjective."

Not only does Comte thus practically ignore the conception of philosophy as a Synthesis of the most general truths of science into a body of universal truths relating to the Cosmos as a whole, but there is reason to believe that had such a conception been distinctly brought before his mind, he would have explicitly condemned it as chimerical. In illustration of this I shall, at the risk of apparent digression, cite one of his conspicuous shortcomings which is peculiarly interesting, not only as throwing light upon his intellectual habits, but also as exemplifying the radical erroneousness of his views concerning the limits of philosophic inquiry. Professor Huxley calls attention to Comte's scornful repudiation of what is known as the "cell-doctrine" in anatomy and physiology. Comte characterized this doctrine as a melancholy instance of the abuse of microscopic investigation, a chimerical attempt to refer all tissues to a single primordial tissue, "formed by the unintelligible assemblage of a sort of organic monads, which are supposed to be the ultimate units of every living body." Now this "chimerical doctrine" is at the present day one of the fundamental doctrines of biology. Other instances are at hand, which Professor Huxley has not cited. For example, Comte condemned as vain and useless all inquiries into the origin of the human race, although, with an inconsistency not unusual with him, he was a warm advocate of that nebular hypothesis which seeks to account for the origin of the solar system. As these two orders of inquiry are philosophically precisely on a level with each other, the former being indeed the one for which we have now the more abundant material, the attempted distinction is proof of the vagueness with which Comte conceived the limits of philosophic inquiry. But what shall we say when we find him asserting the impossibility of a science of stellar astronomy? He tells us that we have not even the first datum for such a science, and in all probability shall never obtain that datum. Until we have ascertained the distance, and calculated the proper motion, of at least one or two fixed stars, we cannot be certain even that the law of gravitation holds in these distant regions. And the distance of a star we shall probably never be able even approximately to estimate. Thus wrote Comte in 1835. But events, with almost malicious rapidity, falsified his words. In less than four years, Bessel had measured the parallax of the star 61 Cygni,—the first of a brilliant series of discoveries which by this time have made the starry heavens comparatively familiar ground to us. What would Comte's scorn have been, had it been suggested to him that within a third of a century we should possess many of the data for a science of stellar chemistry; that we should be able to say, for instance, that Aldebaran contains sodium, magnesium, calcium, iron, bismuth, and antimony, or that all the stars hitherto observed with the spectroscope contain hydrogen, save ß Pegasi and *a* Orionis, which apparently do not! Or what would he have said, had it been told him that, by the aid of the same instrument which now enables us to make with perfect confidence these audacious assertions, we should be able to determine the proper motions of stars which present no parallax! No example could more forcibly illustrate the rashness of prophetically setting limits to the possible future advance of science. Here are truths which, within the memory of young men, seemed wholly out of the reach of observation, but which are already familiar, and will soon become an old story.

I believe it was Comte's neglect of psychological analysis which caused him to be thus over-conservative in accepting new discoveries, and over-confident in setting limits to scientific achievement. He did not clearly distinguish between the rashness of metaphysics and the well-founded boldness of science. He was deeply impressed with the futility of wasting time and mental energy in constructing unverifiable hypotheses; but he did not sufficiently distinguish between hypotheses which are temporarily unverifiable from present lack of the means of observation, and those which are permanently unverifiable from the very nature of the knowing process. There is no ground for supposing that Comte ever thoroughly understood *why* we cannot know the Absolute and the Infinite. He knew, as a matter of historical fact, that all attempts to obtain such knowledge had miserably failed, or ended in nothing better than vain verbal wranglings; but his ignorance of psychology was so great that he probably never knew, or cared to know, why it must necessarily be so. Had he ever once arrived at the knowledge that the process of knowing involves the cognition of likeness, difference, and relation, and that the Absolute, as presenting none of these elements, is trebly unknowable, he would never have confounded purely metaphysical hypotheses with those which are only premature but are nevertheless scientific. He would have seen, for instance, that our inability to say positively whether there are or are not living beings on Saturn results merely from our lack of sufficient data for a complete induction; whereas our inability to frame a tenable hypothesis concerning matter *per se* results from the eternal fact that we can know nothing save under the conditions prescribed by our mental structure. Could we contrive a telescope powerful enough to detect life, or the products of art, upon a distant planet, there is nothing in the constitution of our minds to prevent our appropriating such knowledge; but no patience of observation or cunning of experiment can ever enable us to know the merest pebble as it exists out of relation to our consciousness. Simple and obvious as this distinction appears, there is much reason to believe that Comte never understood it. He inveighs against inquiries into the proximate origin of organic life in exactly the same terms in which he condemns inquiries into the ultimate origin of the universe. He could not have done this had he perceived that the latter question is forever insoluble because it involves absolute beginning; whereas the former is merely a question of a particular combination of molecules, which we cannot solve at present only because we have not yet obtained the requisite knowledge of the interactions of molecular forces, and of the past physical condition of the earth's surface. In short, he would have seen that, while the human mind is utterly impotent in the presence of noumena, it is well-nigh omnipotent in the presence of phenomena. In science we may be said to advance by geometrical progression. Here, in the forty years which have elapsed since Comte wrote on physical science, it is hardly extravagant to say that the progress has been as great as during the seventeen hundred years between Hipparchos and Galileo. If then, in the three or four thousand years which have elapsed since Europe began to emerge from utter barbarism, we have reached a point at which we can begin to describe the chemical constitution of a heavenly body seventy thousand million miles distant, what may not science be destined to achieve in the next four thousand or forty thousand years? We may rest assured that the tale, if we could only read it, would far excel in strangeness anything in the "Arabian Nights" or in the mystic pages of the Bollandists.

But Comte did not understand all this. He, the great overthrower and superseder of metaphysics, did not really apprehend the distinction between metaphysics and science. Hence every hypothesis which went a little way beyond the limited science of his day he wrongly stigmatized as "metaphysical." Hence he heaped contumely upon the cell-doctrine, only three years before Schwann and Schleiden finally established it. And hence, when he had occasion to observe that certain facts were not yet known, he generally added, "and probably they never will be,"—though his prophecy was not seldom confuted, while yet warm from the press.

Toward the close of his life, after he had become sacerdotally inclined, this tendency assumed a moral aspect. These remote and audacious inquiries into the movements of stars, and the development of cellular tissue, and the origin of species should not only be pronounced fruitless, but should be frowned upon and discountenanced by public opinion, as a pernicious waste of time and energy, which might better be devoted to nearer and more practical objects. It is a curious illustration of the effects of discipleship upon the mind, that several of Comte's disciples—Dr. Bridges among others less distinguished—maintain this same opinion, for no earthly reason, I imagine, save that Comte held it. It is certainly a strange opinion for a philosopher to hold. It bears an unlovely resemblance to the prejudice of the Philistines, that all speculation is foolish and empty which does not speedily end in bread-and-butter knowledge. Who can decide what is useful and what is useless? We are told first that we shall never know the distance to a star, and secondly that even if we could know it, the knowledge would be useless, since human interests are at the uttermost bounded by the solar system. Three years suffice to disprove the first part of the prediction. In a little while the second part may also be disproved. We are told by Comte that it makes no difference to us whether organic species are fixed or variable; and yet, as the Darwinian controversy has shown, the decision of this question must affect from beginning to end our general conception of physiology, of psychology, and of history, as well as our estimate of theology. If it were not universally felt to be of practical consequence, it would be argued calmly, and not with the weapons of ridicule and the *odium theologicum*. But this position—the least defensible one which Comte ever occupied—may best be refuted by his own words, written in a healthier frame of mind. "The most important practical results continually flow from theories formed purely with scientific intent, and which have sometimes been pursued for ages without any practical result. A remarkable example is furnished by the beautiful researches of the Greek geometers upon conic sections, which, after a long series of generations, have renovated the science of astronomy, and thus brought the art of navigation to a pitch of perfection which it could never have reached but for the purely theoretic inquiries of Archimedes and Apollonios. As Condorcet well observes, the sailor, whom an exact calculation of longitude preserves from shipwreck, owes his life to a theory conceived two thousand years ago by men of genius who were thinking of nothing but lines and angles." This is the true view; and we need not fear that the scientific world will ever adopt any other. That inborn curiosity which, according to the Hebrew legend, has already made us like gods, knowing good and evil, will continue to inspire us until the last secret of Nature is laid bare; and doubtless, in the untiring search, we shall uncover many priceless jewels, in places where we least expected to find them.

The foregoing examples will suffice to illustrate the vagueness with which Comte conceived the limits of scientific and of philosophic inquiry. I have here cited them, not so much for the sake of exhibiting Comte's mental idiosyncrasies, as for the sake of emphasizing the radical difference between his conception of the scope of philosophy and the conception upon which the Cosmic Philosophy is founded. In giving to Comte the credit which he deserves, for having heralded a new era of speculation in which philosophy should be built up entirely out of scientific materials, we must not forget that his conception of the kind of philosophy thus to be built up was utterly and hopelessly erroneous. Though he insisted upon the all-important truth that philosophy is simply a higher organization of scientific doctrines and methods, he fell into the error of regarding philosophy merely as a logical Organon of the sciences, and he never framed the conception of philosophy as a Universal Science in which the widest truths obtainable by the several sciences are contemplated to-gether as corollaries of a single ultimate truth. Not only did he never frame such a conception, but there can be no doubt that, had it ever been presented to him in all its complete-ness, he would have heaped opprobrium upon it as a meta-physical conception utterly foreign to the spirit of Positive Philosophy. We have just seen him resolutely setting his face against those very scientific speculations to which this con-ception of the scope of philosophy owes its origin; and we need find no difficulty in believing Dr. Bridges when he says that the Doctrine of Evolution would have appeared to his master quite as chimerical as the theories by which Thales and other Greek cosmogonists "sought to deduce all things from the principle of Water or of Fire."

Thus in a way that one would hardly have anticipated, we have disclosed a fundamental and pervading difference be-tween the Positive and the Cosmic conceptions of philosophy. . . . That [Comte's] conception of Philosophy as an Organon was a noble conception, there is no doubt; but that it was radically different from our conception of Philosophy as a Synthesis, is equally undeniable. . . .

CHAUNCEY WRIGHT

After more than a hundred years of Lockeian intuition and anti-Lockeian sentiment, at least one American philosopher rejected both of them as avenues to knowledge when Chauncey Wright (1830–1875) became a follower of John Stuart Mill and Charles Darwin. Acceptance of Mill's thoroughgoing empiricism led Wright to hold that *all* our knowledge is based on experience, including our logical and mathematical knowledge; and agreement with Darwin strengthened Wright's anti-Coleridgian, anti-Transcendentalist conviction that men differ from the brutes only in degree. Wright felt little sympathy with the Lockeian idea that mathematics, morality, and theology rest on self-evident principles; little sympathy with the Germano-Coleridgian view that the Reason is the faculty for perceiving necessary truth; and great antipathy to Scottish intuitionism. On the other hand, Wright was not prepared to use science in behalf of religion in the manner of Paley, nor was he willing to follow Herbert Spencer in regarding philosophy as a super-science which derives all of ordinary science—and especially Darwinian biology—from the conservation principles of physics. For all of these reasons, Wright was an intellectually lonely American in the second

third of the nineteenth century. His friendship with Darwin
and his attachment to John Stuart Mill did not diminish his
sense of intellectual isolation, for in spite of the greatness of
these two Englishmen, most American thinkers were not yet
ready for natural selection and utilitarianism. Those doctrines
were too empirical for most Transcendentalists, and not sufficiently architectonic for readers who liked to sprawl in Spencer's well-upholstered philosophical ark. Wright did not make
himself any more popular by adopting a variety of religious
agnosticism. He held that we cannot know, but at best have
faith in, the existence of God; that faith is a form of sentiment; and that sentiment is radically different from knowledge.

A century after his death, Wright is best viewed as
a clear-headed, scientifically knowledgeable spokesman for
Millian empiricism in philosophy and Darwinism in biology.
He has been called a pragmatist for saying that scientific laws
are "finders, not merely summaries of truth", but such a classification of Wright is not defensible if we identify pragmatism with Peirce's theory of meaning or with James' theory of
truth. Wright is more accurately regarded as an empiricist
who rejected the intuitionism which had become traditionally American by his time; who pricked the bubbles of natural religion and Spencerian super-science; who showed philosophers the great virtues of Darwinian biology; and who
also showed them the importance of learning the details of
science before becoming philosophers of science. His best
writings were primarily critical, deflationary, and monitory;
and he helped remove rubbish from the paths of the master-
builders who followed him, notably his younger Cambridge
friends, Charles Peirce and William James. In the first set of
selections below, Wright argues that Spencer, by lifting scientific terms from their original contexts into his rarefied philosophy, had distorted their meaning; and in the second,
Wright tries to show how critics of Darwinian biology had
failed to understand the notion of accidental variation as well

as the important distinction between the real kinds of Mill's logic and the real species of Linnaean biology.

Against Spencer [1]

It is the opinion of many modern thinkers, besides the so-called Positivists, or avowed followers of M. Comte, that science, as we have defined it, or truth pursued simply in the interests of a rational curiosity, and for the mental discipline and the material utilities of its processes and conclusions, will hereafter occupy more and more the attention of mankind, to the exclusion of the older philosophy. It is also the opinion of these thinkers, that this is not to be regretted, but rather welcomed as a step forward in the advancement of human welfare and civilization; that the pursuit of science and its utilities is capable of inspiring as great and earnest a devotion as those which religious interests have inspired, and which have hitherto determined the destinies of mankind and given form to human thought, and one vastly more beneficent.

Whatever foundations there are for these opinions, it is certain that the claims of science, as a new power in the world, to the regard of thoughtful and earnest men, are receiving a renewed and more candid attention. Through its recent progress, many of the questions which have hitherto remained in the arena of metaphysical disputation are brought forward in new forms and under new auspices. Scientific investigations promise to throw a flood of light on subjects which have interested mankind since the beginning of speculation,—subjects related to universal human interests. History, society, laws, and morality,—all are claimed as topics

---

[1] This selection is made from Wright's long article-review of eight books by Herbert Spencer, "The Philosophy of Herbert Spencer", *The North American Review,* Volume 100 (April 1865). The selection combines passages on pp. 434–36 and pp. 449–60 of that volume. This article-review is reprinted in Chauncey Wright, *Philosophical Discussions,* edited by Charles Eliot Norton (New York, 1877).

with which scientific methods are competent to deal. Scientific solutions are proposed to all the questions of philosophy which scientific illumination may not show to have their origin in metaphysical hallucination.

Prominent in the ranks of the new school stands Mr. Herbert Spencer, whose versatility has already given to the world many ingenious and original essays in this new philosophy, and whose aspiring genius projects many more, which, if his strength does not fail, are to develop the capacities of a scientific method in dealing with all the problems that ought legitimately to interest the human mind.

The programme of his future labors which his publishers have advertised might dispose a prejudiced critic to look with suspicion on what he has already accomplished; but the favorable impression which his works have made, and the plaudits of an admiring public, demand a suspension of judgment; and the extravagance of his pretensions should for the present be credited to the strength of his enthusiasm.

It is through the past labors of an author that we must judge of his qualifications for future work, and the completeness of his preparation. Mr. Spencer's writings evince an extensive knowledge of facts political and scientific, but extensive rather than profound, and all at second hand. It is not, of course, to be expected that a philosopher will be an original investigator in all the departments of knowledge with which he is obliged to have dealings. He must take much at second hand. But original investigations in some department of empirical science are a discipline which best tests and develops even a philosopher's powers. He has in this at least an experience of what is requisite to an adequate comprehension of facts. He learns how to make knowledge profitable to the ascertainment of new truths,—an art in which the modern natural philosopher excels. By new truths must be understood such as are not implied in what we already know, or educible from what is patent to common observation. However skilfully the philosopher may apply his analytical processes to the abstraction of the truths involved in patent facts, the utility of his results will depend not so much on their value and extent as mere abstractions, as on their capacity to enlarge our experience by bringing to notice residual phenomena, and making us observe what we have entirely overlooked, or search out what has eluded our observation. Such is the character of the principles of modern natural philosophy, both mathematical and physical. They are rather the eyes with which nature is seen, than the elements and constituents of the objects discovered. It was in a clear apprehension of this value in the principles of mathematical and experimental science, that the excellence of Newton's genius consisted; and it is this value which the Positive Philosophy most prizes. But this is not the value which we find in Mr. Spencer's speculations.

Mr. Spencer is not a positivist, though that was not a very culpable mistake which confounded his speculations with the writings of this school. For however much he differs from the positivists in his methods and opinions, he is actuated by the same confidence in the capacities of a scientific method, and by the same disrespect for the older philosophies. Mr. Spencer applies a method for the ascertainment of ultimate truths, which a positivist would regard as correct only on the supposition that the materials of truth have all been collected, and that the research of science is no longer for the enlargement of our experience or for the informing of the mind. Until these conditions be realized, the positivist regards such attempts as Mr. Spencer's as not only faulty, but positively pernicious and misleading. Nothing justifies the development of abstract principles in science but their utility in enlarging our concrete knowledge of nature. The ideas on which mathematical Mechanics and the Calculus are founded, the morphological ideas of Natural History, and the theories of Chemistry are such working ideas,—finders, not merely summaries of truth. . . .

The idea which has exercised the profoundest influence on

the course of Mr. Spencer's thought, as well as on all thought in modern times, and one which appears more or less distinctly in nearly all of Mr. Spencer's writings, is the idea which he elaborates in his First Principles as the "Law of Evolution." But what is the origin and value of this idea? Ostensibly it was derived from the investigations of the physiologists in embryology, from Harvey down to the present time. The formula of Von Baer was the first adequate statement of it. This formula Mr. Spencer has elaborated and completed, so as to apply, he thinks, not only to the phenomena of embryology, but to the phenomena of nature generally, and especially, as it appears, to those which we know least about, and to those which we only guess at.

But while this is the ostensible origin and scientific value of this idea, its real origin is a very curious and instructive fact in human nature. Progress is a grand idea,—Universal Progress is a still grander idea. It strikes the key-note of modern civilization. Moral idealism is the religion of our times. What the ideas God, the One and the All, the Infinite First Cause, were to an earlier civilization, such are Progress and Universal Progress to the modern world,—a reflex of its moral ideas and feelings, and not a tradition. Men ever worship the Best, and the consciousness that the Best is attainable is the highest moral consciousness, the most inspiring of truths. And when indications of that attainment are visible not merely to the eye of faith, but in sensible progress, scientifically measurable, civilization is inspired with a new devotion. Faith that moral perfectibility is possible, not in remote times and places, not in the millennium, not in heaven, but in the furtherance of a present progress, is a faith which to possess in modern times does not make a man suspected of folly or fanaticism. He may forget the past, cease to be religious in the conventional sense of the word, but he is the modern prophet.

When Plato forsook the scientific studies of his youth, and found the truest interpretation of nature by asking his own mind what was the best, according to which, he felt sure, the order and framework of nature must be determined, he did but illustrate the influence which strongly impressed moral ideas have on speculative thought at all times; but he did it consciously and avowedly. Modern thinkers may be less conscious of this influence, may endeavor to suppress what consciousness they have of it, warned by the history of philosophy that teleological speculations are exploded follies; nevertheless, the influence surrounds and penetrates them like an atmosphere, unless they be moral phlegmatics and mere lookers-on.

It was Mr. Spencer's aim to free the law of evolution from all teleological implications, and to add such elements and limitations to its definition as should make it universally applicable to the movement of nature. Having done this, as he thinks, he arrives at the following definition: "Evolution is a change from an indefinite incoherent homogeneity to a definite coherent heterogeneity through continuous differentiations and integrations." But teleology is a subtile poison, and lurks where least suspected. The facts of the sciences which Dr. Whewell calls palaetiological, [2] like the various branches of geology, and every actual concrete series of events which together form an object of interest to us, are apt, unless we are fully acquainted with the actual details through observation or by actual particular deductions from well-known particular facts and general laws, to fall into a dramatic procession in our imaginations. The mythic instinct slips into the place of the chronicles at every opportunity. All history is written on dramatic principles. All cosmological speculations are strictly teleological. We never can comprehend the whole of a concrete series of events. What arrests our attention in it is what constitutes the parts of an *order* either real or imagi-

[2] According to William Whewell (1794–1866), palaetiological sciences are those which try to explain actual past events by laws of causation. See his *History of the Inductive Sciences* (London, 1847), Volume III, Book XVIII. [M.W.]

nary, and all merely imaginary orders are dramatic, or are determined by interests which are spontaneous in human life. Our speculations about what we have not really observed, to which we supply the order and most of the facts, are necessarily determined by some principle of order in our minds. Now the most general principle which we can have, included by all others, is this: that the concrete series shall be an intelligible series in its entirety, shall only interest and attract our thoughts and a rational curiosity.

But to suppose that such series exist anywhere but where observation and legitimate particular inferences from observation warrant the supposition, is to commit the same mistake which has given rise to teleological theories of nature. The "law of causation," the postulate of positive science, does not go to this extent. It does not suppose that there are throughout nature unbroken series in causation, forming in their entirety intelligible wholes, determinable in their beginnings, their progressions, and their ends, with a birth, a growth, a maturation, and a decay. It only presumes that the perhaps unintelligible wholes, both in the sequences and the coexistences of natural phenomena, are composed of intelligible elements; that chaos does not subsist at the heart of things; that the order in nature which is discernible vaguely even to the unobservant implies at least a precise *elementary* order, or fixed relations of antecedents and consequents in its ultimate parts and constituents; that the apparently irregular heterogeneous masses, the concrete series of events, are crystalline in their substance.

To discover these elementary fixed relations of antecedents and consequents, is the work of scientific induction; and the only postulate of science is, that these relations are everywhere to be found. To account, as far as possible, for any concrete order, like that of life, intelligible as a whole, or regular, is the work of scientific explanation, by deductions from the elementary fixed relations which induction may have discovered. But to explain any such order by simply defining it

externally in vague, abstract terms, and to postulate such orders as the components of nature and parts of one complete
and intelligible order, is to take a step in advance of legitimate speculation, and a step backward in scientific method,
—is to commit the mistake of the ancient philosophies of nature.

But Mr. Spencer thinks he has established his "Law of
Evolution" by induction. The examples from which he has
analyzed his law, the examples of progress in the development of the several elements of civilization, such as languages, laws, fashions, and ideas,—the hypothetical examples
of the Nebular Hypothesis and the Development Hypothesis,
and the example of embryological development (the only one
our conceptions of which are not liable to be tainted by teleological biases),—are examples which, according to Mr.
Spencer's philosophy, afford both the definition and its justification. In other words, his definitions are only carefully elaborated general descriptions in abstract terms; or statements
of facts which are observed in numerous instances or classes
of instances, in terms detached from all objects, in abstract
terms, of which the intension is fully known, but of which the
extension is unknown except through the descriptions they
embody. This, though a useful, is a precarious kind of induction, and is apt to lead to premature and false generalizations, or extensions of descriptions to what is hypothetical or
unknown. Such inductions are liable to be mistaken for another sort, and to be regarded as not merely general, but universal descriptions, and as applicable to what they do not
really apply to. This liability is strong just in proportion as
prominence is given to such definitions in a philosophical system. No convert to Mr. Spencer's philosophy doubts the sub-
stantial correctness of the Nebular and Development Hypotheses, though these are only hypothetical examples of Mr.
Spencer's law.

The other sort of inductions to which we have referred are
peculiar to the exact inductive sciences. Facts which are not

merely general, but, from their elementary character and their immediate relations to the orderliness of nature, are presumed to be universal facts, are the sort which the positive philosophy most prizes, and of which the law of gravitation is the typical example. The honor must be conceded to Mr. Spencer of having elaborated a precise and very abstract description of certain phenomena, the number, the other characters, and the extent of which are, however, unknown, but are all the more imposing from this circumstance.

The law of gravity was a key which deciphered a vast body of otherwise obscure phenomena, and (what is more to the purpose) was successfully applied to the solution of all the problems these phenomena presented. It is common to ascribe to Newton the merit of having discovered the law of gravity, in the same sense in which Mr. Spencer may be said to have discovered his law. The justness of this praise may well be doubted; for others had speculated and defined the law of gravity before Newton. What he really discovered was the *universality* of this law, or so nearly discovered it that the astronomers who completed the investigation did not hesitate to concede to him the full honor. He established for it such a degree of probability that his successors pursued the verification with unhesitating confidence, and still pursue it in the fulness of faith.

Mr. Spencer's law is founded on examples, of which only one class, the facts of embryology, are properly scientific. The others are still debated as to their real characters. Theories of society and of the character and origin of social progress, theories on the origins and the changes of organic forms, and theories on the origins and the causes of cosmical bodies and their arrangements, are all liable to the taint of teleological and cosmological conceptions,—to spring from the order which the mind imposes upon what it imperfectly observes, rather than from that which the objects, were they better known, would supply to the mind.

To us Mr. Spencer's speculation seems but the abstract

statement of the cosmological conceptions, and that kind of orderliness which the human mind spontaneously supplies in the absence of facts sufficiently numerous and precise to justify sound scientific conclusions. Progress and development, when they mean more than a continuous proceeding, have a meaning suspiciously like what the moral and mythic instincts are inclined to,—something having a beginning, a middle, and an end,—an epic poem, a dramatic representation, a story, a cosmogony. It is not sufficient for the purposes of science that the idea of progress be freed from any reference to human happiness as an end. Teleology does not consist entirely of speculations having happy *dénouements*, save that the perfection or the end to which the progress tends is a happiness to the intellect that contemplates it in its evolution and beauty of orderliness. Plato's astronomical speculations were teleological in this artistic sense.

It is not sufficient for the purposes of science, that the idea of progress be thus purified; and it would be better if science itself were purified of this idea, at least until proof of its extent and reality be borne in upon the mind by the irresistible force of a truly scientific induction. Aristotle exhibited the characteristics of scientific genius in no way more distinctly than in the rejection of this idea, and of all cosmological speculations.

But there is a truth implied in this idea, and an important one,—the truth, namely, that the proper objects of scientific research are all of them processes and the results of processes; not the immutable natures which Plato sought for above a world of confusion and unreality, in the world of his own intelligence, but the immutable elements in the orders of all changes, the permanent relations of coexistences and sequences, which are hidden in the confusions of complex phenomena. Thought itself is a process and the mind a complex series of processes, the immutable elements of which must be discovered, not merely by introspection or by self-consciousness, but by the aid of physiological researches and by indirect observation. Everything out of the mind is a product, the result of some process. Nothing is exempt from change. Worlds are formed and dissipated. Races of organic beings grow up like their constituent individual members, and disappear like these. Nothing shows a trace of an original, immutable nature, except the unchangeable laws of change. These point to no beginning and to no end in time, nor to any bounds in space. All indications to the contrary in the results of physical research are clearly traceable to imperfections in our present knowledge of all the laws of change, and to that disposition to cosmological speculations which still prevails even in science.

We propound these doctrines not as established ones, but as having a warrant from the general results of physical research similar to that which the postulate of science, the law of causation, has in the vaguely discerned order in nature, which forces itself on the attention even of the unobservant. But as a mind unfamiliar with science is easily persuaded that there are phenomena in nature to which the law of causation does not apply, phenomena intrinsically arbitrary and capricious, so even to those most familiar with our present knowledge of physical laws, but who have not attended to the implication of their general characters and relations, the supposition is not incredible that there is a tendency in the forces of nature to a permanent or persistently progressive change in the theatre of their operations, and to an ultimate cessation of all the particular conditions on which their manifestations depend. To show why this is incredible to us would carry us beyond the proper limits of our subject, were it not that our author has speculated in the same direction.

Having developed what he thinks to be the true scientific idea of progress in his "Law of Evolution," Mr. Spencer next considers its relations to ultimate scientific ideas, the ideas of space, time, matter, and force. As evolution is change, and as change, scientifically comprehended, is comprehended in terms of matter, motion, and force, and the conditions necessary to these, or time and space, it is necessary that evolution be further defined in its relations to these ideas. These are only formulating terms, entirely abstract. They imply no ontological theory about the nature or existence of mind or matter; and when Mr. Spencer proposes to formulate the phenomena of mind as well as those of matter in terms of matter, motion, and force, it is because these ideas are the only precise ones in which the phenomena of change can be defined.

Mr. Spencer is not a materialist. Materialism and spiritualism, or psychological idealism, are as dogmatic theories equally self-contradictory and absurd. Mr. Spencer is neither a materialist nor an idealist; neither theist, atheist, nor pantheist. All these doctrines are, he thinks, without sense or reason; and the philosophers who invented them, and the disciples who received and thought they understood them, were deceived. But we are inclined to the opinion that believers, though they may be deceived about their ability to comprehend these theories (for it is easy to mistake meanings), are not deceived about the motives or the spirit which prompts these speculations, and which in fact determines for each his election of what doctrine best suits his character. For within the pale of philosophy, character determines belief, and ideas stand for feelings. We receive the truths of science on compulsion. Nothing but ignorance is able to resist them. In philosophy we are free from every bias, except that of our own characters; and it therefore seems to us becoming in a philosopher, who is solicitous about the moral reputation of his doctrines, who would avoid classification under disreputable categories, that he teach nothing which he does not know, lest the direction of his inquiries be mistaken for that of his dispositions. The vulgar who use these obnoxious terms, materialism, atheism, pantheism, do not pretend to define them; but they somehow have a very definite idea, or at least a strong feeling, about the dangerous character of such speculations, which are none the less reprehensible because inconceivable.

But we must defer the consideration of the moral character of Mr. Spencer's speculations, until we have further examined their scientific grounds.

Terms which the real physicist knows how to use as the terms of mathematical formulas, and which were never even suspected of any heterodox tendencies, terms which have been of inestimable service both in formulating and finding out the secrets of nature, are appropriated by Mr. Spencer to the further elaboration of his vague definitions, and to the abstract description of as much in real nature as they may happen to apply to. As if an inventory of the tools of any craft were a proper account of its handiwork! Out of mathematical formulas these terms lose their definiteness and their utility. They become corrupting and misleading ideas. They are none the less abstract, but they are less clear. They again clothe themselves in circumstance, though vaguely. They appeal to that indefinite consciousness which, as Mr. Spencer says, cannot be formulated, but in which he thinks we have an apprehension of cause and causal agencies.

> "Though along with the extension of generalizations, and concomitant integrations of conceived causal agencies," says Mr. Spencer, "the conceptions of causal agencies grow more indefinite; and though as they gradually coalesce into a universal causal agency they cease to be representable in thought, and are no longer supposed to be comprehensible, yet the consciousness of *cause* remains as dominant to the last as it was at first, and can never be got rid of. The consciousness of cause can be abolished only by abolishing consciousness itself."

This is quoted by himself from his "First Principles," as one of his "reasons for dissenting from the philosophy of M. Comte." Though he seems solicitous to avoid all ontological implications in his use of scientific terms, yet we cannot avoid the impression of a vague metaphysical signification in his speculations, as if he were presenting all the parts of a system of materialism except the affirmative and negative copulas. These are withheld, because we cannot be supposed to believe anything inconceivable, as all ontological dogmas are. He seems to lead us on to the point of requiring our assent to a materialistic doctrine, and then lets us off on account of the infirmities of our minds; presenting materialism to our contemplation rather than to our understandings.

Mr. Spencer regards the ultimate ideas of science as unknowable; and in a sense the meanings of the abstractest terms are unknowable, that is, are not referable to any notions more abstract, nor susceptible of sensuous apprehension or representation as such. But the way to know them is to use them in mathematical formulas to express precisely what we do know. It is true that this cannot yet be done, except in the physical sciences proper, and not always with distinctness in these. It is only in astronomy and mechanical physics that these terms are used with mathematical precision. They change their meanings, or at least lose their definiteness, when we come to chemistry and physiology.

"The indestructibility of matter," "the continuity of motion," "the conservation of force," and "the correlation and equivalence of forces," are ideas which mathematical and physical science has rendered familiar. Beside these, Mr. Spencer has analyzed others, descriptive of the general external characteristics of motion; and he continues with a development of what the Law of Evolution implies. To all the ideas which he adopts from science he adds a new sense, or rather a vagueness, so as to make them descriptive of as much as possible. One of these ideas loses in the process so many of its original features, as well as its name, that we should not have recognized it as the same, but for Mr. Spencer's justification of what he regards as a change of nomenclature. He prefers "persistence of force" to "conservation of force," because the latter "implies a conservator and an act of conserving," and because "it does not imply the existence of the force before that particular manifestation of it with which we commence." Science, we are inclined to believe, will not adopt this emendation, because the conservation it refers to is that whereby the special conditions of the production of any mechanical effect in nature are themselves replaced by the changes through which this effect is manifested; so that if this effect ceases to appear as a motion, it nevertheless exists in the altered antecedents of motions, which may subsequently be developed in the course of natural changes. It is this conservation of the conditions of motion by the operations of nature through the strictest observation of certain mathematical laws, that science wishes to express. The objection (if there be any) to this phrase is in the word "force." This word is used in mathematical mechanics in three different senses, but fortunately they are distinct. They are not here fused together, as they are by Mr. Spencer, into one vague expression of what nobody in fact knows anything about. There is no danger of ambiguities arising from this source in mathematics. The ideas expressed by this word are perfectly distinct and definable. The liability to ambiguity is only when we pass from mathematical formulas to sciences, in which the word has more or less of vagueness and an ontological reference. This liability is somewhat diminished, at least so far as distinct mathematical comprehension is concerned, by the use of the phrases, "conservation of mechanical effect" or "the law of power," which are now employed to express the mathematical theorem which has as one of its corollaries the doctrine that "perpetual motion" is impossible in the sense in which practical mechanics use the words. This theorem is deduced from the fundamental laws of motion, or those transcendental ideas and definitions which have received their proof or justification in their ability to clear up the confusions with which the movements of nature fall upon the senses and present themselves to the undisciplined understanding.

242 Documents in the History of American Philosophy

The phrase "conservation of force" was adopted from mathematical mechanics into chemical physics, with reference to the question of the possibility of "perpetual motion" by means of those natural forces with which chemistry deals. The impossibility of "perpetual motion," or the fact that "in the series of natural processes there is no circuit to be found by which mechanical force can be gained without a corresponding consumption," had been demonstrated only with reference to the so-called "fixed forces" of nature, or those which depend solely on the relative distances of bodies from each other. Chemical forces are not mathematically comprehended, and are therefore utterly unknown, save in their effects, and their laws are unknown, save in the observed invariable orders of these effects. These forces are merely hypotheses, and hypotheses which include little or nothing that is definite or profitable to research. But mechanical forces suggested to physicists a problem perfectly clear and definite. "Are the laws of chemical forces also inconsistent with 'perpetual motion'?" "Are light, heat, electricity, magnetism, and the force of chemical transformations, correlated with each other, and with mechanical motions and forces, as these are among themselves?" Here is something tangible; and the direction which these questions have given to physical researches in recent times mark out a distinct epoch in scientific progress. Here the answer could not be found *a priori*, as a consequent of any known or presumed universal laws of nature. Experiment must establish these presumptions; and it does so with such an overwhelming amount of evidence, that they are made the grounds of prediction, as the law of gravity was in the discovery of the planet Uranus. Physicists have anticipated, on the ground of the impossibility of perpetual motion, such an apparently remote fact as this, "that the freezing temperature in water depends on the pressure to which the water is subjected." Experiment confirms this anticipation.

The processes of such researches are long and intricate, but they are perfectly precise and definite; and it is thus that the law of the "Conservation of Force" is made of value, and not by such use as Mr. Spencer is able to make of it, if indeed his "Persistence of Force" can be regarded as having any meaning in common with it. His principle seems to us to bear a much closer resemblance to the old metaphysical "Principle of Causality," or the impossibility of any change in the quantity of existence (whatever this may mean); and it also seems to us to be as profitless. . . .

In Defense of Darwin
SO-CALLED ACCIDENTAL VARIATIONS
ARE NOT UNCAUSED [3]

. . . There are many facts of variation, numerous cases of abrupt changes in individuals both of natural and domesticated species, which, of course, no Darwinian or physiologist denies, and of which Natural Selection professes to offer no direct explanation. The causes of these phenomena, and their relations to external conditions of existence, are matters quite independent of the principle of Natural Selection, except so far as they may directly affect the animal's or plant's well-being, with the origin of which this principle is alone concerned. . . . The almost universal prevalence of well-marked phenomena of variation in species, the absolutely universal fact that no two individual organisms are exactly alike, and that the description of a species is necessarily abstract and in

[3] This selection is made from Wright's "The Genesis of Species", *The North American Review*, Volume 113 (July 1871), pp. 67–69; p. 78. This is an article-review of the fifth edition of Darwin's *Origin of Species*, of the first edition of Darwin's *The Descent of Man*, of Alfred Russel Wallace's *Contributions to the Theory of Natural Selection*, and of St. George Mivart's *On the Genesis of Species*. The review is reprinted in Wright's *Philosophical Discussions*.

many respects by means of averages,—these facts have received no particular explanations, and might indeed be taken as ultimate facts or highest laws in themselves, were it not that in biological speculations such an assumption would be likely to be misunderstood, as denying the existence of any real determining causes and more ultimate laws, as well as denying any known antecedents or regularities in such phenomena. No physical naturalist would for a moment be liable to such a misunderstanding, but would, on the contrary, be more likely to be off his guard against the possibility of it in minds otherwise trained and habituated to a different kind of studies. Mr. Darwin has undoubtedly erred in this respect. He has not in his works repeated with sufficient frequency his faith in the universality of the law of causation, in the phenomena of general physiology or theoretical biology, as well as in all the rest of physical nature. He has not said often enough, it would appear, that in referring any effect to "accident," he only means that its causes are like particular phases of the weather, or like innumerable phenomena in the concrete course of nature generally, which are quite beyond the power of finite minds to anticipate or to account for in detail, though none the less really determinate or due to regular causes. That he has committed this error appears from the fact that his critic, Mr. Mivart, has made the mistake, which nullifies nearly the whole of his criticism, of supposing that "the theory of Natural Selection may (though it need not) be taken in such a way as to lead men to regard the present organic world as formed, so to speak, *accidentally*, beautiful and wonderful as is confessedly the hap-hazard result." Mr. Mivart, like many another writer, seems to forget the age of the world in which he lives and for which he writes,—the age of "experimental philosophy," the very stand-point of which, its fundamental assumption, is the universality of physical causation. This is so familiar to minds bred in physical studies, that they rarely imagine that they may be mistaken for disciples of Democritus, or for believers in "the fortuitous concourse of atoms," in the sense, at least, which theology has attached to this phrase. If they assent to the truth that may have been meant by the phrase, they would not for a moment suppose that the atoms move fortuitously, but only that their conjunctions, constituting the actual concrete orders of events, could not be anticipated except by a knowledge of the natures and regular histories of each and all of them,—such knowledge as belongs only to omniscience. The very hope of experimental philosophy, its expectation of constructing the sciences into a true philosophy of nature, is based on the induction, or, if you please, the *a priori* presumption, that physical causation is universal; that the constitution of nature is written in its actual manifestations, and needs only to be deciphered by experimental and inductive research; that it is not a latent invisible writing, to be brought out by the magic of mental anticipation or metaphysical meditation. Or, as Bacon said, it is not by the "anticipations of the mind," but by the "interpretation of nature," that natural philosophy is to be constituted; and this is to presume that the order of nature is decipherable, or that causation is everywhere either manifest or hidden, but never absent. . . .

The accidental causes of science are only "accidents" relatively to the intelligence of a man. Eclipses have the least of this character to the astronomer of all the phenomena of nature; yet to the savage they are the most terrible of monstrous accidents. The accidents of monstrous variation, or even of the small and limited variations normal in any race or species, are only accidents relatively to the intelligence of the naturalist, or to his knowledge of general physiology. An accident is what cannot be anticipated from what we know, or by any intelligence, perhaps, which is less than omniscient. . . .

REAL KINDS VERSUS FIXED SPECIES [4]

. . . It was not many years ago that a distinguished writer in criticising the views of Lamarck affirmed that "the majority of naturalists agree with Linnæus in supposing that all the individuals propagated from one stock have certain distinguishing characters in common, which never vary, and which have remained the same since the creation of each species." The influence of this opinion still remains, even with naturalists who would hesitate to assert categorically the opinion itself. This comes, doubtless, from the fact that long-prevalent doctrines often get stamped into the very meanings of words, and thus acquire the character of axioms. The word "species" became synonymous with *real* or *fixed* species, or these adjectives became pleonastic. And this was from the mere force of repetition, and without valid foundation, in fact, or confirmation from proper inductive evidence.

Natural selection does not, of course, account for a fixity that does not exist, but only for the adaptations and the diversities in species, which may or may not be changing at any time. They are fixed only as the "fixed" stars are fixed, of which very many are now known to be slowly moving. Their fixity, when they are fixed, is temporary and through the accident of unchanging external conditions. Such is at least the assumption of the theory of natural selection. Mr. Mivart's theory seems to assume, on the other hand, that unless a species or a character is tied to something it will run away; that there is a necessity for some internal bond to hold it, at least temporarily, or so long as it remains the *same* species. He is entitled, it is true, to challenge the theory of natural selection for proofs of its assumption, that "fixity" is not an essential

---

[4] This selection is made from Wright's "Evolution by Natural Selection", *The North American Review*, Volume 115 (July 1872), pp. 14–19. This is an article-review of the sixth edition of Darwin's *Origin of Species* and of two short pieces by Mivart. The review is reprinted in Wright's *Philosophical Discussions*.

feature of natural species; for, in fact, so far as direct evidence is concerned, this is an open question. Its decision must depend chiefly on the preponderance of indirect and probable evidences in the interpretation of the "geological record," a subject to which much space is devoted, in accordance with its importance, in the "Origin of Species." Technical questions on the classification and description of species afford other evidences, and it is asserted by naturalists that a very large number of specimens, say ten thousand, is sufficient, in some departments of natural history, to break down any definition or discrimination even of living species. Other evidences are afforded by the phenomena of variation under domestication. Mr. Mivart had the right, and may still have it, to resist all this evidence, as not conclusive; but he is not entitled to call upon the theory of natural selection for an explanation of a feature in organic structures which the theory denies in its very elements, the *fixity* of species. . . .

The question of zoölogical philosophy, "Whether species have a real existence in nature," in the decision of which naturalists have so generally agreed with Linnæus, refers directly and explicitly to this question of the fixity of essential characters, and to the assumption that species must remain unaltered in these respects so long as they continue to exist, or until they give birth to new species; or, as was formerly believed, give place in perishing to new independent creations. The distinction involved in this question should not be confounded, as it might easily be, with the distinction in Logic of "real kinds" from other class-names. Logic recognizes a principal division in class-names, according as these are the names of objects which agree with each other and differ from other objects in a very large and indefinite number of particulars or attributes, or are the names of objects which agree only in a few and a definite number of attributes.[5] The

[5] See J. S. Mill, *A System of Logic* (London, 1947), Book I, Chapter VII, Section 4. [M.W.]

former are the names of "real kinds," and include the names of natural species, as man, horse, etc., and of natural genera, as whale, oak, etc. These classes are "real kinds," not because the innumerable particulars in which the individual members of them agree with each other and differ from the members of other classes, are themselves fixed or invariable in time, but because this sort of agreement and difference is fixed or continues to appear. An individual hipparion resembled its immediate parents and the other offspring of them as closely as, or, at least, in the same intimate manner in which one horse resembles another, namely, in innumerable details. But this is not opposed to the conception that the horse is descended from the hipparion by insensible steps of gradation or continuously. For examples of names that are not the names of "real kinds," we may instance such objects as those that are an inch in length, or in breadth, or are colored black, or are square, or (combining these particulars) such objects as black square inches. These may be made of paper, or wood, or ivory, or differ in all other respects except the enumerated and definite particulars. They are not "real" or natural "kinds," but factitious ones.

The confusion which, as we have said, might arise between the "real kinds" of Logic, and the *real* species of biological speculation, would depend on a vagueness in the significance of the word "real," which in common usage combines in uncertain proportions two elementary and more precise ideas, that of fixedness and that of breadth of relationship. Both these marks of reality are applied habitually as tests of it. Thus if an object attests its existence to several of my senses, is seen, heard, touched, and varied in its relations to these senses, and moreover is similarly related to the senses of another person, as evinced by his testimony, then I know that the object is real, and not a mere hallucination or invention of my fantasy; though it may disappear immediately afterwards in an unexplained manner, or be removed by some unknown but supposable agency. Here the judgment of reality depends on breadth of relationship to my experience and sources of knowledge. Or again I may only *see* the object, and consult no other eyes than my own; but seeing it often, day after day, in the same place, I shall judge it a real object, provided its existence is conformable to the general possibilities of experience, or to the test of "breadth." Here the test of reality is "fixity" or continuance in time. That natural species are real in one of these senses, or that individuals of a species are alike in an indefinite number of particulars, or resemble each other intimately, is unquestionable as a fact, and is not an invention of the understanding or classifying faculty, and is moreover the direct natural consequence of the principles of inheritance. In this sense species are equivalent to large natural stocks or races existing for a limited but indeterminate number of generations. That they are real in the other sense, or fixed in time absolutely in respect to any of the particulars of their resemblance, whether these are essential (that is, useful for discrimination and classification) or are not, is far from being the axiom it has seemed to be. It is, on the contrary, highly improbable, though tacitly assumed, as we have seen, in criticisms of the theory of natural selection; and in that significance often attached to the word "species" in which the notions of fixedness and distinctiveness have coalesced. It is true that without this significance in the word "species" the names and descriptions of organic forms could not be permanently applicable. No system of classification, however natural or real, could be final. Classification would, indeed, be wholly inadequate as a representation of the organic world on the whole, or as a sketch of the "plan of creation," and would be falsely conceived as revealing the categories and thoughts of creative intelligence,—a consequence by no means welcome to the devout naturalist, since it seems to degrade the value of his work. But this may be because he has misconceived its true value, and dedicated to the science of divinity what is really the rightful inheritance of natural or physical science.

If instead of implicitly assuming the principle of specific stability in the criticisms of the earlier chapters of his book, and deferring the explicit consideration of it to a later chapter and as a special topic, [Mivart] had undertaken the establishment of it as the essential basis of his theory (as indeed it really is), he would have attacked the theory of natural selection in a most vital point; and if he had succeeded, all further criticism of the theory would have been superfluous. But without success in establishing this essential basis, he leaves his own theory and his general difficulties on the theory of natural selection without adequate foundation. The importance of natural selection in the evolution of organic species (its predominant influence) depends entirely on the truth of the opposite assumption, the *instability* of species. The evidences for and against this position are various, and are not adequately considered in the author's chapter on this subject. Moreover, some of the evidences may be expected to be greatly affected by what will doubtless be the discoveries of the immediate future. Already the difficulties of discrimination and classification in dealing with large collections have become very great in some departments of natural history, and even in paleontology the gradations of fossil forms are becoming finer and finer with almost every new discovery; and this in spite of the fact that nothing at all approaching to evidence of continuity can rationally be expected anywhere from the fragmentary geological record. To this evidence must be added the phenomena of variation under domestication. The apparent limits of the changes which can be effected by artificial selection are not, as they have been thought, proofs of the doctrine of "specific stability," or of the opinion of Linnæus, but only indications of the dependence of variation on physiological causes, and on laws of inheritance; and also of the fact that the laws of variation and the action of natural selection are not suspended by domestication, but may oppose the aims and efforts of artificial selection. The real point of the proof afforded by these phenomena is that permanent changes may be effected in species by insensible degrees. They are permanent, however, only in the sense that no tendency to reversion will restore the original form, except by the action of similar causes. . . .

J. B. STALLO

In 1876, when the first serious history of American Transcendentalism appeared, its author remarked on the fact that a new philosophical order was developing in America, and he was undoubtedly right.[1] Although it is hard to discern a distinctively American philosophical movement between the decline of Transcendentalism and the rise of pragmatism, the intervening period in the history of American thought saw a growth of philosophical interest in the fundamental concepts and methods of science even if no striking new *ism* emerged in that period. We have already seen how biological thought captured the concern of Wright and Fiske, but it is important to observe that the eighteen-seventies also saw the appearance of a series of important papers on the foundations of physics by an extraordinary German-born Cincinnati lawyer, Judge J. B. Stallo (1823–1890).[2] Those papers were later revised

[1] O. B. Frothingham, *Transcendentalism in New England* (New York, 1886; originally published in 1876), p. viii.
[2] Stallo's four papers appeared in *The Popular Science Monthly* for October, November, and December 1873, and for January 1874. The first is in Volume III (pp. 705–17) and the other three are in Volume IV (pp. 92–108; pp. 219–31; and pp. 349–61).

and incorporated in Stallo's book, *The Concepts and Theories of Modern Physics* (1881), which earned an international reputation mainly through the efforts of its most distinguished admirer, the Austrian physicist-philosopher, Ernst Mach. After learning about the book from references to it in Bertrand Russell's *Essay on the Foundations of Geometry* (1897), Mach encouraged someone to translate it into German and wrote an introduction to the resulting translation that appeared in 1901.[3]

Stallo's intellectual development was not unlike that of many nineteenth-century thinkers who passed through a process that may be called "dehegelization". He came to America at the age of sixteen, and at twenty-five published his very Hegelian *General Principles of the Philosophy of Nature*, which bore the weighty subtitle, "*With an Outline of some of its Recent Developments among the Germans, Embracing the Philosophical Systems of Schelling and Hegel, and Oken's System of Nature*". This idealistic work exerted considerable influence on Emerson,[4] but Stallo ruthlessly disowned it in *The Concepts and Theories of Modern Physics*, saying that his later book was "in no sense a further exposition of the doctrines of" his earlier one. The earlier one, he added, "was written while I was under the spell of Hegel's

[3] For comparatively recent discussions of Stallo, see Stillman Drake, "J. B. Stallo and the Critique of Classical Physics", in H. M. Evans, ed., *Men and Moments in the History of Science* (Seattle, 1959), pp. 22–37; Stillman Drake, "John Bernard Stallo", in *The Encyclopedia of Philosophy*, ed. Paul Edwards (New York, 1967), Volume 8, pp. 4–6; P. W. Bridgman, Introduction to The John Harvard Library edition of Stallo's *The Concepts and Theories of Modern Physics* (Cambridge, Mass., 1960), pp. vii–xxix; Loyd D. Easton, *Hegel's First American Followers: The Ohio Hegelians: John B. Stallo, Peter Kaufmann, Moncure Conway, and August Willich, with Key Writings* (Athens, Ohio, 1966), esp. Chapters II–III. [M.W.]

[4] See Easton, *op. cit.*, pp. 43–49; also H. A. Pochmann, *German Culture in America: Philosophical and Literary Influences, 1600–1900* (Madison, Wisc., 1957), pp. 198 ff. [M.W.]

ontological reveries—at a time when I was barely of age and still seriously affected with the metaphysical malady which seems to be one of the unavoidable disorders of intellectual infancy". And although Stallo allowed that there were some things in his *General Principles of the Philosophy of Nature* of which he was not ashamed, he said that he sincerely regretted its publication and hoped that his later work would in some degree atone for it.[5]

Nevertheless, there was more philosophical continuity between the earlier and later Stallo than the later Stallo acknowledged.[6] The main purpose of *The Concepts and Theories of Modern Physics* was to undermine what he called the atomo-mechanical theory of nature, which sought to explain all phenomena by appealing to laws concerning atoms that were supposed to be "absolutely simple, unchangeable, indestructible".[7] Stallo argued that the theory was logically incoherent and incapable of explaining the phenomena it purported to explain; and his argument was similar to one that he leveled in an earlier paper of 1855, published in German under the title "Der Materialismus". The fundamental —and indefensible—principle of materialism, he maintained in that paper, is that only sensibly perceived things are real. This principle he traced back to Locke's doctrine that the senses are the only sources of knowledge, a doctrine, he went on to say, which quickly led to the conclusion that only things in space are real, and thence to the further conclusion that every real thing is made up of atoms or molecules.[8]

[5] J. B. Stallo, *The Concepts and Theories of Modern Physics*, ed. P. W. Bridgman (Cambridge, Mass., 1960), pp. 6–7.
[6] Unlike a number of commentators on Stallo, Easton properly emphasizes this continuity, *op. cit.*, pp. 84–87. [M.W.]
[7] Stallo, *op. cit.*, p. 111.
[8] J. B. Stallo, "Der Materialismus", reprinted in his *Reden, Abhandlungen und Briefe* (New York, 1893), esp. pp. 79–80. Students of German philosophy might prefer to use "actual" instead of "real" as a translation of Stallo's "wirklich". [M.W.]

Stallo's attack on the atomic theory may have been very congenial to the militant anti-atomist, Mach, but it was not supported by later scientific developments. Thus in 1891 Charles Peirce remarked (with more condescension than Stallo deserved): "The brilliant Judge Stallo, a man who did not always rightly estimate his own qualities in accepting tasks for himself, declared war upon the atomic theory in a book well worth careful perusal. To the old arguments in favor of atoms which he found in Fechner's monograph, he was able to make replies of considerable force, though they were not sufficient to destroy those arguments. But against modern proofs he made no headway at all".[9] And in 1960, P. W. Bridgman said in his Introduction to a new edition of *The Concepts and Theories of Modern Physics* that facts discovered after Stallo wrote "were so numerous and so unequivocal that today the thesis of the atomic constitution of matter is universally accepted with no reservations whatever by every competent scientist".[10]

It might be said in Stallo's defense that he did not claim that he was making a contribution to physics itself but rather that he was applying to physics certain "irrefragable truths" of the theory of cognition.[11] Those "truths" are in my opinion neither irrefragable nor original, as the reader may agree when he reads the later parts of the selection below; and therefore, when one reflects on the limitations of Stallo's theory of cognition and on the fact that his onslaught against atomic theory was not vindicated by later scientific developments, it is hard to identify his name with any resounding contribution to philosophy or physics. Nevertheless, his writ-

---

[9] *Collected Papers of Charles Sanders Peirce,* eds. Charles Hartshorne and Paul Weiss (Cambridge, Mass., 1935), Volume VI, paragraph 240. Fechner's monograph was *Ueber die Physikalische und Philosophische Atomenlehre* (Leipzig, 1864).
[10] P. W. Bridgman, Introduction to Stallo, *The Concepts and Theories of Modern Physics*, p. xxi.
[11] *Ibid.*, p. 3.

ings, like those of Chauncey Wright, are filled with very interesting and often profound insights and asides which earn
him an important though not a commanding place in the history of the philosophy of science. For example, Stallo's discussion of the nature of hypotheses and his theory of cognition in the selections below contain many illuminating
remarks about the nature of science even though his attack
on the atomic theory might be thought futile and his theory
of cognition less than irrefragable. Before reproducing those
passages, I should like to exhibit a typical Stallonistic gem
from another part of *The Concepts and Theories of Modern
Physics,* a philosophical remark that deserves to be rescued
from the oblivion of a footnote: "One of the most noteworthy
specimens of ontological reasoning is the argument which infers the existence of absolutely simple substances from the existence of compound substances. Leibnitz places this argument at the head of his 'Monadology.' 'Necesse est,' he says,
'dari substantias simplices quia dantur compositae; neque
enim compositum est nisi aggregatum simplicium.' ['It is necessary that simple substances be posited because composite
ones are likewise posited; for there is no composite which is
not an aggregate of simple ones.'] (Leibnitz, *Opera omnia,*
ed. Dutens, II, 21.) But the enthymeme is obviously a vicious
paralogism—a fallacy of the class known in logic as fallacies
of suppressed relative. The existence of a compound substance certainly proves the existence of component parts
which, *relatively to this substance,* are simple. But it proves
nothing whatever as to the simplicity of these parts in
themselves".[12]

Scientific Hypotheses [13]

A scientific hypothesis may be defined in general terms as
a provisional or tentative explanation of physical phenom-

[12] *Ibid.,* p. 202, n. 2.
[13] This selection, reproduced under my title, is abridged from Chapter
VIII of *The Concepts and Theories of Modern Physics,* edited by

ena.[14] But what is an explanation in the true scientific sense? The answers to this question which are given by logicians and men of science, though differing in their phraseology, are essentially of the same import. Phenomena are explained by an exhibition of their partial or total identity with other phenomena. Science is knowledge; and all knowledge, in the language of Sir William Hamilton,[15] is a "unification of the multiple." "The basis of all scientific explanation," says Bain,[16] "consists in assimilating a fact to some other fact or facts. It is identical with the generalizing process." And "generalization is only the apprehension of the One in the Many." [17] Similarly Jevons: [18] "Science arises from the discovery of identity amid diversity," and [19] "every great advance in science consists in a great generalization pointing out deep and subtle resemblances." The same thing is stated by the author just quoted in another place: [20] "Every act of explanation consists in detecting and pointing out a resemblance between facts, or in showing that a greater or less degree of identity exists between apparently diverse phenomena."

P. W. Bridgman (The John Harvard Library edition, Cambridge, Mass.: The Belknap Press of the Harvard University Press). Copyright 1960 by the President and Fellows of Harvard College. Reprinted by permission. I have reproduced only some of the notes in Bridgman's edition. His editorial addenda, like translations and first names of authors, are put in brackets. [M.W.]

[14] Wundt has lately (*Logik*, I, 403) sought to distinguish hypotheses from "anticipations of fact" and to restrict the term "hypothesis" to a sense which, notwithstanding its etymological warrant, is at variance with ordinary as well as scientific usage.

[15] *Lectures on Metaphysics [and Logic]*, Boston ed. [1860], pp. 47–48.

[16] [Alexander Bain] *Logic,* II (Induction) [London, 1870], chap. xii, § 2.

[17] Hamilton, *Lectures on Metaphysics [and Logic]*, p. 48.

[18] *Principles of Science*, I, 1.

[19] *Ibid.*, II, 281.

[20] *Ibid.*, II, 166.

All this may be expressed in familiar language thus: When a new phenomenon presents itself to the man of science or to the ordinary observer, the question arises in the mind of either: What is it?—and this question simply means: Of what known, familiar fact is this apparently strange, hitherto unknown fact a new presentation—of what known, familiar fact or facts is it a disguise or complication? Or, inasmuch as the partial or total identity of several phenomena is the basis of classification (a class being a number of objects having one or more properties in common), it may also be said that all explanation, including explanation by hypothesis, is in its nature classification.

Such being the essential nature of a scientific explanation of which an hypothesis is a probatory form, it follows that no hypothesis can be valid which does not identify the whole or a part of the phenomenon, for the explanation of which it is advanced, with some other phenomenon or phenomena previously observed. This first and fundamental canon of all hypothetical reasoning in science is formally resolvable into two propositions, the first of which is that every valid hypothesis must be an identification of two terms—the fact to be explained and a fact by which it is explained; and the second that the latter fact must be known to experience.

Tested by the first of these propositions, all hypotheses are futile which merely substitute an assumption for a fact, and thus, in the language of the schoolmen, explain *obscurum per obscurius* ["the obscure by means of the more obscure"], or (the assumption being simply the statement of the fact itself in another form—the "fact over again") illustrate *idem per idem*. And the futility of such hypotheses goes to the verge of mischievous puerility when they replace a single fact by a number of arbitrary assumptions, among which is the fact itself. Some of the uses made of the atomic hypothesis, both in physics and chemistry, which have been discussed in the last chapter, afford conspicuous examples of this class of bootless assumptions; and similar instances abound among the mathematical formulæ that are not infrequently paraded as physical theories. These formulæ are in many cases simply results of a series of transformations of an equation which embodies an hypothesis whose elements are neither more nor less than the elements of the phenomenon to be accounted for, the sole merit of the emerging formula being that it is not in conflict with the initial one.[21]

In order to comply with the first condition of its validity, an hypothesis must bring the fact to be explained into relation with some other fact or facts by identifying the whole or a part of the former with the whole or a part of the latter. In this sense it has been well said that a valid hypothesis reduces the number of the uncomprehended elements of a phenomenon by at least one. In the same sense it is sometimes said that every true theory or hypothesis is in effect a simplification of the data of experience—an assertion which must be understood, however, with due regard to the second proposition to be discussed presently, i. e., with the proviso that the theory be not a mere *asylum ignorantiæ,* of the kind denoted by the schoolmen as a *principium expressivum,* such as the explanation of the phenomena of life by reference to a *vital principle,* or of certain chemical processes by *catalytic action.* True scientific explanations are generally complicated in form, not only because most phenomena, on proper analysis, prove to be complex, but because the simplest fact is not the effect of a single cause, but the product of a great and often indeterminate multiplicity of agencies—the outcome of the

[21] I hope not to be misunderstood as disparaging the services for which physical science is indebted to mathematics. These services—especially those rendered by modern analysis—are incalculable. But there are mathematicians who imagine that they have compassed a solution of all the mysteries involved in a case of physical action when they have reduced it to the form of a differential expression preceded by a group of integral signs. Even when their equations are integrable they should bear in mind that the operations of mathematics are essentially deductive, and, while they may extend, can never deepen a physical theory. . . .

concurrence of numerous conditions. The Newtonian theory of planetary motion is much more intricate than that of Kepler, according to which every planet is conducted along its path by an *angelus rector;* and the account given by modern celestial mechanics of the precession of the equinoxes is far less simple than the announcement that among the great periods originally established by the Author of the universe was the Hipparchian cycle. The old brocard, *simplex veri judicium,* is to be taken with many grains of allowance before it can be trusted as a safe rule in determining the validity or value of scientific doctrines.

I now come to the second requirement of the validity of an hypothesis: that the explanatory phenomenon (i. e., that with which the phenomenon to be explained is identified) must be a datum of experience. This proposition is in substance equivalent to that part of Newton's first *regula philosophandi,*[22] in which he insists that the cause assigned for the explanation of natural things must be a *vera causa*—a term which he does not expressly define in the Principia, but whose import may be gathered from the following passage of his Opticks: [23] "To tell us that every species of things is endowed with an occult specific quality by which it acts and produces manifest effects is to tell us nothing. But to derive two or three general principles of motion *from phenomena* and afterward to tell us how the properties and actions of all corporeal things follow from these manifest principles would be a very great step in philosophy, though the causes of those principles were not yet discovered."

The requirement in question has long been the subject of animated discussion by J. S. Mill, Whewell, and others; but it will be found, I think, that, after making due allowance for necessary implications, there is little real disagreement among thinkers. The recent statement of G. H. Lewes [24] that "an

[22] *Phil. Nat. Princ. Math.,* Book III.
[23] 4th ed., p. 377.
[24] [George Henry Lewes] *Problems of Life and Mind* [Boston, 1879–1880; 2 vols.], II, 7.

explanation to be valid must be expressed in terms of phenomena already observed," and the counter-statement of
Jevons [25] that "agreement with fact (i. e., the fact to be explained) is the one sole and sufficient test of a true hypothesis," are both far too broad, and are, indeed, modified by
Lewes and Jevons themselves in the progress of the discussion; but the claim of Mr. Lewes is nevertheless true in the
sense that no explanation is real unless it is an identification
of experiential data. The confusion which, as in so many
other cases of scientific controversy, is at the bottom of the
seeming disagreement between the contending parties, arises
from a disregard of the circumstance that the identification of
two phenomena may be both partial and indirect—that it
may be effected by showing that the phenomena have some
known feature in common on condition that the existence, in
one or both of the phenomena, of some other feature not yet
directly observed, and perhaps incapable of direct observation, be assumed. The aptest illustration of this is the much-
debated undulatory theory of light. This hypothesis identifies
light with other forms of radiance, and even with sound, by
showing that all these phenomena have the element of vibra-
tion or undulation (which is well known to experience) in
common, on the assumption of an all-pervading material medium, of a kind wholly unknown to experience, as the bearer
of the luminar undulations. In this case, as in all similar cases,
the identity lies, not in the *fictitious* element, the æther, but
in the *real* element, the *undulation*. It consists, not in the
agent, but in *the law of its action.* And it is obvious that
every hypothesis which establishes coincidences between
phenomena in particulars that are purely fictitious is wholly
vain, because it is in no sense an identification of phenomena.
It is worse than vain: it is meaningless—a mere collection of
words or symbols without comprehensive import. As Jevons
expresses it: [26] "No hypothesis can be so much as framed in

[25] *Principles of Science,* II, 138.
[26] *Ibid.,* 141.

the mind, unless it be more or less conformable to experience. As the material of our ideas is undoubtedly derived from sensation so we can not figure to ourselves any existence or agent but as endowed with some of the properties of matter. All that the mind can do in the creation of new existences is to alter combinations, or by analogy to alter the intensity of sensuous properties." J. S. Mill is, therefore, clearly wrong when he says [27] that, "an hypothesis being a mere supposition, there can be no other limits to hypotheses than those of the human imagination," and that "we may, if we please, imagine, by way of accounting for an effect, some cause of a kind utterly unknown and acting according to a law altogether fictitious." The unsoundness of the latter part of this proposition is evidently felt by Mill himself, for he adds at the end of the next sentence that "there is *probably* no hypothesis in the history of science in which both the agent itself and the law of its operation were fictitious." There *certainly* is no such hypothesis—at least none which has in any way subserved the interests of science.

An hypothesis may involve not only one but several fictitious assumptions, provided they bring into relief, or point to the probability, or at least possibility, of an agreement between phenomena in a particular that is real and observable. This is especially legitimate when the agreement thus brought to light is not between two, but a greater number of phenomena, and still more so when the agreement is not merely in one but in several real particulars between diverse phenomena, so that, in the language of Whewell,[28] "the hypotheses which were assumed for one class of cases are found to explain another of a different nature—a consilience of induction." An instance of this is afforded by the hypothesis

[27] [*A System of*] *Logic* [*Ratiocinative and Inductive*], 8th ed. [London, 1872], p. 394.
[28] [William Whewell] *History of the Inductive Sciences*, American ed. [New York, 1858], II, 186.

just referred to of the luminiferous æther, which was at first believed also to explain the retardation of comets. But, while the probability of the truth of an hypothesis is in direct ratio to the number of phenomena thus brought into relation, it is in the inverse ratio of the number of such fictions, or, more accurately, its improbability increases geometrically while the series of independent fictions expands arithmetically.[29]

[29] "En général," says [Antoine Augustin] Cournot (*Traité de l'Enchainement des Idées Fondamentales dans les Sciences et dans l'Histoire* [Paris, 1861], I, 103), "une théorie scientifique quelconque, imaginée pour relier un certain nombre de faits donnés par l'observation, peut être assimilée à la courbe que l'on trace d'après une loi géométrique, en s'imposant la condition de la faire passer par un certain nombre de points donnés d'avance. Le jugement que la raison porte sur la valeur intrinsèque de cette théorie est un jugement probable, une induction dont la probabilité tient d'une part à la simplicité de la formule théorique, d'autre part au nombre des faits ou des groupes de faits qu'elle relie, le même groupe devant comprendre tous les faits qui s'expliquent déjà les uns par les autres, indépendamment de l'hypothèse théorique. *S'il faut compliquer la formule à mesure que de nouveaux faits se révèlent à l'observation, elle devient de moins en moins probable en tant que loi de la Nature;* ce n'est bientôt plus qu'un échafaudage artificiel qui croule enfin lorsque, par un surcroit de complication, elle perd même l'utilité d'un système artificiel, celle d'aider le travail de la pensée et de diriger les recherches. Si au contraire les faits acquis à l'observation postérieurement à la construction de l'hypothèse sont reliés par elle aussi bien que les faits qui ont servi à la construire, si surtout des faits prévus comme conséquences de l'hypothèse reçoivent des observations postérieures une confirmation éclatante, la probabilité de l'hypothèse peut aller jusqu'à ne laisser aucune place au doute dans un esprit éclairé."

["In general, any scientific theory whatever designed to connect a certain number of facts of observation can be represented by a curve traced according to some geometrical law so as to satisfy the condition that it pass through a certain number of points given in advance. The judgment which reason makes on the intrinsic importance of this theory is a judgment made on a probability basis, the probability depending partly on the simplicity of the theoretical formula and partly on the number of facts or groups of facts which it ties together, a single group of facts including all those which are so related that they explain each

This finds illustration again in the undulatory theory of light. The multitude of fictitious assumptions embodied in this hypothesis, in conjunction with the failure of the consiliences by which it appeared at first to be distinguished, can hardly be looked upon otherwise than as a standing impeachment of its validity in its present form. However ready we may be to accede to the demands of the theorist when he asks us to grant that all space is pervaded, and all sensible matter is penetrated, by an adamantine solid exerting at each point in space an elastic force 1,148,000,000,000 times that of air at the earth's surface, and a pressure upon the square inch of 17,000,000,000,000 pounds [30]—a solid which, at the same time, wholly eludes our senses, is utterly impalpable and offers no appreciable resistance to the motions of ordinary bodies—we are appalled when we are told that the alleged existence of this adamantine medium, the æther, does not, after all, explain the observed irregularities in the periods of comets; that, furthermore, not only is the supposed luminiferous æther unavailable as a medium for the origination and propagation of dielectric phenomena, so that for these a distinct all-pervading electriferous æther must be assumed,[31]

other, without reference to the hypothetical theory. *If it becomes necessary to make the formula more complicated in proportion as new facts of observation are discovered, the theory becomes in so far less and less probable as a law of nature;* it quickly becomes merely an artificial scaffolding which finally collapses when, by an excess of complication, it loses even the usefulness of an artificial system in assisting thought or in directing research. If, on the contrary, the facts acquired by observation after the construction of the hypothesis are covered by it as well as the facts used in its construction, and if, above all, facts anticipated as consequences of the hypothesis receive a brilliant confirmation from posterior observation, the probability of the hypothesis becomes so great as to leave no room for doubt in an enlightened mind."]

[30] Cf. [Sir John] Herschel, *Familiar Lectures [on Scientific Subjects* (London and New York, 1866)], p. 282; F. De Wrede (President Royal Academy of Sciences in Stockholm), address, *Phil. Mag.*, 4th ser., XLIV [August 1872], 82.

[31] W. A. Norton, "On Molecular Physics," *ibid.*, XXVIII [1864], 193.

but that it is very questionable whether the assumption of a single æthereal medium is competent to account for all the known facts in optics (as, for instance, the non-interference of two rays originally polarized in different planes when they have been brought to the same plane of polarization, and certain phenomena of double refraction, in view of which it is necessary to suppose that the rigidity of the medium varies with the direction of the strain—a supposition discountenanced by the facts relating to the intensities of reflected light), and that for the adequate explanation of the phenomena of light it is "necessary to consider what we term the æther as consisting of two media, each possessed of equal and enormous self-repulsion or elasticity, and both existing in equal quantities throughout space, whose vibrations take place in perpendicular planes, the two media being mutually indifferent, neither attracting nor repelling." [32] In this endless superfetation of æthereal media upon space and ordinary matter, there are ominous suggestions of the three kinds of æthereal substances postulated by Leibnitz and Cartesius alike as a basis for their vortical systems. There is an impul-

[32] Hudson, "On Wave Theories of Light, Heat, and Electricity," *ibid.*, XLIV [September 1872], 210f. In this article the author also points out the crudeness of the subsidiary hypotheses which have been framed to obviate other difficulties of the undulatory theory, among which are those discussed in the last chapter. "Waves of sound," he says, "in our atmosphere are 10,000 times as long as the waves of light, and their velocity of propagation about 850,000 times less, and, even when air has been raised to a temperature at which waves of red light are propagated from matter, the velocity of sound-waves is only increased to about double what it was at zero centigrade. Even their velocity through glass is 55,000 times less than the speed of the aethereal undulations, and the extreme slowness of change of temperature in the conduction of heat (as contrasted with the rapidity with which the vibrations of the aether exhaust themselves, becoming insensible almost instantly when the action of the existing cause ceases) marks distinctly the essential difference between molecular and aethereal vibrations. It appears to me, therefore, a very crude hypothesis to imagine a combination of aethereo-molecular vibrations as accounting for the very minute difference in the retardation of doubly refracted rays in crystals."

sive whirl in our thoughts, at least, when we are called upon, in the interests of the received form of the undulatory theory, not only to reject all the presumptions arising from our common observation and all the analogies of experience, but to cumulate hypotheses and æthers indefinitely. And we are but partially reassured by the circumstance that the theory in question, besides accounting for the phenomena of optics which had been observed at the time of its promulgation, has the great merit of successful prevision, having led to the prediction of a number of facts subsequently discovered. These predictions, certainly, have not only been numerous, but several of them, such as Hamilton's announcement of conical refraction (afterward verified by Lloyd) and Fresnel's forecast (from the imaginary form of an algebraic formula) of circular polarization after two internal reflections in a rhomb, are very striking. But, although anticipations of this sort justly serve to accredit an hypothesis, they are, as Mill has shown,[33] by no means absolute tests of their truth. Using the word "cause" in the sense in which it is commonly understood, an effect may be due to any one of several causes, and may, therefore, in many cases be accounted for by any one of several conflicting hypotheses, as becomes evident to the most cursory glance at the history of science. When an hypothesis successfully explains a number of phenomena with reference to which it was constructed, it is not strange that it should also explain others connected with them that are subsequently discovered. There are few discarded physical theories that could not boast the prevision of phenomena to which they pointed and which were afterward observed;

[33] *Logic*, p. 356. Long before Mill, Leibnitz observed that success in explaining (or predicting) facts is no proof of the validity of an hypothesis, inasmuch as right conclusions may be drawn from wrong premises —as Leibnitz expresses it, "Comme le vrai peut être tiré du faux" ["As it is possible to deduce the true from the false"]. Cf. *Nouveaux Essais*, chap. xvii, sec. 5—Leibnitz, *Opp.*, ed. Erdmann, p. 397.

among them are the one-fluid theory of electricity and the corpuscular theory of light.

There are, of course, other conditions of the validity of an hypothesis to which I have not yet adverted. Among them are those specified by Sir W. Hamilton, Mill, Bain, and others, such as that the hypothesis must not be contradictory of itself or in conflict with the known laws of nature (which latter requirement is, however, somewhat doubtful, inasmuch as the laws in question may be incomplete inductions from past experience to be supplemented by the very elements postulated by the hypothesis); that it must be of a nature to admit of deductive inferences, etc. Upon all these it is not necessary, in view of my present purpose, to dilate. . . .

The Relation of Thoughts
to Things—the Formation
of Concepts—Metaphysical Theories [34]

It has become evident, I take it, in the course of the preceding discussions, that, while modern physical science is professedly an endeavor to reduce the phenomena of nature to the elements of mass and motion, and thus to exhibit them as results or phases of mechanical action—claiming, on this ground, to be the only mode of dealing with these phenomena that is not in its nature metaphysical—nevertheless all the departments of science which have made decided advances beyond the first classificatory stage proceed upon assumptions and lead to consequences inconsistent with the object of this endeavor and with the fundamental principles of the mechanical theory. We find ourselves in the midst of a confusion, therefore, which is to be cleared up, if at all, by an inquiry into the origin of this theory and by a determination

[34] Below, Chapter IX of *The Concepts and Theories of Modern Physics* is reproduced from Bridgman's edition. This time the title is Stallo's. [M.W.]

of its attitude toward the laws of thought and the forms and conditions of its evolution.

The account given, by ordinary psychologists and logicians, of the nature and operations of thought may, so far as it bears upon the matter now under consideration, be compressed into a few sentences. Thought, in its most comprehensive sense, is the establishment or recognition of relations between phenomena. Foremost among these relations—the foundation, in fact, of all others, such as those of exclusion and inclusion, coexistence and sequence, cause and effect, means and end—are the relations of identity and difference. The difference between phenomena is a primary datum of sensation. The very act of sensation is based upon it. It is one of the many acute observations of Hobbes that "it is all one to be always sensible of the same thing and not to be sensible of anything." [35] "We only know anything," says J. S. Mill, [36] "by knowing it as distinguished from something else; all consciousness is of difference; two objects are the smallest number required to constitute consciousness; a thing is only seen to be what it is by contrast with what it is not."

While the apprehension of phenomenal difference (which, however, may be, and in most cases is, replaced by its reproduction in memory) is the basis or prerequisite of thought, thought proper, i. e., discursive thought, begins with the apprehension of identity amid phenomenal difference. Objects are *perceived* as different; they are *conceived* as identical by an attention of the mind to their point or points of agreement. They are thus classified, the points of agreement, i.e., those properties of the objects of cognition which belong to them in common, serving as the basis of classification. When the number of objects classified is great, and some of these

[35] "Sentire semper idem et non sentire ad idem recidunt." Hobbes, *Physica* (iv, 25), *Opp.*, ed. Molesworth, I, 321.
[36] *Examination of Sir William Hamilton's Philosophy,* American ed. [Boston, 1865], I, 14.

objects have more properties in common than others, a series of classes is formed. The objects are first divided into groups (called by the logicians *infimae species*) severally embracing such objects as are characterized by the greatest number of common properties consistent with their difference; these groups are then collected and distributed into higher groups or species having a less number of properties in common, and so on, until we arrive at the least number of properties in which all objects embraced in (*logicè* subsumed under) the *infimae species* and the intermediate species agree, so as to characterize the highest class, or *summum genus*.

From this it follows that, in proportion as we ascend the scale of classification from the *infimae species* to the *summum genus*, the number of objects embraced in the successive classes (species or genera) increases, while the number of characteristic properties decreases. Now, the complement of properties characteristic of a particular class is termed a *concept;* the number of objects denoted by each concept is called its *extension* or *breadth;* and the number of properties (which, as constituents of a concept, bear the name of attributes) connoted by it its *intension, comprehension* or *depth;* whence springs the law of logic that, the greater the extension of a concept, i.e., the greater the number of objects denoted, the less its comprehension, i. e., the number of attributes connoted; or, expressed with mathematical accuracy, that the extension varies in geometrical ratio inversely as the comprehension varies in arithmetical ratio.[37]

It is readily seen that the ascent from a lower (more comprehensive, but less extensive) to a higher (more extensive but less comprehensive) class is effected by a progressive segregation and ideal union of those attributes which the respec-

[37] For an exact statement of the law in question, see [Moritz Wilhelm] Drobisch, *Neue Darstellung der Logik* ["New Exposition of Logic"], 3rd ed. [Leipzig, 1836], Logico-mathematical Appendix, p. 206.

tive classes have in common; and this process is termed abstraction.

In the sense of the foregoing exposition, thought proper has been defined as "the act of knowing or judging of things by means of concepts," [38] a concept being "a collection of attributes united by a sign and representing a possible object of intuition." [39] This definition of a concept, however, is obnoxious to criticism, as being either too wide or too narrow. It may be said, on the one hand, to be too wide: for it applies to the total array of attributes constituting the mental representation of a single object, without reference to the question whether or not they are shared by any other object, as well as to the factitious selection or collection of attributes characteristic of a class, i.e., of a plurality of objects. In other words, it is a definition of *singular concepts* (expressed by singular terms) as well as of *general concepts* (expressed by general terms, or, as Mill would say, class names). In the language of the old logicians, it includes *infimae species,* and may stand for any singular object or singular quality, irrespective of the fact or degree of its generality. This criticism would be avoided by defining a concept, with Sir William Hamilton,[40] as "the cognition of the general character, point or points in which a plurality of objects coincide." On the other hand, the word "concept" is very generally employed in a sense for which Mansel's definition is too narrow. German logicians, for example, habitually designate not only every mental reproduction of a presentation of sense, in so far as it is or may be an element of a judgment or logical proposition, as a concept (*Begriff*), but also the last result of any series of abstractions. And the last results of abstraction, the *summa genera,* are excluded by the definition of Mansel. It is neither neces-

---

[38] [Henry Longueville] Mansel, *Prolegomena Logica* [first pub. 1851; an American ed. pub. Boston and New York in 1860], p. 22.
[39] *Ibid.,* p. 60.
[40] *Lectures on* [*Metaphysics and*] *Logic,* American ed., p. 87.

sary nor practicable here to attempt a minute discussion of the questions arising upon these divergences in the use of terms; nor can I stop to weigh the objections recently urged by Tauschinsky, Lotze, Sigwart, Wundt and others to the theory of conception as founded upon classification or subsumption. The controversies on this head between the logicians of the old and those of the new school, as well as the interminable disputes between the nominalists and the conceptualists to which so large a space is devoted in the writings of J. S. Mill,[41] are in the main mere wars of words, and the points of disagreement are foreign to the investigation upon which I am about to enter. To one or two of these points I may have occasion to recur hereafter; for the present my brief summary of the incidents of logical conception is to serve only as a clew to the meaning of certain logical terms I am constrained to employ, whenever this meaning is not sufficiently apparent from the context.

Now, in any discussion of the operations of thought, it is of the utmost importance to bear in mind the following irrefragable truths, some of which—although all of them seem to be obvious—have not been clearly apprehended until very recent times:

1. Thought deals, not with things as they are, or are supposed to be, in themselves, but with our mental representations of them. Its elements are, not pure objects, but their intellectual counterparts. What is present in the mind in the act of thought is never a thing, but always a state or states of consciousness. However much, and in whatever sense, it may be contended that the intellect and its object are both real and distinct entities, it can not for a moment be denied that the object, of which the intellect has cognizance, is a synthesis of objective and subjective elements, and is thus primarily, in the very act of its apprehension and to the full

[41] Cf. Mill's *Examination of Sir William Hamilton's Philosophy*, chap. xvii.

extent of its cognizable existence, affected by the determinations of the cognizing faculty. Whenever, therefore, we speak of a thing, or a property of a thing, it must be understood that we mean a product of two factors neither of which is capable of being apprehended by itself. In this sense all knowledge is said to be relative.

2. Objects are known only through their relations to other objects. They have, and can have, no properties, and their concepts can include no attributes, save these relations, or rather, our mental representations of them. Indeed, an object can not be known or conceived otherwise than as a complex of such relations. In mathematical phrase: things and their properties are known only as functions of other things and properties. In this sense, also relativity is a necessary predicate of all objects of cognition.

3. A particular operation of thought never involves the entire complement of the known or knowable properties of a given object, but only such of them as belong to a definite class of relations. In mechanics, for instance, a body is considered simply as a mass of determinate weight and volume (and in some cases figure), without reference to its other physical or chemical properties. In like manner each of the several other departments of knowledge effects a classification of objects upon its own peculiar principles, thereby giving rise to different series of concepts in which each concept represents that attribute or group of attributes—that aspect of the object —which it is necessary, in view of the question in hand, to bring into view. Our thoughts of things are thus, in the language of Leibnitz, adopted by Sir William Hamilton, and after him by Herbert Spencer, *symbolical,* not (or, at least, not only) because a complete mental representation of the properties of an object is precluded by their number and the incapacity of the mind to hold them in simultaneous grasp, but because many (and in most cases the greater part) of them are irrelevant to the mental operation in progress.

Again: the attributes comprised in the concept of an object

being the representations of its relations to other objects, and the number of these objects being unlimited, it follows that the number of attributes is also unlimited, and that, consequently, there is no concept of an object in which its cognizable properties are exhaustively exhibited. In this connection it is worthy of mention that the ordinary doctrinal statement of the relation of concepts to judgments is liable to serious objection. A judgment is said to be "a comparison of two notions (concepts), with a resulting declaration of their agreement or disagreement" (Whately), or "a recognition of the relation of congruence or confliction between two concepts" (Hamilton). Here it is assumed that the concepts preëxist to the act of judgment, and that this act simply determines the fact or degree of their congruence or confliction. But the truth is that every concept is the result of a judgment, or of a series of judgments, the initial judgment being the recognition of a relation between two data of experience. In most cases, indeed, a judgment is a collation of two concepts; but every synthetic judgment (i. e., every judgment in which the predicate is more than a mere display of one or more of the attributes connoted by the subject) transforms both concepts which it brings into relation, by either amplifying or restricting their respective implications.[42] When a boy learns that "a

---

[42] That this did not escape the attention of Sir William Hamilton, notwithstanding his definition of a judgment, appears from the following passage of his *Lectures on* [*Metaphysics and*] *Logic*, p. 84: "A concept is a judgment: for, on the one hand it is nothing but the result of a foregone judgment, or series of judgments, fixed and recorded in a word, a sign, and it is only amplified by the annexation of a new attribute through a continuance of the same process." Among German thinkers [Johann Friedrich] Herbart had a clear view of the same truth. "Die Ausbildung der Begriffe," he says (*Lehrbuch zur Psychologie* [1816], § 189, *Werke*, V, 130), "ist der langsame, allmaelige Erfolg des immer fort gehenden Urtheilens." ["The development of a concept is the slow, gradual result of continuously progressing judgment."] In another place (*Ibid.*, § 79, *Werke*, V, 59): "Es fragt sich, ob die Begriffe im strengen logischen Sinn nicht vielmehr logische Ideale seien,

274 Documents in the History of American Philosophy

whale is a mammal," his notions, both of a whale and of a mammal, undergo a material change. From the judgment of Thomas Graham that "hydrogen is a metal," both the term "hydrogen" and the term "metal" emerged with new meanings. The announcement by Sterry Hunt, that "just as solution is chemical combination so chemical combination is mutual solution," extended the concept "solution" as well as the concept "chemical combination."

It is apparent, from these considerations, that the concepts of a given object are terms or links in numberless series or chains of abstractions varying in kind and diverging in direction with the comparisons instituted between it and other objects; that the import and scope of any one of these concepts are dependent, not only on the number, but also on the nature of the relations with reference to which the classification of objects is effected; and that for this reason, too, all thoughts of things are fragmentary and symbolic representations of realities whose thorough comprehension in any single mental act, or series of acts, is impossible. And this is true, *a fortiori*, because the relations of which any object of cognition is the entirety, besides being endless in number, are also variable—because, in the language of Herakleitos, all things are in a perpetual flux.

All metaphysical or ontological speculation is based upon a disregard of some or all of the truths here set forth. Metaphysical thinking is an attempt to deduce the true nature of things from our concepts of them. Whatever diversity may

denen sich unser logisches Denken mehr und mehr annaehern soll. . . . Es wird sich ueberdiess zeigen, dass die Urtheile es sind, wodurch die Begriffe dem Ideal mehr und mehr angenaehert werden, daher sie den letzten in gewissem Sinne vorangehn." ["It is to be asked whether concepts in the strictly logical sense are not rather logical ideals, to which our logical thinking is to approach ever more closely. . . . It is moreover obvious that it is through our judgments that our concepts approach ever closer to the ideal; that is why in a certain sense judgment precedes concept."]

exist between metaphysical systems, they are all founded upon the express or implied supposition that there is a fixed correspondence between concepts and their filiations on the one hand and things and their modes of interdependence on the other. This fundamental error is, in great part, due to a delusory view of the function of language as an aid to the formation and fixation of concepts. Roughly stated, concepts are the meanings of words; and the circumstance that words primarily designate things, or at least objects of sensation and their sensible interactions, has given rise to certain fallacious assumptions which, unlike the ordinary infractions of the laws of logic, are in a sense natural outgrowths of the evolution of thought (not without analogy to the organic diseases incident to bodily life) and may be termed structural fallacies of the intellect. These assumptions are:

1. That every concept is the counterpart of a distinct objective reality, and that hence there are as many things, or natural classes of things, as there are concepts or notions.

2. That the more general or extensive concepts and the realities corresponding to them preëxist to the less general, more comprehensive concepts and their corresponding realities; and that the latter concepts and realities are derived from the former, either by a successive addition of attributes or properties, or by a process of evolution, the attributes or properties of the former being taken as implications of those of the latter.

3. That the order of the genesis of concepts is identical with the order of the genesis of things.

4. That things exist independently of and antecedently to their relations; that all relations are between absolute terms; and that, therefore, whatever reality belongs to the properties of things is distinct from that of the things themselves.

By the aid of these preliminaries I hope to be able to assign to the mechanical theory its true character and position in the history of the evolution of thought. Before I proceed to this, however, it may not be without interest, in connection with the preceding inquiry into the relation between concepts and their corresponding objects, to consider the question which has long been the subject of eager debate, whether and to what extent conceivability is a test of possible reality. It is contended by J. S. Mill and his followers, that our incapacity of conceiving a thing is no proof of its impossibility; while Whewell and Herbert Spencer maintain (though not strictly in the same sense and on the same grounds) that what is inconceivable can not be real or true.[43] A trustworthy judgment on the merits of this controversy can only be formed after a careful determination of the conditions of conceivability as indicated by the nature of the process of conception which I have attempted to describe.

It has been shown that all true conception consists in the establishment of relations of partial or total identity between the fact to be conceived and other known facts of experience. The first condition of conceivability, therefore, is that the thing or phenomenon in question be susceptible of classification, i. e., of total or partial identification with objects or phenomena previously observed.

A second and very obvious condition of conceivability is the consistency of the elements of the concept to be formed with each other. It is clear that two attributes, one of which is the negation of the other, can not simultaneously belong to the same subject and thus be parts of the same concept.

These two are the only conditions which are directly deducible from the theory of conception, and may, therefore, with some propriety be termed theoretical conditions. But there is a third, practical condition: the consistency of the new con-

---

[43] The precise form of Spencer's test of truth, which he terms the "Universal Postulate," is the "Inconceivability of the Opposite." Expressed in the strict language of logic, his thesis is that every proposition whose contradictory is inconceivable must be true. But, inasmuch as every negation of a proposition is the affirmation of its contradictory, this is equivalent to the general statement that whatever is inconceivable can not be true.

cept with previously-formed concepts bearing upon the same subject-matter. As I have said, this is a practical condition—not so much a condition of conceivability as of ready conceivability. For the old concepts may be defective or erroneous; the very concept with which they conflict may supplement or supplant, rectify or destroy them.

Now, it is easily seen that fulfillment of the first condition can not be a test of reality. Facts or phenomena may present themselves to observation which are wholly unlike any fact of phenomenon theretofore observed, or whose likeness to the prior data of experience has not yet been detected. The history of science is full of startling discoveries; every period of active research brings to light phenomena which are not only unlooked-for, but without apparent analogy to other known facts. In view of this Liebig said: "The secret of all those who make discoveries is that they regard nothing as impossible." [44]

Thus far, then, I agree with Mr. Mill. But I can not follow him when he also rejects compliance with the second condition as a criterion of possibility, and refuses or neglects to distinguish between the case of inconceivability by reason of the apparent or real incongruity of a new fact or phenomenon with the data of past experience and the very different case of inconceivability on the ground of inconsistency between the several elements of a proposed concept. He instances the concept "a round square" as one which we are unable to form, and alleges that this inability is due solely to the inveteracy of our experience. "We can not conceive a round square," he says,[45] "not merely because no such object has ever presented itself in our experience, for that would not be enough. Neither, for anything we know, are the two ideas in themselves incompatible. To conceive a body all black and yet all white, would only be to conceive two different sensa-

---

[44] [Justus von Liebig] *Annalen der Pharmacie*, X, 179.
[45] *Examination of Sir William Hamilton's Philosophy*, I, 88.

tions as produced in us simultaneously by the same object—a conception familiar to our experience—and we should probably be as well able to conceive a round square as a hard square, or a heavy square, if it were not that in our uniform experience, at the instant when a thing begins to be round, it ceases to be square, so that the beginning of the one impression is inseparably associated with the departure or cessation of the other. Thus our inability to form a conception always arises from our being compelled to form another contradictory to it."

Our inability to conceive a round square due to the fact "that in our uniform experience at the instant when a thing begins to be round it ceases to be square," and to the inseparable association between incipient roundness and departing squareness! Whether any one has ever had such experience as is here spoken of, I do not know; but, if he has, I am confident that, even after being reënforced by a large inheritance of ancestral experience in the light of the modern theory of evolution, it will prove insufficient to account for the inseparable association which Mill brings into play. The simple truth is, that a round square is an absurdity, a contradiction in terms. A square is a figure bounded by four equal straight lines intersecting at right angles; a round figure is a figure bounded by a curve; and the oldest definition of a curve is that of "a line which is neither a straight line nor made up of straight lines."

Mill's claim is, in effect, if not in express words, a denial of the validity of the laws of non-contradiction and excluded middle, or (as he himself would prefer to say) an assertion that the fundamental laws of logic are, like all so-called laws of nature, mere experiential inductions, uniformity of experience being their only warrant. But, if these laws are not absolutely and universally binding as constitutive principles of thought and speech—if the same thing may, at the same time, be and not be, and if its affirmation and denial are not strict alternatives—we are fairly landed in the regions of utter nonsense, where all thinking is at an end and all language without meaning. The laws in question are principles constitutive of, because they are tacit conventions preliminary to, distinct thought and intelligible speech; and they are no more to be suspended in favor of Mill's theory of inseparable association than to be abrogated in furtherance of Hegel's dialectic process.

It ought to be said that there are expressions in the same chapter of Mill's book, from which I have just quoted, which show that the author was very ill at ease in the presence of his own theory. For instance, he says: [46] "These things are literally inconceivable to us, our minds and our experience being what they are. Whether they would be inconceivable if our minds were the same, but our experience different, is open to discussion. A distinction may be made which I think will be found pertinent to the question. That the same thing should at once be and not be—that identically the same statement should be both true and false—is not only inconceivable to us, *but we can not conceive that it could be made conceivable*."

How strange that sentences like these should come from the pen of John Stuart Mill! First he denies that inconceivability is, in any sense or in any case, a test of truth or reality; but then he says it may be otherwise if the inconceivability itself is inconceivable! That is to say: a witness is utterly untrustworthy; but, when he makes a declaration respecting his own trustworthiness, he ought to be believed!

The whole theory of inseparable association, as here advanced and applied by Mill, is simply groundless, it being impossible, under his theory, to know what the experience of his numerous readers has been, except again by experience which he can not have had, since most of these readers were utterly unknown to him. And all attempts to argue questions with any one on such a basis are supremely foolish, Mill

[46] *Ibid.*, p. 88.

being bound, by his own doctrine, to accept the answer, "My experience has been otherwise," as conclusive. Mill's theory is thus subversive of itself, and every earnest sentence he has ever written is its practical refutation.

In reference to the case of inconceivability just discussed, and others analogous to it, it is to be observed that much of the perplexity and confusion which is characteristic of the disputes between Mill and his antagonists arises from the failure of the disputants to discriminate between purely formal concepts and the mental representations of physical realities. There is a very wide distinction between the relation of a concept to the object of thought in mathematics, for example, and the corresponding relation between a concept of a material object and that object itself. In mathematics, as in all the sciences which are conversant about single relations or groups of relations established (and, within the limits of the constitutive laws of the mind, *arbitrarily* established) by the mind itself, certain concepts are exhaustive in the sense that they imply, if they do not explicitly exhibit, all the properties belonging to the object of thought. Not only the constituents of such an object, but also the laws of their interdependence, being determined by the intellect, a single concept may be expanded into a series of others. Thus, a parabola is a line every point in which is equidistant from a fixed point and a given straight line: that is one of its concepts. And in this all the properties of the parabola—that it is a conic section formed by cutting a cone parallel to one of its sides, that the area of any one of its segments is equal to two thirds of its circumscribed rectangle, etc.—are implied, and from it they may be deduced. One of its attributes is an implication of all the others. Our concepts of material objects, on the contrary, as I have shown, are never exhaustive, for their complement of attributes is of necessity both incomplete and variable. To what strange vagaries this confusion has given rise in other departments of speculation we shall see in a future chapter.

I come now to the third condition of conceivability: the

consistency of the concept to be formed with previous concepts *in pari materia.* By far the greatest number of the cases of alleged inconceivability are traceable to a breach of this condition—to the incompatibility of new facts or views with our intellectual prepossessions. Accordingly, most of the cases adduced by Mill in support of his theory are taken from this class. But he does not always apprehend their true character, and most of them are very imperfectly, if at all, accounted for by his theory. One of his instances is that of the denial, once all but universal, of the possibility of antipodes, on the ground of their inconceivability. According to Mill, this inconceivability has now vanished; we not only readily conceive them as possible, but know them to be real. This is true enough; but it finds its explanation, not in the law of inseparable association to which it is referred by Mill, but in the fact that our ancestors held an erroneous concept of the action of gravity. They supposed that the direction in which gravity acted was an absolute direction in space; they did not realize that it was a direction toward the earth's center of gravity; *downward* to them meant something very different from the sense we attach to that word. With this erroneous concept they could not reconcile the fact that the force of gravity held our antipodes in position as well as ourselves; nor can we. But we have a juster concept of gravity, and the mode and direction of its action; the spurious notion with which the notion of antipodes was inconsistent has been removed, and the inconceivability of antipodes is at an end.

Similar observations apply to another example brought forward by Mill: the inability to conceive *actio in distans,* to which extended reference has already been made in a preceding chapter. This inability results from the inconsistency of this concept with the prevailing notions respecting material presence. If we reverse the proposition that a body acts where it is, and say that a body is where it acts, the inconceivability disappears at once. One of the wisest utterances on this subject is the saying of Thomas Carlyle (quoted by Mill himself in another place): "You say that a body can not act where it is not? With all my heart; but, pray where is it?" Of course, a reconstitution of our familiar concepts of material presence, in the sense here indicated, would preclude the mechanical construction of matter from elements absolutely limited, hard, unchangeable and separated from each other by absolutely void spaces.

It is hardly necessary to add that, generally speaking, the inconceivability of a physical fact arising from its incongruity with preconceived notions is no proof of its impossibility or want of reality. Intellectual progress consists almost wholly in the rectification or subversion of old ideas not a few of which are held to be self-evident during long intellectual periods. The instances already cited from Mill are apt illustrations of this; and they may be cumulated without limit. Until the discovery of the composition of water, of the true theory of combustion, and of the relative affinities of potassium and hydrogen for oxygen, it was impossible to conceive a substance which would ignite on contact with water, it being one of the recognized attributes of water—in other words, a part of the concept water—that it antagonized fire. This previous concept was spurious, and, when it had been destroyed, the inconceivability of a substance like potassium disappeared. Similarly, we are now unable to conceive a warmblooded animal without a respiratory system, because we conceive the idiothermic condition of an animal organism to depend mainly on the chemical changes taking place within it, chief among which is the oxidation of the blood, which requires some form of contact between the blood and the air, and therefore some form of respiration. If, however, future researches should destroy this latter concept—if it should be shown that the heat of a living body may be produced in sufficient quantity by mechanical agencies, such as friction—a non-respiring warm-blooded animal would at once become conceivable.

While thus a physical phenomenon, however little we may be able to conceive it without violence to our familiar ideas, may be real, it is otherwise in the domain of the formal sciences, such as logic and mathematics. There we find concepts founded upon fundamental postulates or axiomatic truths with which all new concepts, to be valid, must be consistent. The fact is that, in the sphere of the ideal relations of space and time, the third condition of conceivability is at bottom identical with the second, inasmuch as there all minor concepts are, by implication at least, constituents of some higher, more comprehensive concept whose validity requires their consistency with each other. All this is equally true of those purely formal concepts which constitute the theoretical basis of some of the physical sciences, such as the general propositions of kinematics or phoronomics; within the limits of their proper application they are authoritative tests of possibility. And even among the physical truths based upon induction there are many whose universality is so well established as to afford strong, if not conclusive presumption against the legitimacy of concepts and the reality of alleged phenomena which would invalidate them.

The foregoing discussion of the question of conceivability as a test of truth is by no means exhaustive. There are topics connected with it upon which it is not my province to enter. One of these topics is the specification of the conditions under which the inconsistency between the elements of a proposed concept becomes apparent. In many cases the inconsistency is latent and emerges only upon thorough exhibition of all the implications of these elements and their colligation—upon an explication which is familiarly known as *reductio ad absurdum*. The procedure, in such cases, is in effect a reduction of the propositions into which the concept may be resolved to their last degree of homogeneity, so that the conflict between them, if it exists, becomes explicit. The details of this subject, however, belong to treatises on logic.

Part 5: Pragmatism: *A Tough and Tender Philosophy*

CHARLES PEIRCE

Charles Peirce is best known as the founder of pragmatism, although he was also a distinguished mathematical logician, a trained chemist, an accomplished historian of science, and a metaphysician who hoped to construct a philosophical edifice that would "outlast the vicissitudes of time". During his lifetime he failed to receive his due in the American academic world, but posterity has tried to help him achieve the immortality he sought. It has tried to make amends for an earlier generation's indifference by collecting his papers in several impressive volumes, by establishing a Charles Peirce Society to do him the kind of honor traditionally reserved for figures like Aristotle and Kant, and by extensive exegesis of work that he himself might have preferred to keep from the world's eyes. Some of this posthumous adulation of Peirce may be explained by the fact that America has had too few distinguished philosophers to neglect any of them, but a good deal of it is unquestionably merited by the brilliance of Peirce's ideas. There are those who are disturbed by the scattered quality of his work and by its obscurity, but no one can read Peirce without being aware of both his logical power and his philosophical acuity—a combination that is not as common as sometimes supposed.

Peirce was born in Cambridge, Massachusetts, in 1839 and died in 1914 after a life that could hardly be called very happy or successful even by standards that philosophers are sometimes content to use. In spite of the efforts of William James, his loyal friend, admirer, and fellow pragmatist, Peirce was never appointed to a permanent academic position; not even at his *alma mater*, Harvard, where his father, Benjamin Peirce, had been an eminent professor of mathematics, and where Peirce's own mathematico-logical talents were sorely needed in the days of James, Royce, and Santayana. Peirce was forced to eke out an approximation to a living by working for the United States Coast and Geodetic Survey, by itinerant lecturing, and by badly paying journalism. He was never able to produce a philosophical book, but his papers, published and unpublished, are testimony to his great philosophical distinction. One of them, "How To Make Our Ideas Clear", published in 1878, has become a classic in the history of philosophy; and in spite of making a strenuous effort to avoid reprinting it because it is a great favorite of all anthologists, I have decided to reprint it once again because no other work more effectively communicates the gist of Peirce's pragmatism or his quality as a writer. However, since Peirce —for whom consistency was not a hobgoblin—changed his mind about one of the crucial points in that essay, I have also reproduced some other passages in which he abandons what he later came to think of as the excessively nominalistic implications of the formulation of pragmatism in "How To Make Our Ideas Clear". In those passages he makes a number of other useful comments on his pragmatism or "pragmaticism" as he later came to call it.

In one of its later forms, Peirce's pragmatism was a general recipe for translating statements like "This diamond is hard" into an equivalent like "If any normal person were to try to scratch this diamond, he would see no indentation on it shortly after trying". The chief virtue of such translation, Peirce held, was that it transforms the original statement about the diamond into one that makes it easier to see whether the original statement is true or false. His point was that the conditional statement into which the original is translated by the pragmatist reports what sensible experience —in this case seeing no indentation on the diamond—would ensue upon the performance of a specified operation; and that such a statement may be tested by going through the indicated experiment. The recipe was pragmatic insofar as it called for the performance of a deliberate operation; it was empirical because it required sensory observation of the result of the operation; and it emphasized the importance of publicity by calling for an experiment which disputing parties could openly perform together. One of the effects of using his pragmatic recipe or maxim, Peirce predicted, would be the speedy disappearance of idle and meaningless debate in both science and philosophy.

At one point in "How To Make Our Ideas Clear", Peirce is led to ask a puzzling question about a diamond which has been crystallized in the midst of a cushion of soft cotton and which has remained there until finally burned up, so that no one has been able to try to scratch it. He asks: "Would it be false to say that the diamond was soft?" The later Peirce would have immediately answered "yes" but the earlier Peirce said that one may answer "yes" or "no", depending on how one wishes to use language and to arrange one's thoughts. In short, on Peirce's earlier view one could call that diamond hard or soft, as one wished. His earlier view therefore implied that the hardness of that diamond was not real, Peirce later said, precisely because anything which is not independent of our thought is not real. Furthermore, Peirce said, the denial of the reality of hardness was nominalism, a doctrine he wished to repudiate. The later Peirce insisted that the hardness of the diamond that no one tried to scratch was real, and therefore he called himself a scholastic realist. He emphasized that according to the mature version of the pragmatic recipe, to say that a diamond is hard is to say that if anybody *were* to try to scratch it, he would fail; and not that everybody who *actually* tested it failed. Peirce's point was that we must not neglect the fact that the hardness of a diamond is a disposition or potentiality which is real even though not manifested when no one has tried to scratch the diamond. And, he continued, since dispositions are universals, universals are real, as some scholastics said they were. Furthermore, he thought that they were the efficient causes of phenomena and that we should not scoff at those who say that opium puts people to sleep because it has the dormitive virtue.

Peirce's insistence that scholastic realism is an essential consequence of his pragmatic theory of meaning can surprise only those who hold that as a nineteenth-century logician and scientist who emphasized the importance of experiment, Peirce was bound to be what William James called "tough-minded"—a supporter of such doctrines as nominalism, materialism, fatalism, and atheism. The fact is, however, that Peirce defended none of these doctrines and went out of his way to attack all those tough-minded thinkers who gave the impression that science was on their side. For this reason, one is inclined to take half-seriously his jesting remark that he might have been infected by the bacilli of Transcendentalism while growing up near Emerson's Concord. Indeed, it would have greatly pleased the Concord sage to know that the first two famous American philosophers to follow him— Peirce and, as we shall see, James—believed in free will and in a divine being whose reality, according to Peirce, was to be detected by a "perceptive organ" which he called the heart. Also, it might have pleased the Emerson who called Jesus a minister of *Pure* Reason to know that Peirce remarked of his pragmatic maxim: "It has been said to be a sceptical and materialistic principle. But it is only an application of the sole principle of logic which was recommended by Jesus; 'Ye may know them by their fruits', and is very intimately allied with the ideas of the gospel".

The selections below are taken from Volume V of the *Collected Papers of Charles Sanders Peirce,* edited by Charles Hartshorne and Paul Weiss, and published by Harvard University Press. Titles supplied by the editors are marked with the superscript "E", footnotes by the editors are indicated by various typographical signs, and footnotes by Peirce are indicated by numerals. The year in which Peirce added a note is indicated by the editors at the end of the note. They have also supplied numerals for sections. Where sections are referred to in footnotes they are designated by the Arabic numeral of the volume in Peirce's *Collected Papers,* followed by a decimal point, followed by the numeral of the section. Where the reference is made to a section in Volume V the initial "5" is omitted.

How To Make Our Ideas Clear °

§1. CLEARNESS AND DISTINCTNESS *E*

388. Whoever has looked into a modern treatise on logic of the common sort,[1] will doubtless remember the two distinctions between *clear* and *obscure* conceptions, and between *distinct* and *confused* conceptions. They have lain in the books now for nigh two centuries, unimproved and unmodified, and are generally reckoned by logicians as among the gems of their doctrine.

° *Popular Science Monthly,* vol. 12, pp. 286–302 (1878); the second of the papers on the "Illustrations of the Logic of Science"; with corrections and notes from revised versions, one of which was intended as ch. 16 of the "Grand Logic" of 1893 and as Essay IX of the "Search for a Method" of 1893. This selection comes from *Collected Papers of Charles Sanders Peirce,* Volume V, edited by Charles Hartshorne and Paul Weiss (Cambridge, Mass.: The Belknap Press of Harvard University Press), pp. 248–71. Copyright 1934, 1962 by the President and Fellows of Harvard College. Reprinted by permission.

[1] One of the treatises upon logic dating from *L'Art de Penser* of the Port Royalists down to very recent times.—1893.

389. A clear idea is defined as one which is so apprehended that it will be recognized wherever it is met with, and so that no other will be mistaken for it. If it fails of this clearness, it is said to be obscure.

This is rather a neat bit of philosophical terminology; yet, since it is clearness that they were defining, I wish the logicians had made their definition a little more plain. Never to fail to recognize an idea, and under no circumstances to mistake another for it, let it come in how recondite a form it may, would indeed imply such prodigious force and clearness of intellect as is seldom met with in this world. On the other hand, merely to have such an acquaintance with the idea as to have become familiar with it, and to have lost all hesitancy in recognizing it in ordinary cases, hardly seems to deserve the name of clearness of apprehension, since after all it only amounts to a subjective feeling of mastery which may be entirely mistaken. I take it, however, that when the logicians speak of "clearness," they mean nothing more than such a familiarity with an idea, since they regard the quality as but a small merit, which needs to be supplemented by another, which they call *distinctness*.

390. A distinct idea is defined as one which contains nothing which is not clear. This is technical language; by the *contents* of an idea logicians understand whatever is contained in its definition. So that an idea is *distinctly* apprehended, according to them, when we can give a precise definition of it, in abstract terms. Here the professional logicians leave the subject; and I would not have troubled the reader with what they have to say, if it were not such a striking example of how they have been slumbering through ages of intellectual activity, listlessly disregarding the enginery of modern thought, and never dreaming of applying its lessons to the improvement of logic. It is easy to show that the doctrine that familiar use and abstract distinctness make the perfection of apprehension has its only true place in philosophies which have long been extinct; and it is now time to formulate

the method of attaining to a more perfect clearness of thought, such as we see and admire in the thinkers of our own time.

391. When Descartes set about the reconstruction of philosophy, his first step was to (theoretically) permit scepticism and to discard the practice of the schoolmen of looking to authority as the ultimate source of truth. That done, he sought a more natural fountain of true principles, and thought he found ° it in the human mind; thus passing, in the directest way, from the method of authority to that of apriority, as described in my first paper.† Self-consciousness was to furnish us with our fundamental truths, and to decide what was agreeable to reason. But since, evidently, not all ideas are true, he was led to note, as the first condition of infallibility, that they must be clear. The distinction between an idea *seeming* clear and really being so, never occurred to him. Trusting to introspection, as he did, even for a knowledge of external things, why should he question its testimony in respect to the contents of our own minds? But then, I suppose, seeing men, who seemed to be quite clear and positive, holding opposite opinions upon fundamental principles, he was further led to say that clearness of ideas is not sufficient, but that they need also to be distinct, i.e., to have nothing unclear about them. What he probably meant by this (for he did not explain himself with precision) was, that they must sustain the test of dialectical examination; that they must not only seem clear at the outset, but that discussion must never be able to bring to light points of obscurity connected with them.

392. Such was the distinction of Descartes, and one sees that it was precisely on the level of his philosophy. It was somewhat developed by Lebnitz. This great and singular genius was as remarkable for what he failed to see as for what

° "thought he found" originally "professed to find."
† See 383.

he saw. That a piece of mechanism could not do work perpetually without being fed with power in some form, was a thing perfectly apparent to him; yet he did not understand that the machinery of the mind can only transform knowledge, but never originate it, unless it be fed with facts of observation. He thus missed the most essential point of the Cartesian philosophy, which is, that to accept propositions which seem perfectly evident to us is a thing which, whether it be logical or illogical, we cannot help doing. Instead of regarding the matter in this way, he sought to reduce the first principles of science to two ° classes, those which cannot be denied without self-contradiction, and those which result from the principle of sufficient reason (of which more anon),° and was apparently unaware of the great difference between his position and that of Descartes.[1] So he reverted to the old trivialities † of logic; and, above all, abstract definitions played a great part in his philosophy. It was quite natural, therefore, that on observing that the method of Descartes labored under the difficulty that we may seem to ourselves to have clear apprehensions of ideas which in truth are very hazy, no better remedy occurred to him than to require an abstract definition of every important term. Accordingly, in adopting the distinction of *clear* and *distinct* notions, he described the latter quality as the clear apprehension of everything contained in the definition; and the books have ever since copied his words.‡ There is no danger that his chimeri-

° "two . . . anon" originally "formulas which cannot be denied without self-contradiction."

[1] He was, however, above all, one of the minds that grow; while at first he was an extreme nominalist, like Hobbes, and dabbled in the nonsensical and impotent *Ars magna* of Raymond Lully, he subsequently embraced the law of continuity and other doctrines opposed to nominalism. I speak here of his earlier views.—1903.

† Originally "formalities."

‡ Cf. his "Meditationes de Cognitione," *Die Philosophische Schriften von Leibniz*, her. von C. I. Gerhardt, Bd. IV, S. 422–427; *Nouveaux Essais*, II, 29.

cal scheme will ever again be over-valued. Nothing new can ever be learned by analyzing definitions. Nevertheless, our existing beliefs can be set in order by this process, and order is an essential element of intellectual economy, as of every other. It may be acknowledged, therefore, that the books are right in making familiarity with a notion the first step toward clearness of apprehension, and the defining of it the second. But in omitting all mention of any higher perspicuity of thought, they simply mirror a philosophy which was exploded a hundred years ago. That much-admired "ornament of logic"—the doctrine of clearness and distinctness—may be pretty enough, but it is high time to relegate to our cabinet of curiosities the antique *bijou,* and to wear about us something better adapted to modern uses.

393.[1] The very first lesson that we have a right to demand that logic shall teach us is, how to make our ideas clear; and a most important one it is, depreciated only by minds who stand in need of it. To know what we think, to be masters of our own meaning, will make a solid foundation for great and weighty thought. It is most easily learned by those whose ideas are meagre and restricted; and far happier they than such as wallow helplessly in a rich mud of conceptions. A nation, it is true, may, in the course of generations, overcome the disadvantage of an excessive wealth of language and its natural concomitant, a vast, unfathomable deep of ideas. We may see it in history, slowly perfecting its literary forms, sloughing at length its metaphysics, and, by virtue of the untirable patience which is often a compensation, attaining great excellence in every branch of mental acquirement. The page of history is not yet unrolled that * is to tell us whether such a people will or will not in the long run prevail over one whose ideas (like the words of their language) are few, but which possesses a wonderful mastery over those which it has.

[1] Delete this paragraph.—1903.
* Originally "which."

For an individual, however, there can be no question that a few clear ideas are worth more than many confused ones. A young man would hardly be persuaded to sacrifice the greater part of his thoughts to save the rest; and the muddled head is the least apt to see the necessity of such a sacrifice. Him we can usually only commiserate, as a person with a congenital defect. Time will help him, but intellectual maturity with regard to clearness is apt to ° come rather late. This seems † an unfortunate arrangement of Nature, inasmuch as clearness is of less use to a man settled in life, whose errors have in great measure had their effect, than it would be to one whose path lay ‡ before him. It is terrible to see how a single unclear idea, a single formula without meaning, lurking in a young man's head, will sometimes act like an obstruction of inert matter in an artery, hindering the nutrition of the brain, and condemning its victim to pine away in the fullness of his intellectual vigor and in the midst of intellectual plenty. Many a man has cherished for years as his hobby some vague shadow of an idea, too meaningless to be positively false; he has, nevertheless, passionately loved it, has made it his companion by day and by night, and has given to it his strength and his life, leaving all other occupations for its sake, and in short has lived with it and for it, until it has become, as it were, flesh of his flesh and bone of his bone; and then he has waked up some bright morning to find it gone, clean vanished away like the beautiful Melusina of the fable, and the essence of his life gone with it. I have myself known such a man; and who can tell how many histories of circle-squarers, metaphysicians, astrologers, and what not, may not be told in the old German [French!] story?

° "is apt to" not in the original.
† "This seems" not in the original, replacing a semicolon.
‡ Originally "lies."

§2. THE PRAGMATIC MAXIM[E]

394. The principles set forth in the first part of this essay [*]
lead, at once, to a method of reaching a clearness of thought
of [†] higher grade than the "distinctness" of the logicians. It
was there noticed [‡] that the action of thought is excited by
the irritation of doubt, and ceases when belief is attained; so
that the production of belief is the sole function of thought.[§]
All these words, however, are too strong for my purpose. It is
as if I had described the phenomena as they appear under a
mental microscope. Doubt and Belief, as the words are commonly employed, relate to religious or other grave discussions. But here I use them to designate the starting of any
question, no matter how small or how great, and the resolu-
tion of it. If, for instance, in a horse-car, I pull out my purse
and find a five-cent nickel and five coppers, I decide, while
my hand is going to the purse, in which way I will pay my
fare. To call such a question Doubt, and my decision Belief,
is certainly to use words very disproportionate to the occasion. To speak of such a doubt as causing an irritation which
needs to be appeased, suggests a temper which is uncomfortable to the verge of insanity. Yet, looking at the matter minutely, it must be admitted that, if there is the least hesitation
as to whether I shall pay the five coppers or the nickel (as
there will be sure to be, unless I act from some previously
contracted habit in the matter), though irritation is too strong
a word, yet I am excited to such small mental activity as may
be necessary to deciding how I shall act. Most frequently
doubts arise from some indecision, however momentary, in

[*] "part . . . essay" originally "of these papers."
[†] "a far," followed "of" in the original.
[‡] Originally "We have there found."
[§] See 371ff.

our action. Sometimes it is not so. I have, for example, to wait
in a railway-station, and to pass the time I read the advertise-
ments on the walls. I compare the advantages of different
trains and different routes which I never expect to take,
merely fancying myself to be in a state of hesitancy, because
I am bored with having nothing to trouble me. Feigned hesitancy, whether feigned for mere amusement or with a lofty
purpose, plays a great part in the production of scientific inquiry. However the doubt may originate, it stimulates the
mind to an activity which may be slight or energetic, calm or
turbulent. Images pass rapidly through consciousness, one incessantly melting into another, until at last, when all is over
—it may be in a fraction of a second, in an hour, or after long
years—we find ourselves decided as to how we should act
under such circumstances as those which occasioned our hesitation. In other words, we have attained belief.

395. In this process we observe two sorts of elements of
consciousness, the distinction between which may best be
made clear by means of an illustration. In a piece of music
there are the separate notes, and there is the air. A single
tone may be prolonged for an hour or a day, and it exists as
perfectly in each second of that time as in the whole taken
together; so that, as long as it is sounding, it might be present
to a sense from which everything in the past was as completely absent as the future itself. But it is different with the
air, the performance of which occupies a certain time, during
the portions of which only portions of it are played. It consists in an orderliness in the succession of sounds which strike
the ear at different times; and to perceive it there must be
some continuity of consciousness which makes the events of a
lapse of time present to us. We certainly only perceive the air
by hearing the separate notes; yet we cannot be said to directly hear it, for we hear only what is present at the instant,
and an orderliness of succession cannot exist in an instant.
These two sorts of objects, what we are *immediately* conscious of and what we are *mediately* conscious of, are found

in all consciousness. Some elements (the sensations) are completely present at every instant so long as they last, while others (like thought) are actions having beginning, middle, and end, and consist in a congruence in the succession of sensations which flow through the mind. They cannot be immediately present to us, but must cover some portion of the past or future. Thought is a thread of melody running through the succession of our sensations.

396. We may add that just as a piece of music may be written in parts, each part having its own air, so various systems of relationship of succession subsist together between the same sensations. These different systems are distinguished by having different motives, ideas, or functions. Thought is only one such system, for its sole motive, idea, and function is to produce belief, and whatever does not concern that purpose belongs to some other system of relations. The action of thinking may incidentally have other results; it may serve to amuse us, for example, and among *dilettanti* it is not rare to find those who have so perverted thought to the purposes of pleasure that it seems to vex them to think that the questions upon which they delight to exercise it may ever get finally settled; and a positive discovery which takes a favorite subject out of the arena of literary debate is met with ill-concealed dislike. This disposition is the very debauchery of thought. But the soul and meaning of thought, abstracted from the other elements which accompany it, though it may be voluntarily thwarted, can never be made to direct itself toward anything but the production of belief. Thought in action has for its only possible motive the attainment of thought at rest; and whatever does not refer to belief is no part of the thought itself.

397. And what, then, is belief? It is the demi-cadence which closes a musical phrase in the symphony of our intellectual life. We have seen that it has just three properties: First, it is something that we are aware of; second, it appeases the irritation of doubt; and, third, it involves the es-

tablishment in our nature of a rule of action, or, say for short, a *habit*. As it appeases the irritation of doubt, which is the motive for thinking, thought relaxes, and comes to rest for a moment when belief is reached. But, since belief is a rule for action, the application of which involves further doubt and further thought, at the same time that it is a stopping-place, it is also a new starting-place for thought. That is why I have permitted myself to call it thought at rest, although thought is essentially an action. The *final* upshot of thinking is the exercise of volition, and of this thought no longer forms a part; but belief is only a stadium of mental action, an effect upon our nature due to thought, which will influence future thinking.

398. The essence of belief is the establishment of a habit; and different beliefs are distinguished by the different modes of action to which they give rise. If beliefs do not differ in this respect, if they appease the same doubt by producing the same rule of action, then no mere differences in the manner of consciousness of them can make them different beliefs, any more than playing a tune in different keys is playing different tunes. Imaginary distinctions are often drawn between beliefs which differ only in their mode of expression;—the wrangling which ensues is real enough, however. To believe that any objects are arranged among themselves ° as in Fig. 1, and to believe that they are arranged [as] in Fig. 2, are one and the same belief; yet it is conceivable that a man should assert one proposition and deny the other. Such false distinctions do as much harm as the confusion of beliefs really different, and are among the pitfalls of which we ought constantly to beware, especially when we are upon metaphysical ground. One singular deception of this sort, which often occurs, is to mistake the sensation produced by our own unclearness of thought for a character of the object we are thinking. Instead of perceiving that the obscurity is purely subjective, we fancy

° "among themselves" not in the original.

that we contemplate a quality of the object which is essentially mysterious; and if our conception be afterward presented to us in a clear form we do not recognize it as the same, owing to the absence of the feeling of unintelligibility. So long as this deception lasts, it obviously puts an impassable barrier in the way of perspicuous thinking; so that it equally interests the opponents of rational thought to perpetuate it, and its adherents to guard against it.

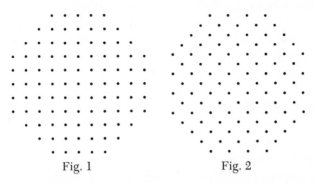

Fig. 1   Fig. 2

399. Another such deception is to mistake a mere difference in the grammatical construction of two words for a distinction between the ideas they express. In this pedantic age, when the general mob of writers attend so much more to words than to things, this error is common enough. When I just said that thought is an *action,* and that it consists in a *relation,* although a person performs an action but not a relation, which can only be the result of an action, yet there was no inconsistency in what I said, but only a grammatical vagueness.

400. From all these sophisms we shall be perfectly safe so long as we reflect that the whole function of thought is to produce habits of action; and that whatever there is connected with a thought, but irrelevant to its purpose, is an accretion to it, but no part of it. If there be a unity among our sensations which has no reference to how we shall act on a given occasion, as when we listen to a piece of music, why

we do not call that thinking. To develop its meaning, we have, therefore, simply to determine what habits it produces, for what a thing means is simply what habits it involves. Now, the identity of a habit depends on how it might lead us to act, not merely under such circumstances as are likely to arise, but under such as might possibly occur, no matter how improbable they may be.° What the habit is depends on *when* and *how* it causes us to act. As for the *when*, every stimulus to action is derived from perception; as for the *how*, every purpose of action is to produce some sensible result. Thus, we come down to what is tangible and † conceivably † practical, as the root of every real distinction of thought, no matter how subtle it may be; and there is no distinction of meaning so fine as to consist in anything but a possible difference of practice.

401. To see what this principle leads to, consider in the light of it such a doctrine as that of transubstantiation. The Protestant churches generally hold that the elements of the sacrament are flesh and blood only in a tropical sense; they nourish our souls as meat and the juice of it would our bodies. But the Catholics maintain that they are literally just meat and blood ‡; although they possess all the sensible qualities of wafercakes and diluted wine. But we can have no conception of wine except what may enter into a belief, either—

1. That this, that, or the other, is wine; or,
2. That wine possesses certain properties.

Such beliefs are nothing but self-notifications that we should, upon occasion, act in regard to such things as we believe to be wine according to the qualities which we believe wine to possess. The occasion of such action would be some sensible perception, the motive of it to produce some sensible result.

° No matter if contrary to all previous experience.—marginal note, 1893.
† Not in the original.
‡ "meat and blood" originally "that."

Thus our action has exclusive reference to what affects the senses, our habit has the same bearing as our action, our belief the same as our habit, our conception the same as our belief; and we can consequently mean nothing by wine but what has certain effects, direct or indirect, upon our senses; and to talk of something as having all the sensible characters of wine, yet being in reality blood, is senseless jargon. Now, it is not my object to pursue the theological question; and having used it as a logical example I drop it, without caring to anticipate the theologian's reply. I only desire to point out how impossible it is that we should have an idea in our minds which relates to anything but conceived sensible effects of things. Our idea of anything *is* our idea of its sensible effects; and if we fancy that we have any other we deceive ourselves, and mistake a mere sensation accompanying the thought for a part of the thought itself. It is absurd to say that thought has any meaning unrelated to its only function. It is foolish for Catholics and Protestants to fancy themselves in disagreement about the elements of the sacrament, if they agree in regard to all their sensible effects, here and ° hereafter.†

402. It appears, then, that the rule for attaining the third grade of clearness of apprehension is as follows: Consider what effects, that ‡ might conceivably have practical bearings, we conceive the object of our conception to have. Then, our conception of these effects is the whole of our conception of the object.[1,2,3]

° Originally "or."
† Cf. 541.
‡ Originally "which."
[1] Long addition refuting what comes next.—1903. [This seems to refer to the following, which was written ten years earlier on a different sheet.]
[2] Before we undertake to apply this rule, let us reflect a little upon what it implies. It has been said to be a sceptical and materialistic principle. But it is only an application of the sole principle of logic which was recommended by Jesus; "Ye may know them by their fruits," and it is very intimately allied with the ideas of the gospel. We must certainly

§3. SOME APPLICATIONS OF THE PRAGMATIC MAXIM [B]

403. Let us illustrate this rule by some examples; and, to begin with the simplest one possible, let us ask what we mean by calling a thing *hard*. Evidently that it will not be scratched by many other substances. The whole conception of this quality, as of every other, lies in its conceived effects.

guard ourselves against understanding this rule in too individualistic a sense. To say that man accomplishes nothing but that to which his endeavors are directed would be a cruel condemnation of the great bulk of mankind, who never have leisure to labor for anything but the necessities of life for themselves and their families. But, without directly striving for it, far less comprehending it, they perform all that civilization requires, and bring forth another generation to advance history another step. Their fruit is, therefore, collective; it is the achievement of the whole people. What is it, then, that the whole people is about, what is this civilization that is the outcome of history, but is never completed? We cannot expect to attain a complete conception of it; but we can see that it is a gradual process, that it involves a realization of ideas in man's consciousness and in his works, and that it takes place by virtue of man's capacity for learning, and by experience continually pouring upon him ideas he has not yet acquired. We may say that it is the process whereby man, with all his miserable littlenesses, becomes gradually more and more imbued with the Spirit of God, in which Nature and History are rife. We are also told to believe in a world to come; but the idea is itself too vague to contribute much to the perspicuity of ordinary ideas. It is a common observation that those who dwell continually upon their expectations are apt to become oblivious to the requirements of their actual station. The great principle of logic is self-surrender, which does not mean that self is to lay low for the sake of an ultimate triumph. It may turn out so; but that must not be the governing purpose.

When we come to study the great principle of continuity [see vol. 6, Bk. I, B.] and see how all is fluid and every point directly partakes the being of every other, it will appear that individualism and falsity are one and the same. Meantime, we know that man is not whole as long as he is single, that he is essentially a possible member of society. Especially, one man's experience is nothing, if it stands alone. If he sees what others cannot, we call it hallucination. It is not "my" experience, but "our" experience that has to be thought of; and this "us" has indefinite possibilities.

There is absolutely no difference between a hard thing and a soft thing so long as they are not brought to the test. Suppose, then, that a diamond could be crystallized in the midst of a cushion of soft cotton, and should remain there until it was finally burned up. Would it be false to say that that diamond was soft? This seems a foolish question, and would be so, in fact, except in the realm of logic. There such questions are often of the greatest utility as serving to bring logical principles into sharper relief than real discussions ever could.

Neither must we understand the practical in any low and sordid sense. Individual action is a means and not our end. Individual pleasure is not our end; we are all putting our shoulders to the wheel for an end that none of us can catch more than a glimpse at—that which the generations are working out. But we can see that the development of embodied ideas is what it will consist in.—1893.

3 Note that in these three lines one finds, "conceivably," "conceive," "conception," "conception," "conception." Now I find there are many people who detect the authorship of my unsigned screeds; and I doubt not that one of the marks of my style by which they do so is my inordinate reluctance to repeat a word. This employment five times over of derivates of *concipere* must then have had a purpose. In point of fact it had two. One was to show that I was speaking of meaning in no other sense than that of *intellectual purport*. The other was to avoid all danger of being understood as attempting to explain a concept by percepts, images, schemata, or by anything but concepts. I did not, therefore, mean to say that acts, which are more strictly singular than anything, could constitute the purport, or adequate proper interpretation, of any symbol. I compared action to the finale of the symphony of thought, belief being a demi-cadence. Nobody conceives that the few bars at the end of a musical movement are the *purpose* of the movement. They may be called its upshot. But the figure obviously would not bear detailed application. I only mention it to show that the suspicion I myself expressed (Baldwin's *Dictionary* Article, *Pragmatism*) [see 3] after a too hasty rereading of the forgotten magazine paper, that it expressed a stoic, that is, a nominalistic, materialistic, and utterly philistine state of thought, was quite mistaken.

No doubt, Pragmaticism [see 414] makes thought ultimately *apply* to action exclusively—to *conceived* action. But between admitting that and either saying that it makes thought, in the sense of the purport of symbols, to consist in acts, or saying that the true ultimate purpose of thinking is action, there is much the same difference as there is be-

In studying logic we must not put them aside with hasty answers, but must consider them with attentive care, in order to make out the principles involved. We may, in the present case, modify our question, and ask what prevents us from saying that all hard bodies remain perfectly soft until they are touched, when their hardness increases with the pressure until they are scratched. Reflection will show that the reply is this: there would be no *falsity* in such modes of speech. They would involve a modification of our present usage of speech with regard to the words hard and soft, but not of their meanings. For they represent no fact to be different from what it is; only they involve arrangements of facts which would be exceedingly maladroit.° This leads us to remark that the question of what would occur under circumstances

tween saying that the artist-painter's living art is applied to dabbing paint upon canvas, and saying that that art-life consists in dabbing paint, or that its ultimate aim is dabbing paint. Pragmaticism makes thinking to consist in the living inferential metaboly of symbols whose purport lies in conditional general resolutions to act. As for the ultimate purpose of thought, which must be the purpose of everything, it is beyond human comprehension; but according to the stage of approach which my thought has made to it—with aid from many persons, among whom I may mention Royce (in his *World and Individual*), Schiller (in his *Riddles of the Sphinx*) as well, by the way, as the famous poet [Friedrich Schiller] (in his *Aesthetische Briefe*), Henry James the elder (in his *Substance and Shadow* and in his conversations), together with Swedenborg himself—it is by the indefinite replication of self-control upon self-control that the *vir* is begotten, and by action, through thought, he grows an esthetic ideal, not for the behoof of his own poor noddle merely, but as the share which God permits him to have in the work of creation.

This ideal, by modifying the rules of self-control modifies action, and so experience too—both the man's own and that of others, and this centrifugal movement thus rebounds in a new centripetal movement, and so on; and the whole is a bit of what has been going on, we may presume, for a time in comparison with which the sum of the geological ages is as the surface of an electron in comparison with that of a planet.—From "Consequences of Pragmaticism," 1906.

° But see 453, 457.

which do not actually arise is not a question of fact, but only of the most perspicuous arrangement of them. For example, the question of free-will and fate in its simplest form, stripped of verbiage, is something like this: I have done something of which I am ashamed; could I, by an effort of the will, have resisted the temptation, and done otherwise? The philosophical reply is, that this is not a question of fact, but only of the arrangement of facts.° Arranging them so as to exhibit what is particularly pertinent to my question—namely, that I ought to blame myself for having done wrong—it is perfectly true to say that, if I had willed to do otherwise than I did, I should have done otherwise. On the other hand, arranging the facts so as to exhibit another important consideration, it is equally true that, when a temptation has once been allowed to work, it will, if it has a certain force, produce its effect, let me struggle how I may. There is no objection to a contradiction in what would result from a false supposition. The *reductio ad absurdum* consists in showing that contradictory results would follow from a hypothesis which is consequently judged to be false. Many questions are involved in the free-will discussion, and I am far from desiring to say that both sides are equally right. On the contrary, I am of opinion that one side denies important facts, and that the other does not. But what I do say is, that the above single question was the origin of the whole doubt; that, had it not been for this question, the controversy would never have arisen; and that this question is perfectly solved in the manner which I have indicated.

Let us next seek a clear idea of Weight. This is another very easy case. To say that a body is heavy means simply that, in the absence of opposing force, it will fall. This (neglecting certain specifications of how it will fall, etc., which exist in the mind of the physicist who uses the word) is evidently the whole conception of weight. It is a fair question whether some particular facts may not *account* for gravity;

°Cf. 339.

but what we mean by the force itself is completely involved in its effects.

404. This leads us to undertake an account of the idea of Force in general. This is the great conception which, developed in the early part of the seventeenth century from the rude idea of a cause, and constantly improved upon since, has shown us how to explain all the changes of motion which bodies experience, and how to think about all physical phenomena; which has given birth to modern science, and changed the face of the globe; and which, aside from its more special uses, has played a principal part in directing the course of modern thought, and in furthering modern social development. It is, therefore, worth some pains to comprehend it. According to our rule, we must begin by asking what is the immediate use of thinking about force; and the answer is, that we thus account for changes of motion. If bodies were left to themselves, without the intervention of forces, every motion would continue unchanged both in velocity and in direction. Furthermore, change of motion never takes place abruptly; if its direction is changed, it is always through a curve without angles; if its velocity alters, it is by degrees. The gradual changes which are constantly taking place are conceived by geometers to be compounded together according to the rules of the parallelogram of forces. If the reader does not already know what this is, he will find it, I hope, to his advantage to endeavor to follow the following explanation; but if mathematics are insupportable to him, pray let him skip three paragraphs rather than that we should part company here.

A *path* is a line whose beginning and end are distinguished. Two paths are considered to be equivalent, which, beginning at the same point, lead to the same point. Thus the two paths, *ABCDE* and *AFGHE* (Fig. 3), are equivalent. Paths which do *not* begin at the same point are considered to be equivalent, provided that, on moving either of them without turning it, but keeping it always parallel to its original position, when its beginning coincides with that of the other path, the ends also coincide. Paths are considered as geometrically added together, when one begins where the other ends; thus the path *AE* is conceived to be a sum of *AB*, *BC*, *CD*, and *DE*. In the parallelogram of Fig. 4 the diagonal *AC* is the sum of *AB* and *BC*; or, since *AD* is geometrically equivalent to *BC*, *AC* is the geometrical sum of *AB* and *AD*.

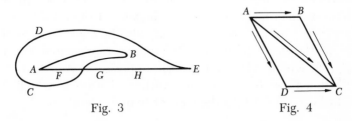

Fig. 3   Fig. 4

All this is purely conventional. It simply amounts to this: that we choose to call paths having the relations I have described equal or added. But, though it is a convention, it is a convention with a good reason. The rule for geometrical addition may be applied not only to paths, but to any other things which can be represented by paths. Now, as a path is determined by the varying direction and distance of the point which moves over it from the starting-point, it follows that anything which from its beginning to its end is determined by a varying direction and a varying magnitude is capable of being represented by a line. Accordingly, *velocities* may be represented by lines, for they have only directions and rates. The same thing is true of *accelerations*, or changes of velocities. This is evident enough in the case of velocities; and it becomes evident for accelerations if we consider that precisely what velocities are to positions—namely, states of change of them—that accelerations are to velocities.

The so-called "parallelogram of forces" is simply a rule for compounding accelerations. The rule is, to represent the accelerations by paths, and then to geometrically add the paths. The geometers, however, not only use the "parallelogram of

forces" to compound different accelerations, but also to resolve one acceleration into a sum of several. Let *AB* (Fig. 5)
be the path which represents a certain acceleration—say,
such a change in the motion of a body that at the end of one
second the body will, under the influence of that change, be
in a position different from what it would have had if its motion had continued unchanged such that a path equivalent to
AB would lead from the latter position to the former. This acceleration may be considered as the sum of the accelerations
represented by *AC* and *CB*. It may also be considered as the
sum of the very different accelerations represented by *AD*
and *DB*, where *AD* is almost the opposite of *AC*. And it is
clear that there is an immense variety of ways in which *AB*
might be resolved into the sum of two accelerations.

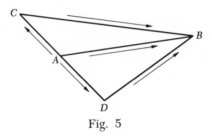

Fig. 5

After this tedious explanation, which I hope, in view of the
extraordinary interest of the conception of force, may not
have exhausted the reader's patience, we are prepared at last
to state the grand fact which this conception embodies. This
fact is that if the actual changes of motion which the different particles of bodies experience are each resolved in its appropriate way, each component acceleration is precisely such
as is prescribed by a certain law of Nature, according to
which bodies, in the relative positions which the bodies in
question actually have at the moment,[1] always receive certain accelerations, which, being compounded by geometrical

[1] Possibly the velocities also have to be taken into account.

addition, give the acceleration which the body actually experiences.

This is the only fact which the idea of force represents, and whoever will take the trouble clearly to apprehend what this fact is, perfectly comprehends what force is. Whether we ought to say that a force *is* an acceleration, or that it *causes* an acceleration, is a mere question of propriety of language, which has no more to do with our real meaning than the difference between the French idiom *"Il fait froid"* and its English equivalent *"It is cold."* Yet it is surprising to see how this simple affair has muddled men's minds. In how many profound treatises is not force spoken of as a "mysterious entity," which seems to be only a way of confessing that the author despairs of ever getting a clear notion of what the word means! In a recent admired work on *Analytic Mechanics* ° it is stated that we understand precisely the effect of force, but what force itself is we do not understand! This is simply a self-contradiction. The idea which the word force excites in our minds has no other function than to affect our actions, and these actions can have no reference to force otherwise than through its effects. Consequently, if we know what the effects of force are, we are acquainted with every fact which is implied in saying that a force exists, and there is nothing more to know. The truth is, there is some vague notion afloat that a question may mean something which the mind cannot conceive; and when some hair-splitting philosophers have been confronted with the absurdity of such a view, they have invented an empty distinction between positive and negative conceptions, in the attempt to give their non-idea a form not obviously nonsensical. The nullity of it is sufficiently plain from the considerations given a few pages back; and, apart from those considerations, the quibbling character of the distinction must have struck every mind accustomed to real thinking.

° Kirchhoff's *Vorlesungen über math. Physik,* Bd. I, Vorrede.

§4. REALITY [E]

405. Let us now approach the subject of logic, and consider a conception which particularly concerns it, that of *reality*. Taking clearness in the sense of familiarity, no idea could be clearer than this. Every child uses it with perfect confidence, never dreaming that he does not understand it. As for clearness in its second grade, however, it would probably puzzle most men, even among those of a reflective turn of mind, to give an abstract definition of the real. Yet such a definition may perhaps be reached by considering the points of difference between reality and its opposite, fiction. A figment is a product of somebody's imagination; it has such characters as his thought impresses upon it. That those characters are independent of how you or I think is an external reality. There are, however, phenomena within our own minds, dependent upon our thought, which are at the same time real in the sense that we really think them. But though their characters depend on how we think, they do not depend on what we think those characters to be. Thus, a dream has a real existence as a mental phenomenon, if somebody has really dreamt it; that he dreamt so and so, does not depend on what anybody thinks was dreamt, but is completely independent of all opinion on the subject. On the other hand, considering, not the fact of dreaming, but the thing dreamt, it retains its peculiarities by virtue of no other fact than that it was dreamt to possess them. Thus we may define the real as that whose characters are independent of what anybody may think them to be.

406. But, however satisfactory such a definition may be found, it would be a great mistake to suppose that it makes the idea of reality perfectly clear. Here, then, let us apply our rules. According to them, reality, like every other quality, consists in the peculiar sensible effects which things partaking of it produce. The only effect which real things have is to cause belief, for all the sensations which they excite emerge

into consciousness in the form of beliefs. The question therefore is, how is true belief (or belief in the real) distinguished from false belief (or belief in fiction). Now, as we have seen in the former paper,° the ideas of truth and falsehood, in their full development, appertain exclusively to the experiential † method of settling opinion. A person who arbitrarily chooses the propositions which he will adopt can use the word truth only to emphasize the expression of his determination to hold on to his choice. Of course, the method of tenacity ‡ never prevailed exclusively; reason is too natural to men for that. But in the literature of the dark ages we find some fine examples of it. When Scotus Erigena is commenting upon a poetical passage in which hellebore is spoken of as having caused the death of Socrates, he does not hesitate to inform the inquiring reader that Helleborus and Socrates were two eminent Greek philosophers, and that the latter, having been overcome in argument by the former, took the matter to heart and died of it! What sort of an idea of truth could a man have who could adopt and teach, without the qualification of a perhaps, an opinion taken so entirely at random? The real spirit of Socrates, who I hope would have been delighted to have been "overcome in argument," because he would have learned something by it, is in curious contrast with the naïve idea of the glossist, for whom (as for "the born missionary" of today) § discussion would seem to have been simply a struggle. When philosophy began to awake from its long slumber, and before theology completely dominated it, the practice seems to have been for each professor to seize upon any philosophical position he found unoccupied and which seemed a strong one, to intrench himself in it, and to sally forth from time to time to give battle to the others.

° In 385.
† Originally "scientific."
‡ See 377f.
§ The parenthesized phrase was not in the original.

Thus, even the scanty records we possess of those disputes enable us to make out a dozen or more opinions held by different teachers at one time concerning the question of nominalism and realism. Read the opening part of the *Historia Calamitatum* of Abelard,* who was certainly as philosophical as any of his contemporaries, and see the spirit of combat which it breathes. For him, the truth is simply his particular stronghold. When the method of authority † prevailed, the truth meant little more than the Catholic faith. All the efforts of the scholastic doctors are directed toward harmonizing their faith in Aristotle and their faith in the Church, and one may search their ponderous folios through without finding an argument which goes any further. It is noticeable that where different faiths flourish side by side, renegades are looked upon with contempt even by the party whose belief they adopt; so completely has the idea of loyalty replaced that of truth-seeking. Since the time of Descartes, the defect in the conception of truth has been less apparent. Still, it will sometimes strike a scientific man that the philosophers have been less intent on finding out what the facts are, than on inquiring what belief is most in harmony with their system. It is hard to convince a follower of the *a priori* method by adducing facts; but show him that an opinion he is defending is inconsistent with what he has laid down elsewhere, and he will be very apt to retract it. These minds do not seem to believe that disputation is ever to cease; they seem to think that the opinion which is natural for one man is not so for another, and that belief will, consequently, never be settled. In contenting themselves with fixing their own opinions by a method which would lead another man to a different result, they betray their feeble hold of the conception of what truth is.

* *Patrologia Latina*, vol. 178, p. 114 et seq., (1885).
† See 379f.

407. On the other hand, all the followers of science are animated by a cheerful hope ° that the processes of investigation, if only pushed far enough, will give one certain solution to each † question to which they apply it. ‡ One man may investigate the velocity of light by studying the transits of Venus and the aberration of the stars; another by the oppositions of Mars and the eclipses of Jupiter's satellites; a third by the method of Fizeau; a fourth by that of Foucault; a fifth by the motions of the curves of Lissajoux; a sixth, a seventh, an eighth, and a ninth, may follow the different methods of comparing the measures of statical and dynamical electricity. They may at first obtain different results, but, as each perfects his method and his processes, the results are found to move § steadily together toward a destined centre. So with all scientific research. Different minds may set out with the most antagonistic views, but the progress of investigation carries them by a force outside of themselves to one and the same conclusion. This activity of thought by which we are carried, not where we wish, but to a fore-ordained goal, is like the operation of destiny. No modification of the point of view taken, no selection of other facts for study, no natural bent of mind even, can enable a man to escape the predestinate opinion. This great hope ¶ is embodied in the conception of truth and reality. The opinion which is fated [1] to be ultimately agreed to by all who investigate, is what we mean by the truth, and the object represented in this opinion is the real. That is the way I would explain reality.

° "are . . . hope" originally "are fully persuaded."
† Originally "every."
‡ "apply it" originally "can be applied."
§ "are . . . move" originally "will move."
¶ Originally "law."
[1] Fate means merely that which is sure to come true, and can nohow be avoided. It is a superstition to suppose that a certain sort of events are ever fated, and it is another to suppose that the word fate can never be freed from its superstitious taint. We are all fated to die.

408. But it may be said that this view is directly opposed to the abstract definition which we have given of reality, inasmuch as it makes the characters of the real depend on what is ultimately thought about them. But the answer to this is that, on the one hand, reality is independent, not necessarily of thought in general, but only of what you or I or any finite number of men may think about it; and that, on the other hand, though the object of the final opinion depends on what that opinion is, yet what that opinion is does not depend on what you or I or any man thinks. Our perversity and that of others may indefinitely postpone the settlement of opinion; it might even conceivably cause an arbitrary proposition to be universally accepted as long as the human race should last. Yet even that would not change the nature of the belief, which alone could be the result of investigation carried sufficiently far; and if, after the extinction of our race, another should arise with faculties and disposition for investigation, that true opinion must be the one which they would ultimately come to. "Truth crushed to earth shall rise again," and the opinion which would finally result from investigation does not depend on how anybody may actually think. But the reality of that which is real does depend on the real fact that investigation is destined to lead, at last, if continued long enough, to a belief in it.

409. But I may be asked what I have to say to all the minute facts of history, forgotten never to be recovered, to the lost books of the ancients, to the buried secrets.

> Full many a gem of purest ray serene
>> The dark, unfathomed caves of ocean bear;
> Full many a flower is born to blush unseen,
>> And waste its sweetness on the desert air.

Do these things not really exist because they are hopelessly beyond the reach of our knowledge? And then, after the universe is dead (according to the prediction of some scientists), and all life has ceased forever, will not the shock of atoms continue though there will be no mind to know it? To this I reply that, though in no possible state of knowledge can any number be great enough to express the relation between the amount of what rests unknown to the amount of the known, yet it is unphilosophical to suppose that, with regard to any given question (which has any clear meaning), investigation would not bring forth a solution of it, if it were carried far enough. Who would have said, a few years ago, that we could ever know of what substances stars are made whose light may have been longer in reaching us than the human race has existed? Who can be sure of what we shall not know in a few hundred years? Who can guess what would be the result of continuing the pursuit of science for ten thousand years, with the activity of the last hundred? And if it were to go on for a million, or a billion, or any number of years you please, how is it possible to say that there is any question which might not ultimately be solved?

But it may be objected, "Why make so much of these remote considerations, especially when it is your principle that only practical distinctions have a meaning?" Well, I must confess that it makes very little difference whether we say that a stone on the bottom of the ocean, in complete darkness, is brilliant or not—that is to say, that it *probably* makes no difference, remembering always that that stone *may* be fished up tomorrow. But that there are gems at the bottom of the sea, flowers in the untraveled desert, etc., are propositions which, like that about a diamond being hard when it is not pressed, concern much more the arrangement of our language than they do the meaning of our ideas.

410. It seems to me, however, that we have, by the application of our rule, reached so clear an apprehension of what we mean by reality, and of the fact which the idea rests on, that we should not, perhaps, be making a pretension so presumptuous as it would be singular, if we were to offer a metaphysical theory of existence for universal acceptance among those who employ the scientific method of fixing belief. How-

ever, as metaphysics is a subject much more curious than useful, the knowledge of which, like that of a sunken reef, serves chiefly to enable us to keep clear of it, I will not trouble the reader with any more Ontology at this moment. I have already been led much further into that path than I should have desired; and I have given the reader such a dose of mathematics, psychology, and all that is most abstruse, that I fear he may already have left me, and that what I am now writing is for the compositor and proof-reader exclusively. I trusted to the importance of the subject. There is no royal road to logic, and really valuable ideas can only be had at the price of close attention. But I know that in the matter of ideas the public prefer the cheap and nasty; and in my next paper ° I am going to return to the easily intelligible, and not wander from it again. The reader who has been at the pains of wading through this paper, shall be rewarded in the next one by seeing how beautifully what has been developed in this tedious way can be applied to the ascertainment of the rules of scientific reasoning.

We have, hitherto, not crossed the threshold of scientific logic. It is certainly important to know how to make our ideas clear, but they may be ever so clear without being true. How to make them so, we have next to study. How to give birth to those vital and procreative ideas which multiply into a thousand forms and diffuse themselves everywhere, advancing civilization and making the dignity of man, is an art not yet reduced to rules, but of the secret of which the history of science affords some hints.

Pragmatism and Scholastic Realism

WHAT PRAGMATISM IS †

§1. THE EXPERIMENTALISTS' VIEW OF ASSERTION[B]

411. The writer of this article has been led by much expe-

° See vol. 2, bk. III, ch. 6.

† *The Monist,* vol. 15, pp. 161–81 (1905). The first of three articles. Parts of the second follow below in this anthology on pages 327–29.

rience to believe that every physicist, and every chemist, and, in short, every master in any department of experimental science, has had his mind moulded by his life in the laboratory to a degree that is little suspected. The experimentalist himself can hardly be fully aware of it, for the reason that the men whose intellects he really knows about are much like himself in this respect. With intellects of widely different training from his own, whose education has largely been a thing learned out of books, he will never become inwardly intimate, be he on ever so familiar terms with them; for he and they are as oil and water, and though they be shaken up together, it is remarkable how quickly they will go their several mental ways, without having gained more than a faint flavor from the association. Were those other men only to take skillful soundings of the experimentalist's mind—which is just what they are unqualified to do, for the most part—they would soon discover that, excepting perhaps upon topics where his mind is trammelled by personal feeling or by his bringing up, his disposition is to think of everything just as everything is thought of in the laboratory, that is, as a question of experimentation. Of course, no living man possesses in their fullness all the attributes characteristic of his type: it is not the typical doctor whom you will see every day driven in buggy or coupé, nor is it the typical pedagogue that will be met with in the first schoolroom you enter. But when you have found, or ideally constructed upon a basis of observation, the typical experimentalist, you will find that whatever assertion you may make to him, he will either understand as meaning that if a given prescription for an experiment ever can be and ever is carried out in act, an experience of a given description will result, or else he will see no sense at all in

This composite selection is made from *Collected Papers of Charles Sanders Peirce*, Volume V, edited by Charles Hartshorne and Paul Weiss (Cambridge, Mass.: The Belknap Press of the Harvard University Press), pp. 272–74, 276–77, 281–85, 305–6, 309–10. Copyright 1934, 1962 by the President and Fellows of Harvard College. Reprinted by permission. [M.W.]

what you say. If you talk to him as Mr. Balfour talked not long ago to the British Association ° saying that "the physicist . . . seeks for something deeper than the laws connecting possible objects of experience," that "his object is physical reality" unrevealed in experiments, and that the existence of such non-experiential reality "is the unalterable faith of science," to all such ontological meaning you will find the experimentalist mind to be color-blind. What adds to that confidence in this, which the writer owes to his conversations with experimentalists, is that he himself may almost be said to have inhabited a laboratory from the age of six until long past maturity; and having all his life associated mostly with experimentalists, it has always been with a confident sense of understanding them and of being understood by them.

412. That laboratory life did not prevent the writer (who here and in what follows simply exemplifies the experimentalist type) from becoming interested in methods of thinking; and when he came to read metaphysics, although much of it seemed to him loosely reasoned and determined by accidental prepossessions, yet in the writings of some philosophers, especially Kant, Berkeley, and Spinoza, he sometimes came upon strains of thought that recalled the ways of thinking of the laboratory, so that he felt he might trust to them; all of which has been true of other laboratory-men.

Endeavoring, as a man of that type naturally would, to formulate what he so approved, he framed the theory that a *conception,* that is, the rational purport of a word or other expression, lies exclusively in its conceivable bearing upon the conduct of life; so that, since obviously nothing that might not result from experiment can have any direct bearing upon conduct, if one can define accurately all the conceivable experimental phenomena which the affirmation or

° *Reflections Suggested by the New Theory of Matter;* Presidential Address, British Association for the Advancement of Science, August 17, 1904.

denial of a concept could imply, one will have therein a complete definition of the concept, and *there is absolutely nothing more in it*. For this doctrine he invented the name *pragmatism*. Some of his friends wished him to call it *practicism* or *practicalism* (perhaps on the ground that πρακτικός is better Greek than πραγματικός). But for one who had learned philosophy out of Kant, as the writer, along with nineteen out of every twenty experimentalists who have turned to philosophy, had done, and who still thought in Kantian terms most readily, *praktisch* and *pragmatisch* were as far apart as the two poles, the former belonging in a region of thought where no mind of the experimentalist type can ever make sure of solid ground under his feet, the latter expressing relation to some definite human purpose. Now quite the most striking feature of the new theory was its recognition of an inseparable connection between rational cognition and rational purpose; and that consideration it was which determined the preference for the name *pragmatism*. . . .

§3. PRAGMATICISM[E]

414. After awaiting in vain, for a good many years, some particularly opportune conjuncture of circumstances that might serve to recommend his notions of the ethics of terminology, the writer has now, at last, dragged them in over head and shoulders, on an occasion when he has no specific proposal to offer nor any feeling but satisfaction at the course usage has run without any canons or resolutions of a congress. His word "pragmatism" has gained general recognition in a generalized sense that seems to argue power of growth and vitality. The famed psychologist, James, first took it up,[*] seeing that his "radical empiricism" substantially answered to the writer's definition of pragmatism, albeit with a certain difference in the point of view. Next, the admirably clear and

---

[*] See his *Pragmatism*, p. 47.

brilliant thinker, Mr. Ferdinand C. S. Schiller, casting about for a more attractive name for the "anthropomorphism" of his *Riddle of the Sphinx*, lit, in that most remarkable paper of his on *Axioms as Postulates*,° upon the same designation "pragmatism," which in its original sense was in generic agreement with his own doctrine, for which he has since found the more appropriate specification "humanism," while he still retains "pragmatism" in a somewhat wider sense. So far all went happily. But at present, the word begins to be met with occasionally in the literary journals, where it gets abused in the merciless way that words have to expect when they fall into literary clutches. Sometimes the manners of the British have effloresced in scolding at the word as ill-chosen—ill-chosen, that is, to express some meaning that it was rather designed to exclude. So then, the writer, finding his bantling "pragmatism" so promoted, feels that it is time to kiss his child good-by and relinquish it to its higher destiny; while to serve the precise purpose of expressing the original definition, he begs to announce the birth of the word "pragmaticism," which is ugly enough to be safe from kidnappers.[1] . . .

422. Let us now hasten to the exposition of pragmaticism itself. Here it will be convenient to imagine that somebody to whom the doctrine is new, but of rather preternatural perspicacity, asks questions of a pragmaticist. Everything that might give a dramatic illusion must be stripped off, so that the result will be a sort of cross between a dialogue and a

---

° In *Personal Idealism*, ed. by H. Sturt, p. 63 (1902).

[1] To show how recent the general use of the word "pragmatism" is, the writer may mention that, to the best of his belief, he never used it in copy for the press before today, except by particular request, in *Baldwin's Dictionary*. [See 1–4.] Toward the end of 1890, when this part of the *Century Dictionary* appeared, he did not deem that the word had sufficient status to appear in that work. [But see 13n.] But he has used it continually in philosophical conversation since, perhaps, the mid-seventies.

catechism, but a good deal liker the latter—something rather painfully reminiscent of Mangnall's *Historical Questions.*

Questioner: I am astounded at your definition of your pragmatism, because only last year I was assured by a person above all suspicion of warping the truth—himself a pragmatist—that your doctrine precisely was "that a conception is to be tested by its practical effects." You must surely, then, have entirely changed your definition very recently.

Pragmatist: If you will turn to Vols. VI and VII of the *Revue Philosophique,* or to the *Popular Science Monthly* for November 1877 and January 1878, . . . you will be able to judge for yourself whether the interpretation you mention was not then clearly excluded. The exact wording of the English enunciation, (changing only the first person into the second), was: "Consider what effects that might conceivably have practical bearing you conceive the object of your conception to have. Then your conception of those effects is the WHOLE of your conception of the object." °

Questioner: Well, what reason have you for asserting that this is so?

Pragmatist: That is what I specially desire to tell you. But the question had better be postponed until you clearly understand what those reasons profess to prove.

423. *Questioner:* What, then, is the *raison d'être* of the doctrine? What advantage is expected from it?

Pragmatist: It will serve to show that almost every proposition of ontological metaphysics is either meaningless gibberish—one word being defined by other words, and they by still others, without any real conception ever being reached—or else is downright absurd; so that all such rubbish being swept away, what will remain of philosophy will be a series of problems capable of investigation by the observational methods of the true sciences—the truth about which

° See 402.

can be reached without those interminable misunderstandings and disputes which have made the highest of the positive sciences a mere amusement for idle intellects, a sort of chess—idle pleasure its purpose, and reading out of a book its method. In this regard, pragmaticism is a species of prope-positivism. But what distinguishes it from other species is, first, its retention of a purified philosophy; secondly, its full acceptance of the main body of our instinctive beliefs; and thirdly, its strenuous insistence upon the truth of scholastic realism (or a close approximation to that, well-stated by the late Dr. Francis Ellingwood Abbot in the Introduction to his *Scientific Theism*). So, instead of merely jeering at metaphysics, like other prope-positivists, whether by long drawn-out parodies or otherwise, the pragmaticist extracts from it a precious essence, which will serve to give life and light to cosmology and physics. At the same time, the moral applications of the doctrine are positive and potent; and there are many other uses of it not easily classed. On another occasion, instances may be given to show that it really has these effects.

424. *Questioner:* I hardly need to be convinced that your doctrine would wipe out metaphysics. Is it not as obvious that it must wipe out every proposition of science and everything that bears on the conduct of life? For you say that the only meaning that, for you, any assertion bears is that a certain experiment has resulted in a certain way: Nothing else but an experiment enters into the meaning. Tell me, then, how can an experiment, in itself, reveal anything more than that something once happened to an individual object and that subsequently some other individual event occurred?

Pragmatist: That question is, indeed, to the purpose—the purpose being to correct any misapprehensions of pragmaticism. You speak of an experiment in itself, emphasising *"in itself."* You evidently think of each experiment as isolated from every other. It has not, for example, occurred to you, one might venture to surmise, that every connected series of experiments constitutes a single collective experiment. What are the essential ingredients of an experiment? First, of course, an experimenter of flesh and blood. Secondly, a verifiable hypothesis. This is a proposition [1] relating to the universe environing the experimenter, or to some well-known part of it and affirming or denying of this only some experimental possibility or impossibility. The third indispensable ingredient is a sincere doubt in the experimenter's mind as to the truth of that hypothesis.

Passing over several ingredients on which we need not dwell, the purpose, the plan, and the resolve, we come to the act of choice by which the experimenter singles out certain identifiable objects to be operated upon. The next is the external (or quasi-external) ACT by which he modifies those objects. Next, comes the subsequent *reaction* of the world upon the experimenter in a perception; and finally, his recognition of the teaching of the experiment. While the two chief parts of the event itself are the action and the reaction, yet the unity of essence of the experiment lies in its purpose and plan, the ingredients passed over in the enumeration.

425. Another thing: in representing the pragmaticist as making rational meaning to consist in an experiment (which you speak of as an event in the past), you strikingly fail to catch his attitude of mind. Indeed, it is not in an experiment, but in *experimental phenomena,* that rational meaning is said to consist. When an experimentalist speaks of a *phenomenon,* such as "Hall's phenomenon," "Zeemann's phenomenon" and its modification, "Michelson's phenomenon," or "the chess-

---

[1] The writer, like most English logicians, invariably uses the word *proposition* not as the Germans define their equivalent, *Satz,* as the language-expression of a judgment (*Urtheil*), but as that which is related to any assertion, whether mental and self-addressed or outwardly expressed, just as any possibility is related to its actualisation. The difficulty of the, at best, difficult problem of the essential nature of a Proposition has been increased, for the Germans, by their *Urtheil,* confounding, under one designation, the mental *assertion* with the *assertible* [cf. 2.315].

board phenomenon," he does not mean any particular event
that did happen to somebody in the dead past, but what
surely will happen to everybody in the living future who
shall fulfill certain conditions. The phenomenon consists in
the fact that when an experimentalist shall come to *act* according to a certain scheme that he has in mind, then will
something else happen, and shatter the doubts of sceptics,
like the celestial fire upon the altar of Elijah.

426. And do not overlook the fact that the pragmaticist
maxim says nothing of single experiments or of single experimental phenomena (for what is conditionally true *in futuro*
can hardly be singular), but only speaks of *general kinds* of
experimental phenomena. Its adherent does not shrink from
speaking of general objects as real, since whatever is true
represents a real. Now the laws of nature are true.

427. The rational meaning of every proposition lies in the
future. How so? The meaning of a proposition is itself a proposition. Indeed, it is no other than the very proposition of
which it is the meaning: it is a translation of it. But of the
myriads of forms into which a proposition may be translated,
what is that one which is to be called its very meaning? It is,
according to the pragmaticist, that form in which the proposition becomes applicable to human conduct, not in these or
those special circumstances, nor when one entertains this or
that special design, but that form which is most directly applicable to self-control under every situation, and to every
purpose. This is why he locates the meaning in future time;
for future conduct is the only conduct that is subject to self-
control. But in order that that form of the proposition which
is to be taken as its meaning should be applicable to every
situation and to every purpose upon which the proposition
has any bearing, it must be simply the general description of
all the experimental phenomena which the assertion of the
proposition virtually predicts. For an experimental phenomenon is the fact asserted by the proposition that action of a
certain description will have a certain kind of experimental

result; and experimental results are the only results that can affect human conduct. No doubt, some unchanging idea may come to influence a man more than it had done; but only because some experience equivalent to an experiment has brought its truth home to him more intimately than before. Whenever a man acts purposively, he acts under a belief in some experimental phenomenon. Consequently, the sum of the experimental phenomena that a proposition implies makes up its entire bearing upon human conduct. Your question, then, of how a pragmaticist can attribute any meaning to any assertion other than that of a single occurrence is substantially answered. . . .

453. [A] doctrine which is involved in Pragmaticism as an essential consequence of it, but which the writer defended . . . before he had formulated, even in his own mind, the principle of pragmaticism, is the scholastic doctrine of realism. This is usually defined as the opinion that there are real objects that are general, among the number being the modes of determination of existent singulars, if, indeed, these be not the only such objects. . . . The article of January 1878 ° endeavored to gloze over this point as unsuited to the exoteric public addressed; or perhaps the writer wavered in his own mind. He said that if a diamond were to be formed in a bed of cotton-wool, and were to be consumed there without ever having been pressed upon by any hard edge or point, it would be merely a question of nomenclature whether that diamond should be said to have been hard or not. No doubt this is true, except for the abominable falsehood in the word MERELY, implying that symbols are unreal. Nomenclature involves classification; and classification is true or false, and the generals to which it refers are either reals in the one case, or figments in the other. For if the reader will turn to the original maxim of pragmaticism at the beginning of this article, he will see that the question is, not what *did* happen, but

° See 403.

whether it would have been well to engage in any line of conduct whose successful issue depended upon whether that diamond *would* resist an attempt to scratch it, or whether all other logical means of determining how it ought to be classed *would* lead to the conclusion which, to quote the very words of that article, would be "the belief which alone could be the result of investigation carried *sufficiently far*." *

457. Let us now take up the case of that diamond which, having been crystallized upon a cushion of jeweler's cotton, was accidentally consumed by fire before the crystal of corundum that had been sent for had had time to arrive, and indeed without being subjected to any other pressure than that of the atmosphere and its own weight. The question is, was that diamond *really* hard? It is certain that no discernible *actual* fact determined it to be so. But is its hardness not, nevertheless, a *real* fact? To say, as the article of January 1878 seems to intend, that it is just as an arbitrary "usage of speech" chooses to arrange its thoughts, is as much as to decide against the reality of the property, since the real is that which is such as it is regardless of how it is, at any time, thought to be. Remember that this diamond's condition is not an isolated fact. There is no such thing; and an isolated fact could hardly be real. It is an unsevered . . . part of the unitary fact of nature. Being a diamond, it was a mass of pure carbon, in the form of a more or less transparent crystal (brittle, and of facile octahedral cleavage, unless it was of an unheard-of variety), which, if not trimmed after one of the fashions in which diamonds may be trimmed, took the shape of an octahedron, apparently regular (I need not go into minutiæ), with grooved edges, and probably with some curved faces. Without being subjected to any considerable pressure, it could be found to be insoluble, very highly refractive, showing under radium rays (and perhaps under "dark light" and X-rays) a peculiar bluish phosphorescence, having as

* See 408.

high a specific gravity as realgar or orpiment, and giving off during its combustion less heat than any other form of carbon would have done. From some of these properties hardness is believed to be inseparable. For like it they bespeak the high polemerization of the molecule. But however this may be, how can the hardness of all other diamonds fail to bespeak *some* real relation among the diamonds without which a piece of carbon would not be a diamond? Is it not a monstrous perversion of the word and concept *real* to say that the accident of the non-arrival of the corundum prevented the hardness of the diamond from having the *reality* which it otherwise, with little doubt, would have had?

At the same time, we must dismiss the idea that the occult state of things (be it a relation among atoms or something else), which constitutes the reality of a diamond's hardness can possibly consist in anything but in the truth of a general conditional proposition. For to what else does the entire teaching of chemistry relate except to the "behavior" of different possible kinds of material substance? And in what does that behavior consist except that if a substance of a certain kind should be exposed to an agency of a certain kind, a certain kind of sensible result *would* ensue, according to our experiences hitherto. As for the pragmaticist, it is precisely his position that nothing else than this can be so much as *meant* by saying that an object possesses a character. . . .

WILLIAM JAMES

Anyone who has studied the history of American philosophy may well conclude that William James (1842–1910) was his country's greatest philosopher. He lacked the great dialectical power that Edwards and Peirce were blessed with, he was not the full-time sage that Emerson was, he lacked the historical learning that Royce possessed, he was not the esthete that Santayana was nor the practical reformer that Dewey was; but he combined all of their different powers and qualities in such high degree that he became the one American who could walk upon the stage of world philosophy in company with its most majestic figures. And I venture to add that no other American philosopher is likely to push James out of this position in the foreseeable future. Specialists in logic and semantics may dispute this judgment because of their high opinion of Peirce, religious men may be more sympathetic to Edwards, literary men more respectful of Emerson and Santayana, and reformers and educators may favor Dewey; but so long as men cling to the idea that philosophy is not identical with logic, that it is not simply a form of literature, and that it is not to be confused with its own history, William James will remain its greatest American hero.

James' synoptic philosophical power may well have been related to the fact that he studied many different things before he chose the career of philosopher. Painting, medicine, physiology, and psychology in turn claimed his attention before he became a teacher of philosophy at the age of thirty-seven. Also, he was the son of the Swedenborgian religious thinker, Henry James, and the brother of Henry James the novelist. Contact with them, with painting, and with natural science put William James in close touch with almost every important part of the intellectual life save mathematics—an exception which his friend Charles Peirce took great pleasure in twitting him about. In addition, James was more deeply interested in ordinary human beings and their anxieties than most philosophers ever manage to be. James' philosophical doctrines reflected the great breadth of his education, the depth of his experience, his democratic openness, and his sympathy for human beings. He hoped to create a philosophy that would felicitously communicate to the ordinary man and the professional philosopher some idea of the roles that reason, experience, and sentiment play in the intellectual life. In doing so, James thought, he would mediate between what he called tough-minded and tender-minded people, and formulate a philosophy that would serve as a "happy harmonizer of empiricist ways of thinking with the more religious demands of human beings".[1]

Primarily under the influence of Charles Peirce, James called himself a pragmatist, but his main contribution to philosophy was not as closely connected with Peirce's pragmatic theory of meaning as might be supposed. James did not take very seriously Peirce's demand that all statements attributing objective properties should be translatable into statements reporting what would be experienced by a normal human being under certain conditions. The closest James came to that was in his pragmatic theory of truth. He held that a true

[1] William James, *Pragmatism* (New York, 1907), p. 69.

belief is one that ought to be held; and that a belief which ought to be held is one which, if held, would lead to satisfactory experiences on the part of the believer. There is therefore some temptation to suppose that James was merely applying Peirce's pragmatic maxim to the concept of truth and that the Jamesian analysis of the term "true" is quite analogous to the Peirceian analysis of the term "hard". It might be said that whereas Peirce holds that "This diamond is hard" means the same as "If anybody were to try to scratch this diamond, he would see no indentation on it shortly after trying", James would say that "The statement 'This is hard' is true" means the same as "If anybody were to try accepting the statement 'This is hard', he would have satisfactory experiences". Yet, in spite of some indication that James may have had something like this in mind, I am less inclined than I once was to interpret him in this way.[2] It now seems to me more in keeping with what James says to regard his theory of truth not as an effort to define the notion of true statement, but rather as an effort to give a description of the psychological process whereby men come to accept beliefs they regard as true.[3]

In my opinion, James' thought on this subject went through two main phases. In *The Principles of Psychology* of 1890 and in the essays he collected in *The Will To Believe* of 1897, he seems to favor what may be called a *trialistic* view, according to which we are (1) coerced into accepting some beliefs by external reality; (2) coerced into accepting other beliefs—notably those in logic and mathematics—by the relationships between what James calls ideal concepts; and (3) free to accept still other beliefs by appealing to our senti-

---

[2] See Morton White, ed., *The Age of Analysis* (Boston, 1955), pp. 157–58.

[3] Here I agree with A. J. Ayer's view in *The Origins of Pragmatism: Studies in the Philosophy of Charles Sanders Peirce and William James* (London, 1968), pp. 198–99.

ments just because we are not coerced into believing them in
the ways just mentioned. In his *Psychology* and in *The Will
To Believe,* James tended to include metaphysical beliefs like
"Every event has a cause", theological beliefs, and moral beliefs in the third category, so the net effect of his thinking
was a trichotomy which allowed for three fundamentally different ways of testing different kinds of beliefs.

It is also my opinion that although James seems to defend
a trialistic point of view in some parts of his *Pragmatism* of
1907, in other parts of that work he argues that the process of
accepting a belief must be viewed as one in which a whole
stock of the believer's opinions is under scrutiny. To see how
this involves a departure from trialism, it is best to examine
what James says about the acceptance of a theory in natural
science. According to James, a physicist who tests a theory by
performing what is sometimes called a crucial experiment
tacitly makes other assumptions which—because he is so confident of them—he treats as not questionable for the moment.
If the experiment should turn out in a certain way, the physicist may reject the theory which he regards as the one ostensibly being tested, but there is always the possibility that he
may decide to hold on to that theory and to surrender instead one or more of the assumptions which he had treated
for the moment as fixed or stable. There are, in short, more
ways of dealing with a recalcitrant experience than the obvious one. This approach led James to the view that among
the stable assumptions in the stock of opinions that men test
there may be beliefs of logic, of mathematics, of metaphysics,
of religion, and even of morals. He also seems to have held
that when we test such an amplified stock of opinions, we do
not test it by appealing to sensory experience only; we may
also appeal to sentiments associated with the satisfaction of
our desires or with their failure to be satisfied.

Once James' pragmatic theory of truth is put forward as a
description of a process in which an apparently isolated belief
is treated as part of a whole stock any member of which may

be abandoned, once we see that the stock may include opinions from different disciplines, and once we see that the data which the stock is supposed to accommodate consists of desires or feelings as well as observations, then that theory of truth becomes incompatible with trialism. For example, so long as James allows that a new sensory experience may result in the abandonment of a logical or mathematical belief—and he says that it may—he cannot hold that logical and mathematical beliefs are inevitably tested by examining the relationships among ideal concepts. James' very strong point is that a candid examination of the habits of thinking men will show that they may respond to many different demands or claims when they are considering the adoption of a belief. They respond, James holds, to the demand that the new belief or hypothesis derange older beliefs as little as possible, especially those as old as the beliefs of logic; to the demand that sensory experience be taken into account; to the demand that the new hypothesis be elegant or simple; and even to the demand that its acceptance should not clash with moral feelings or with moral beliefs that may occupy a well-entrenched position in the stock of opinions. Because James views the process of testing a belief as one in which these different kinds of demands are satisfied, he concludes that the belief which is usually accepted must strike a balance among all of these different demands. And striking such a balance is what James had in mind when he said that the belief which we accept as true is the one whose consequences are most satisfactory after an overall assessment of the kind I have just described. When James is interpreted in this way, it becomes more difficult to lampoon him as the patron saint of wishful thinking and easy to see why he was a philosopher who could respond to the needs of the whole man without lapsing into the excesses of romantic irrationalism.

Before presenting extended selections from James' writings, I shall quote a passage from an early essay in which he describes the formation of *philosophical* opinions. By giving intellect *some* say in the choice of such opinions, this passage departs from the tendency in James' earlier writings to let sentiment be virtually the sole basis for choosing a metaphysics. However, the passage succinctly formulates James' later view as to how *all* opinions are formed by "the whole man within us". James declares: "Pretend what we may, the whole man within us is at work when we form our philosophical opinions. Intellect, will, taste, and passion co-operate just as they do in practical affairs; and lucky it is if the passion be not something as petty as a love of personal conquest over the philosopher across the way. The absurd abstraction of an intellect verbally formulating all its evidence and carefully estimating the probability thereof by a vulgar fraction by the size of whose denominator and numerator alone it is swayed, is ideally as inept as it is actually impossible. It is almost incredible that men who are themselves working philosophers should pretend that any philosophy can be, or ever has been, constructed without the help of personal preference, belief, or divination".[4]

In the first of the passages below, taken from *The Principles of Psychology,* James expresses his early view that metaphysical principles are more like esthetic and moral principles than they are like the beliefs of mathematics or natural science insofar as many metaphysical principles rest on feeling. In the second passage, taken from his famous essay, "The Dilemma of Determinism," he applies this view to a metaphysical debate and defends indeterminism. In the third passage, taken from *Pragmatism,* we see James' later position that beliefs in metaphysics, theology, and morals are not sharply separated from those of natural science, logic, and mathematics insofar as all of them may be members of a stock of opinions which is evaluated for its capacity to organize sensations and feelings.

[4] *The Will To Believe and Other Essays in Popular Philosophy* (New York, 1897), pp. 92–93.

The Nature of Metaphysical Axioms [5]

METAPHYSICAL AXIOMS

[A]longside of . . . ideal relations between terms which the world verifies, there are other ideal relations not as yet so verified. I refer to those propositions . . . which are formulated in such metaphysical and æsthetic axioms as "The Principle of things is one;" "The quantity of existence is unchanged;" "Nature is simple and invariable;" "Nature acts by the shortest ways;" "*Ex nihilo nihil fit;*" "Nothing can be evolved which was not involved;" "Whatever is in the effect must be in the cause;" "A thing can only work where it is;" "A thing can only affect another of its own kind;" "*Cessante causa, cessat et effectus;*" "Nature makes no leaps;" "Things belong to discrete and permanent kinds;" "Nothing is or happens without a reason;" "The world is throughout rationally intelligible;" etc., etc., etc. Such principles as these, which might be multiplied to satiety, are properly to be called *postulates of rationality*, not propositions of fact. If nature *did* obey them, she *would* be *pro tanto* more intelligible; and we seek meanwhile so to conceive her phenomena as to show that she does obey them. To a certain extent we succeed. For example, instead of the 'quantity of existence' so vaguely postulated as unchanged, Nature allows us to suppose that curious sum of distances and velocities which for want of a better term we call 'energy.' For the effect being 'contained in the cause,' nature lets us substitute 'the effect *is* the cause,' so soon as she lets us conceive both effect and cause as the same molecules, in two successive positions.—But all around these incipient successes (as all around the molecular world, so soon as we add to it as its 'effects' those illusory 'things' of

---

[5] This selection comes from William James, *The Principles of Psychology* (New York, 1890), Volume II, pp. 669–75. I have omitted footnotes.

common-sense which we had to butcher for its sake), there still spreads a vast field of irrationalized fact whose items simply *are* together, and from one to another of which we can pass by no ideally 'rational' way.

It is not that these more metaphysical postulates of rationality are absolutely barren—though barren enough they were when used, as the scholastics used them, as immediate propositions of fact. They have a fertility as ideals, and keep us uneasy and striving always to recast the world of sense until its lines become more congruent with theirs. Take for example the principle that 'nothing can happen without a cause.' We have no definite idea of what we mean by cause, or of what causality consists in. But the principle expresses a demand for *some* deeper sort of inward connection between phenomena than their merely habitual time-sequence seems to us to be. The word 'cause' is, in short, an altar to an unknown god; an empty pedestal still marking the place of a hoped-for statue. *Any* really inward belonging-together of the sequent terms, if discovered, would be accepted as what the word cause was meant to stand for. So we seek, and seek; and in the molecular systems we find a sort of inward belonging in the notion of identity of matter with change of collocation. Perhaps by still seeking we may find other sorts of inward belonging, even between the molecules and those 'secondary qualities,' etc., which they produce upon our minds.

It cannot be too often repeated that the triumphant application of any one of our ideal systems of rational relations to the real world justifies our hope that other systems may be found also applicable. Metaphysics should take heart from the example of physics, simply confessing that hers is the longer task. Nature *may* be remodelled, nay, certainly will be remodelled, far beyond the point at present reached. Just how far?—is a question which only the whole future history of Science and Philosophy can answer. Our task being Psychology, we cannot even cross the threshold of that larger problem.

Besides the mental structure which results in such meta-physical principles as those just considered, there is a mental structure which expresses itself in

ÆSTHETIC AND MORAL PRINCIPLES

The æsthetic principles are at bottom such axioms as that a note sounds good with its third and fifth, or that potatoes need salt. We are once for all so made that when certain impressions come before our mind, one of them will seem to call for or repel the others as its companions. To a certain extent the principle of habit will explain these æsthetic connections. When a conjunction is repeatedly experienced, the cohesion of its terms grows grateful, or at least their disruption grows unpleasant. But to explain *all* æsthetic judgments in this way would be absurd; for it is notorious how seldom natural experiences come up to our æsthetic demands. Many of the so-called metaphysical principles are at bottom only expressions of æsthetic feeling. Nature is simple and invariable; makes no leaps, or makes nothing but leaps; is rationally intelligible; neither increases nor diminishes in quantity; flows from one principle, etc., etc.,—what do all such principles express save our sense of how pleasantly our intellect would feel if it had a Nature of that sort to deal with? The subjectivity of which feeling is of course quite compatible with Nature also turning out objectively to be of that sort, later on.

The *moral* principles which our mental structure engenders are quite as little explicable *in toto* by habitual experiences having bred inner cohesions. Rightness is not *mere* usualness, wrongness not *mere* oddity, however numerous the facts which might be invoked to prove such identity. Nor are the moral judgments those most invariably and emphatically impressed on us by public opinion. The most characteristically and peculiarly moral judgments that a man is ever called on to make are in unprecedented cases and lonely emergencies, where no popular rhetorical maxims can avail, and the hidden oracle alone can speak; and it speaks often in favor of conduct quite unusual, and suicidal as far as gaining popular approbation goes. The forces which conspire to this resultant are subtle harmonies and discords between the elementary ideas which form the data of the case. Some of these harmonies, no doubt, have to do with habit; but in respect to most of them our sensibility must assuredly be a phenomenon of supernumerary order, correlated with a brain-function quite as secondary as that which takes cognizance of the diverse excellence of elaborate musical compositions. No more than the higher musical sensibility can the higher moral sensibility be accounted for by the frequency with which outer relations have cohered. Take judgments of justice or equity, for example. Instinctively, one judges everything differently, according as it pertains to one's self or to some one else. Empirically one notices that everybody else does the same. But little by little there dawns in one the judgment "nothing can be right for me which would not be right for another similarly placed;" or "the fulfilment of my desires is intrinsically no more imperative than that of anyone else's;" or "what it is reasonable that another should do for me, it is also reasonable that I should do for him;" and forthwith the whole mass of the habitual gets overturned. It gets *seriously* overturned only in a few fanatical heads. But its overturning is due to a back-door and not to a front-door process. Some minds are preternaturally sensitive to logical consistency and inconsistency. When they have ranked a thing under a kind, they *must* treat it as of that kind's kind, or feel all out of tune. In many respects we do class ourselves with other men, and call them and ourselves by a common name. They agree with us in having the same Heavenly Father, in not being consulted about their birth, in not being themselves to thank or blame for their natural gifts, in having the same desires and pains and pleasures, in short in a host of fundamental relations. Hence, *if these things be our essence,* we should be substitutable for other men, and they for us, in any proposition in which either of us is involved. The more fundamental and common the essence chosen, and the more simple the reasoning, the more wildly radical and unconditional will the justice be which is aspired to. Life is one long struggle between conclusions based on abstract ways of conceiving cases, and opposite conclusions prompted by our instinctive perception of them as individual facts. The logical stickler for justice always seems pedantic and mechanical to the man who goes by tact and the particular instance, and who usually makes a poor show at argument. Sometimes the abstract conceiver's way is better, sometimes that of the man of instinct. But just as in our study of reasoning we found it impossible to lay down any mark whereby to distinguish *right* conception of a concrete case from *confusion,* so here we can give no general rule for deciding when it is morally useful to treat a concrete case as *sui generis,* and when to lump it with others in an abstract class.

An adequate treatment of the way in which we come by our æsthetic and moral judgments would require a separate chapter, which I cannot conveniently include in this book. Suffice it that these judgments express inner harmonies and discords between objects of thought; and that whilst outer cohesions frequently repeated will often seem harmonious, all harmonies are not thus engendered, but our feeling of many of them is a secondary and incidental function of the mind. Where harmonies are asserted of the real world, they are obviously mere postulates of rationality, so far as they transcend experience. Such postulates are exemplified by the ethical propositions that the individual and universal good are one, and that happiness and goodness are bound to coalesce in the same subject.

Against Determinism [6]

A common opinion prevails that the juice has ages ago been pressed out of the free-will controversy, and that no

[6] This selection comes from James' *The Will To Believe and Other Essays in Popular Philosophy* (1897), pp. 145–53; pp. 158–64; pp. 175–80. The essay is "The Dilemma of Determinism".

new champion can do more than warm up stale arguments
which every one has heard. This is a radical mistake. I know
of no subject less worn out, or in which inventive genius has
a better chance of breaking open new ground,—not, perhaps,
of forcing a conclusion or of coercing assent, but of deepen-
ing our sense of what the issue between the two parties really
is, of what the ideas of fate and of free-will imply. At our
very side almost, in the past few years, we have seen falling
in rapid succession from the press works that present the alternative in entirely novel lights. Not to speak of the English
disciples of Hegel, such as Green and Bradley; not to speak
of Hinton and Hodgson, nor of Hazard here,—we see in the
writings of Renouvier, Fouillée, and Delbœuf [7] how completely changed and refreshed is the form of all the old disputes. I cannot pretend to vie in originality with any of the
masters I have named, and my ambition limits itself to just
one little point. If I can make two of the necessarily implied
corollaries of determinism clearer to you than they have been
made before, I shall have made it possible for you to decide
for or against that doctrine with a better understanding of
what you are about. And if you prefer not to decide at all,
but to remain doubters, you will at least see more plainly
what the subject of your hesitation is. I thus disclaim openly
on the threshold all pretension to prove to you that the freedom of the will is true. The most I hope is to induce some of
you to follow my own example in assuming it true, and acting as if it were true. If it be true, it seems to me that this is
involved in the strict logic of the case. Its truth ought not to
be forced willy-nilly down our indifferent throats. It ought to
be freely espoused by men who can equally well turn their
backs upon it. In other words, our first act of freedom, if we
are free, ought in all inward propriety to be to affirm that we
are free. This should exclude, it seems to me, from the free-
will side of the question all hope of a coercive demonstration,

---

[7] Here James adds in a note: "And I may now say Charles S.
Peirce,—see the Monist, for 1892–93". [M.W.]

—a demonstration which I, for one, am perfectly contented to go without.

With thus much understood at the outset, we can advance. But not without one more point understood as well. The arguments I am about to urge all proceed on two suppositions: first, when we make theories about the world and discuss them with one another, we do so in order to attain a conception of things which shall give us subjective satisfaction; and, second, if there be two conceptions, and the one seems to us, on the whole, more rational than the other, we are entitled to suppose that the more rational one is the truer of the two. I hope that you are all willing to make these suppositions with me; for I am afraid that if there be any of you here who are not, they will find little edification in the rest of what I have to say. I cannot stop to argue the point; but I myself believe that all the magnificent achievements of mathematical and physical science—our doctrines of evolution, of uniformity of law, and the rest—proceed from our indomitable desire to cast the world into a more rational shape in our minds than the shape into which it is thrown there by the crude order of our experience. The world has shown itself, to a great extent, plastic to this demand of ours for rationality. How much farther it will show itself plastic no one can say. Our only means of finding out is to try; and I, for one, feel as free to try conceptions of moral as of mechanical or of logical rationality. If a certain formula for expressing the nature of the world violates my moral demand, I shall feel as free to throw it overboard, or at least to doubt it, as if it disappointed my demand for uniformity of sequence, for example; the one demand being, so far as I can see, quite as subjective and emotional as the other is. The principle of causality, for example,—what is it but a postulate, an empty name covering simply a demand that the sequence of events shall some day manifest a deeper kind of belonging of one thing with another than the mere arbitrary juxtaposition which now phenomenally appears? It is as much an altar to an unknown god as the one that Saint

Paul found at Athens. All our scientific and philosophic ideals
are altars to unknown gods. Uniformity is as much so as is
free-will. If this be admitted, we can debate on even terms.
But if any one pretends that while freedom and variety are,
in the first instance, subjective demands, necessity and uniformity are something altogether different, I do not see how
we can debate at all.

To begin, then, I must suppose you acquainted with all the
usual arguments on the subject. I cannot stop to take up the
old proofs from causation, from statistics, from the certainty
with which we can foretell one another's conduct, from the
fixity of character, and all the rest. But there are two *words*
which usually encumber these classical arguments, and which
we must immediately dispose of if we are to make any progress. One is the eulogistic word *freedom,* and the other is
the opprobrious word *chance.* The word 'chance' I wish to
keep, but I wish to get rid of the word 'freedom.' Its eulogistic associations have so far overshadowed all the rest of its
meaning that both parties claim the sole right to use it, and
determinists to-day insist that they alone are freedom's cham-
pions. Old-fashioned determinism was what we may call *hard*
determinism. It did not shrink from such words as fatality,
bondage of the will, necessitation, and the like. Nowadays,
we have a *soft* determinism which abhors harsh words, and,
repudiating fatality, necessity, and even predetermination,
says that its real name is freedom; for freedom is only necessity understood, and bondage to the highest is identical with
true freedom. Even a writer as little used to making capital
out of soft words as Mr. Hodgson hesitates not to call himself
a 'free-will determinist.'

Now, all this is a quagmire of evasion under which the real
issue of fact has been entirely smothered. Freedom in all
these senses presents simply no problem at all. No matter
what the soft determinist mean by it,—whether he mean the
acting without external constraint; whether he mean the act-

ing rightly, or whether he mean the acquiescing in the law of the whole,—who cannot answer him that sometimes we are free and sometimes we are not? But there *is* a problem, an issue of fact and not of words, an issue of the most momentous importance, which is often decided without discussion in one sentence,—nay, in one clause of a sentence,—by those very writers who spin out whole chapters in their efforts to show what 'true' freedom is; and that is the question of determinism, about which we are to talk to-night.

Fortunately, no ambiguities hang about this word or about its opposite, indeterminism. Both designate an outward way in which things may happen, and their cold and mathematical sound has no sentimental associations that can bribe our partiality either way in advance. Now, evidence of an external kind to decide between determinism and indeterminism is, as I intimated a while back, strictly impossible to find. Let us look at the difference between them and see for ourselves. What does determinism profess?

It professes that those parts of the universe already laid down absolutely appoint and decree what the other parts shall be. The future has no ambiguous possibilities hidden in its womb: the part we call the present is compatible with only one totality. Any other future complement than the one fixed from eternity is impossible. The whole is in each and every part, and welds it with the rest into an absolute unity, an iron block, in which there can be no equivocation or shadow of turning. . . .

Indeterminism, on the contrary, says that the parts have a certain amount of loose play on one another, so that the laying down of one of them does not necessarily determine what the others shall be. It admits that possibilities may be in excess of actualities, and that things not yet revealed to our knowledge may really in themselves be ambiguous. Of two alternative futures which we conceive, both may now be really possible; and the one become impossible only at the very moment when the other excludes it by becoming real itself. Indeterminism thus denies the world to be one unbending unit of fact. It says there is a certain ultimate pluralism in it; and, so saying, it corroborates our ordinary unsophisticated view of things. To that view, actualities seem to float in a wider sea of possibilities from out of which they are chosen; and, *somewhere,* indeterminism says, such possibilities exist, and form a part of truth.

Determinism, on the contrary, says they exist *nowhere,* and that necessity on the one hand and impossibility on the other are the sole categories of the real. Possibilities that fail to get realized are, for determinism, pure illusions: they never were possibilities at all. There is nothing inchoate, it says, about this universe of ours, all that was or is or shall be actual in it having been from eternity virtually there. The cloud of alternatives our minds escort this mass of actuality withal is a cloud of sheer deceptions, to which 'impossibilities' is the only name that rightfully belongs.

The issue, it will be seen, is a perfectly sharp one, which no eulogistic terminology can smear over or wipe out. The truth *must* lie with one side or the other, and its lying with one side makes the other false.

The question relates solely to the existence of possibilities, in the strict sense of the term, as things that may, but need not, be. Both sides admit that a volition, for instance, has occurred. The indeterminists say another volition might have occurred in its place: the determinists swear that nothing could possibly have occurred in its place. Now, can science be called in to tell us which of these two point-blank contradicters of each other is right? Science professes to draw no conclusions but such as are based on matters of fact, things that have actually happened; but how can any amount of assurance that something actually happened give us the least grain of information as to whether another thing might or might not have happened in its place? Only facts can be proved by other facts. With things that are possibilities and not facts, facts have no concern. If we have no other evidence than the evidence of existing facts, the possibility-question must remain a mystery never to be cleared up.

And the truth is that facts practically have hardly anything to do with making us either determinists or indeterminists. Sure enough, we make a flourish of quoting facts this way or that; and if we are determinists, we talk about the infallibility with which we can predict one another's conduct; while if we are indeterminists, we lay great stress on the fact that it is just because we cannot foretell one another's conduct, either in war or statecraft or in any of the great and small intrigues and businesses of men, that life is so intensely anxious and hazardous a game. But who does not see the wretched insufficiency of this so-called objective testimony on both sides? What fills up the gaps in our minds is something not objective, not external. What divides us into possibility men and anti-possibility men is different faiths or postulates,—postulates of rationality. To this man the world seems more rational with possibilities in it,—to that man more rational with possibilities excluded; and talk as we will about having to yield to evidence, what makes us monists or pluralists, determinists or indeterminists, is at bottom always some sentiment like this.

The stronghold of the deterministic sentiment is the antipathy to the idea of chance. As soon as we begin to talk indeterminism to our friends, we find a number of them shaking their heads. This notion of alternative possibility, they say, this admission that any one of several things may come to pass, is, after all, only a roundabout name for chance; and chance is something the notion of which no sane mind can for an instant tolerate in the world. What is it, they ask, but barefaced crazy unreason, the negation of intelligibility and law? And if the slightest particle of it exist anywhere, what is to prevent the whole fabric from falling together, the stars from going out, and chaos from recommencing her topsy-turvy reign? . . . The quarrel which determinism has with chance . . . is a quarrel altogether metaphysical. Determinism denies the ambiguity of future volitions, because it affirms that nothing future can be ambiguous. But we have said enough to meet the issue. Indeterminate future volitions *do* mean chance. Let us not fear to shout it from the house-tops if need be; for we now know that the idea of chance is, at bottom, exactly the same thing as the idea of gift,—the one simply being a disparaging, and the other a eulogistic, name for anything on which we have no effective *claim*. And whether the world be the better or the worse for having either chances or gifts in it will depend altogether on *what* these uncertain and unclaimable things turn out to be.

And this at last brings us within sight of our subject. We have seen what determinism means: we have seen that indeterminism is rightly described as meaning chance; and we have seen that chance, the very name of which we are urged to shrink from as from a metaphysical pestilence, means only the negative fact that no part of the world, however big, can claim to control absolutely the destinies of the whole. But although, in discussing the word 'chance,' I may at moments have seemed to be arguing for its real existence, I have not meant to do so yet. We have not yet ascertained whether this be a world of chance or no; at most, we have agreed that it seems so. And I now repeat what I said at the outset, that, from any strict theoretical point of view, the question is insoluble. To deepen our theoretic sense of the *difference* between a world with chances in it and a deterministic world is the most I can hope to do; and this I may now at last begin upon, after all our tedious clearing of the way.

I wish first of all to show you just what the notion that this is a deterministic world implies. The implications I call your attention to are all bound up with the fact that it is a world in which we constantly have to make what I shall, with your permission, call judgments of regret. Hardly an hour passes in which we do not wish that something might be otherwise;

and happy indeed are those of us whose hearts have never echoed the wish of Omar Khayam—

> "That we might clasp, ere closed, the book of fate,
>   And make the writer on a fairer leaf
>   Inscribe our names, or quite obliterate.

> "Ah! Love, could you and I with fate conspire
>   To mend this sorry scheme of things entire,
>   Would we not shatter it to bits, and then
>   Remould it nearer to the heart's desire?"

Now, it is undeniable that most of these regrets are foolish, and quite on a par in point of philosophic value with the criticisms on the universe of that friend of our infancy, the hero of the fable The Atheist and the Acorn,—

> "Fool! had that bough a pumpkin bore,
>   Thy whimsies would have worked no more," etc.

Even from the point of view of our own ends, we should probably make a botch of remodelling the universe. How much more then from the point of view of ends we cannot see! Wise men therefore regret as little as they can. But still some regrets are pretty obstinate and hard to stifle,—regrets for acts of wanton cruelty or treachery, for example, whether performed by others or by ourselves. Hardly any one can remain *entirely* optimistic after reading the confession of the murderer at Brockton the other day: how, to get rid of the wife whose continued existence bored him, he inveigled her into a desert spot, shot her four times, and then, as she lay on the ground and said to him, "You didn't do it on purpose, did you, dear?" replied, "No, I didn't do it on purpose," as he raised a rock and smashed her skull. Such an occurrence, with the mild sentence and self-satisfaction of the prisoner, is a field for a crop of regrets, which one need not take up in detail. We feel that, although a perfect mechanical fit to the rest of the universe, it is a bad moral fit, and that something else would really have been better in its place.

But for the deterministic philosophy the murder, the sentence, and the prisoner's optimism were all necessary from eternity; and nothing else for a moment had a ghost of a chance of being put into their place. To admit such a chance, the determinists tell us, would be to make a suicide of reason; so we must steel our hearts against the thought. And here our plot thickens, for we see the first of those difficult implications of determinism and monism which it is my purpose to make you feel. If this Brockton murder was called for by the rest of the universe, if it had to come at its preappointed hour, and if nothing else would have been consistent with the sense of the whole, what are we to think of the universe? Are we stubbornly to stick to our judgment of regret, and say, though it *couldn't* be, yet it *would* have been a better universe with something different from this Brockton murder in it? That, of course, seems the natural and spontaneous thing for us to do; and yet it is nothing short of deliberately espousing a kind of pessimism. The judgment of regret calls the murder bad. Calling a thing bad means, if it mean anything at all, that the thing ought not to be, that something else ought to be in its stead. Determinism, in denying that anything else can be in its stead, virtually defines the universe as a place in which what ought to be is impossible,—in other words, as an organism whose constitution is afflicted with an incurable taint, an irremediable flaw. The pessimism of a Schopenhauer says no more than this,—that the murder is a symptom; and that it is a vicious symptom because it belongs to a vicious whole, which can express its nature no otherwise than by bringing forth just such a symptom as that at this particular spot. Regret for the murder must transform itself, if we are determinists and wise, into a larger regret. It is absurd to regret the murder alone. Other things being what they are, *it* could not be different. What we should regret is that whole frame of things of which the murder is one member. I see no escape whatever from this pessimistic conclusion, if, being determinists, our judgment of regret is to be allowed to stand at all.

The only deterministic escape from pessimism is everywhere to abandon the judgment of regret. That this can be done, history shows to be not impossible. The devil, *quoad existentiam*, may be good. That is, although he be a *principle* of evil, yet the universe, with such a principle in it, may practically be a better universe than it could have been without. On every hand, in a small way, we find that a certain amount of evil is a condition by which a higher form of good is brought. There is nothing to prevent anybody from generalizing this view, and trusting that if we could but see things in the largest of all ways, even such matters as this Brockton murder would appear to be paid for by the uses that follow in their train. An optimism *quand même*, a systematic and infatuated optimism like that ridiculed by Voltaire in his Candide, is one of the possible ideal ways in which a man may train himself to look on life. Bereft of dogmatic hardness and lit up with the expression of a tender and pathetic hope, such an optimism has been the grace of some of the most religious characters that ever lived.

> "Throb thine with Nature's throbbing breast,
> And all is clear from east to west."

Even cruelty and treachery may be among the absolutely blessed fruits of time, and to quarrel with any of their details may be blasphemy. The only real blasphemy, in short, may be that pessimistic temper of the soul which lets it give way to such things as regrets, remorse, and grief.

Thus, our deterministic pessimism may become a deterministic optimism at the price of extinguishing our judgments of regret.

But does not this immediately bring us into a curious logical predicament? Our determinism leads us to call our judgments of regret wrong, because they are pessimistic in implying that what is impossible yet ought to be. But how then about the judgments of regret themselves? If they are wrong, other judgments, judgments of approval presumably, ought to be in their place. But as they are necessitated, nothing else *can* be in their place; and the universe is just what it was before,—namely, a place in which what ought to be appears impossible. We have got one foot out of the pessimistic bog, but the other one sinks all the deeper. We have rescued our actions from the bonds of evil, but our judgments are now held fast. When murders and treacheries cease to be sins, regrets are theoretic absurdities and errors. The theoretic and the active life thus play a kind of see-saw with each other on the ground of evil. The rise of either sends the other down. Murder and treachery cannot be good without regret being bad: regret cannot be good without treachery and murder being bad. Both, however, are supposed to have been foredoomed; so something must be fatally unreasonable, absurd, and wrong in the world. It must be a place of which either sin or error forms a necessary part. From this dilemma there seems at first sight no escape. Are we then so soon to fall back into the pessimism from which we thought we had emerged? And is there no possible way by which we may, with good intellectual consciences, call the cruelties and the treacheries, the reluctances and the regrets, *all* good together?

Certainly there is such a way, and you are probably most of you ready to formulate it yourselves. . . . The only consistent way of representing a pluralism and a world whose parts may affect one another through their conduct being either good or bad is the indeterministic way. What interest, zest, or excitement can there be in achieving the right way, unless we are enabled to feel that the wrong way is also a possible and a natural way,—nay, more, a menacing and an imminent way? And what sense can there be in condemning ourselves for taking the wrong way, unless we need have done nothing of the sort, unless the right way was open to us as well? I cannot understand the willingness to act, no matter how we feel, without the belief that acts are really good and bad. I cannot understand the belief that an act is bad, without regret at its happening. I cannot understand regret without the admission of real, genuine possibilities in the world. Only *then* is it other than a mockery to feel, after we have failed to do our best, that an irreparable opportunity is gone from the universe, the loss of which it must forever after mourn.

If you insist that this is all superstition, that possibility is in the eye of science and reason impossibility, and that if I act badly 'tis that the universe was foredoomed to suffer this defect, you fall right back into the dilemma . . . from out of whose toils we have just wound our way. Now, we are of course free to fall back, if we please. For my own part, though, whatever difficulties may beset the philosophy of objective right and wrong, and the indeterminism it seems to imply, determinism . . . contains difficulties that are greater still. But you will remember that I expressly repudiated awhile ago the pretension to offer any arguments which could be coercive in a so-called scientific fashion in this matter. And I consequently find myself, at the end of this long talk, obliged to state my conclusions in an altogether personal way. This personal method of appeal seems to be among the very conditions of the problem; and the most any one can do is to confess as candidly as he can the grounds for the faith that is in him, and leave his example to work on others as it may.

Let me, then, without circumlocution say just this. The world is enigmatical enough in all conscience, whatever theory we may take up toward it. The indeterminism I defend, the free-will theory of popular sense based on the judgment of regret, represents that world as vulnerable, and liable to be injured by certain of its parts if they act wrong. And it represents their acting wrong as a matter of possibility or accident, neither inevitable nor yet to be infallibly warded off. In all this, it is a theory devoid either of transparency or of stability. It gives us a pluralistic, restless universe, in which no single point of view can ever take in the whole scene; and to a mind possessed of the love of unity at any cost, it will, no doubt, remain forever inacceptable. A friend with such a mind once told me that the thought of my universe made him sick, like the sight of the horrible motion of a mass of maggots in their carrion bed.

But while I freely admit that the pluralism and the restlessness are repugnant and irrational in a certain way, I find that every alternative to them is irrational in a deeper way. The indeterminism with its maggots, if you please to speak so about it, offends only the native absolutism of my intellect,— an absolutism which, after all, perhaps, deserves to be snubbed and kept in check. But the determinism with its necessary carrion, to continue the figure of speech, and with no possible maggots to eat the latter up, violates my sense of moral reality through and through. When, for example, I imagine such carrion as the Brockton murder, I cannot conceive it as an act by which the universe, as a whole, logically and necessarily expresses its nature without shrinking from complicity with such a whole. And I deliberately refuse to keep on terms of loyalty with the universe by saying blankly that the murder, since it does flow from the nature of the whole, is not carrion. There are *some* instinctive reactions which I, for one, will not tamper with. . . . Make as great an uproar about chance as you please, I know that chance means pluralism and nothing more. If some of the members of the pluralism are bad, the philosophy of pluralism, whatever broad views it may deny me, permits me, at least, to turn to the other members with a clean breast of affection and an unsophisticated moral sense. And if I still wish to think of the world as a totality, it lets me feel that a world with a *chance* in it of being altogether good, even if the chance never come to pass, is better than a world with no such chance at all. That 'chance' whose very notion I am exhorted and conjured to banish from my view of the future as the suicide of reason concerning it, that 'chance' is—what? Just this,—the chance that in moral respects the future may be other and better than the past has been. This is the only chance we have any motive for supposing to exist. Shame, rather, on its repudiation and its denial! For its presence is the vital air which lets the world live, the salt which keeps it sweet.

And here I might legitimately stop, having expressed all I care to see admitted by others to-night. But I know that if I do stop here, misapprehensions will remain in the minds of some of you, and keep all I have said from having its effect; so I judge it best to add a few more words.

In the first place, in spite of all my explanations, the word 'chance' will still be giving trouble. Though you may yourselves be adverse to the deterministic doctrine, you wish a pleasanter word than 'chance' to name the opposite doctrine by; and you very likely consider my preference for such a word a perverse sort of a partiality on my part. It certainly *is* a bad word to make converts with; and you wish I had not thrust it so butt-foremost at you,—you wish to use a milder term.

Well, I admit there may be just a dash of perversity in its choice. The spectacle of the mere wordgrabbing game played by the soft determinists has perhaps driven me too violently the other way; and, rather than be found wrangling with them for the good words, I am willing to take the first bad one which comes along, provided it be unequivocal. The question is of things, not of eulogistic names for them; and the best word is the one that enables men to know the quickest whether they disagree or not about the things. But the word 'chance,' with its singular negativity, is just the word for this purpose. Whoever uses it instead of 'freedom,' squarely and resolutely gives up all pretence to control the things he says are free. For *him*, he confesses that they are no better than mere chance would be. It is a word of *impotence*, and is therefore the only sincere word we can use, if, in granting freedom to certain things, we grant it honestly, and really risk the game. "Who chooses me must give and forfeit all he hath." Any other word permits of quibbling, and lets us, after the fashion of the soft determinists, make a pretence of restoring the caged bird to liberty with one hand, while with the other we anxiously tie a string to its leg to make sure it does not get beyond our sight.

Pragmatism: "A Happy Harmonizer" [8]

One of the most successfully cultivated branches of philosophy in our time is what is called inductive logic, the study of the conditions under which our sciences have evolved. Writers on this subject have begun to show a singular unanimity as to what the laws of nature and elements of fact mean, when formulated by mathematicians, physicists and chemists. When the first mathematical, logical, and natural uniformities, the first *laws*, were discovered, men were so carried away by the clearness, beauty and simplification that resulted, that they believed themselves to have deciphered authentically the eternal thoughts of the Almighty. His mind also thundered and reverberated in syllogisms. He also thought in conic sections, squares and roots and ratios, and geometrized like Euclid. He made Kepler's laws for the planets to follow; he made velocity increase proportionally to the time in falling bodies; he made the law of the sines for light to obey when refracted; he established the classes, orders, families and genera of plants and animals, and fixed the distances between them. He thought the archetypes of all things, and devised their variations; and when we rediscover any one of these his wondrous institutions, we seize his mind in its very literal intention.

But as the sciences have developed farther the notion has gained ground that most, perhaps all, of our laws are only approximations. The laws themselves, moreover, have grown so

[8] This selection comes from James' *Pragmatism* (1907), pp. 55–81.

numerous that there is no counting them; and so many rival formulations are proposed in all the branches of science that investigators have become accustomed to the notion that no theory is absolutely a transcript of reality, but that any one of them may from some point of view be useful. Their great use is to summarize old facts and to lead to new ones. They are only a man-made language, a conceptual shorthand, as some one calls them, in which we write our reports of nature; and languages, as is well known, tolerate much choice of expression and many dialects.

Thus human arbitrariness has driven divine necessity from scientific logic. If I mention the names of Sigwart, Mach, Ostwald, Pearson, Milhaud, Poincaré, Duhem, Ruyssen, those of you who are students will easily identify the tendency I speak of, and will think of additional names.

Riding now on the front of this wave of scientific logic Messrs. Schiller and Dewey appear with their pragmatistic account of what truth everywhere signifies. Everywhere, these teachers say, 'truth' in our ideas and beliefs means the same thing that it means in science. It means, they say, nothing but this, *that ideas (which themselves are but parts of our* experience) *become true just in so far as they help us to get into satisfactory relation with other parts of our experience,* to summarize them and get about among them by conceptual short-cuts instead of following the interminable succession of particular phenomena. Any idea upon which we can ride, so to speak; any idea that will carry us prosperously from any one part of our experience to any other part, linking things satisfactorily, working securely, simplifying, saving labor; is true for just so much, true in so far forth, true *instrumentally*. This is the 'instrumental' view of truth taught so successfully at Chicago, the view that truth in our ideas means their power to 'work,' promulgated so brilliantly at Oxford.

Messrs. Dewey, Schiller and their allies, in reaching this general conception of all truth, have only followed the example of geologists, biologists and philologists. In the establishment of these other sciences, the successful stroke was always to take some simple process actually observable in operation —as denudation by weather, say, or variation from parental type, or change of dialect by incorporation of new words and pronunciations—and then to generalize it, making it apply to all times, and produce great results by summating its effects through the ages.

The observable process which Schiller and Dewey particularly singled out for generalization is the familiar one by which any individual settles into *new opinions*. The process here is always the same. The individual has a stock of old opinions already, but he meets a new experience that puts them to a strain. Somebody contradicts them; or in a reflective moment he discovers that they contradict each other; or he hears of facts with which they are incompatible; or desires arise in him which they cease to satisfy. The result is an inward trouble to which his mind till then had been a stranger, and from which he seeks to escape by modifying his previous mass of opinions. He saves as much of it as he can, for in this matter of belief we are all extreme conservatives. So he tries to change first this opinion, and then that (for they resist change very variously), until at last some new idea comes up which he can graft upon the ancient stock with a minimum of disturbance of the latter, some idea that mediates between the stock and the new experience and runs them into one another most felicitously and expediently.

This new idea is then adopted as the true one. It preserves the older stock of truths with a minimum of modification, stretching them just enough to make them admit the novelty, but conceiving that in ways as familiar as the case leaves possible. An *outrée* explanation, violating all our preconceptions, would never pass for a true account of a novelty. We should scratch round industriously till we found something less excentric. The most violent revolutions in an individual's beliefs leave most of his old order standing. Time and space, cause and effect, nature and history, and one's own biography remain untouched. New truth is always a go-between, a smoother-over of transitions. It marries old opinion to new fact so as ever to show a minimum of jolt, a maximum of continuity. We hold a theory true just in proportion to its success in solving this 'problem of maxima and minima.' But success in solving this problem is eminently a matter of approximation. We say this theory solves it on the whole more satisfactorily than that theory; but that means more satisfactorily to ourselves, and individuals will emphasize their points of satisfaction differently. To a certain degree, therefore, everything here is plastic.

The point I now urge you to observe particularly is the part played by the older truths. Failure to take account of it is the source of much of the unjust criticism levelled against pragmatism. Their influence is absolutely controlling. Loyalty to them is the first principle—in most cases it is the only principle; for by far the most usual way of handling phenomena so novel that they would make for a serious re-arrangement of our preconception is to ignore them altogether, or to abuse those who bear witness for them.

You doubtless wish examples of this process of truth's growth, and the only trouble is their superabundance. The simplest case of new truth is of course the mere numerical addition of new kinds of facts, or of new single facts of old kinds, to our experience—an addition that involves no alteration in the old beliefs. Day follows day, and its contents are simply added. The new contents themselves are not true, they simply *come* and *are*. Truth is *what we say about* them, and when we say that they have come, truth is satisfied by the plain additive formula.

But often the day's contents oblige a re-arrangement. If I should now utter piercing shrieks and act like a maniac on this platform, it would make many of you revise your ideas as to the probable worth of my philosophy. 'Radium' came the other day as part of the day's content, and seemed for a moment to contradict our ideas of the whole order of nature, that order having come to be identified with what is called the conservation of energy. The mere sight of radium paying heat away indefinitely out of its own pocket seemed to violate that conservation. What to think? If the radiations from it were nothing but an escape of unsuspected 'potential' energy, pre-existent inside of the atoms, the principle of conservation would be saved. The discovery of 'helium' as the radiation's outcome, opened a way to this belief. So Ramsay's view is generally held to be true, because, although it extends our old ideas of energy, it causes a minimum of alteration in their nature.

I need not multiply instances. A new opinion counts as 'true' just in proportion as it gratifies the individual's desire to assimilate the novel in his experience to his beliefs in stock. It must both lean on old truth and grasp new fact; and its success (as I said a moment ago) in doing this, is a matter for the individual's appreciation. When old truth grows, then, by new truth's addition, it is for subjective reasons. We are in the process and obey the reasons. That new idea is truest which performs most felicitously its function of satisfying our double urgency. It makes itself true, gets itself classed as true, by the way it works; grafting itself then upon the ancient body of truth, which thus grows much as a tree grows by the activity of a new layer of cambium.

Now Dewey and Schiller proceed to generalize this observation and to apply it to the most ancient parts of truth. They also once were plastic. They also were called true for human reasons. They also mediated between still earlier truths and what in those days were novel observations. Purely objective truth, truth in whose establishment the function of giving human satisfaction in marrying previous parts of experience with newer parts played no rôle whatever, is nowhere to be found. The reasons why we call things true is the reason why they *are* true, for 'to be true' *means* only to perform this marriage-function.

The trail of the human serpent is thus over everything.

Truth independent; truth that we *find* merely; truth no longer malleable to human need; truth incorrigible, in a word; such truth exists indeed superabundantly—or is supposed to exist by rationalistically minded thinkers; but then it means only the dead heart of the living tree, and its being there means only that truth also has its paleontology, and its 'prescription,' and may grow stiff with years of veteran service and petrified in men's regard by sheer antiquity. But how plastic even the oldest truths nevertheless really are has been vividly shown in our day by the transformation of logical and mathematical ideas, a transformation which seems even to be invading physics. The ancient formulas are reinterpreted as special expressions of much wider principles, principles that our ancestors never got a glimpse of in their present shape and formulation. . . .

You will probably be surprised to learn, then, that Messrs. Schiller's and Dewey's theories have suffered a hailstorm of contempt and ridicule. All rationalism has risen against them. In influential quarters Mr. Schiller, in particular, has been treated like an impudent schoolboy who deserves a spanking. I should not mention this, but for the fact that it throws so much sidelight upon that rationalistic temper to which I have opposed the temper of pragmatism. Pragmatism is uncomfortable away from facts. Rationalism is comfortable only in the presence of abstractions. This pragmatist talk about truths in the plural, about their utility and satisfactoriness, about the success with which they 'work,' etc., suggests to the typical intellectualist mind a sort of coarse lame second-rate makeshift article of truth. Such truths are not real truth. Such tests are merely subjective. As against this, objective truth must be something nonutilitarian, haughty, refined, remote, august, exalted. It must be an absolute correspondence of our thoughts with an equally absolute reality. It must be what we *ought* to think unconditionally. The conditioned ways in which we *do* think are so much irrelevance and matter for psychology. Down with psychology, up with logic, in all this question!

See the exquisite contrast of the types of mind! The pragmatist clings to facts and concreteness, observes truth at its work in particular cases, and generalizes. Truth, for him, becomes a class-name for all sorts of definite working-values in experience. For the rationalist it remains a pure abstraction, to the bare name of which we must defer. When the pragmatist undertakes to show in detail just *why* we must defer, the rationalist is unable to recognize the concretes from which his own abstraction is taken. He accuses us of *denying* truth; whereas we have only sought to trace exactly why people follow it and always ought to follow it. Your typical ultra-abstractionist fairly shudders at concreteness: other things equal, he positively prefers the pale and spectral. If the two universes were offered, he would always choose the skinny outline rather than the rich thicket of reality. It is so much purer, clearer, nobler.

I hope that as these lectures go on, the concreteness and closeness to facts of the pragmatism which they advocate may be what approves itself to you as its most satisfactory peculiarity. It only follows here the example of the sister-sciences, interpreting the unobserved by the observed. It brings old and new harmoniously together. It converts the absolutely empty notion of a static relation of 'correspondence' . . . between our minds and reality, into that of a rich and active commerce (that any one may follow in detail and understand) between particular thoughts of ours, and the great universe of other experiences in which they play their parts and have their uses.

But enough of this at present? . . . I wish now to add a word in further explanation of the claim . . . that pragmatism may be a happy harmonizer of empiricist ways of thinking with the more religious demands of human beings.

Men who are strongly of the fact-loving temperament . . . are liable to be kept at a distance by the small sympathy with facts which that philosophy from the present-day fashion of idealism offers them. It is far too intellectualistic. Old fashioned theism was bad enough, with its notion of God as an exalted monarch, made up of a lot of unintelligible or preposterous 'attributes'; but, so long as it held strongly by the argument from design, it kept some touch with concrete realities. Since, however, darwinism has once for all displaced design from the minds of the 'scientific,' theism has lost that foothold; and some kind of an immanent or pantheistic deity working *in* things rather than above them is, if any, the kind recommended to our contemporary imagination. Aspirants to a philosophic religion turn, as a rule, more hopefully nowadays towards idealistic pantheism than towards the older dualistic theism, in spite of the fact that the latter still counts able defenders.

But . . . the brand of pantheism offered is hard for them to assimilate if they are lovers of facts, or empirically minded. It is the absolutistic brand, spurning the dust and reared upon pure logic. It keeps no connexion whatever with concreteness. Affirming the Absolute Mind, which is its substitute for God, to be the rational presupposition of all particulars of fact, whatever they may be, it remains supremely indifferent to what the particular facts in our world actually are. Be they what they may, the Absolute will father them. Like the sick lion in Esop's fable, all footprints lead into his den, but *nulla vestigia retrorsum.* You cannot redescend into the world of particulars by the Absolute's aid, or deduce any necessary consequences of detail important for your life from your idea of his nature. He gives you indeed the assurance that all is well with *Him,* and for his eternal way of thinking; but thereupon he leaves you to be finitely saved by your own temporal devices.

Far be it from me to deny the majesty of this conception, or its capacity to yield religious comfort to a most respectable class of minds. But from the human point of view, no one can pretend that it doesn't suffer from the faults of remoteness and abstractness. It is eminently a product of what I have ventured to call the rationalistic temper. It disdains empiricism's needs. It substitutes a pallid outline for the real world's richness. It is dapper, it is noble in the bad sense, in the sense in which to be noble is to be inapt for humble service. In this real world of sweat and dirt, it seems to me that when a view of things is 'noble,' that ought to count as a presumption against its truth, and as a philosophic disqualification. The prince of darkness may be a gentleman, as we are told he is, but whatever the God of earth and heaven is, he can surely be no gentleman. His menial services are needed in the dust of our human trials, even more than his dignity is needed in the empyrean.

Now pragmatism, devoted though she be to facts, has no such materialistic bias as ordinary empiricism labors under. Moreover, she has no objection whatever to the realizing of abstractions, so long as you get about among particulars with their aid and they actually carry you somewhere. Interested in no conclusions but those which our minds and our experiences work out together, she has no *a priori* prejudices against theology. *If theological ideas prove to have a value for concrete life, they will be true, for pragmatism, in the sense of being good for so much. For how much more they are true, will depend entirely on their relations to the other truths that also have to be acknowledged.*

What I said just now about the Absolute, of transcendental idealism, is a case in point. First, I called it majestic and said it yielded religious comfort to a class of minds, and then I accused it of remoteness and sterility. But so far as it affords such comfort, it surely is not sterile; it has that amount of value; it performs a concrete function. As a good pragmatist, I myself ought to call the Absolute true 'in so far forth,' then; and I unhesitatingly now do so.

But what does *true in so far forth* mean in this case? To answer, we need only apply the pragmatic method. What do believers in the Absolute mean by saying that their belief affords them comfort? They mean that since, in the Absolute finite evil is 'overruled' already, we may, therefore, whenever we wish, treat the temporal as if it were potentially the eternal, be sure that we can trust its outcome, and, without sin, dismiss our fear and drop the worry of our finite responsibility. In short, they mean that we have a right ever and anon to take a moral holiday, to let the world wag in its own way, feeling that its issues are in better hands than ours and are none of our business.

The universe is a system of which the individual members may relax their anxieties occasionally, in which the don't-care mood is also right for men, and moral holidays in order,— that, if I mistake not, is part, at least, of what the Absolute is 'known-as,' that is the great difference in our particular experiences which his being true makes, for us, that is his cash-value when he is pragmatically interpreted. Farther than that the ordinary lay-reader in philosophy who thinks favorably of absolute idealism does not venture to sharpen his conceptions. He can use the Absolute for so much, and so much is very precious. He is pained at hearing you speak incredulously of the Absolute, therefore, and disregards your criticisms because they deal with aspects of the conception that he fails to follow.

If the Absolute means this, and means no more than this, who can possibly deny the truth of it? To deny it would be to insist that men should never relax, and that holidays are never in order.

I am well aware how odd it must seem to some of you to hear me say that an idea is 'true' so long as to believe it is profitable to our lives. That it is *good*, for as much as it profits, you will gladly admit. If what we do by its aid is good, you will allow the idea itself to be good in so far forth, for we are the better for possessing it. But is it not a strange misuse of the word 'truth,' you will say, to call ideas also 'true' for this reason?

To answer this difficulty fully is impossible at this stage of my account. You touch here upon the very central point of

Messrs. Schiller's, Dewey's and my own doctrine of truth.
. . . Let me now say only this, that truth is *one species of good*, and not, as is usually supposed, a category distinct from good, and co-ordinate with it. *The true is the name of whatever proves itself to be good in the way of belief, and good, too, for definite, assignable reasons.* Surely you must admit this, that if there were *no* good for life in true ideas, or if the knowledge of them were positively disadvantageous and false ideas the only useful ones, then the current notion that truth is divine and precious, and its pursuit a duty, could never have grown up or become a dogma. In a world like that, our duty would be to *shun* truth, rather. But in this world, just as certain foods are not only agreeable to our taste, but good for our teeth, our stomach, and our tissues; so certain ideas are not only agreeable to think about, or agreeable as supporting other ideas that we are fond of, but they are also helpful in life's practical struggles. If there be any life that it is really better we should lead, and if there be any idea which, if believed in, would help us to lead that life, then it would be really *better for us* to believe in that idea, *unless, indeed, belief in it incidentally clashed with other greater vital benefits.*

'What would be better for us to believe'! This sounds very like a definition of truth. It comes very near to saying 'what we *ought* to believe': and in *that* definition none of you would find any oddity. Ought we ever not to believe what it is *better for us* to believe? And can we then keep the notion of what is better for us, and what is true for us, permanently apart?

Pragmatism says no, and I fully agree with her. Probably you also agree, so far as the abstract statement goes, but with a suspicion that if we practically did believe everything that made for good in our own personal lives, we should be found indulging all kinds of fancies about this world's affairs, and all kinds of sentimental superstitions about a world hereafter.

Your suspicion here is undoubtedly well founded, and it is evident that something happens when you pass from the abstract to the concrete that complicates the situation.

I said just now that what is better for us to believe is true *unless the belief incidentally clashes with some other vital benefit.* Now in real life what vital benefits is any particular belief of ours most liable to clash with? What indeed except the vital benefits yielded by *other beliefs* when these prove incompatible with the first ones? In other words, the greatest enemy of any one of our truths may be the rest of our truths. Truths have once for all this desperate instinct of self-preservation and of desire to extinguish whatever contradicts them. My belief in the Absolute, based on the good it does me, must run the gauntlet of all my other beliefs. Grant that it may be true in giving me a moral holiday. Nevertheless, as I conceive it,—and let me speak now confidentially, as it were, and merely in my own private person,—it clashes with other truths of mine whose benefits I hate to give up on its account. It happens to be associated with a kind of logic of which I am the enemy, I find that it entangles me in metaphysical paradoxes that are inacceptable, etc., etc. But as I have enough trouble in life already without adding the trouble of carrying these intellectual inconsistencies, I personally just give up the Absolute. I just *take* my moral holidays; or else as a professional philosopher, I try to justify them by some other principle.

If I could restrict my notion of the Absolute to its bare holiday-giving value, it wouldn't clash with my other truths. But we can not easily thus restrict our hypotheses. They carry supernumerary features, and these it is that clash so. My disbelief in the Absolute means then disbelief in those other supernumerary features, for I fully believe in the legitimacy of taking moral holidays.

You see by this what I meant when I called pragmatism a mediator and reconciler and said, borrowing the word from Papini, that she 'unstiffens' our theories. She has in fact no prejudices whatever, no obstructive dogmas, no rigid canons of what shall count as proof. She is completely genial. She will entertain any hypothesis, she will consider any evidence. It follows that in the religious field she is at a great advantage both over positivistic empiricism, with its anti-theological bias, and over religious rationalism, with its exclusive interest in the remote, the noble, the simple, and the abstract in the way of conception.

In short, she widens the field of search for God. Rationalism sticks to logic and the empyrean. Empiricism sticks to the external senses. Pragmatism is willing to take anything, to follow either logic or the senses and to count the humblest and most personal experiences. She will count mystical experiences if they have practical consequences. She will take a God who lives in the very dirt of private fact—if that should seem a likely place to find him.

Her only test of probable truth is what works best in the way of leading us, what fits every part of life best and combines with the collectivity of experience's demands, nothing being omitted. If theological ideas should do this, if the notion of God, in particular, should prove to do it, how could pragmatism possibly deny God's existence? She could see no meaning in treating as 'not true' a notion that was pragmatically so successful. What other kind of truth could there be, for her, than all this agreement with concrete reality? . . . [Y]ou see . . . how democratic she is. Her manners are as various and flexible, her resources as rich and endless, and her conclusions as friendly as those of mother nature.

Part 6: *Absolute Idealism*

JOSIAH ROYCE

In the nineteenth century the English-speaking philosophical world experienced two Germanic invasions. The first was joyously welcomed by literary men like Coleridge and Carlyle in Britain and by the Transcendentalists in America; the second was more sedately welcomed by academic English philosophers like T. H. Green (1836–1882), F. H. Bradley (1846–1924), and J. M. E. McTaggart (1866–1925). In America the most formidable champion of the second idealistic invasion was Josiah Royce (1855–1916). A Californian by birth, he was invited to Harvard mainly through the efforts of William James in spite of the great philosophical gulf that separated their doctrines; and from the eighties to the first decade of the twentieth century Royce helped James and George Santayana form what is called the Golden Age of American philosophy. In a series of heavy books, Royce defended the idealistic doctrine that the existence of an all-knowing Absolute Mind is postulated in every scientific statement we make, and that such a postulate may be logically demonstrated as true. To say that a rose is red, Royce held, is to say that it appears red to an Absolute Mind and not merely to the normal human mind that Peirce was content to appeal to in his theory of meaning. Royce went on to argue by the method of *reductio ad absurdum* that a denial of the existence of the Absolute leads by logic to an affirmation of its existence. James, as we have seen, did not agree.

As will be evident in some of the passages below, Royce was a dialectically trained spokesman for a doctrine that Emerson and his literary friends had defended by the use of what Royce disparaged as fantastic methods. In their place Royce used whatever tough techniques of modern logic, mathematics, and natural science he could muster; and therefore he appeared to be the most formidable academic philosopher of the Golden Age. He was armed to the hilt and determined to defend idealism in every branch of philosophy from metaphysics to ethics. Indeed, so formidable did Royce seem at the turn of the century, that he was singled out by young American philosophers as *the* man to refute by equally technical means if one wished to defend realism, naturalism, pragmatism, or any of the other doctrines which were soon to dominate the Anglo-American world. Consequently, these American rebels attacked Royce with the same ferocity that the young Bertrand Russell and G. E. Moore used in attacking Bradley and McTaggart in England. The main object of the Americans' attack was Royce's Absolute, which fell very quickly; and when it fell, a second Germanic invasion of American philosophy seemed to have been repelled. A wave which had moved powerfully through American thought for about three-quarters of a century after Emerson's *Nature* at last appeared to be spent.

I have chosen to illustrate Royce's Absolute Idealism by reprinting large portions of "The Conception of God," a lecture delivered by Royce before the Philosophical Union of his *alma mater*, The University of California, in 1895. In contrast to some of Royce's exceedingly verbose treatments of this subject—notably his two-volume *The World and the Individual* (1899–1901)—this essay is, the reader may be surprised to hear, a comparatively terse account of his Absolute Idealism and of its relationships with science and with Christianity.

God and Science [1]

The Conception of God—this is our immediate topic. And I begin its consideration by saying that, to my mind, a really fruitful philosophical study of the conception of God is inseparable from an attempt to estimate what evidence there is for the existence of God. When one conceives of God, one does so because one is interested, not in the bare definition of a purely logical or mathematical notion, but in the attempt to make out what sort of real world this is in which you and I live. If it is worth while even to speak of God before the forum of the philosophical reason, it is so because one hopes to be able, in a measure, to translate into articulate terms the central mystery of our existence, and to get some notion about what is at the heart of the world. Therefore, when tonight I speak of the conception of God, I mean to do so in the closest relation to a train of thought concerning the philosophical proof that this conception corresponds to some living Reality. It is useless in this region to define unless one wishes to show that, corresponding to the definition, there is a reality. And, on the other hand, the proof that one can offer for God's presence at the heart of the world constitutes also the best exposition that one can suggest regarding what one means by the conception of God.

Yet, of course, some preliminary definition of what one has in mind when one uses the word "God" is of value, since our proof will then involve a development of the fuller meaning

[1] This selection comes from *The Conception of God: A Philosophical Discussion Concerning the Nature of the Divine Idea as a Demonstrable Reality*, by Josiah Royce, Joseph LeConte, G. H. Howison, and Sidney Edward Mezes (New York, 1909; originally published in 1897), pp. 6–16; pp. 23–50.

of just this preliminary definition. For this preliminary purpose, I propose to define, in advance, what we mean under the name "God," by means of using what tradition would call one of the Divine Attributes. I refer here to what has been called the attribute of Omniscience, or of the Divine Wisdom. By the word "God" I shall mean, then, in advance of any proof of God's existence, a being who is conceived as possessing to the full all logically possible knowledge, insight, wisdom. Our problem, then, becomes at once this: Does there demonstrably exist an Omniscient Being? or is the conception of an Omniscient Being, for all that we can say, a bare ideal of the human mind?

Why I choose this so-called attribute of Omniscience as constituting for the purposes of this argument the primary attribute of the Divine Being, students of philosophy—who remember, for instance, that the Aristotelian God, however his existence was proved, was defined by that thinker principally in terms of the attribute of Omniscience—will easily understand. . . . But, for the present, let this selection of the attribute of Omniscience, as giving us a preliminary definition of God, appear, if you will, as just the arbitrary choice of this address. What we here need to see from the outset, however, is that this conceived attribute of Omniscience, if it were once regarded as expressing the nature of a real being, would involve as a consequence the concurrent presence, in such a being, of attributes that we could at pleasure express under other names; such, for instance, as what is rationally meant by Omnipotence, by Self-Consciousness, by Self-Possession— yes, I should unhesitatingly add, by Goodness, by Perfection, by Peace. . . .

An Omniscient Being would be one who simply found presented to him, not by virtue of fragmentary and gradually completed processes of inquiry, but by virtue of an all-embracing, direct, and transparent insight into his own truth,— who found thus presented to him, I say, the complete, the fulfilled answer to every genuinely rational question. . . .

[T]o answer to the full, and with direct insight, any question, means to get your ideas, just in so far as they turn out to be true ideas, fulfilled, confirmed, verified by your experiences. When with full and complete insight you answer a question, then you get into the direct presence of facts, of experiences, which you behold as the confirmation or fulfillment of certain ideas, as the verification of certain thoughts. Take your mere ideas, as such, alone by themselves, and you have to question whether or no they are true accounts of facts. Answer your questions, wholly for yourself, without intermediation, and then you have got your ideas, your thoughts, somehow into the presence of experienced facts. There are thus two factors or elements in completed and genuine knowing, namely: fact, or something experienced, on the one hand; and mere idea, or pure thought about actual or possible experience, on the other hand. Divorce those two elements of knowledge, let the experienced fact, actual or possible, be remote from the idea or thought about it, and then the being who merely thinks, questions, and, so far, can only question. His state is such that he wonders: Is my idea true? But let the divorce be completely overcome, and then the being who fully knows answers questions, in so far as he simply sees his ideas fulfilled in the facts of his experience, and beholds his experiences as the fulfilment of his ideas.

Very well, then, an Omniscient Being is defined as one in whom these two factors of knowledge, so often divorced in us, are supposed to be fully and universally joined. Such a being, I have said, would behold answered, in the facts present to his experience, all rational, all logically possible questions. That is, for him, all genuinely significant, all truly thinkable ideas would be seen as directly fulfilled, and fulfilled in his own experience.

These two factors of his knowledge would, however, still remain distinguishable. He would think, or have ideas,—richer ideas than our present fragments of thought, I need not say; but he would think. And he would experience. That is, he would have, in perfect fulness, what we call feeling—a world of immediate data of consciousness, presented as facts. This his world of feeling, of presented fact, would be richer than our fragments of scattered sensation, as I also need not say; but he would experience. Only,—herein lies the essence of his conceived Omniscience,—in him and for him these facts would not be, as they often are in us, merely felt, but they would be seen as fulfilling his ideas; as answering what, were he not omniscient, would be his mere questions.

But now, in us, our ideas, our thoughts, our questions, not merely concern what experienced facts might come to us through our senses, but also concern the value, the worth, the relations, the whole significance, ethical or æsthetic, of our particular experiences themselves. We ask: Shall I win success? And the question implies the idea of an experience of success which we now have not. We ask: What ought I to do? And the question involves the idea of an experience of doing, which we conceive as fulfilling the idea of right. Misfortune comes to us, and we ask: What means this horror of my fragmentary experience?—why did this happen to me? The question involves the idea of an experience that, if present, would answer the question. Now such an experience, if it were present to us, would be an experience of a certain passing through pain to peace, of a certain winning of triumph through partial defeat, of a certain far more exceeding weight of glory that would give even this fragmentary horror its place in an experience of triumph and of self-possession. In brief, every time we are weak, downcast, horror-stricken, alone with our sin, the victims of evil fortune or of our own baseness, we stand, as we all know, not only in presence of agonising fragmentary experiences, but in presence of besetting problems, which in fact constitute the very heart of our calamity. We are beset by questions to which we now get no answers. Those questions could only be answered, those bitter problems that pierce our hearts with the keen edge of doubt and of wonder,—when friends part, when lovers weep, when the lightning of fortune blasts our hopes, when remorse and failure make desolate the lonely hours of our private despair,—such questions, such problems, I say, could only be answered if the flickering ideas then present in the midst of our darkness shone steadily in the presence of some world of superhuman experience, of which ours would then seem to be only the remote hint. Such superhuman experience might in its wholeness at once contain the answer to our questions, and the triumph over—yes, and through—our fragmentary experience. But, as we are, we can only question.

Well, then,—if the divorce of idea and experience characterises every form of our human consciousness of finitude, of weakness, of evil, of sin, of despair,—you see that Omniscience, involving, by definition, the complete and final fulfilment of idea in experience, the unity of thought and fact, the illumination of feeling by comprehension, would be an attribute implying, for the being who possessed it, much more than a universally clear but absolutely passionless insight. An Omniscient Being could answer your bitter *Why?* when you mourn, with an experience that would not simply ignore your passion. For your passion, too, is a fact. It is experienced. The experience of the Omniscient Being would therefore include it. Only his insight, unlike yours, would comprehend it, and so would answer whatever is rational about your present question.

This is what I mean by saying that the definition of God by means of the attribute of Omniscience would involve far more than the phrase "mere omniscience" at first easily suggests. As a fact, in order to have the attribute of Omniscience, a being would necessarily be conceived as essentially world-possessing,—as the source and principle of the universe of truth,—not merely as an external observer of a world of foreign truth. As such, he would be conceived as omnipotent, and also in possession of just such experience as ideally ought to be; in other words, as good and perfect.

So much, then, for the mere preliminary definition. To this

definition I should here add a word or two of more technical analysis. We mortals have an incomplete experience. This means that the ideas awakened in us by our experience far transcend what we are now able to verify. We think, then, of actual or of possible experience that is not now ours. But an Omniscient Being would have no genuine or logically permissible ideas of any experience actually beyond his own or remote from his own. We express this by saying, technically, that an Omniscient Being would possess an Absolute Experience; that is, a wholly complete or self-contained experience, not a mere part of some larger whole. Again, the Omniscient Being would be, as we have said, a thinker. But we, as thinkers, are limited, both in so far as there is possible thought not yet attained by us, and in so far as we often do not know what ones amongst our thoughts or ideas have a genuine meaning, or correspond to what an absolute experience would fulfil. But the Omniscient Being would not be thus limited as to his thinking. Accordingly, he would possess what we may call an Absolute Thought; that is, a self-contained thought, sufficient unto itself, and needing no further comment, supplement, or correction. As the union of such an Absolute Thought and Absolute Experience, our Omniscient Being is technically to be named simply the Absolute; that is, the being sufficient unto himself. Moreover, I should also say that the experience and thought of this being might be called completely or fully *organised*. For us, namely, facts come in a disjointed way, out of connexion; and our thoughts, equally, seek a connexion which they do not now possess. An Omniscient Being would have to have present to himself all the conceivable relations amongst facts, so that in his world nothing would be fragmentary, disunited, confused, unrelated. To the question: What is the connexion of this and this in the world? the Omniscient Being would simply always find present the fulfilled answer. His experience, then, would form one whole. There would be endless variety in this whole, but the whole, as such, would fulfil an all-embracing unity, a single system of ideas. This is what I mean by calling his Experience, as we here conceive it, an absolutely organised experience, his Thought an absolutely organised thought.

And now our question returns. We have defined the Omniscient Being. The question is: Does such a being exist? We turn from the ideal to the hard fact that we mortals find ourselves very ignorant beings. What can such as we are hope to know of the Absolute? . . .

Yes, the vast extent of our human ignorance, the limitations of our finite knowledge,—these great facts, so familiar to the present generation, confront us at the outset of every inquiry into our knowledge about God, or about any absolute issue. So little am I disposed to neglect these great facts of our limitation, that . . . philosophy seems to me, primarily, to be as much the theory of human ignorance as it is the theory of human knowledge. In fact, it is a small thing to say that man is ignorant. It is a great thing to undertake to comprehend the essence, the form, the implications, the meaning, of human ignorance. Let us make a beginning in this task as we approach the problem of Theism. For my thesis to-night will be that the very nature of human ignorance is such that you cannot conceive or define it apart from the assertion that there is, in truth, at the heart of the world, an Absolute and Universal Intelligence, for which thought and experience, so divided in us, are in complete and harmonious unity. . . .

The fortune of our empirical science has been, that as we men have wrought together upon the data of our senses, we have gradually woven a vast web of what we call relatively connected, united, or organised knowledge. . . . This organised knowledge has a very curious relation to our more direct experience. In the first place, wherever this organised knowledge seems best developed, we find it undertaking to deal with a world of truth, of so-called reality, or at least of apparent truth and reality, which is very remote from the actual sensory data that any man of us has ever beheld. Our organised science, as many have pointed out ever since Plato's first naïve but permanently important observations upon this topic, deals very largely with conceived—with ideal—realities, that transcend actual human observation. Atoms, ether-waves, geological periods, processes of evolution,—these are to-day some of the most important constituents of our conceived phenomenal universe. Spatial relations, far more exactly describable than they are directly verifiable, mathematical formulæ that express again the exactly describable aspects of vast physical processes of change—such are the topics with which our exacter science is most immediately concerned. In whose sensory experience are such objects and relationships at all directly pictured? The ideal world of Plato, the product of a more elementary sort of infant science, was made up of simpler contents than these; but still, when thus viewed, our science does indeed seem as if absorbed in the contemplation of a world of pure,—yes, I repeat, of Platonic ideas. For such realities get directly presented to no man's senses.

But of course, on the other hand, we no sooner try to define the work of our science in these terms than we are afresh reminded that this realm of pure Platonic ideas would be a mere world of fantastic shadows if we had not good reason to say that these ideas, these laws, these principles, these ideal objects of science, remote as they seem from our momentary sensory experiences, still have a real and, in the end, a verifiable relation to actual experience. One uses the scientific conceptions because, as one says, one can verify their reality. And to verify must mean to confirm in sensory terms. Only, to be sure, such verification always has to be for us men an extremely indirect one. The conceived realities of constructive science,—atoms, molecules, ether-waves, geological periods, processes of change whose type is embodied in mathematical formulæ,—these are never directly presented to any moment of our verifying sensory experience. But nevertheless we say that science does verify these conceptions; for science computes that if they are true, then, under given conditions, particular sensory experiences, of a predictable character, will occur in somebody's individual experience. Such predictions trained observers can and do successfully undertake to verify. The verification is itself, indeed, no direct acquaintance with the so-called realities that the aforesaid Platonic ideas define. But it appears to involve an indirect knowledge about such realities.

Yet our direct experience, as it actually comes, remains at best but a heap of fragments. And when one says that our science reduces our experience to order, one is still talking in relatively ideal terms. For our science does not in the least succeed in effectively reducing this chaos of our finite sensory life to any directly presented orderly wholeness. For think, I beg you, of what our concrete human experience is, as it actually comes, even at its best. Here we are all only too much alike. The sensory experience of a scientific man is, on the whole, nearly as full of immediately experienced disorder and fragmentariness as is that of his fellow the layman. For the scientific student too, the dust of the moment flies, and this dust often fills his eyes, and blinds him with its whirl of chance almost as much as it torments his neighbour who knows no Platonic ideas. I insist: Science throughout makes use of the contrast between this flying experience which we have, and which we call an experience of unreality, and the ideal experience, the higher sort of organised experience which we have not, and which we call an experience of reality. Upon this contrast the whole confession of our human ignorance depends. Let us still dwell a little on this contrast. Remember how full of mere chance the experience of nearly every moment seems to be; and that, too, even in a laboratory; much more, in a day's walk or in a lecture-room. The wind that sighs; the cart or the carriage that rumbles by; yonder dress or paper that rustles; the chair or boot that squeaks; the twinge that one suddenly feels; the confusions of our associative mental process, "fancy unto fancy linking"; the accidents that filled to-day's newspapers,—of such stuff, I beg you to notice, our immediate experience is naturally made up. The isolating devices of the laboratory, the nightly silence of the lonely observatory, the narrowness of the microscopic field, and, best of all, the control of a fixed and well-trained attention, often greatly diminish, but simply cannot annul, the disorder of this outer and inner chaos. But, on the other hand, all such efforts to secure order rest on the presupposition that this disorder means fragmentariness— random selection from a world of data that our science aims to view indirectly as a world of orderly experience. But even such relative reduction of the chaos as we get never lasts long and continuously in the life of any one person. Your moments of unfragmentary and more scientific experience fill of themselves only fragments of your life. A wandering attention, the interruption of intruding sensations,—such fragments may at any time be ready, by their intrusion, to destroy the orderliness of even the best-equipped scientific experience. The student of science, like other men, knows in fragments, and prophesies in fragments. But—and here we come again in sight of our goal—the world of truth that he wants to know is a world where that which is in part is to be taken away. He calls that the world of an organised experience. But he sees that world as through a glass,—darkly. He has to ignore his and our ignorance whenever he speaks of such a world as if it were the actual object of any human experience whatever. As a fact, direct human experience, apart from the elaborately devised indirect contrivances of conceptual thought, knows nothing of it. . . .

All our actual sensory experience comes in passing moments, and is fragmentary. Our science, wherever it has taken any form, contrasts with this immediate fragmentariness of our experience the assertion of a world of phenomenal truth, which is first of all characterised by the fact that for us it is a conceptual world, and not a world directly experienced by any one of us. Yet this ideal world is not an arbitrary world. It is linked to our actual experience by the fact that its conceptions are accounts, as exact as may be, of systems of possible experience, whose contents would be presented, in a certain form and order, to beings whom we conceive as including our fragmentary moments in some sort of definite unity of experience. That these scientific accounts of this world of organised experience are true, at least in a measure, we are said to verify, in so far as, first, we predict that, if they are true, certain other fragmentary phenomena will get presented to us under certain definable conditions, and in so far as, secondly, we successfully proceed to fulfil such predictions. Thus all of our knowledge of natural truth depends upon contrasting our actually fragmentary and stubbornly chaotic individual and momentary experience with a conceived world of organised experience, inclusive of all our fragments, but reduced in its wholeness to some sort of all-embracing unity. The contents and objects of this unified experience, we discover first by means of hypotheses as to what these contents and objects are, and then by means of verifications which depend upon a successful retranslation of our hypotheses as to organised experience into terms which our fragmentary experience can, under certain conditions, once more fulfil.

If, however, this is the work of all our science, then the conception of our human ignorance easily gets a provisional restatement. You are ignorant, in so far as you desire a knowledge that you cannot now get. Now, the knowledge you desire is, from our present point of view, no longer any knowledge of a reality foreign to all possible experience; but it is an adequate knowledge of the contents and the objects of a certain conceived or ideal sort of experience, called by you organised experience. And an organised experience would be one that found a system of ideas fulfilled in and by its facts. This sort of knowledge, you, as human being, can only define indirectly, tentatively, slowly, fallibly. And you get at it thus imperfectly,—why? Because your immediate experience, as it comes, is always fleeting, fragmentary. This is the sort of direct knower that you are,—a being who can of himself verify only fragments. But you can conceive infinitely more than you can directly verify. In thought you therefore construct conceptions which start, indeed, in your fragmentary experience, but which transcend it infinitely, and which so do inevitably run into danger of becoming mere shadows —pure Platonic ideas. But you don't mean your conceptions to remain thus shadowy. By the devices of hypothesis, prediction, and verification, you seek to link anew the concept and the presentation, the ideal order and the stubborn chaos, the conceived truth and the immediate datum, the contents of the organised experience and the fragments of your momentary flight of sensations. In so far as you succeed in this effort, you say that you have science. In so far as you are always, in presented experience, limited to your chaos, you admit that your sensations are of subjective moment and often delude you. But in so far as your conceptions of the contents of the ideal organised experience get verified, you say that you acquire the aforesaid indirect knowledge of the contents of the ideal and organised experience. We men know all things through contrasts. It is the contrast of your supposed indirect knowledge of the contents of the ideal organised experience with your direct and actual, but fragmentary, passing experience, that enables you to confess your ignorance. Were you merely ignorant, you could not know the fact. Because you are indirectly assured of the truth of an insight that you cannot directly share, you accuse your direct experience of illusory fragmentariness. But in so doing you contrast the contents of your individual experience, not with any mere reality apart from any possible experience, but with the conceived object of an ideal organised experience—an object conceived to be present to that experience as directly as your sensory experiences are present to you. . . .

In the light of such considerations, our notion of the infinitely remote goal of human knowledge gets a transformation of a sort very familiar to all students of philosophical Idealism. And this transformation relates to two aspects of our conception of knowledge, viz.: first, to our notion of what reality is, and secondly to our notion of what we mean by that Organised Experience. In the first place, the reality that we seek to know has always to be defined as that which either is or would be present to a sort of experience which we ideally define as an organised—that is, a united and transparently reasonable—experience. We have, in point of fact, no conception of reality capable of definition except this one. In case of an ordinary illusion of the senses we often say: This object seems thus or so; but in reality it is *thus*. Now, here the seeming is opposed to the reality only in so far as the chance experience of one point of view gets contrasted with what would be, or might be, experienced from some larger, more rationally permanent, or more inclusive and uniting point of view. Just so, the temperature of the room seems to a fevered patient to vary thus or thus; but the real temperature remains all the while nearly constant. Here the seeming is the content of the patient's momentary experience. The real temperature is a fact that either is, or conceivably might be, present to a larger, a more organised and scientific and united experience, such as his physician may come nearer than himself to possessing. The sun seems to rise and set; but in reality the earth turns on its axis. Here the apparent movement of the sun is somewhat indirectly presented to a narrow sort of human experience. A wider experience, say an experience defined from an extra-terrestrial point of view, would have presented to it the earth's rotation as immediately as we now can get the sunrise presented to us. To conceive any human belief as false—say, the belief of a lunatic, a fanatic, a philosopher, or a theologian—is to conceive this opinion as either possibly or actually corrected from some higher point of view, to which a larger whole of experience is considered as present.

Passing to the limit in this direction, we can accordingly say that by the absolute reality we can only mean either that which is present to an absolutely organised experience inclusive of all possible experience, or that which would be presented as the content of such an experience if there were one. If there concretely is such an absolute experience, then there concretely is such a reality present to it. If the absolute experience, however, remains to the end barely possible, then the concept of reality must be tainted by the same bare possibility. But the two concepts are strictly correlated. To conceive, for instance, absolute reality as containing no God, means simply that an absolutely all-embracing experience, if there were one, would find nothing Divine in the world. To assert that all human experience is illusory, is to say that an absolutely inclusive experience, if there were one, would have present, as part of its content, something involving the utter failure of our experience to attain that absolute content as such. To conceive that absolute reality consists of material atoms and ether, is to say that a complete experience of the universe would find presented to it nothing but experiences analogous to those that we have when we talk of matter in motion. In short, one must be serious with this concept of experience. Reality, as opposed to illusion, means simply an actual or possible content of experience, not in so far as this experience is supposed to be transient and fleeting, but in so far as it is conceived to be somehow inclusive and organised, the fulfilment of a system of ideas, the answer to a scheme of rational questions.

It remains, however, to analyse the other member of our related pair of terms, viz.: the conception of this organised sort of experience itself. In what sense can there be any meaning or truth about this conception? . . .

The conception of organised experience, in the limited and relative form in which the special sciences possess it, is unquestionably through and through a conception that for us men, as we are, has a social origin. No man, if isolated, could develope the sort of thoughtfulness that would lead him to appeal from experience as it comes to him to experience as it ideally ought to come, or would come, to him in case he could widely organise a whole world of experience in clear relation to a single system of conceptions. Man begins his intelligent life by imitatively appealing to his fellow's experience. The life-blood of science is distrust of individual belief as such. A common definition of a relatively organised experience is, the consensus of the competent observers. Deeper than our belief in any physical truth is our common-sense assurance that the experience of our fellows is as genuine as our own, is in actual relation to our own, has present to it objects identical with those that we ourselves experience, and consequently supplements our own. Apart from our social consciousness, I myself should hold that we men, growing up as we do, can come to have no clear conception of truth, nor any definite power clearly to think at all. Every man verifies for himself. But what he verifies,—the truth that he believes himself to be making out when he verifies,—this he conceives as a truth either actually or possibly verifiable by his fellow or by some still more organised sort of experience. And it becomes for him a concrete truth, and not a merely conceived possibility, precisely so far as he believes that his fellow or some other concrete mind does verify it.

My fellow's experience, however, thus supplements my own in two senses; namely, as actual and as possible experience. First, in so far as I am a social being, I take my fellow's experience to be as live and real an experience as is mine. In appealing to the consensus of other men's experiences, I am so far appealing to what I regard as a real experience other than my own momentary experience, and not as a merely possible experience. But in this sense, to be sure, human experience is not precisely an organised whole. Other men experience in passing moments, just as I do. Their consensus, in so far as it is reached, is no one whole of organised experience at all. But, on the other hand, the fact of the consensus of the various experiences of men, so far as such consensus appears to have been reached, suggests to our conception an ideal—the ideal of an experience which should be not only manifold but united, not only possessed of chance agreements but reduced to an all-embracing connectedness. As a fact, this ideal is the one constantly used by anyone who talks of the "verdict of science." This significant, whole, and connected experience remains, to us mortals, a conceived ideal, —always sought, never present. The ultimate question is: Is this conception a mere ideal?—or does it stand for a genuine sort of concrete experience? The social origin of the conception, as we mortals have come to get it, suggests in an ambiguous way both alternatives. The experience to which, as a social being, I first appeal when I learn to talk of truth, is the live actual experience of other men, which I, as an imitative being, primarily long to share, and which I therefore naturally regard as in many respects the norm for my experience. In society, in so far as I am plastic, my primary feeling is that I ought, on the whole, to experience what the other men experience. But in the course of more thoughtful mental growth, we have come to appeal from what the various men do experience to what they all ought to experience, or would experience if their experiences were in unity; that is, if all their moments were linked expressions of one universal meaning which was present to one Universal Subject, of whose insight their own experiences were but fragments. Such an ideally united experience, if it could but absolutely define its own contents, would know reality. And by reality we mean merely the contents that would be present to such an ideal unity of experience. But now, on this side, the conception of the ideally organised experience does indeed at first look like a mere ideal of a barely possible unity. The problem still is: Is this unity more than a bare possibility? Has it any such concrete genuineness as the life of our fellows is believed to possess?

Observe, however, that our question: Is there any such real unity of organised experience? is precisely equivalent to the question: Is there, not as a mere possibility, but as a genuine

truth, any reality? The question: Is there an absolutely organised experience? is equivalent to the question: Is there an absolute reality? You cannot first say: There is a reality now unknown to us mortals, and then go on to ask whether there is
an experience to which such reality is presented. The terms
"reality" and "organised experience" are correlative terms.
The one can only be defined as the object, the content, of the
other. Drop either, and the other vanishes. Make one a bare
ideal, and the other becomes equally such. If the organised
experience is a bare and ideal possibility, then the reality is a
mere seeming. If what I ought to experience, and should experience were I not ignorant, remains only a possibility, then
there is no absolute reality, but only possibility, in the universe, apart from your passing feelings and mine. Our actual
issue, then, is: Does a real world ultimately exist at all? If it
does, then it exists as the object of some sort of concretely actual organised experience, of the general type which our science indirectly and ideally defines, only of this type carried
to its absolute limit of completeness.

The answer to the ultimate question now before us—the
question: Is there an absolutely organised experience?—is
suggested by two very significant considerations. Of these
two considerations, the first runs as follows:

The alternative to saying that there is such a real unity of
experience is the assertion that such a unity is a bare and
ideal possibility. But, now, there can be no such thing as a
merely possible *truth*, definable apart from some actual experience. To say: So and so is possible, is to say: There is, somewhere in experience, an actuality some aspect of which can
be defined in terms of this possibility. A possibility is a truth
expressed in terms of a proposition beginning with *if*, or a hypothetical proposition,—an *is* expressed in terms of an *if*. But
every hypothetical proposition involves a categorical proposition. Every *if* implies an *is*. For you cannot define a truth as
concretely true unless you define it as really present to some
experience. Thus, for instance, I can easily define my actual

experience by expressing some aspect of it in the form of a supposition, even if the supposition be one contrary to fact, but I cannot believe in the truth of such a supposition without believing in some concrete and experienced fact. The suitor asks for the daughter. The father replies: "I will give thee my daughter *if* thou canst touch heaven." Here the father expresses his actually experienced intention in the form of a hypothetical proposition each member of which he believes to be false. The suitor cannot touch heaven, and is not to get the gift of the daughter. Yet the hypothetical proposition is to be true. Why? Because it expresses in terms of an *if* what the father experiences in terms of an *is*, namely, the obdurate inner will of the forbidding parent himself. Just so with any *if* proposition. Its members, antecedent and consequent, may be false. But it is true only in case there corresponds to its fashion of assertion some real experience.

And now, to apply this thought to our central problem: You and I, whenever we talk of reality as opposed to mere seeming, assert of necessity, as has just been shown, that *if* there were an organised unity of experience, this organised experience *would have* present to it as part of its content the fact whose reality we assert. This proposition cannot, as a merely hypothetical proposition, have any real truth unless to its asserted possibility there corresponds some actual experience, present somewhere in the world, not of barely possible, but of concretely actual experience. And this is the first of our two considerations. In fine, if there is an actual experience to which an absolute reality corresponds, then you can indeed translate this actuality into the terms of bare possibility. But unless there is such an actual experience, the bare possibility expresses no truth.

The second consideration appears when we ask our finite experience whereabouts, in its limited circle, is in any wise even suggested the actually experienced fact of which that hypothetical proposition relating to the ideal or absolute experience is the expression. What in finite experience suggests the truth that if there were an absolute experience it would find a certain unity of facts? . . .

To the foregoing question, my answer is this: Any finite experience either regards itself as suggesting some sort of truth, or does not so regard itself. If it does not regard itself as suggesting truth, it concerns us not here. Enough, one who thinks, who aims at truth, who means to know anything, is regarding his experience as suggesting truth. Now, to regard our experience as suggesting truth is, as we have seen, to mean that our experience indicates what a higher or inclusive, *i.e.* a more organised, experience would find presented thus or thus to itself. It is this meaning, this intent, this aim, this will to find in the moment the indication of what a higher experience directly grasps,—it is this that embodies for us the fact of which our hypothetical proposition aforesaid is the expression. But you may here say: "This aim, this will, is all. As a fact, you and I aim at the absolute experience; that is what we mean by wanting to know absolute truth; but the absolute experience," so you may insist, "is just a mere ideal. There need be no such experience as a concrete actuality. The aim, the intent, is the known fact. The rest is silence,— perhaps error. Perhaps there is no absolute truth, no ideally united and unfragmentary experience."

But hereupon one turns upon you with the inevitable dialectic of our problem itself. Grant hypothetically, if you choose, for a moment, that there is no universal experience as a concrete fact, but only the hope of it, the definition of it, the will to win it, the groaning and travail of the whole of finite experience in the search for it, in the error of believing that it is. Well, what will that mean? This ultimate limitation, this finally imprisoned finitude, this absolute fragmentariness and error, of the actual experience that aims at the absolute experience when there is no absolute experience at which to aim,—this absolute finiteness and erroneousness of the real experience, I say, will itself be a fact, a truth, a reality, and, as such, just the absolute truth. But this supposed ultimate truth will exist for whose experience? For the finite experience? No, for although our finite experience knows itself to be limited, still, just in so far as it is finite, it cannot know that there is no unity beyond its fragmentariness. For if any experience actually knew (that is, actually experienced) itself to be the whole of experience, it would have to experience how and why it were so. And if it knew this, it would be *ipso facto* an absolute, *i.e.* a completely self-possessed, experience, for which there was no truth that was not, as such, a datum, —no ideal of a beyond that was not, as such, judged by the facts to be meaningless,—no thought to which a presentation did not correspond, no presentation whose reality was not luminous to its comprehending thought. Only such an absolute experience could say with assurance: "Beyond my world there is no further experience actual." But if, by hypothesis, there is to be no such an experience, but only a limited collection of finite experiences, the question returns: The reality of this final limitation, the existence of no experience beyond the broken mass of finite fragments,—this is to be a truth,—but for whose experience is it to be a truth? Plainly, in the supposed case, it will be a truth nowhere presented—a truth for nobody. But, as we saw before, to assert any absolute reality as real is simply to assert an experience—and, in fact, just in so far as the reality is absolute, an absolute experience—for which this reality exists. To assert a truth as more than possible is to assert the concrete reality of an experience that knows this truth. Hence,—and here, indeed, is the conclusion of the whole matter,—the very effort hypothetically to assert that the whole world of experience is a world of fragmentary and finite experience is an effort involving a contradiction. Experience must constitute, in its entirety, one self-determined and consequently absolute and organised whole.

Otherwise put: All concrete or genuine, and not barely possible truth is, as such, a truth somewhere experienced. This is the inevitable result of the view with which we started when we said that without experience there is no knowledge. For truth *is,* so far as it is *known*. Now, this proposition applies as well to the totality of the world of finite experience as it does to the parts of that world. There must, then, be an experience to which is present the constitution (*i.e.* the actual limitation and narrowness) of all finite experience, just as surely as there is such a constitution. That there is nothing at all beyond this limited constitution must, as a fact, be present to this final experience. But this fact that the world of finite experience has no experience beyond it could not be present, as a fact, to any but an absolute experience which knew all that is or that genuinely can be known; and the proposition that a totality of finite experience could exist without there being any absolute experience, thus proves to be simply self-contradictory. . . .

Let us sum up, in a few words, our whole argument. There is, for us as we are, experience. Our thought undertakes the interpretation of this experience. Every intelligent interpretation of an experience involves, however, the appeal from this experienced fragment to some more organised whole of experience, in whose unity this fragment is conceived as finding its organic place. To talk of any reality which this fragmentary experience indicates, is to conceive this reality as the content of the more organised experience. To assert that there is any absolutely real fact indicated by our experience, is to regard this reality as presented to an absolutely organised experience, in which every fragment finds its place.

So far, indeed, in speaking of reality and an absolute experience, one talks of mere conceptual objects,—one deals, as the mathematical sciences do, with what appear to be only shadowy Platonic ideas. The question arises: Do these Platonic ideas of the absolute reality, and of the absolutely organised experience, stand for anything but merely ideal or possible entities? The right answer to this question comes, if one first assumes, for argument's sake, that such answer is negative, and that there is no organised, but only a fragmentary experience. For then one has to define the alternative that is to be opposed to the supposedly erroneous conception of an absolute experience. That alternative, as pointed out, is a world of fragmentary experiences, whose limited nature is not determined by any all-pervading idea. Such a world of finite experiences is to be merely what it happens to be,—is to contain only what chances here or there to be felt. But hereupon arises the question: What reality has this fact of the limitation and fragmentariness of the actual world of experiences? If every reality has to exist just in so far as there is experience of its existence, then the determination of the world of experience to be this world and no other, the fact that reality contains no other facts than these, is, as the supposed final reality, itself the object of one experience, for which the fragmentariness of the finite world appears as a presented and absolute fact, beyond which no reality is to be viewed as even genuinely possible. For this final experience, the conception of any possible experience beyond is known as an ungrounded conception, as an actual impossibility. But so, this final experience is by hypothesis forthwith defined as One, as all-inclusive, as determined by nothing beyond itself, as assured of the complete fulfilment of its own ideas concerning what is,—in brief, it becomes an absolute experience. The very effort to deny an absolute experience involves, then, the actual assertion of such an absolute experience.

Our result, then, is: There is an Absolute Experience, for which the conception of an absolute reality, *i.e.* the conception of a system of ideal truth, is fulfilled by the very contents that get presented to this Experience. This Absolute Experience is related to our experience as an organic whole to its own fragments. It is an experience which finds fulfilled all that the completest thought can rationally conceive as genuinely possible. Herein lies its definition as an Absolute. For the Absolute Experience, as for ours, there are data, contents, facts. But these data, these contents, express, for the Absolute Experience, its own meaning, its thought, its ideas. Contents beyond these that it possesses, the Absolute Experience knows to be, in genuine truth, impossible. Hence its contents are indeed particular,—a selection from the world of bare or merely conceptual possibilities,—but they form a self-determined whole, than which nothing completer, more organic, more fulfilled, more transparent, or more complete in meaning, is concretely or genuinely possible. On the other hand, these contents are not foreign to those of our finite experience, but are inclusive of them in the unity of one life. . . .

The conception now reached I regard as the philosophical conception of God. Some of you may observe that in the foregoing account I have often, in defining the Absolute, made use of the terms lately employed by Mr. Bradley,[2] rather than of the terms used in either of my two published discussions of the topic, *i.e.* either in [my *Religious Aspect of Philosophy*] or in my *Spirit of Modern Philosophy*. Such variation of the terms employed involves indeed an enrichment, but certainly no essential change in the conception. The argument here used is essentially the same as the one before employed. You can certainly, and, as I still hold, quite properly, define the Absolute as Thought. But then you mean, as in my book I explicitly showed, a thought that is no longer, like ours in the exact sciences, concerned with the shadowy Platonic ideas, viewed as conceptional possibilities, but a thought that sees its own fulfilment in the world of its self-possessed life,—in other words, a thought whose Ideas are not mere shadows, but have an aspect in which they are felt as well as meant, appreciated as well as described,—yes, I should unhesitatingly say, loved as well as conceived, willed as well as viewed. Such an Absolute Thought you can also call, in its wholeness, a Self; for it beholds the fulfilment of its own thinking, and views the determined character of its living experience as identical with what its universal concep-

[2] Here Royce refers to F. H. Bradley's *Appearance and Reality* (London, 1893). [M.W.]

tions mean. All these names: "Absolute Self," "Absolute Thought," "Absolute Experience," are not, indeed, mere indifferent names for the inexpressible truth; but, when carefully defined through the very process of their construction, they are equally valuable expressions of different aspects of the same truth. God is known as Thought fulfilled; as Experience absolutely organised, so as to have one ideal unity of meaning; as Truth transparent to itself; as Life in absolute accordance with idea; as Selfhood eternally obtained. And all this the Absolute is in concrete unity, not in mere variety.

Yet our purpose here is not religious but speculative. It is not mine to-night to declare the glory of the Divine Being, but simply to scrutinise the definition of the Absolute. The heart of my whole argument . . . has been the insistence that all these seemingly so transcendent and imprudent speculations about the Absolute are, as a fact, the mere effort to express, as coherently as may be, the commonplace implications of our very human ignorance itself. People think it very modest to say: We cannot know what the Absolute Reality is. They forget that to make this assertion implies—unless one is using idle words without sense—that one knows what the term "Absolute Reality" means. People think it easy to say: We can be sure of only what our own finite experience presents. They forget that if a world of finite experience exists at all, this world must have a consistently definable constitution, in order that it may exist. Its constitution, however, turns out to be such that an Absolute Experience—namely, an experience acquainted with limitation only in so far as this limitation is determined by the organised and transparent constitution of this experience—is needed as that for which the fragmentary constitution of the finite world of experience exists. The very watchword, then, of our whole doctrine is this: All knowledge is of something experienced. For this means that nothing actually exists save what is somewhere experienced. If this be true, then the total limitation, the determination, the fragmentariness, the ignorance, the error,—yes (as forms or cases of ignorance and error), the evil, the pain, the horror, the longing, the travail, the faith, the devotion, the endless flight from its own worthlessness,—that constitutes the very essence of the world of finite experience, is, as a positive reality, somewhere so experienced in its wholeness that this entire constitution of the finite appears as a world beyond which, in its whole constitution, nothing exists or can exist. But, for such an experience, this constitution of the finite is a fact determined from an absolute point of view, and every finite incompleteness and struggle appears as a part of a whole in whose wholeness the fragments find their true place, the ideas their realisation, the seeking its fulfilment, and our whole life its truth, and so its eternal rest,—that peace which transcends the storms of its agony and its restlessness. For this agony and restlessness are the very embodiment of an incomplete experience, of a finite ignorance.

Do you ask, then: Where in our human world does God get revealed?—what manifests his glory? I answer: Our ignorance, our fallibility, our imperfection, and so, as forms of this ignorance and imperfection, our experience of longing, of strife, of pain, of error,—yes, of whatever, as finite, declares that its truth lies in its limitation, and so lies beyond itself. These things, wherein we taste the bitterness of our finitude, are what they are because they mean more than they contain, imply what is beyond them, refuse to exist by themselves, and, at the very moment of confessing their own fragmentary falsity, assure us of the reality of that fulfilment which is the life of God.

The conception of God thus reached offers itself to you, not as destroying, but as fulfilling, the large collection of slowly evolving notions that have appeared in the course of history in connection with the name of God.

The foregoing definition of God as an Absolute Experience transparently fulfilling a system of organised ideas, is, as you all doubtless are aware, in essence identical with the conception first reached, but very faintly and briefly developed, by

Aristotle. Another definition of God, as the Absolute (or Perfect) Reality, long struggled in the history of speculation with this idea of God as Fulfilled Thought, or as Self-possessed Experience. The interrelation of these two central definitions has long occupied philosophical thinking. Their rational identification is the work of recent speculation. The all-powerful and righteous World-Creator of the Old and New Testaments was first conceived, not speculatively, but ethically; and it is to the rich experience of Christian mysticism that the historical honour belongs, of having bridged the gulf that seemed to separate, and that to many minds still separates, the God of practical faith from the God of philosophical definition. Mysticism is not philosophy; but, as a stage of human experience, it is the link that binds the contemplative to the practical in the history of religion, since the saints have taken refuge in it, and the philosophers have endeavoured to emerge from its mysteries to the light of clearer insight. To St. Thomas Aquinas belongs the credit of the first explicit and fully developed synthesis of the Aristotelian and the Christian conception of God. The Thomistic proofs of God's existence—repeated, diluted, and thus often rendered very trivial, by popular apologetic writers—have now, at best, lost much of their speculative interest. But the conception of the Divine that St. Thomas reached remains in certain important respects central, and in essence identical, I think, with the definition that I have here tried to repeat; and that, too, despite the paradoxes and the errors involved in the traditional concept of the creation of the world.

For the rest, let me in closing be perfectly frank with you. I myself am one of those students whom a more modern and radical scepticism has, indeed, put in general very much out of sympathy with many of what seem to me the unessential accidents of religious tradition as represented in the historical faith; and for such students this scepticism has transformed, in many ways, our methods of defining our relation to truth. But this scepticism has not thrown even the most radical of us, if we are enlightened, out of a close, a rational, a spiritually intelligent relation to those deep ideas that, despite all these accidents, have moulded the heart of the history of religion. In brief, then, the foregoing conception of God undertakes to be distinctly theistic, and not pantheistic. It is not the conception of any Unconscious Reality, into which finite beings are absorbed; nor of a Universal Substance, in whose law our ethical independence is lost; nor of an Ineffable Mystery, which we can only silently adore. On the contrary, every ethical predicate that the highest religious faith of the past has attributed to God is capable of exact interpretation in terms of our present view. For my own part, then, while I wish to be no slave of any tradition, I am certainly disposed to insist that what the faith of our fathers has genuinely meant by God, is, despite all the blindness and all the unessential accidents of religious tradition, identical with the inevitable outcome of a reflective philosophy.

Part 7: Naturalism: The Revolt against Gentility and Dualism

GEORGE SANTAYANA

George Santayana (1863–1952) was the youngest of the triumvir that ruled American philosophy in its "Golden Age" from the eighteen-eighties to almost the beginning of the First World War. And although James wrote brilliantly and Royce wrote *The Feud of Oakfield Creek: A Novel of California Life* (1887), Santayana was unquestionably *the* literary man of the three. He wrote affecting poetry and penetrating criticism, and in his seventies published a well-received novel, *The Last Puritan* (1936), which treated nothing as wild as Royce's native California. Santayana's novel began with the sentence: "A little below the State House in Boston, where Beacon Street consents to bend slightly and begins to run down hill, and where across the Mall the grassy shoulder of the Common slopes almost steeply down to the Frog Pond, there stood about the year 1870—and for all I know there may still stand—a pair of old brick houses, flatter and plainer than the rest". And the words "for all I know there may still stand" epitomized a lifetime of spiritual distance separating Santayana from the Boston to which he was brought from Spain as a boy. In 1912, upon inheriting some money, Santayana resigned his Harvard professorship; but just before he left he dissected the New England mind in "The Genteel Tradition in America", one of the best and most influential pieces he ever wrote.

In spite of Santayana's distaste for America, his best work was done there while he focused on what he called "the vicissitudes of human belief" and before he attempted to construct an ambitious metaphysics and epistemology in unsuccessful imitation of the great philosophers. Santayana's *Interpretations of Poetry and Religion* (1900), *The Life of Reason* (1905–6), and his essay on the genteel tradition included trenchant analyses of the larger aspects of civilization, and in particular of religion. He approached it as a Catholic who was an atheist and a materialist might, insisting that it should not be regarded as a competitor of science but rather as an allegorical, poetic vehicle of moral philosophy. And in spite of his distaste for the genteel tradition, which in his view included Emerson as one of its great pillars, Santayana ironically appears in the history of American philosophy as a materialistic opposite number of Emerson, whom he once described as "a Puritan mystic with a poetic fancy and a gift for observation and epigram". Santayana was no mystic, but he did possess a poetic fancy and a gift for observation and epigram; and he reveals this in good measure in the selections to follow. With John Dewey—unlike Santayana as he was in very important respects—Santayana led the American revolt against the genteel tradition under the banner of naturalism. In the period covered by this volume they were among the few major American philosophers not to believe literally in God, and the most persuasive opponents of an absolute idealism that even William James could not defeat on his own.

The Genteel Tradition [1]

Ladies and Gentlemen,—The privilege of addressing you to-day is very welcome to me, not merely for the honour of it,

[1] Below there appears in its entirety Santayana's "The Genteel Tradition in American Philosophy", originally delivered as an address before

which is great, nor for the pleasures of travel, which are many, when it is California that one is visiting for the first time, but also because there is something I have long wanted to say which this occasion seems particularly favourable for saying. America is still a young country, and this part of it is especially so; and it would have been nothing extraordinary if, in this young country, material preoccupations had altogether absorbed people's minds, and they had been too much engrossed in living to reflect upon life, or to have any philosophy. The opposite, however, is the case. Not only have you already found time to philosophise in California, as your society proves, but the eastern colonists from the very beginning were a sophisticated race. As much as in clearing the land and fighting the Indians they were occupied, as they expressed it, in wrestling with the Lord. The country was new, but the race was tried, chastened, and full of solemn memories. It was an old wine in new bottles; and America did not have to wait for its present universities, with their departments of academic philosophy, in order to possess a living philosophy—to have a distinct vision of the universe and definite convictions about human destiny.

Now this situation is a singular and remarkable one, and has many consequences, not all of which are equally fortunate. America is a young country with an old mentality: it has enjoyed the advantages of a child carefully brought up and thoroughly indoctrinated; it has been a wise child. But a wise child, an old head on young shoulders, always has a comic and an unpromising side. The wisdom is a little thin and verbal, not aware of its full meaning and grounds; and physical and emotional growth may be stunted by it, or even deranged. Or when the child is too vigorous for that, he will develop a fresh mentality of his own, out of his observations

the Philosophical Union of the University of California on August 25, 1911. It was first printed in *The University of California Chronicle,* Volume 13 (October 1911), pp. 357–80 and later in Santayana's *Winds of Doctrine* (New York, 1913). Reprinted by permission of J. M. Dent and Sons, Ltd., London.

and actual instincts; and this fresh mentality will interfere with the traditional mentality, and tend to reduce it to something perfunctory, conventional, and perhaps secretly despised. A philosophy is not genuine unless it inspires and expresses the life of those who cherish it. I do not think the hereditary philosophy of America has done much to atrophy the natural activities of the inhabitants; the wise child has not missed the joys of youth or of manhood; but what has happened is that the hereditary philosophy has grown stale, and that the academic philosophy afterwards developed has caught the stale odour from it. America is not simply, as I said a moment ago, a young country with an old mentality: it is a country with two mentalities, one a survival of the beliefs and standards of the fathers, the other an expression of the instincts, practice, and discoveries of the younger generations. In all the higher things of the mind—in religion, in literature, in the moral emotions—it is the hereditary spirit that still prevails, so much so that Mr. Bernard Shaw finds that America is a hundred years behind the times. The truth is that one-half of the American mind, that not occupied intensely in practical affairs, has remained, I will not say highand-dry, but slightly becalmed; it has floated gently in the back-water, while, alongside, in invention and industry and social organisation, the other half of the mind was leaping down a sort of Niagara Rapids. This division may be found symbolised in American architecture: a neat reproduction of the colonial mansion—with some modern comforts introduced surreptitiously—stands beside the sky-scraper. The American Will inhabits the sky-scraper; the American Intellect inhabits the colonial mansion. The one is the sphere of the American man; the other, at least predominantly, of the American woman. The one is all aggressive enterprise; the other is all genteel tradition.

Now, with your permission, I should like to analyse more fully how this interesting situation has arisen, how it is qualified, and whither it tends. And in the first place we should remember what, precisely, that philosophy was which the first settlers brought with them into the country. In strictness there was more than one; but we may confine our attention to what I will call Calvinism, since it is on this that the current academic philosophy has been grafted. I do not mean exactly the Calvinism of Calvin, or even of Jonathan Edwards; for in their systems there was much that was not pure philosophy, but rather faith in the externals and history of revelation. Jewish and Christian revelation was interpreted by these men, however, in the spirit of a particular philosophy, which might have arisen under any sky, and been associated with any other religion as well as with Protestant Christianity. In fact, the philosophical principle of Calvinism appears also in the Koran, in Spinoza, and in Cardinal Newman; and persons with no very distinctive Christian belief, like Carlyle or like Professor Royce, may be nevertheless, philosophically, perfect Calvinists. Calvinism, taken in this sense, is an expression of the agonised conscience. It is a view of the world which an agonised conscience readily embraces, if it takes itself seriously, as, being agonised, of course it must. Calvinism, essentially, asserts three things: that sin exists, that sin is punished, and that it is beautiful that sin should exist to be punished. The heart of the Calvinist is therefore divided between tragic concern at his own miserable condition, and tragic exultation about the universe at large. He oscillates between a profound abasement and a paradoxical elation of the spirit. To be a Calvinist philosophically is to feel a fierce pleasure in the existence of misery, especially of one's own, in that this misery seems to manifest the fact that the Absolute is irresponsible or infinite or holy. Human nature, it feels, is totally depraved: to have the instincts and motives that we necessarily have is a great scandal, and we must suffer for it; but that scandal is requisite, since otherwise the serious importance of being as we ought to be would not have been vindicated.

To those of us who have not an agonised conscience this

system may seem fantastic and even unintelligible; yet it is logically and intently thought out from its emotional premises. It can take permanent possession of a deep mind here and there, and under certain conditions it can become epidemic. Imagine, for instance, a small nation with an intense vitality, but on the verge of ruin, ecstatic and distressful, having a strict and minute code of laws, that paints life in sharp and violent chiaroscuro, all pure righteousness and black abominations, and exaggerating the consequences of both perhaps to infinity. Such a people were the Jews after the exile, and again the early Protestants. If such a people is philosophical at all, it will not improbably be Calvinistic. Even in the early American communities many of these conditions were fulfilled. The nation was small and isolated; it lived under pressure and constant trial; it was acquainted with but a small range of goods and evils. Vigilance over conduct and an absolute demand for personal integrity were not merely traditional things, but things that practical sages, like Franklin and Washington, recommended to their countrymen, because they were virtues that justified themselves visibly by their fruits. But soon these happy results themselves helped to relax the pressure of external circumstances, and indirectly the pressure of the agonised conscience within. The nation became numerous; it ceased to be either ecstatic or distressful; the high social morality which on the whole it preserved took another colour; people remained honest and helpful out of good sense and good will rather than out of scrupulous adherence to any fixed principles. They retained their instinct for order, and often created order with surprising quickness; but the sanctity of law, to be obeyed for its own sake, began to escape them; it seemed too unpractical a notion, and not quite serious. In fact, the second and native-born American mentality began to take shape. The sense of sin totally evaporated. Nature, in the words of Emerson, was all beauty and commodity; and while operating on it laboriously, and drawing quick returns, the American began to drink in inspiration from it æsthetically. At the same time, in so broad a continent, he had elbow-room. His neighbours helped more than they hindered him; he wished their number to increase. Good will became the great American virtue; and a passion arose for counting heads, and square miles, and cubic feet, and minutes saved—as if there had been anything to save them for. How strange to the American now that saying of Jonathan Edwards, that men are naturally God's enemies! Yet that is an axiom to any intelligent Calvinist, though the words he uses may be different. If you told the modern American that he is totally depraved, he would think you were joking, as he himself usually is. He is convinced that he always has been, and always will be, victorious and blameless.

Calvinism thus lost its basis in American life. Some emotional natures, indeed, reverted in their religious revivals or private searchings of heart to the sources of the tradition; for any of the radical points of view in philosophy may cease to be prevalent, but none can cease to be possible. Other natures, more sensitive to the moral and literary influences of the world, preferred to abandon parts of their philosophy, hoping thus to reduce the distance which should separate the remainder from real life.

Meantime, if anybody arose with a special sensibility or a technical genius, he was in great straits; not being fed sufficiently by the world, he was driven in upon his own resources. The three American writers whose personal endowment was perhaps the finest—Poe, Hawthorne, and Emerson —had all a certain starved and abstract quality. They could not retail the genteel tradition; they were too keen, too perceptive, and too independent for that. But life offered them little digestible material, nor were they naturally voracious. They were fastidious, and under the circumstances they were starved. Emerson, to be sure, fed on books. There was a great catholicity in his reading; and he showed a fine tact in his comments, and in his way of appropriating what he read. But he read transcendentally, not historically, to learn what he himself felt, not what others might have felt before him. And to feed on books, for a philosopher or a poet, is still to starve. Books can help him to acquire form, or to avoid pitfalls; they cannot supply him with substance, if he is to have any. Therefore the genius of Poe and Hawthorne, and even of Emerson, was employed on a sort of inner play, or digestion of vacancy. It was a refined labour, but it was in danger of being morbid, or tinkling, or self-indulgent. It was a play of intra-mental rhymes. Their mind was like an old music-box, full of tender echoes and quaint fancies. These fancies expressed their personal genius sincerely, as dreams may; but they were arbitrary fancies in comparison with what a real observer would have said in the premises. Their manner, in a word, was subjective. In their own persons they escaped the mediocrity of the genteel tradition, but they supplied nothing to supplant it in other minds.

The churches, likewise, although they modified their spirit, had no philosophy to offer save a new emphasis on parts of what Calvinism contained. The theology of Calvin, we must remember, had much in it besides philosophical Calvinism. A Christian tenderness, and a hope of grace for the individual, came to mitigate its sardonic optimism; and it was these evangelical elements that the Calvinistic churches now emphasised, seldom and with blushes referring to hell-fire or infant damnation. Yet philosophic Calvinism, with a theory of life that would perfectly justify hell-fire and infant damnation if they happened to exist, still dominates the traditional metaphysics. It is an ingredient, and the decisive ingredient, in what calls itself idealism. But in order to see just what part Calvinism plays in current idealism, it will be necessary to distinguish the other chief element in that complex system, namely, transcendentalism.

Transcendentalism is the philosophy which the romantic era produced in Germany, and independently, I believe, in America also. Transcendentalism proper, like romanticism, is not any particular set of dogmas about what things exist; it is not a system of the universe regarded as a fact, or as a collection of facts. It is a method, a point of view, from which any world, no matter what it might contain, could be approached by a self-conscious observer. Transcendentalism is systematic subjectivism. It studies the perspectives of knowledge as they radiate from the self; it is a plan of those avenues of inference by which our ideas of things must be reached, if they are to afford any systematic or distant vistas. In other words, transcendentalism is the critical logic of science. Knowledge, it says, has a station, as in a watchtower; it is always seated here and now, in the self of the moment. The past and the future, things inferred and things conceived, lie around it, painted as upon a panorama. They cannot be lighted up save by some centrifugal ray of attention and present interest, by some active operation of the mind.

This is hardly the occasion for developing or explaining this delicate insight; suffice it to say, lest you should think later that I disparage transcendentalism, that as a method I regard it as correct and, when once suggested, unforgettable. I regard it as the chief contribution made in modern times to speculation. But it is a method only, an attitude we may always assume if we like and that will always be legitimate. It is no answer, and involves no particular answer, to the question: What exists; in what order is what exists produced; what is to exist in the future? This question must be answered by observing the object, and tracing humbly the movement of the object. It cannot be answered at all by harping on the fact that this object, if discovered, must be discovered by somebody, and by somebody who has an interest in discovering it. Yet the Germans who first gained the full transcendental insight were romantic people; they were more or less frankly poets; they were colossal egotists, and wished to make not only their own knowledge but the whole universe centre about themselves. And full as they were of their romantic isolation and romantic liberty, it occurred to them to imagine that all reality might be a transcendental self and a romantic dreamer like themselves; nay, that it might be just their own transcendental self and their own romantic dreams extended indefinitely. Transcendental logic, the method of discovery for the mind, was to become also the method of evolution in nature and history. Transcendental method, so abused, produced transcendental myth. A conscientious critique of knowledge was turned into a sham system of nature. We must therefore distinguish sharply the transcendental grammar of the intellect, which is significant and potentially correct, from the various transcendental systems of the universe, which are chimeras.

In both its parts, however, transcendentalism had much to recommend it to American philosophers, for the transcendental method appealed to the individualistic and revolutionary temper of their youth, while transcendental myths enabled them to find a new status for their inherited theology, and to give what parts of it they cared to preserve some semblance of philosophical backing. This last was the use to which the transcendental method was put by Kant himself, who first brought it into vogue, before the terrible weapon had got out of hand, and become the instrument of pure romanticism. Kant came, he himself said, to remove knowledge in order to make room for faith, which in his case meant faith in Calvinism. In other words, he applied the transcendental method to matters of fact, reducing them thereby to human ideas, in order to give to the Calvinistic postulates of conscience a metaphysical validity. For Kant had a genteel tradition of his own, which he wished to remove to a place of safety, feeling that the empirical world had become too hot for it; and this place of safety was the region of transcendental myth. I need hardly say how perfectly this expedient suited the needs of philosophers in America, and it is no accident if the influence of Kant soon became dominant here. To embrace this philosophy was regarded as a sign of profound metaphysical insight, although the most mediocre minds found no difficulty in embracing it. In truth it was a sign of having been brought up in the genteel tradition, of feeling it weak, and of wishing to save it.

But the transcendental method, in its way, was also sympathetic to the American mind. It embodied, in a radical form, the spirit of Protestantism as distinguished from its inherited doctrines; it was autonomous, undismayed, calmly revolutionary; it felt that Will was deeper than Intellect; it focussed everything here and now, and asked all things to show their credentials at the bar of the young self, and to prove their value for this latest born moment. These things are truly American; they would be characteristic of any young society with a keen and discursive intelligence, and they are strikingly exemplified in the thought and in the person of Emerson. They constitute what he called self-trust. Self-trust, like other transcendental attitudes, may be expressed in metaphysical fables. The romantic spirit may imagine itself to be an absolute force, evoking and moulding the plastic world to express its varying moods. But for a pioneer who is actually a world-builder this metaphysical illusion has a partial warrant in historical fact; far more warrant than it could boast of in the fixed and articulated society of Europe, among the moonstruck rebels and sulking poets of the romantic era. Emerson was a shrewd Yankee, by instinct on the winning side; he was a cheery, child-like soul, impervious to the evidence of evil, as of everything that it did not suit his transcendental individuality to appreciate or to notice. More, perhaps, than anybody that has ever lived, he practised the transcendental method in all its purity. He had no system. He opened his eyes on the world every morning with a fresh sincerity, marking how things seemed to him then, or what they suggested to his spontaneous fancy. This fancy, for being spontaneous, was not always novel; it was guided by the habits and training of his mind, which were those of a preacher. Yet he never insisted on his notions so as to turn them into settled dogmas; he felt in his bones that they were myths. Sometimes, indeed,

the bad example of other transcendentalists, less true than he
to their method, or the pressing questions of unintelligent
people, or the instinct we all have to think our ideas final, led
him to the very verge of system-making; but he stopped
short. Had he made a system out of his notion of compensation, or the over-soul, or spiritual laws, the result would have
been as thin and forced as it is in other transcendental systems. But he coveted truth; and he returned to experience, to
history, to poetry, to the natural science of his day, for new
starting-points and hints toward fresh transcendental mus-
ings.

To covet truth is a very distinguished passion. Every philosopher says he is pursuing the truth, but this is seldom the
case. As Mr. Bertrand Russell has observed, one reason why
philosophers often fail to reach the truth is that often they do
not desire to reach it. Those who are genuinely concerned in
discovering what happens to be true are rather the men of
science, the naturalists, the historians; and ordinarily they
discover it, according to their lights. The truths they find are
never complete, and are not always important; but they are
integral parts of the truth, facts and circumstances that help
to fill in the picture, and that no later interpretation can invalidate or afford to contradict. But professional philosophers
are usually only apologists: that is, they are absorbed in defending some vested illusion or some eloquent idea. Like lawyers or detectives, they study the case for which they are
retained, to see how much evidence or semblance of evidence
they can gather for the defence, and how much prejudice
they can raise against the witnesses for the prosecution; for
they know they are defending prisoners suspected by the
world, and perhaps by their own good sense, of falsification.
They do not covet truth, but victory and the dispelling of
their own doubts. What they defend is some system, that is,
some view about the totality of things, of which men are actually ignorant. No system would have ever been framed if
people had been simply interested in knowing what is true,

whatever it may be. What produces systems is the interest in maintaining against all comers that some favourite or inherited idea of ours is sufficient and right. A system may contain an account of many things which, in detail, are true enough; but as a system, covering infinite possibilities that neither our experience nor our logic can prejudge, it must be a work of imagination and a piece of human soliloquy. It may be expressive of human experience, it may be poetical; but how should any one who really coveted truth suppose that it was true?

Emerson had no system; and his coveting truth had another exceptional consequence: he was detached, unworldly, contemplative. When he came out of the conventicle or the reform meeting, or out of the rapturous close atmosphere of the lecture-room, he heard Nature whispering to him: "Why so hot, little sir?" No doubt the spirit or energy of the world is what is acting in us, as the sea is what rises in every little wave; but it passes through us, and cry out as we may, it will move on. Our privilege is to have perceived it as it moves. Our dignity is not in what we do, but in what we understand. The whole world is doing things. We are turning in that vortex; yet within us is silent observation, the speculative eye before which all passes, which bridges the distances and compares the combatants. On this side of his genius Emerson broke away from all conditions of age or country and represented nothing except intelligence itself.

There was another element in Emerson, curiously combined with transcendentalism, namely, his love and respect for Nature. Nature, for the transcendentalist, is precious because it is his own work, a mirror in which he looks at himself and says (like a poet relishing his own verses), "What a genius I am! Who would have thought there was such stuff in me?" And the philosophical egotist finds in his doctrine a ready explanation of whatever beauty and commodity nature actually has. No wonder, he says to himself, that nature is sympathetic, since I made it. And such a view, one-sided and even fatuous as it may be, undoubtedly sharpens the vision of a poet and a moralist to all that is inspiriting and symbolic in the natural world. Emerson was particularly ingenious and clear-sighted in feeling the spiritual uses of fellowship with the elements. This is something in which all Teutonic poetry is rich and which forms, I think, the most genuine and spontaneous part of modern taste, and especially of American taste. Just as some people are naturally enthralled and refreshed by music, so others are by landscape. Music and landscape make up the spiritual resources of those who cannot or dare not express their unfulfilled ideals in words. Serious poetry, profound religion (Calvinism, for instance), are the joys of an unhappiness that confesses itself; but when a genteel tradition forbids people to confess that they are unhappy, serious poetry and profound religion are closed to them by that; and since human life, in its depths, cannot then express itself openly, imagination is driven for comfort into abstract arts, where human circumstances are lost sight of, and human problems dissolve in a purer medium. The pressure of care is thus relieved, without its quietus being found in intelligence. To understand oneself is the classic form of consolation; to elude oneself is the romantic. In the presence of music or landscape human experience eludes itself; and thus romanticism is the bond between transcendental and naturalistic sentiment. The winds and clouds come to minister to the solitary ego.

Have there been, we may ask, any successful efforts to escape from the genteel tradition, and to express something worth expressing behind its back? This might well not have occurred as yet; but America is so precocious, it has been trained by the genteel tradition to be so wise for its years, that some indications of a truly native philosophy and poetry are already to be found. I might mention the humorists, of whom you here in California have had your share. The humorists, however, only half escape the genteel tradition; their humour would lose its savour if they had wholly escaped it.

They point to what contradicts it in the facts; but not in order to abandon the genteel tradition, for they have nothing solid to put in its place. When they point out how ill many facts fit into it, they do not clearly conceive that this militates against the standard, but think it a funny perversity in the facts. Of course, did they earnestly respect the genteel tradition, such an incongruity would seem to them sad, rather than ludicrous. Perhaps the prevalence of humour in America, in and out of season, may be taken as one more evidence that the genteel tradition is present pervasively, but everywhere weak. Similarly in Italy, during the Renaissance, the Catholic tradition could not be banished from the intellect, since there was nothing articulate to take its place; yet its hold on the heart was singularly relaxed. The consequence was that humorists could regale themselves with the foibles of monks and of cardinals, with the credulity of fools, and the bogus miracles of the saints; not intending to deny the theory of the church, but caring for it so little at heart that they could find it infinitely amusing that it should be contradicted in men's lives and that no harm should come of it. So when Mark Twain says, "I was born of poor but dishonest parents," the humour depends on the parody of the genteel Anglo-Saxon convention that it is disreputable to be poor; but to hint at the hollowness of it would not be amusing if it did not remain at bottom one's habitual conviction.

The one American writer who has left the genteel tradition entirely behind is perhaps Walt Whitman. For this reason educated Americans find him rather an unpalatable person, who they sincerely protest ought not to be taken for a representative of their culture; and he certainly should not, because their culture is so genteel and traditional. But the foreigner may sometimes think otherwise, since he is looking for what may have arisen in America to express, not the polite and conventional American mind, but the spirit and the inarticulate principles that animate the community, on which its own genteel mentality seems to sit rather lightly. When the foreigner opens the pages of Walt Whitman, he thinks that he has come at last upon something representative and original. In Walt Whitman democracy is carried into psychology and morals. The various sights, moods, and emotions are given each one vote; they are declared to be all free and equal, and the innumerable commonplace moments of life are suffered to speak like the others. Those moments formerly reputed great are not excluded, but they are made to march in the ranks with their companions—plain foot-soldiers and servants of the hour. Nor does the refusal to discriminate stop there; we must carry our principle further down, to the animals, to inanimate nature, to the cosmos as a whole. Whitman became a pantheist; but his pantheism, unlike that of the Stoics and of Spinoza, was unintellectual, lazy, and self-indulgent; for he simply felt jovially that everything real was good enough, and that he was good enough himself. In him Bohemia rebelled against the genteel tradition; but the reconstruction that alone can justify revolution did not ensue. His attitude, in principle, was utterly disintegrating; his poetic genius fell back to the lowest level, perhaps, to which it is possible for poetic genius to fall. He reduced his imagination to a passive sensorium for the registering of impressions. No element of construction remained in it, and therefore no element of penetration. But his scope was wide; and his lazy, desultory apprehension was poetical. His work, for the very reason that it is so rudimentary, contains a beginning, or rather many beginnings, that might possibly grow into a noble moral imagination, a worthy filling for the human mind. An American in the nineteenth century who completely disregarded the genteel tradition could hardly have done more.

But there is another distinguished man, lately lost to this country, who has given some rude shocks to this tradition and who, as much as Whitman, may be regarded as representing the genuine, the long silent American mind—I mean William James. He and his brother Henry were as tightly swaddled in the genteel tradition as any infant geniuses could be, for they were born before 1850, and in a Swedenborgian household. Yet they burst those bands almost entirely. The ways in which the two brothers freed themselves, however, are interestingly different. Mr. Henry James has done it by adopting the point of view of the outer world, and by turning the genteel American tradition, as he turns everything else, into a subject-matter for analysis. For him it is a curious habit of mind, intimately comprehended, to be compared with other habits of mind, also well known to him. Thus he has overcome the genteel tradition in the classic way, by understanding it. With William James too this infusion of worldly insight and European sympathies was a potent influence, especially in his earlier days; but the chief source of his liberty was another. It was his personal spontaneity, similar to that of Emerson, and his personal vitality, similar to that of nobody else. Convictions and ideas came to him, so to speak, from the subsoil. He had a prophetic sympathy with the dawning sentiments of the age, with the moods of the dumb majority. His scattered words caught fire in many parts of the world. His way of thinking and feeling represented the true America, and represented in a measure the whole ultra-modern, radical world. Thus he eluded the genteel tradition in the romantic way, by continuing it into its opposite. The romantic mind, glorified in Hegel's dialectic (which is not dialectic at all, but a sort of tragi-comic history of experience), is always rendering its thoughts unrecognisable through the infusion of new insights, and through the insensible transformation of the moral feeling that accompanies them, till at last it has completely reversed its old judgments under cover of expanding them. Thus the genteel tradition was led a merry dance when it fell again into the hands of a genuine and vigorous romanticist like William James. He restored their revolutionary force to its neutralised elements, by picking them out afresh, and emphasising them separately, according to his personal predilections.

For one thing, William James kept his mind and heart wide open to all that might seem, to polite minds, odd, personal, or visionary in religion and philosophy. He gave a sincerely respectful hearing to sentimentalists, mystics, spiritualists, wizards, cranks, quacks, and impostors—for it is hard to draw the line, and James was not willing to draw it prematurely. He thought, with his usual modesty, that any of these might have something to teach him. The lame, the halt, the blind, and those speaking with tongues could come to him with the certainty of finding sympathy; and if they were not healed, at least they were comforted, that a famous professor should take them so seriously; and they began to feel that after all to have only one leg, or one hand, or one eye, or to have three, might be in itself no less beauteous than to have just two, like the stolid majority. Thus William James became the friend and helper of those groping, nervous, half-educated, spiritually disinherited, passionately hungry individuals of which America is full. He became, at the same time, their spokesman and representative before the learned world; and he made it a chief part of his vocation to recast what the learned world has to offer, so that as far as possible it might serve the needs and interests of these people.

Yet the normal practical masculine American, too, had a friend in William James. There is a feeling abroad now, to which biology and Darwinism lend some colour, that theory is simply an instrument for practice, and intelligence merely a help toward material survival. Bears, it is said, have fur and claws, but poor naked man is condemned to be intelligent, or he will perish. This feeling William James embodied in that theory of thought and of truth which he called pragmatism. Intelligence, he thought, is no miraculous, idle faculty, by which we mirror passively any or everything that happens to be true, reduplicating the real world to no purpose. Intelligence has its roots and its issue in the context of events; it is one kind of practical adjustment, an experimental act, a form of vital tension. It does not essentially serve to picture other parts of reality, but to connect them. This view was not worked out by William James in its psychological and historical details; unfortunately he developed it chiefly in controversy against its opposite, which he called intellectualism, and which he hated with all the hatred of which his kind heart was capable. Intellectualism, as he conceived it, was pure pedantry; it impoverished and verbalised everything, and tied up nature in red tape. Ideas and rules that may have been occasionally useful it put in the place of the full-blooded irrational movement of life which had called them into being; and these abstractions, so soon obsolete, it strove to fix and to worship for ever. Thus all creeds and theories and all formal precepts sink in the estimation of the pragmatist to a local and temporary grammar of action; a grammar that must be changed slowly by time, and may be changed quickly by genius. To know things as a whole, or as they are eternally, if there is anything eternal in them, is not only beyond our powers, but would prove worthless, and perhaps even fatal to our lives. Ideas are not mirrors, they are weapons; their function is to prepare us to meet events, as future experience may unroll them. Those ideas that disappoint us are false ideas; those to which events are true are true themselves.

This may seem a very utilitarian view of the mind; and I confess I think it a partial one, since the logical force of beliefs and ideas, their truth or falsehood as assertions, has been overlooked altogether, or confused with the vital force of the material processes which these ideas express. It is an external view only, which marks the place and conditions of the mind in nature, but neglects its specific essence; as if a jewel were defined as a round hole in a ring. Nevertheless, the more materialistic the pragmatist's theory of the mind is, the more vitalistic his theory of nature will have to become. If the intellect is a device produced in organic bodies to expedite their processes, these organic bodies must have interests and a chosen direction in their life; otherwise their life could not be expedited, nor could anything be useful to it. In other words

—and this is a third point at which the philosophy of William James has played havoc with the genteel tradition, while ostensibly defending it—nature must be conceived anthropomorphically and in psychological terms. Its purposes are not to be static harmonies, self-unfolding destinies, the logic of spirit, the spirit of logic, or any other formal method and abstract law; its purposes are to be concrete endeavours, finite efforts of souls living in an environment which they transform and by which they, too, are affected. A spirit, the divine spirit as much as the human, as this new animism conceives it, is a romantic adventurer. Its future is undetermined. Its scope, its duration, and the quality of its life are all contingent. This spirit grows; it buds and sends forth feelers, sounding the depths around for such other centres of force or life as may exist there. It has a vital momentum, but no predetermined goal. It uses its past as a stepping-stone, or rather as a diving-board, but has an absolutely fresh will at each moment to plunge this way or that into the unknown. The universe is an experiment; it is unfinished. It has no ultimate or total nature, because it has no end. It embodies no formula or statable law; any formula is at best a poor abstraction, describing what, in some region and for some time, may be the most striking characteristic of existence; the law is a description *a posteriori* of the habit things have chosen to acquire, and which they may possibly throw off altogether. What a day may bring forth is uncertain; uncertain even to God. Omniscience is impossible; time is real; what had been omniscience hitherto might discover something more to-day. "There shall be news," William James was fond of saying with rapture, quoting from the unpublished poem of an obscure friend, "there shall be news in heaven!" There is almost certainly, he thought, a God now; there may be several gods, who might exist together, or one after the other. We might, by our conspiring sympathies, help to make a new one. Much in us is doubtless immortal; we survive death for some time in a recognisable form; but what our career and transformations may be in the sequel we cannot tell, although we may help to determine them by our daily choices. Observation must be continual if our ideas are to remain true. Eternal vigilance is the price of knowledge; perpetual hazard, perpetual experiment keep quick the edge of life.

This is, so far as I know, a new philosophical vista; it is a conception never before presented, although implied, perhaps, in various quarters, as in Norse and even Greek mythology. It is a vision radically empirical and radically romantic; and as William James himself used to say, the visions and not the arguments of a philosopher are the interesting and influential things about him. William James, rather too generously, attributed this vision to M. Bergson, and regarded him in consequence as a philosopher of the first rank, whose thought was to be one of the turning-points in history. M. Bergson had killed intellectualism. It was his book on creative evolution, said James with humorous emphasis, that had come at last to *"écraser l'infâme."* We may suspect, notwithstanding, that intellectualism, infamous and crushed, will survive the blow; and if the author of the Book of Ecclesiastes were now alive, and heard that there shall be news in heaven, he would doubtless say that there may possibly be news there, but that under the sun there is nothing new—not even radical empiricism or radical romanticism, which from the beginning of the world has been the philosophy of those who as yet had had little experience; for to the blinking little child it is not merely something in the world that is new daily, but everything is new all day.

I am not concerned with the rights and wrongs of that controversy; my point is only that William James, in this genial evolutionary view of the world, has given a rude shock to the genteel tradition. What! The world a gradual improvisation? Creation unpremeditated? God a sort of young poet or struggling artist? William James is an advocate of theism; pragmatism adds one to the evidences of religion; that is excellent. But is not the cool abstract piety of the genteel getting more than it asks for? This empirical naturalistic God is too crude and positive a force; he will work miracles, he will answer prayers, he may inhabit distinct places, and have distinct conditions under which alone he can operate; he is a neighbouring being, whom we can act upon, and rely upon for specific aids, as upon a personal friend, or a physician, or an insurance company. How disconcerting! Is not this new theology a little like superstition? And yet how interesting, how exciting, if it should happen to be true! I am far from wishing to suggest that such a view seems to me more probable than conventional idealism or than Christian orthodoxy. All three are in the region of dramatic system-making and myth to which probabilities are irrelevant. If one man says the moon is sister to the sun, and another that she is his daughter, the question is not which notion is more probable, but whether either of them is at all expressive. The so-called evidences are devised afterwards, when faith and imagination have prejudged the issue. The force of William James's new theology, or romantic cosmology, lies only in this: that it has broken the spell of the genteel tradition, and enticed faith in a new direction, which on second thoughts may prove no less alluring than the old. The important fact is not that the new fancy might possibly be true—who shall know that?—but that it has entered the heart of a leading American to conceive and to cherish it. The genteel tradition cannot be dislodged by these insurrections; there are circles to which it is still congenial, and where it will be preserved. But it has been challenged and (what is perhaps more insidious) it has been discovered. No one need be browbeaten any longer into accepting it. No one need be afraid, for instance, that his fate is sealed because some young prig may call him a dualist; the pint would call the quart a dualist, if you tried to pour the quart into him. We need not be afraid of being less profound, for being direct and sincere. The intellectual world may be traversed in many directions; the whole has not been surveyed; there is a great career in it open to talent. That is a sort of knell, that tolls the passing of the genteel tradition. Something else is now in the field; something else can appeal to the imagination, and be a thousand times more idealistic than academic idealism, which is often simply a way of white-washing and adoring things as they are. The illegitimate monopoly which the genteel tradition had established over what ought to be assumed and what ought to be hoped for has been broken down by the first-born of the family, by the genius of the race. Henceforth there can hardly be the same peace and the same pleasure in hugging the old proprieties. Hegel will be to the next generation what Sir William Hamilton was to the last. Nothing will have been disproved, but everything will have been abandoned. An honest man has spoken, and the cant of the genteel tradition has become harder for young lips to repeat.

With this I have finished such a sketch as I am here able to offer you of the genteel tradition in American philosophy. The subject is complex, and calls for many an excursus and qualifying footnote; yet I think the main outlines are clear enough. The chief fountains of this tradition were Calvinism and transcendentalism. Both were living fountains; but to keep them alive they required, one an agonised conscience, and the other a radical subjective criticism of knowledge. When these rare metaphysical preoccupations disappeared— and the American atmosphere is not favourable to either of them—the two systems ceased to be inwardly understood; they subsisted as sacred mysteries only; and the combination of the two in some transcendental system of the universe (a contradiction in principle) was doubly artificial. Besides, it could hardly be held with a single mind. Natural science, history, the beliefs implied in labour and invention, could not be disregarded altogether; so that the transcendental philosopher was condemned to a double allegiance, and to not letting his left hand know the bluff that his right hand was making. Nevertheless, the difficulty in bringing practical inarticulate convictions to expression is very great, and the genteel tradition has subsisted in the academic mind for want of anything equally academic to take its place.

The academic mind, however, has had its flanks turned. On the one side came the revolt of the Bohemian temperament, with its poetry of crude naturalism; on the other side came an impassioned empiricism, welcoming popular religious witnesses to the unseen, reducing science to an instrument of success in action, and declaring the universe to be wild and young, and not to be harnessed by the logic of any school.

This revolution, I should think, might well find an echo among you, who live in a thriving society, and in the presence of a virgin and prodigious world. When you transform nature to your uses, when you experiment with her forces, and reduce them to industrial agents, you cannot feel that nature was made by you or for you, for then these adjustments would have been pre-established. Much less can you feel it when she destroys your labour of years in a momentary spasm. You must feel, rather, that you are an offshoot of her life; one brave little force among her immense forces. When you escape, as you love to do, to your forests and your sierras, I am sure again that you do not feel you made them, or that they were made for you. They have grown, as you have grown, only more massively and more slowly. In their non-human beauty and peace they stir the sub-human depths and the superhuman possibilities of your own spirit. It is no transcendental logic that they teach; and they give no sign of any deliberate morality seated in the world. It is rather the vanity and superficiality of all logic, the needlessness of argument, the relativity of morals, the strength of time, the fertility of matter, the variety, the unspeakable variety, of possible life. Everything is measurable and conditioned, indefinitely repeated, yet, in repetition, twisted somewhat from its old form. Everywhere is beauty and nowhere permanence, everywhere an incipient harmony, nowhere an intention, nor a responsibility, nor a plan. It is the irresistible suasion of this daily spectacle, it is the daily discipline of contact with things, so different from the verbal discipline of the schools, that will, I trust, inspire the philosophy of your children. A Californian whom I had recently the pleasure of meeting observed that, if the philosophers had lived among your mountains their systems would have been different from what they are. Certainly, I should say, very different from what those systems are which the European genteel tradition has handed down since Socrates; for these systems are egotistical; directly or indirectly they are anthropocentric, and inspired by the conceited notion that man, or human reason, or the human distinction between good and evil, is the centre and pivot of the universe. That is what the mountains and the woods should make you at last ashamed to assert. From what, indeed, does the society of nature liberate you, that you find it so sweet? It is hardly (is it?) that you wish to forget your past, or your friends, or that you have any secret contempt for your present ambitions. You respect these, you respect them perhaps too much; you are not suffered by the genteel tradition to criticise or to reform them at all radically. No; it is the yoke of this genteel tradition itself that these primeval solitudes lift from your shoulders. They suspend your forced sense of your own importance not merely as individuals, but even as men. They allow you, in one happy moment, at once to play and to worship, to take yourselves simply, humbly, for what you are, and to salute the wild, indifferent, non-censorious infinity of nature. You are admonished that what you can do avails little materially, and in the end nothing. At the same time, through wonder and pleasure, you are taught speculation. You learn what you are really fitted to do, and where lie your natural dignity and joy, namely, in representing many things, without being them, and in letting your imagination, through sympathy, celebrate and echo their life. Because the peculiarity of man is that his machinery for reaction on external things has involved an imaginative transcript of these things, which is preserved and suspended in his fancy; and the interest and beauty of this inward landscape, rather than any fortunes that may await his body in the outer world, constitute his proper happiness. By their mind, its scope, quality, and temper, we estimate men, for by the mind only do we exist as men, and are more than so many storage-batteries for material energy. Let us therefore be frankly human. Let us be content to live in the mind.

The Poetry of Christian Dogma [2]

Now, the great characteristic of Christianity, inherited from Judaism, was that its scheme was historical. Not exis-tences but events were the subject of its primary interest. It presented a story, not a cosmology. It was an epic in which there was, of course, superhuman machinery, but of which the subject was man, and, notable circumstance, the Hero was a man as well. Like Buddhism, it gave the highest hon-our to a man who could lead his fellow-men to perfection. What had previously been the divine reality—the engine of Nature—now became a temporary stage, built for the exigen-cies of a human drama. What had been before a detail of the edifice—the life of man—now became the argument and pur-pose of the whole creation. Notable transformation, on which the philosopher cannot meditate too much.

Was Christianity right in saying that the world was made for man? Was the account it adopted of the method and causes of Creation conceivably correct? Was the garden of Eden a historical reality, and were the Hebrew prophecies announcements of the advent of Jesus Christ? Did the deluge come because of man's wickedness, and will the last day coin-cide with the dramatic dénouement of the Church's history?

[2] This selection comes from an essay in Santayana's *Interpretations of Poetry and Religion* (New York, 1922; first published, 1900), pp. 90–109; pp. 115–17. The essay is called "The Poetry of Christian Dogma". Reprinted by permission of Charles Scribner's Sons and Con-stable and Co., Ltd., London.

In other words, is the spiritual experience of man the explanation of the universe? Certainly not, if we are thinking of a scientific, not of a poetical explanation. As a matter of fact, man is a product of laws which must also destroy him, and which, as Spinoza would say, infinitely exceed him in their scope and power. His welfare is indifferent to the stars, but dependent on them. And yet that counter-Copernican revolution accomplished by Christianity—a revolution which Kant should hardly have attributed to himself—which put man in the centre of the universe and made the stars circle about him, must have some kind of justification. And indeed its justification (if we may be so brief on so great a subject) is that what is false in the science of facts may be true in the science of values. While the existence of things must be understood by referring them to their causes, which are mechanical, their functions can only be explained by what is interesting in their results, in other words, by their relation to human nature and to human happiness.

The Christian drama was a magnificent poetic rendering of this side of the matter, a side which Socrates had envisaged by his admirable method, but which now flooded the consciousness of mankind with torrential emotions. Christianity was born under an eclipse, when the light of Nature was obscured; but the star that intercepted that light was itself luminous, and shed on succeeding ages a moonlike radiance, paler and sadder than the other, but no less divine, and meriting no less to be eternal. Man now studied his own destiny, as he had before studied the sky, and the woods, and the sunny depths of water; and as the earlier study produced in his soul . . . the images of Zeus, Pan, and Nereus, so the later study produced the images of Jesus and of Mary, of Heaven and Hell, of miracles and sacraments. The observation was no less exact, the translation into poetic images no less wonderful here than there. To trace the endless transfiguration, with all its unconscious ingenuity and harmony, might be the theme of a fascinating science. Let not the reader fancy that

in Christianity everything was settled by records and traditions. The idea of Christ himself had to be constructed by the
imagination in response to moral demands, tradition giving
only the barest external points of attachment. The facts were
nothing until they became symbols; and nothing could turn
them into symbols except an eager imagination on the watch
for all that might embody its dreams.

The crucifixion, for example, would remain a tragic incident without further significance, if we regard it merely as a
historical fact; to make it a religious mystery, an idea capable
of converting the world, the moral imagination must transform it into something that happens for the sake of the soul,
so that each believer may say to himself that Christ so suffered for the love of him. And such a thought is surely the
objectification of an inner impulse; the idea of Christ becomes something spiritual, something poetical. What literal
meaning could there be in saying that one man or one God
died for the sake of each and every other individual? By
what effective causal principle could their salvation be
thought to necessitate his death, or his death to make possible their salvation? By [a reversal] natural to the imagination. . . . Christ's death is a symbol of human life. Men could
"believe in" his death, because it was a figure and premoni-
tion of the burden of their experience. That is why, when
some Apostle told them the story, they could say to him: "Sir,
I perceive that thou art a prophet: thou hast told me all
things whatsoever I have felt." Thus the central fact of all
Christ's history, narrated by every Evangelist, could still be
nothing but a painful incident, as unessential to the Christian
religion as the death of Socrates to the Socratic philosophy,
were it not transformed by the imagination of the believer
into the counterpart of his own moral need. Then, by ceasing
to be viewed as a historical fact, the death of Christ becomes
a religious inspiration. The whole of Christian doctrine is
thus religious and efficacious only when it becomes poetry,

because only then is it the felt counterpart of personal experience and a genuine expansion of human life.

Take, as another example, the doctrine of eternal rewards and punishments. Many perplexed Christians of our day try to reconcile this spirited fable with their modern horror of physical suffering and their detestation of cruelty; and it must be admitted that the image of men suffering unending tortures in retribution for a few ignorant and sufficiently wretched sins is, even as poetry, somewhat repellent. The idea of torments and vengeance is happily becoming alien to our society and is therefore not a natural vehicle for our religion. Some accordingly reject altogether the Christian doctrine on this point, which is too strong for their nerves. Their objection, of course, is not simply that there is no evidence of its truth. If they asked for evidence, would they believe anything? Proofs are the last thing looked for by a truly religious mind which feels the imaginative fitness of its faith and knows instinctively that, in such a matter, imaginative fitness is all that can be required. The reason men reject the doctrine of eternal punishment is that they find it distasteful or unmeaning. They show, by the nature of their objections, that they acknowledge poetic propriety or moral truth to be the sole criterion of religious credibility.

But, passing over the change of sentiment which gives rise to this change of doctrine, let us inquire of what reality Christian eschatology was the imaginative rendering. What was it in the actual life of men that made them think of themselves as hanging between eternal bliss and eternal perdition? Was it not the diversity, the momentousness, and the finality of their experience here? No doubt the desire to make the reversal of the injustices of this world as melodramatic and picturesque as possible contributed to the adoption of this idea; the ideal values of life were thus contrasted with its apparent values in the most absolute and graphic manner. But we may say that beneath this motive, based on the exigences of exposition and edification, there was a deeper intuition. There was the genuine moralist's sympathy with a philosophic and logical view of immortality rather than with a superstitious and sentimental one. Another life exists and is infinitely more important than this life; but it is reached by the intuition of ideals, not by the multiplication of phenomena; it is an eternal state not an indefinite succession of changes. Transitory life ends for the Christian when the balance-sheet of his individual merits and demerits is made up, and the eternity that ensues is the eternal reality of those values.

For the Oriental, who believed in transmigration, the individual dissolved into an infinity of phases; he went on actually and perpetually, as Nature does; his immortality was a long Purgatory behind which a shadowy Hell and Heaven scarcely appeared in the form of annihilation or absorption. This happened because the Oriental mind has no middle; it oscillates between extremes and passes directly from sense to mysticism, and back again; it lacks virile understanding and intelligence creative of form. But Christianity, following in this the Socratic philosophy, rose to the conception of eternal essences, forms suspended above the flux of natural things and expressing the ideal suggestions and rational goals of experience. Each man, for Christianity, has an immortal soul; each life has the potentiality of an eternal meaning, and as this potentiality is or is not actualized, as this meaning is or is not expressed in the phenomena of this life, the soul is eternally saved or lost. As the tree falleth, so it lieth. The finality of this brief and personal experiment, the consequent awful solemnity of the hour of death when all trial is over and when the eternal sentence is passed, has always been duly felt by the Christian. The Church, indeed, in answer to the demand for a more refined and discriminating presentation of its dogma, introduced the temporary discipline of Purgatory, in which the virtues already stamped on the soul might be brought to greater clearness and rid of the alloy of imperfection; but this purification allowed no essential development, no change of character or fate; the soul in Purgatory was already saved, already holy.

The harshness of the doctrine of eternal judgment is therefore a consequence of its symbolic truth. The Church might have been less absolute in the matter had she yielded more, as she did in the doctrine of Purgatory, to the desire for merely imaginary extensions of human experience. But her better instincts kept her, after all, to the moral interpretation of reality; and the facts to be rendered were uncompromising enough. Art is long, life brief. To have told men they would have infinite opportunities to reform and to advance would have been to feed them on gratuitous fictions without raising them, as it was the function of Christianity to do, to a consciousness of the spiritual meaning and upshot of existence. To have speculated about the infinite extent of experience and its endless transformations, after the manner of the barbarous religions, and never to have conceived its moral essence, would have been to encourage a dream which may by chance be prophetic, but which is as devoid of ideal meaning as of empirical probability. Christian fictions were at least significant; they beguiled the intellect, no doubt, and were mistaken for accounts of external fact; but they enlightened the imagination; they made man understand, as never before or since, the pathos and nobility of his life, the necessity of discipline, the possibility of sanctity, the transcendence and the humanity of the divine. For the divine was reached by the idealization of the human. The supernatural was an allegory of the natural, and rendered the values of transitory things under the image of eternal existences. Thus the finality of our activity in this world, together with the eternity of its ideal meanings, was admirably rendered by the Christian dogma of a final judgment.

But there was another moral truth which was impressed upon the believer by that doctrine and which could not be enforced in any other way without presupposing in him an unusual philosophic acumen and elevation of mind. That is the truth that moral distinctions are absolute. A cool philosophy suffices to show us that moral distinctions exist, since men prefer some experiences to others and can by their action bring these good and evil experiences upon themselves and upon their fellows. But a survey of Nature may at the same time impress us with the fact that these goods and evils are singularly mixed, that there is hardly an advantage gained which is not bought by some loss, or any loss which is not an opportunity for the attainment of some advantage. While it would be chimerical to pretend that such compensation was always adequate, and that, in consequence, no one condition was ever really preferable to any other, yet the perplexities into which moral aspiration is thrown by these contradictory vistas is often productive of the desire to reach some other point of view, to escape into what is irrationally thought to be a higher category than the moral. The serious consideration of those things which are right according to human reason and interest may then yield to a fanatical reliance on some facile general notion.

It may be thought, for instance, that what is regular or necessary or universal is therefore right and good; thus a dazed contemplation of the actual may take the place of the determination of the ideal. Mysticism in regard to the better and the worse, by which good and bad are woven into a seamless garment of sorry magnificence in which the whole universe is wrapped up, is like mysticism on other subjects; it consists in the theoretic renunciation of a natural attitude, in this case of the natural attitude of welcome and repulsion in the presence of various things. But this category is the most fundamental of all those that the human mind employs, and it cannot be surrendered so long as life endures. It is indeed the conscious echo of those vital instincts by whose operation we exist. Levity and mysticism may do all they can—and they can do much—to make men think moral distinctions unauthoritative, because moral distinctions may be either ignored or transcended. Yet the essential assertion that one thing is really better than another remains involved in every act of every living being. It is involved even in the operation of abstract thinking, where a cogent conclusion, being still coveted, is assumed to be a good, or in that æsthetic and theoretic enthusiasm before cosmic laws, which is the human foundation of this mysticism itself.

It is accordingly a moral truth which no subterfuge can elude, that some things are really better than others. In the daily course of affairs we are constantly in the presence of events which by turning out one way or the other produce a real, an irrevocable, increase of good or evil in the world. The complexities of life, struggling as it does amidst irrational forces, may make the attainment of one good the cause of the unattainableness of another; they cannot destroy the essential desirability of both. The niggardliness of Nature cannot sterilize the ideal; the odious circumstances which make the attainment of many goods conditional on the perpetration of some evil, and which punish every virtue by some incapacity or some abuse,—these odious circumstances cannot rob any good of its natural sweetness, nor all goods together of their conceptual harmony. To the heart that has felt it and that is the true judge, every loss is irretrievable and every joy indestructible. Eventual compensations may obliterate the memory of these values but cannot destroy their reality. The future can only furnish further applications of the principle by which they arose and were justified.

Now, how utter this moral truth imaginatively, how clothe it in an image that might render its absoluteness and its force? Could any method be better than to say: Your eternal destiny is hanging in the balance: the grace of God, the influences of others, and your own will reacting upon both are shaping at every moment issues of absolute importance. What happens here and now decides not merely incidental pains and pleasures—which perhaps a brave and careless spirit might alike despise—but helps to determine your eternal destiny of joy or anguish, and the eternal destiny of your neighbour. In place of the confused vistas of the empirical world, in which the threads of benefit and injury might seem to be mingled and lost, the imagination substituted the clear vision of Hell and Heaven; while the determination of our destiny was made to depend upon obedience to recognized duties.

Now these duties may often have been far from corresponding to those which reason would impose; but the intention and the principle at least were sound. It was felt that the actions and passions of this world breed momentous values, values which being ideal are as infinite as values can be in the estimation of reason—the values of truth, of love, of rationality, of perfection—although both the length of the experience in which they arise and the number of persons who share that experience may be extremely limited. But the mechanical measure of experience in length, intensity, or multiplication has nothing to do with its moral significance in realizing truth or virtue. Therefore the difference in dignity between the satisfactions of reason and the satisfactions of sense is fittingly rendered by the infinite disproportion between heavenly and earthly joys. In our imaginative translation we are justified in saying that the alternative between infinite happiness and infinite misery is yawning before us, because the alternative between rational failure or success is actually present. The decisions we make from moment to moment, on which the ideal value of our life and character depends, actually constitute in a few years a decision which is irrevocable.

The Christian doctrine of rewards and punishments is thus in harmony with moral truths which a different doctrine might have obscured. The good souls that wish to fancy that everybody will be ultimately saved, subject a fable to standards appropriate to matters of fact, and thereby deprive the fable of that moral significance which is its excuse for being. If every one is ultimately saved, there is nothing truly momentous about alternative events: all paths lead more or less circuitously to the same end. The only ground which then remains for discriminating the better from the worse is the pleasantness or unpleasantness of the path to salvation. All moral meanings inhere, then, in this life, and the other life is without significance. Heaven comes to replace life empirically without fulfilling it ideally. We are reduced for our moral standards to phenomenal values, to the worth of life in transitory feeling. These values are quite real, but they are not those which poetry and religion have for their object. They are values present to sense, not to reason and imagination.

The ideal of a supervening general bliss presents indeed an abstract desideratum, but not the ideal involved in the actual forces of life; that end would have no rational relation to its primary factors; it would not be built on our instinctive preferences but would abolish them by a miraculous dream, following alike upon every species of activity. Moral differences would have existed merely to be forgotten; for if we say they were remembered, but transcended and put to rest, we plunge into an even worse contradiction to the conscience and the will. For if we say that the universal bliss consists in the assurance, mystically received, that while individual experiences may differ in value they all equally conduce to the perfection of the universe, we deny not merely the momentousness but even the elementary validity of moral distinctions. We assert that the best idea of God is that least like the ideal of man, and that the nearer we come to the vision of truth the farther we are from the feeling of preference. In our attempt to extend the good we thus abolish its essence. Our religion consists in denying the authority of the ideal, which is its only rational foundation; and thus that religion, while gaining nothing in empirical reality, comes to express a moral falsehood instead of a moral truth.

If we looked in religion for an account of facts, as most people do, we should have to pass a very different judgment on these several views. The mechanical world is a connected system and Nature seems to be dynamically one; the intuitions on which mysticism feeds are therefore true intuitions. The expectation of a millennium is on the other hand quite visionary, because the evidence of history, while it shows undeniable progress in many directions, shows that this progress is essentially relative, partial, and transitory. As for the Christian doctrine of the judgment, it is something wholly out of relation to empirical facts, it assumes the existence of a supernatural sphere, and is beyond the reach of scientific evidence of any kind. But if we look on religion as on a kind of poetry, as we have decided here to do,—as on a kind of poetry that expresses moral values and reacts beneficently upon life,—we shall see that the Christian doctrine is alone justified. For mysticism is not an imaginative construction at all but a renunciation or confusion of our faculties; here a surrender of the human ideal in the presence of a mechanical force that is felt, and correctly felt, to tend to vaguer results or rather to tend to nothing in particular. Mysticism is not a religion but a religious disease. The idea of universal salvation, on the other hand, is the expression of a feeble sentimentality, a pleasant reverie without structure or significance. But the doctrine of eternal rewards and punishments is, as we have tried to show, an expression of moral truth, a poetic rendering of the fact that rational values are ideal, momentous, and irreversible.

It would be easy to multiply examples and to exhibit the various parts of Christianity as so many interpretations of human life in its ideal aspects. But we are not attempting to narrate facts so much as to advance an idea, and the illustrations given will perhaps suffice to make our conception intelligible. There is, however, a possible misunderstanding which we should be careful to avoid in this dangerous field of philosophic interpretation. In saying that a given religion was the poetic transformation of an experience, we must not imagine that it was thought to be such—for it is evident that every sincere Christian believed in the literal and empirical reality of all that the Christian epic contained. Nor should we imagine that philosophic ideas, or general reflections on life, were the origin of religion, and that afterward certain useful myths, known to be such by their authors, were mistaken for history and for literal prophecy. That sometimes happens, when historians, poets, or philosophers are turned by the unintelligent veneration of posterity into religious prophets. Such was the fate of Plato, for instance, or of the writer of the "Song of Solomon"; but no great and living religion was ever founded in that way.

Had Christianity or any other religion had its basis in literary or philosophical allegories, it would never have become a religion, because the poetry of it would never have been interwoven with the figures and events of real life. No tomb, no relic, no material miracle, no personal derivation of authority, would have existed to serve as the nucleus of devotion and the point of junction between this world and the other. The origin of Christian dogma lay in historic facts and in doctrines literally meant by their authors. It is one of the greatest possible illusions in these matters to fancy that the meaning which we see in parables and mysteries was the meaning they had in the beginning, but which later misinterpretation had obscured. On the contrary—as a glance at any incipient religious movement now going on will show us—the authors of doctrines, however obvious it may be to every one else that these doctrines have only a figurative validity, are the first dupes to their own intuitions. This is no less true of metaphysical theories than of spontaneous superstitions: did their promulgator understand the character of their justification he would give himself out for a simple poet, appeal only to cultivated minds, and never turn his energies to stimulating private delusions, not to speak of public fanaticisms. The best philosophers seldom perceive the poetic merit of their systems.

So among the ancients it was not an abstract observation of Nature, with conscious allegory supervening, that was the origin of mythology, but the interpretation was spontaneous, the illusion was radical, a consciousness of the god's presence was the first impression produced by the phenomenon. Else, in this case too, poetry would never have become superstition; what made it superstition was the initial incapacity in people to discriminate the objects of imagination from those of the understanding. The fancy thus attached its images, without distinguishing their ideal locus, to the visible world, and men became superstitious not because they had too much imagination, but because they were not aware that they had any.

In what sense, then, are we justified in saying that religion expresses moral ideals? In the sense that moral significance, while not the source of religions, is the criterion of their value and the reason why they may deserve to endure. Far as the conception of an allegory may be from the minds of prophets, yet the prophecy can only take root in the popular imagination if it recommends itself to some human interest. There must be some correspondence between the doctrine announced or the hopes set forth, and the natural demands of the human spirit. Otherwise, although the new faith might be preached, it would not be accepted. The significance of religious doctrines has therefore been the condition of their spread, their maintenance, and their development, although not the condition of their origin. In Darwinian language, moral significance has been a spontaneous variation of superstition, and this variation has insured its survival as a religion. For religion differs from superstition not psychologically but morally, not in its origin but in its worth. This worth, when actually felt and appreciated, becomes of course a dynamic factor and contributes like other psychological elements to the evolution of events; but being a logical harmony, a rational beauty, this worth is only appreciable by a few minds, and those the least primitive and the least capable of guiding popular movements. Reason is powerless to found religions, although it is alone competent to judge them. Good religions are therefore the product of unconscious rationality, of imaginative impulses fortunately moral. . . .

The great success which Christianity achieved in this immense undertaking makes it, after classic antiquity, the most important phase in the history of mankind. It is clear, however, that this success was not complete. That fallacy from which the Pagan religion alone has been free, . . . the natural but hopeless misunderstanding of imagining that poetry in order to be religion, in order to be the inspiration of life, must first deny that it is poetry and deceive us about the facts with which we have to deal—this misunderstanding has marred the work of the Christian imagination and condemned it, if we may trust appearances, to be transitory. For by this misunderstanding Christian doctrine was brought into conflict with reality, of which it pretends to prejudge the character, and also into conflict with what might have been its own elements, with all excluded religious instincts and imaginative ideals. Human life is always essentially the same, and therefore a religion which, like Christianity, seizes the essence of that life, ought to be an eternal religion. But it may forfeit that privilege by entangling itself with a particular account of matters of fact, matters irrelevant to its ideal significance, and further by intrenching itself, by virtue of that entanglement, in an inadequate regimen or a too narrow imaginative development, thus putting its ideal authority in jeopardy by opposing it to other intuitions and practices no less religious than its own.

Can Christianity escape these perils? Can it reform its claims, or can it overwhelm all opposition and take the human heart once more by storm? The future alone can decide. The greatest calamity, however, would be that which seems, alas! not unlikely to befall our immediate posterity, namely, that while Christianity should be discredited no other religion, more disillusioned and not less inspired, should come to take its place. Until the imagination should have time to recover and to reassert its legitimate and kindly power, the European races would then be reduced to confessing that while they had mastered the mechanical forces of Nature, both by science and by the arts, they had become incapable of mastering or understanding themselves, and that, bewildered like the beasts by the revolutions of the heavens and by their own irrational passions, they could find no way of uttering the ideal meaning of their life.

JOHN DEWEY

John Dewey was born in 1859, four years before Santayana, and died in 1952, the same year as that in which Santayana died. They were not much younger than Royce, who was born in 1855; but since Royce died in 1916, Peirce in 1914, and James in 1910, it was left to Santayana and Dewey to be joint *doyens* of American philosophy for many years after Royce had disappeared from the American scene. Because Santayana fled this country in 1912 and inevitably diminished his influence by doing so, it was Dewey who became the chief figure of American philosophy. True, in 1924 Alfred North Whitehead came to these shores at the age of sixty-three; and several so-called realists who were younger than Dewey played important parts in the development of twentieth-century American philosophy. But in my opinion there are good reasons for treating Whitehead and the American realists in another place; and also for ending this volume with John Dewey. One of the main reasons for ending with Dewey is that although he was a rebel against much of the earlier American tradition, he was, in a very important respect, the last representative of that tradition. I mean that although he disagreed with some of the most important substantive doctrines of his American predecessors, his conception of the task of philosophy was much closer to theirs than it was to the conception shared by those who have dominated American philosophy since his death. I shall turn first to Dewey the rebel.

In breaking with the theism of his predecessors, Dewey (and his fellow naturalist, Santayana) broke with a tradition of religiosity that had persisted from the days of Plymouth Rock to the days of Josiah Royce. While Europe was producing figures like Hume, Voltaire, Marx, and John Stuart Mill, America was listening to Calvinists, Transcendentalists, Absolute Idealists, and even Pragmatists who were eager to establish the existence of the supernatural. Against all of this Dewey rebelled by launching an attack on all forms of supernaturalistic dualism in metaphysics and the theory of knowledge. Just as he declined to believe in a supernatural deity, so he declined to believe in Platonic forms or in what he called transcendental values that were radically different from concrete things. And just as he did not think that there are extra-scientific ways of arriving at theological truth, so he denied that moral judgments could be established by special methods. In spite of some lapses in his writing, it is fair to say that he tended on the whole to deny that there are fundamentally different kinds of entities and that there are fundamentally different ways of arriving at truth. Although he was James' epistemological ally in supporting the idea that testing a hypothesis involves testing a whole stock of opinions, Dewey did not support James' application of this idea to the theological question. In other words, Dewey was not led by his acceptance of pragmatism to a belief in God, and hence not to any negotiated agreement with his American predecessors on this vital topic.

However, this must not obscure the continuity between them and Dewey—a continuity to which I have previously called attention. That continuity sprang from Dewey's firm retention of the notion that a philosopher should range widely in his interests, that he should be concerned with the broader aspects of civilization, and that his technical concerns should be seriously connected with the concerns of ordinary men. Edwards followed that policy, Emerson did, James did, Royce did, and Santayana did. Dewey continued this American tradition of what would today be called relevance in philosophy. Dewey began his philosophical career under the influence of Hegel; but even after he abandoned Hegelian doctrines, he continued to think of a philosopher as one who, like Hegel, discourses on science, history, law, art, politics, education, and religion in an effort to provide a notion of how they are related to each other. Dewey sought to achieve the large vision he associated with philosophy by developing a unified conception of these various forms of human activity. Dewey's interest in achieving this may well have been influenced by Hegel's idea of a social mind that dominates a civilization, but it was probably more closely connected with Dewey's idea that the main social task of the philosopher is to encourage people to use their intelligence in resolving such large problems as are involved in the conflict between order and freedom, or between religion and science. These issues, which affect a whole society, cannot have their solutions advanced by a philosopher who is not familiar with the main ingredients of a civilization.

The passages below were written by Dewey at the height of his career in 1919, when he delivered a course of lectures at Tokyo University. In them he urged philosophy to abandon the dualistic doctrines which separated it from the world, and asked it to help mankind make the world a better place. It is of course a melancholy thought that the "world war" to which he refers in these hopeful pages is the First World War. Still, it is heartening to think that for the next thirty years, while he was living to be more than ninety and while mankind was making dubious the proposition that it possessed "a sympathetic and integral intelligence", Dewey wisely and courageously argued that if it did not use such intelligence it would destroy itself

Logic and Science [1]

If thinking is the way in which deliberate reorganization of experience is secured, then logic is such a clarified and systematized formulation of the procedures of thinking as will enable the desired reconstruction to go on more economically and efficiently. In language familiar to students, logic is both a science and an art; a science so far as it gives an organized and tested descriptive account of the way in which thought actually goes on; an art, so far as on the basis of this description it projects methods by which future thinking shall take advantage of the operations that lead to success and avoid those which result in failure.

Thus is answered the dispute whether logic is empirical or normative, psychological or regulative. It is both. Logic is based on a definite and executive supply of empirical material. Men have been thinking for ages. They have observed, inferred, and reasoned in all sorts of ways and to all kinds of results. Anthropology, the study of the origin of myth, legend and cult; linguistics and grammar; rhetoric and former logical compositions all tell us how men have thought and what have been the purposes and consequences of different kinds of thinking. Psychology, experimental and pathological, makes important contributions to our knowledge of how thinking goes on and to what effect. Especially does the record of the growth of the various sciences afford instruction in those concrete ways of inquiry and testing which have led men astray and which have proved efficacious. Each science from mathematics to history exhibits typical fallacious meth-

[1] This selection is from Dewey's *Reconstruction in Philosophy* (New York, 1920), pp. 134–51; pp. 155–60. Enlarged edition copyright 1948 by the Beacon Press. Reprinted by permission.

ods and typical efficacious methods in special subject-matters. Logical theory has thus a large, almost inexhaustible field of empirical study.

The conventional statement that experience only tells us how men have thought or *do* think, while logic is concerned with norms, with how men *should* think, is ludicrously inept. Some sorts of thinking are shown *by* experience to have got nowhere, or worse than nowhere—into systematized delusion and mistake. Others have proved in manifest experience that they lead to fruitful and enduring discoveries. It is precisely in experience that the different consequences of different methods of investigation and ratiocination are convincingly shown. The parrot-like repetition of the distinction between an empirical description of what is and a normative account of what should be merely neglects the most striking fact about thinking as it empirically is—namely, its flagrant exhibition of cases of failure and success—that is, of good thinking and bad thinking. Any one who considers this empirical manifestation will not complain of lack of material from which to construct a *regulative* art. The more study that is given to empirical records of actual thought, the more apparent becomes the connection between the specific features of thinking which have produced failure and success. Out of this relationship of cause and effect as it is empirically ascertained grow the norms and regulations of an art of thinking.

Mathematics is often cited as an example of purely normative thinking dependent upon *a priori* canons and supraempirical material. But it is hard to see how the student who approaches the matter historically can avoid the conclusion that the status of mathematics is as empirical as that of metallurgy. Men began with counting and measuring things just as they began with pounding and burning them. One thing, as common speech profoundly has it, led to another. Certain ways were successful—not merely in the immediately practical sense, but in the sense of being interesting, of arousing attention, of exciting attempts at improvement. The present-day mathematical logician may present the structure of mathematics as if it had sprung all at once from the brain of a Zeus whose anatomy is that of pure logic. But, nevertheless, this very structure is a product of long historic growth, in which all kinds of experiments have been tried, in which some men have struck out in this direction and some in that, and in which some exercises and operations have resulted in confusion and others in triumphant clarifications and fruitful growths; a history in which matter and methods have been constantly selected and worked over on the basis of empirical success and failure.

The structure of alleged normative *a priori* mathematics is in truth the crowned result of ages of toilsome experience. The metallurgist who should write on the most highly developed method of dealing with ores would not, in truth, proceed any differently. He too selects, refines, and organizes the methods which in the past have been found to yield the maximum of achievement. Logic is a matter of profound human importance precisely because it is empirically founded and experimentally applied. So considered, the problem of logical theory is none other than the problem of the possibility of the development and employment of intelligent method in inquiries concerned with deliberate reconstruction of experience. And it is only saying again in more specific form what has been said in general form to add that while such a logic has been developed in respect to mathematics and physical science, intelligent method, logic, is still far to seek in moral and political affairs.

Assuming, accordingly, this idea of logic without argument, let us proceed to discuss some of its chief features. First, light is thrown by the *origin* of thinking upon a logic which shall be a method of intelligent guidance of experience. In line with what has already been said about experience being a matter primarily of behavior, a sensori-motor matter, is the fact that thinking takes its departure from specific conflicts in experience that occasion perplexity and trouble. Men do not, in their natural estate, think when they have no troubles to cope with, no difficulties to overcome. A life of ease, of success without effort, would be a thoughtless life, and so also would a life of ready omnipotence. Beings who think are beings whose life is so hemmed in and constricted that they cannot directly carry through a course of action to victorious consummation. Men also do not tend to think when their action, when they are amid difficulties, is dictated to them by authority. Soldiers have difficulties and restrictions in plenty, but *qua soldiers* (as Aristotle would say) they are not notorious for being thinkers. Thinking is done for them, higher up. The same is too true of most workingmen under present economic conditions. Difficulties occasion thinking only when thinking is the imperative or urgent way out, only when it is the indicated road to a solution. Wherever external authority reigns, thinking is suspected and obnoxious.

Thinking, however, is not the only way in which a personal solution of difficulties is sought. . . . [D]reams, reveries, emotional idealizations are roads which are taken to escape the strain of perplexity and conflict. According to modern psychology, many systematized delusions and mental disorders, probably hysteria itself, originate as devices for getting freedom from troublesome conflicting factors. Such considerations throw into relief some of the traits essential to thinking as a way of responding to difficulty. The short-cut "solutions" alluded to do not get rid of the conflict and problems; they only get rid of the feeling of it. They cover up consciousness of it. Because the conflict remains in fact and is evaded in thought, disorders arise.

The first distinguishing characteristic of thinking then is facing the facts—inquiry, minute and extensive scrutinizing, observation. Nothing has done greater harm to the successful conduct of the enterprise of thinking (and to the logics which reflect and formulate the undertaking) than the habit of treating observation as something outside of and prior to thinking, and thinking as something which can go on in the head without *including* observation of new facts as part of itself. Every approximation to such "thinking" is really an approach to the method of escape and self-delusion just referred to. It substitutes an emotionally agreeable and rationally self-consistent train of meanings for inquiry into the features of the situation which cause the trouble. It leads to that type of Idealism which has well been termed intellectual somnambulism. It creates a class of "thinkers" who are remote from practice and hence from testing their thought by application—a socially superior and irresponsible class. This is the condition causing the tragic division of theory and practice, and leading to an unreasonable exaltation of theory on one side and an unreasonable contempt for it on the other. It confirms current practice in its hard brutalities and dead routines just because it has transferred thinking and theory to a separate and nobler region. Thus has the idealist conspired with the materialist to keep actual life impoverished and inequitable.

The isolation of thinking from confrontation with facts encourages that kind of observation which merely accumulates brute facts, which occupies itself laboriously with mere details, but never inquires into their meaning and consequences—a safe occupation, for it never contemplates any use to be made of the observed facts in determining a plan for changing the situation. Thinking which is a method of reconstructing experience treats observation of facts, on the other hand, as the indispensable step of defining the problem, of locating the trouble, of forcing home a definite, instead of a merely vague emotional, sense of what the difficulty is and where it lies. It is not aimless, random, miscellaneous, but purposeful, specific and limited by the character of the trouble undergone. The purpose is so to clarify the disturbed and confused situation that reasonable ways of dealing with it may be suggested. When the scientific man appears to observe aimlessly, it is merely that he is so in love with problems as sources and guides of inquiry, that he is striving to turn up a problem where none appears on the surface: he is, as we say, hunting for trouble because of the satisfaction to be had in coping with it.

Specific and wide observation of concrete fact always, then, corresponds not only with a sense of a problem or difficulty, but with some vague sense of the *meaning* of the difficulty, that is, of what it imports or signifies in subsequent experience. It is a kind of anticipation or prediction of what is coming. We speak, very truly, of *impending* trouble, and in observing the signs of what the trouble is, we are at the same time expecting, forecasting—in short, framing an *idea*, becoming aware of meaning. When the trouble is not only impending but completely actual and present, we are overwhelmed. We do not think, but give way to depression. The kind of trouble that occasions thinking is that which is incomplete and developing, and where what is found already in existence can be employed as a sign from which to infer what is likely to come. When we intelligently observe, we are, as we say apprehensive, as well as apprehending. We are on the alert for something still to come. Curiosity, inquiry, investigation, are directed quite as truly into what is going to happen next as into what has happened. An intelligent interest in the latter is an interest in getting evidence, indications, symptoms for inferring the former. Observation is diagnosis and diagnosis implies an interest in anticipation and preparation. It makes ready in advance an attitude of response so that we shall not be caught unawares.

That which is not already in existence, that which is only anticipated and inferred, cannot be observed. It does not have the status of fact, of something given, a datum, but of a meaning, an idea. So far as ideas are not fancies, framed by emotionalized memory for escape and refuge, they are precisely anticipations of something still to come aroused by looking into the facts of a developing situation. The blacksmith watches his iron, its color and texture, to get evidence of what it is getting ready to pass into; the physician observes his patient to detect symptoms of change in some definite direction; the scientific man keeps his attention upon his laboratory material to get a clue as to what *will* happen under certain conditions. The very fact that observation is not an end in itself but a search for evidence and signs shows that along with observation goes inference, anticipatory forecast —in short an idea, thought or conception.

In a more technical context, it would be worth while to see what light this logical correspondence of observed fact and projected idea or meaning throws upon certain traditional philosophical problems and puzzles, including that of subject and predicate in judgment, object and subject in knowledge, "real" and "ideal" generally. But at this time, we must confine ourselves to pointing out that this view of the correlative origin and function of observed fact and projected idea in experience, commits us to some very important consequences concerning the nature of ideas, meanings, conceptions, or whatever word may be employed to denote the specifically *mental* function. Because they are suggestions of something that may happen or eventuate, they are (as we saw in the case of ideals generally) platforms of response to what is going on. The man who detects that the cause of his difficulty is an automobile bearing down upon him is not guaranteed safety; he may have made his observation-forecast too late. But if his anticipation-perception comes in season, he has the basis for doing something which will avert threatening disaster. Because he foresees an impending result, he may do something that will lead to the situation eventuating in some other way. All intelligent thinking means an increment of freedom in action—an emancipation from chance and fatality. "Thought" represents the suggestion of a way of response that is different from that which would have been followed if intelligent observation had not effected an inference as to the future.

Now a method of action, a mode of response, intended to produce a certain result—that is, to enable the blacksmith to

give a certain form to his hot iron, the physician to treat the
patient so as to facilitate recovery, the scientific experimenter
to draw a conclusion which will apply to other cases,—is by
the nature of the case tentative, uncertain till tested by its results. The significance of this fact for the theory of truth will
be discussed below. Here it is enough to note that notions,
theories, systems, no matter how elaborate and self-consistent
they are, must be regarded as hypotheses. They are to be accepted as bases of actions which test them, not as finalities.
To perceive this fact is to abolish rigid dogmas from the
world. It is to recognize that conceptions, theories and systems of thought are always open to development through use.
It is to enforce the lesson that we must be on the lookout
quite as much for indications to alter them as for opportunities to assert them. They are tools. As in the case of all tools,
their value resides not in themselves but in their capacity to
work shown in the consequences of their use.

Nevertheless, inquiry is free only when the interest in
knowing is so developed that thinking carries with it something worth while for itself, something having its own esthetic and moral interest. Just because knowing is not self-
enclosed and final but is instrumental to reconstruction of
situations, there is always danger that it will be subordinated
to maintaining some preconceived purpose or prejudice.
Then reflection ceases to be complete; it falls short. Being
precommitted to arriving at some special result, it is not sincere. It is one thing to say that all knowing has an end beyond itself, and another thing, a thing of a contrary kind, to
say that an act of knowing has a particular end which it is
bound, in advance, to reach. Much less is it true that the instrumental nature of thinking means that it exists for the sake
of attaining some private, one-sided advantage upon which
one has set one's heart. Any limitation whatever of the end
means limitation in the thinking process itself. It signifies that
it does not attain its full growth and movement, but is
cramped, impeded, interfered with. The only situation in

which knowing is fully stimulated is one in which the end is developed in the process of inquiry and testing.

Disinterested and impartial inquiry is then far from meaning that knowing is self-enclosed and irresponsible. It means that there is no particular end set up in advance so as to shut in the activities of observation, forming of ideas, and application. Inquiry is emancipated. It is encouraged to attend to every fact that is relevant to defining the problem or need, and to follow up every suggestion that promises a clue. The barriers to free inquiry are so many and so solid that mankind is to be congratulated that the very act of investigation is capable of itself becoming a delightful and absorbing pursuit, capable of enlisting on its side man's sporting instincts.

Just in the degree in which thought ceases to be held down to ends fixed by social custom, a social division of labor grows up. Investigation has become a dominant life occupation for some persons. Only superficially, however, does this confirm the idea that theory and knowledge are ends in themselves. They are, relatively speaking, ends in themselves for some persons. But these persons represent a social division of labor; and their specialization can be trusted only when such persons are in unobstructed co-operation with other social occupations, sensitive to others' problems and transmitting results to them for wider application in action. When this social relationship of persons particularly engaged in carrying on the enterprise of knowing is forgotten and the class becomes isolated, inquiry loses stimulus and purpose. It degenerates into sterile specialization, a kind of intellectual busy work carried on by socially absent-minded men. Details are heaped up in the name of science, and abstruse dialectical developments of systems occur. Then the occupation is "rationalized" under the lofty name of devotion to truth for its own sake. But when the path of true science is retaken these things are brushed aside and forgotten. They turn out to have been the toyings of vain and irresponsible men. The only guarantee of impartial, disinterested inquiry is the social sensitiveness of the inquirer to the needs and problems of those with whom he is associated.

As the instrumental theory is favorable to high esteem for impartial and disinterested inquiry, so, contrary to the impressions of some critics, it sets much store upon the apparatus of deduction. It is a strange notion that because one says that the cognitive value of conceptions, definitions, generalizations, classifications and the development of consecutive implications is not self-resident, that therefore one makes light of the deductive function, or denies its fruitfulness and necessity. The instrumental theory only attempts to state with some scrupulousness *where* the value is found and to prevent its being sought in the wrong place. It says that knowing begins with specific observations that define the problem and ends with specific observations that test a hypothesis for its solution. But that the idea, the meaning, which the original observations suggest and the final ones test, itself requires careful scrutiny and prolonged development, the theory would be the last to deny. To say that a locomotive is an agency, that it is intermediate between a need in experience and its satisfaction, is not to depreciate the worth of careful and elaborate construction of the locomotive, or the need of subsidiary tools and processes that are devoted to introducing improvements into its structure. One would rather say that *because* the locomotive is intermediary in experience, not primary and not final, it is impossible to devote too much care to its constructive development.

Such a deductive science as mathematics represents the perfecting of method. That a method to those concerned with it should present itself as an end on its own account is no more surprising than that there should be a distinct business for making any tool. Rarely are those who invent and perfect a tool those who employ it. There is, indeed, one marked difference between the physical and the intellectual instrumentality. The development of the latter runs far beyond any immediately visible use. The artistic interest in perfecting the method by itself is strong—as the utensils of civilization may themselves become works of finest art. But from the practical standpoint this difference shows that the advantage as an instrumentality is on the side of the intellectual tool. Just because it is not formed with a special application in mind, because it is a highly generalized tool, it is the more flexible in adaptation to unforeseen uses. It can be employed in dealing with problems that were not anticipated. The mind is prepared in advance for all sorts of intellectual emergencies, and when the new problem occurs it does not have to wait till it can get a special instrument ready.

More definitely, abstraction is indispensable if one experience is to be applicable in other experiences. Every concrete experience in its totality is unique; it is itself, non-reduplicable. Taken in its full concreteness, it yields no instruction, it throws no light. What is called abstraction means that some phase of it is selected for the sake of the aid it gives in grasping something else. Taken by itself, it is a mangled fragment, a poor substitute for the living whole from which it is extracted. But viewed teleologically or practically, it represents the only way in which one experience can be made of any value for another—the only way in which something enlightening can be secured. What is called false or vicious abstractionism signifies that the *function* of the detached fragment is forgotten and neglected, so that it is esteemed barely in itself as something of a higher order than the muddy and irregular concrete from which it was wrenched. Looked at functionally, not structurally and statically, abstraction means that something has been released from one experience for transfer to another. Abstraction is liberation. The more theoretical, the more abstract, an abstraction, or the farther away it is from anything experienced in its concreteness, the better fitted it is to deal with any one of the indefinite variety of things that may later present themselves. Ancient mathematics and physics were much nearer the gross concrete experience than are modern. For that very reason they were more impotent in affording any insight into and control over such concretes as present themselves in new and unexpected forms.

Abstraction and generalization have always been recognized as close kin. It may be said that they are the negative and positive sides of the same function. Abstraction sets free some factor so that it may be used. Generalization is the use. It carries over and extends. It is always in some sense a leap in the dark. It is an adventure. There can be no assurance in advance that what is extracted from one concrete can be fruitfully extended to another individual case. Since these other cases are individual and concrete they *must* be dissimilar. The trait of flying is detached from the concrete bird. This abstraction is then carried over to the bat, and it is expected in view of the application of the quality to have some of the other traits of the bird. This trivial instance indicates the essence of generalization, and also illustrates the riskiness of the proceeding. It transfers, extends, applies, a result of some former experience to the reception and interpretation of a new one. Deductive processes define, delimit, purify and set in order the conceptions through which this enriching and directive operation is carried on, but they cannot, however perfect, guarantee the outcome. . . .

Little time is left to speak of the account of the nature of truth given by the experimental and functional type of logic. This is less to be regretted because this account is completely a corollary from the nature of thinking and ideas. If the view held as to the latter is understood, the conception of truth follows as a matter of course. If it be not understood, any attempt to present the theory of truth is bound to be confusing, and the theory itself to seem arbitrary and absurd. *If* ideas, meanings, conceptions, notions, theories, systems are instrumental to an active reorganization of the given environment, to a removal of some specific trouble and perplexity, then the test of their validity and value lies in accomplishing this work. If they succeed in their office, they are reliable, sound,

valid, good, true. If they fail to clear up confusion, to elimi-
nate defects, if they increase confusion, uncertainty and evil
when they are acted upon, then are they false. Confirmation,
corroboration, verification lie in works, consequences. Handsome is that handsome does. By their fruits shall ye *know*
them. That which guides us truly is true—demonstrated capacity for such guidance is precisely what is meant by truth.
The adverb "truly" is more fundamental than either the
adjective, true, or the noun, truth. An adverb expresses a
way, a mode of acting. Now an idea or conception is a claim
or injunction or plan to *act* in a certain way as the way to arrive at the clearing up of a specific situation. When the claim
or pretension or plan is acted upon *it guides us truly or
falsely;* it leads us to our end or away from it. Its active, dynamic function is the all-important thing about it, and in the
quality of activity induced by it lies all its truth and falsity.
The hypothesis that works is the *true* one; and *truth* is an abstract noun applied to the collection of cases, actual, foreseen
and desired, that receive confirmation in their works and
consequences.

So wholly does the worth of this conception of truth depend upon the correctness of the prior account of thinking
that it is more profitable to consider why the conception
gives offence than to expound it on its own account. Part of
the reason why it has been found so obnoxious is doubtless its
novelty and defects in its statement. Too often, for example,
when truth has been thought of as satisfaction, it has been
thought of as merely emotional satisfaction, a private comfort, a meeting of purely personal need. But the satisfaction
in question means a satisfaction of the needs and conditions
of the problem out of which the idea, the purpose and
method of action, arises. It includes public and objective conditions. It is not to be manipulated by whim or personal idio-
syncrasy. Again when truth is defined as utility, it is often
thought to mean utility for some purely personal end, some
profit upon which a particular individual has set his heart. So

repulsive is a conception of truth which makes it a mere tool of private ambition and aggrandizement, that the wonder is that critics have attributed such a notion to sane men. As matter of fact, truth as utility means service in making just that contribution to reorganization in experience that the idea or theory claims to be able to make. The usefulness of a road is not measured by the degree in which it lends itself to the purposes of a highwayman. It is measured by whether it actually functions *as* a road, as a means of easy and effective public transportation and communication. And so with the serviceableness of an idea or hypothesis as a measure of its truth.

Turning from such rather superficial misunderstandings, we find, I think, the chief obstacle to the reception of this notion of truth in an inheritance from the classic tradition that has become so deeply engrained in men's minds. In just the degree in which existence is divided into two realms, a higher one of perfect being and a lower one of seeming, phenomenal, deficient reality, truth and falsity are thought of as fixed, ready-made static properties of things themselves. Supreme Reality is true Being, inferior and imperfect Reality is false Being. It makes claims to Reality which it cannot substantiate. It is deceitful, fraudulent, inherently unworthy of trust and belief. Beliefs are false not because they mislead us; they are not mistaken ways of thinking. They are false because they admit and adhere to false existences or subsistences. Other notions are true because they do have to do with true Being—with full and ultimate Reality. Such a notion lies at the back of the head of every one who has, in however an indirect way, been a recipient of the ancient and medieval tradition. This view is radically challenged by the pragmatic conception of truth, and the impossibility of reconciliation or compromise is, I think, the cause of the shock occasioned by the newer theory.

This contrast, however, constitutes the importance of the new theory as well as the unconscious obstruction to its acceptance. The older conception worked out practically to identify truth with authoritative dogma. A society that chiefly esteems order, that finds growth painful and change disturbing, inevitably seeks for a fixed body of superior truths upon which it may depend. It looks backward, to something already in existence, for the source and sanction of truth. It falls back upon what is antecedent, prior, original, *a priori*, for assurance. The thought of looking ahead, toward the eventual, toward consequences, creates uneasiness and fear. It disturbs the sense of rest that is attached to the ideas of fixed Truth already in existence. It puts a heavy burden of responsibility upon us for search, unremitting observation, scrupulous development of hypotheses and thoroughgoing testing. In physical matters men have slowly grown accustomed in all specific beliefs to identifying the true with the verified. But they still hesitate to recognize the implication of this identification and to derive the definition of truth from it. For while it is nominally agreed upon as a commonplace that definitions ought to spring from concrete and specific cases rather than be invented in the empty air and imposed upon particulars, there is a strange unwillingness to act upon the maxim in defining truth. To generalize the recognition that the true means the verified and means nothing else places upon men the responsibility for surrendering political and moral dogmas, and subjecting to the test of consequences their most cherished prejudices. Such a change involves a great change in the seat of authority and the methods of decision in society.

Reconstruction in Philosophy [2]

It has been noted that human experience is made human through the existence of associations and recollections, which are strained through the mesh of imagination so as to suit the

[2] This selection is from *Reconstruction in Philosophy*, pp. 103–31.

demands of the emotions. A life that is humanly interesting is, short of the results of discipline, a life in which the tedium of vacant leisure is filled with images that excite and satisfy. It is in this sense that poetry preceded prose in human experience, religion antedated science, and ornamental and decorative art while it could not take the place of utility early reached a development out of proportion to the practical arts. In order to give contentment and delight, in order to feed present emotion and give the stream of conscious life intensity and color, the suggestions which spring from past experiences are worked over so as to smooth out their unpleasantnesses and enhance their enjoyableness. Some psychologists claim that there is what they call a natural tendency to obliviscence of the disagreeable—that men turn from the unpleasant in thought and recollection as they do from the obnoxious in action. Every serious-minded person knows that a large part of the effort required in moral discipline consists in the courage needed to acknowledge the unpleasant consequences of one's past and present acts. We squirm, dodge, evade, disguise, cover up, find excuses and palliations—anything to render the mental scene less uncongenial. In short, the tendency of spontaneous suggestion is to idealize experience, to give it in consciousness qualities which it does not have in actuality. Time and memory are true artists; they remould reality nearer to the heart's desire.

As imagination becomes freer and less controlled by concrete actualities, the idealizing tendency takes further flights unrestrained by the rein of the prosaic world. The things most emphasized in imagination as it reshapes experience are things which are absent in reality. In the degree in which life is placid and easy, imagination is sluggish and bovine. In the degree in which life is uneasy and troubled, fancy is stirred to frame pictures of a contrary state of things. By reading the characteristic features of any man's castles in the air you can make a shrewd guess as to his underlying desires which are frustrated. What is difficulty and disappointment in real life becomes conspicuous achievement and triumph in revery; what is negative in fact will be positive in the image drawn by fancy; what is vexation in conduct will be compensated for in high relief in idealizing imagination.

These considerations apply beyond mere personal psychology. They are decisive for one of the most marked traits of classic philosophy:—its conception of an ultimate supreme Reality which is essentially ideal in nature. Historians have more than once drawn an instructive parallel between the developed Olympian Pantheon of Greek religion and the Ideal Realm of Platonic philosophy. The gods, whatever their origin and original traits, became idealized projections of the selected and matured achievements which the Greeks admired among their mortal selves. The gods were like mortals, but mortals living only the lives which men would wish to live, with power intensified, beauty perfected, and wisdom ripened. When Aristotle criticized the theory of Ideas of his master, Plato, by saying that the Ideas were after all only things of sense eternalized, he pointed out in effect the parallelism of philosophy with religion and art to which allusion has just been made. And save for matters of merely technical import, is it not possible to say of Aristotle's Forms just what he said of Plato's Ideas? What are they, these Forms and Essences which so profoundly influenced for centuries the course of science and theology, save the objects of ordinary experience with their blemishes removed, their imperfections eliminated, their lacks rounded out, their suggestions and hints fulfilled? What are they in short but the objects of familiar life divinized because reshaped by the idealizing imagination to meet the demands of desire in just those respects in which actual experience is disappointing?

That Plato, and Aristotle in somewhat different fashion, and Plotinus and Marcus Aurelius and Saint Thomas Aquinas, and Spinoza and Hegel all taught that Ultimate Reality is either perfectly Ideal and Rational in nature, or else has absolute ideality and rationality as its necessary attribute, are facts well known to the student of philosophy. They need no exposition here. But it is worth pointing out that these great systematic philosophies defined perfect Ideality in conceptions that express the opposite of those things which make life unsatisfactory and troublesome. What is the chief source of the complaint of poet and moralist with the goods, the values and satisfactions of experience? Rarely is the complaint that such things do not exist; it is that although existing they are momentary, transient, fleeting. They do not stay; at worst they come only to annoy and tease with their hurried and disappearing taste of what might be; at best they come only to inspire and instruct with a passing hint of truer reality. This commonplace of the poet and moralist as to the impermanence not only of sensuous enjoyment, but of fame and civic achievements was profoundly reflected upon by philosophers, especially by Plato and Aristotle. The results of their thinking have been wrought into the very fabric of western ideas. Time, change, movement are signs that what the Greeks called Non-Being somehow infect true Being. The phraseology is now strange, but many a modern who ridicules the conception of Non-Being repeats the same thought under the name of the Finite or Imperfect.

Wherever there is change, there is instability, and instability is proof of something the matter, of absence, deficiency, incompleteness. These are the ideas common to the connection between change, becoming and perishing, and Non-Being, finitude and imperfection. Hence complete and true Reality must be changeless, unalterable, so full of Being that it always and forever maintains itself in fixed rest and repose. As Bradley, the most dialectically ingenious Absolutist of our own day, expresses the doctrine "Nothing that is perfectly real moves." And while Plato took, comparatively speaking, a pessimistic view of change as mere lapse and Aristotle a complacent view of it as tendency to realization, yet Aristotle doubted no more than Plato that the fully realized reality, the divine and ultimate, is changeless. Though it is called Activity or Energy, the Activity knew no change, the energy did nothing. It was the activity of an army forever marking time and never going anywhere.

From this contrast of the permanent with the transient arise other features which mark off the Ultimate Reality from the imperfect realities of practical life. Where there is change, there is of necessity numerical plurality, multiplicity, and from variety comes opposition, strife. Change is alteration, or "othering" and this means diversity. Diversity means division, and division means two sides and their conflict. The world which is transient *must* be a world of discord, for in lacking stability it lacks the government of unity. Did unity completely rule, these would remain an unchanging totality. What alters has parts and partialities which, not recognizing the rule of unity, assert themselves independently and make life a scene of contention and discord. Ultimate and true Being on the other hand, since it is changeless is Total, All-Comprehensive and One. Since it is One, it knows only harmony, and therefore enjoys complete and eternal Good. It *is* Perfection.

Degrees of knowledge and truth correspond with degrees of reality point by point. The higher and more complete the Reality the truer and more important the knowledge that refers to it. Since the world of becoming, of origins and perishings, is deficient in true Being, it cannot be known in the best sense. To know it means to neglect its flux and alteration and discover some permanent form which limits the processes that alter in time. The acorn undergoes a series of changes; these are knowable only in reference to the fixed form of the oak which is the same in the entire oak species in spite of the numerical diversity of trees. Moreover, this form limits the flux of growth at both ends, the acorn coming from the oak as well as passing into it. Where such unifying and limiting eternal forms cannot be detected, there is mere aimless variation and fluctuation, and knowledge is out of the question. On the other hand, as objects are approached in which there is no movement at all, knowledge becomes really demonstrative, certain, perfect—truth pure and unalloyed. The heavens can be more truly known than the earth, God the unmoved mover than the heavens.

From this fact follows the superiority of contemplative to practical knowledge, of pure theoretical speculation to experimentation, and to any kind of knowing that depends upon changes in things or that induces change in them. Pure knowing is pure beholding, viewing, noting. It is complete in itself. It looks for nothing beyond itself; it lacks nothing and hence has no aim or purpose. It is most emphatically its own excuse for being. Indeed, pure contemplative knowing is so much the most truly self-enclosed and self-sufficient thing in the universe that it is the highest and indeed the only attribute that can be ascribed to God, the Highest Being in the scale of Being. Man himself is divine in the rare moments when he attains to purely self-sufficient theoretical insight.

In contrast with such knowing, the so-called knowing of the artisan is base. He has to bring about changes in things, in wood and stone, and this fact is of itself evidence that his material is deficient in Being. What condemns his knowledge even more is the fact that it is not disinterestedly for its own sake. It has reference to results to be attained, food, clothing, shelter, etc. It is concerned with things that perish, the body and its needs. It thus has an ulterior aim, and one which itself testifies to imperfection. For want, desire, affection of every sort, indicate lack. Where there is need and desire—as in the case of all practical knowledge and activity—there is incompleteness and insufficiency. While civic or political and moral knowledge rank higher than do the conceptions of the artisan, yet intrinsically considered they are a low and untrue type. Moral and political action is practical; that is, it implies needs and effort to satisfy them. It has an end beyond itself. Moreover, the very fact of association shows lack of self-sufficiency; it shows dependence upon others. Pure knowing is alone solitary, and capable of being carried on in complete, self-sufficing independence.

In short, the measure of the worth of knowledge according to Aristotle, whose views are here summarized, is the degree in which it is purely contemplative. The highest degree is attained in knowing ultimate Ideal Being, pure Mind. This is Ideal, the Form of Forms, because it has no lacks, no needs, and experiences no change or variety. It has no desires because in it all desires are consummated. Since it is perfect Being, it is perfect Mind and perfect Bliss;—the acme of rationality and ideality. One point more and the argument is completed. The kind of knowing that concerns itself with this ultimate reality (which is also ultimate ideality) is philosophy. Philosophy is therefore the last and highest term in pure contemplation. Whatever may be said for any other kind of knowledge, philosophy is self-enclosed. It has nothing to do beyond itself; it has no aim or purpose or function—except to be philosophy—that is, pure, self-sufficing beholding of ultimate reality. There is of course such a thing as philosophic *study* which falls short of this perfection. Where there is learning, there is change and becoming. But the function of study and learning of philosophy is, as Plato put it, to convert the eye of the soul from dwelling contentedly upon the images of things, upon the inferior realities that are born and that decay, and to lead it to the intuition of supernal and eternal Being. Thus the mind of the knower is transformed. It becomes assimilated to what it knows.

Through a variety of channels, especially Neo-Platonism and St. Augustine, these ideas found their way into Christian theology; and great scholastic thinkers taught that the end of man is to know True Being, that knowledge is contemplative, that True Being is pure Immaterial Mind, and to know it is Bliss and Salvation. While this knowledge cannot be achieved in this stage of life nor without supernatural aid, yet so far as it is accomplished it assimilates the human mind to the divine essence and so constitutes salvation. Through this taking over of the conception of knowledge as Contemplative into the dominant religion of Europe, multitudes were affected who were totally innocent of theoretical philosophy. There was bequeathed to generations of thinkers as an unquestioned axiom the idea that knowledge is intrinsically a mere beholding or viewing of reality—the spectator conception of knowledge. So deeply engrained was this idea that it prevailed for centuries after the actual progress of science had demonstrated that knowledge is power to transform the world, and centuries after the practice of effective knowledge had adopted the method of experimentation.

Let us turn abruptly from this conception of the measure of true knowledge and the nature of true philosophy to the existing practice of knowledge. Nowadays if a man, say a physicist or chemist, wants to know something, the last thing he does is merely to contemplate. He does not look in however earnest and prolonged way upon the object expecting that thereby he will detect its fixed and characteristic form. He does not expect any amount of such aloof scrutiny to reveal to him any secrets. He proceeds to *do* something, to bring some energy to bear upon the substance to see how it reacts; he places it under unusual conditions in order to induce some change. While the astronomer cannot change the remote stars, even he no longer merely gazes. If he cannot change the stars themselves, he can at least by lens and prism change their light as it reaches the earth; he can lay traps for discovering changes which would otherwise escape notice. Instead of taking an antagonistic attitude toward change and denying it to the stars because of their divinity and perfection, he is on constant and alert watch to find some change through which he can form an inference as to the formation of stars and systems of stars.

Change in short is no longer looked upon as a fall from grace, as a lapse from reality or a sign of imperfection of Being. Modern science no longer tries to find some fixed form or essence behind each process of change. Rather, the experimental method tries to break down apparent fixities and to induce changes. The form that remains unchanged to sense, the form of seed or tree, is regarded not as the key to knowledge of the thing, but as a wall, an obstruction to be broken down. Consequently the scientific man experiments with this and that agency applied to this and that condition until something begins to happen; until there is, as we say, something doing. He assumes that there is change going on all the time, that there is movement within each thing in seeming repose; and that since the process is veiled from perception the way to know it is to bring the thing into novel circumstances until change becomes evident. In short, the thing which is to be accepted and paid heed to is not what is originally given but that which emerges after the thing has been set under a great variety of circumstances in order to see how it behaves.

Now this marks a much more general change in the human attitude than perhaps appears at first sight. It signifies nothing less than that the world or any part of it as it presents itself at a given time is accepted or acquiesced in only as *material* for change. It is accepted precisely as the carpenter, say, accepts things as he finds them. If he took them as things to be observed and noted for their own sake, he never would be a carpenter. He would observe, describe, record the structures, forms and changes which things exhibit to him, and leave the matter there. If perchance some of the changes going on should present him with a shelter, so much the better. But what makes the carpenter a *builder* is the fact that he notes things not just as objects in themselves, but with reference to what he wants to do to them and with them; to the end he has in mind. Fitness to effect certain special changes that he wishes to see accomplished is what concerns him in the wood and stones and iron which he observes. His attention is directed to the changes they undergo and the changes they make other things undergo so that he may select that combination of changes which will yield him his desired result. It is only by these processes of active manipulation of things in order to realize his purpose that he discovers what the properties of things are. If he forgoes his own purpose and in the name of a meek and humble subscription to things as they "really are" refuses to bend things as they "are" to his own purpose, he not only never achieves his purpose but he never learns what the things themselves are. They *are* what they can do and what can be done with them,—things that can be found by deliberate trying.

The outcome of this idea of the right way to know is a profound modification in man's attitude toward the natural world. Under differing social conditions, the older or classic conception sometimes bred resignation and submission; sometimes contempt and desire to escape; sometimes, notably in the case of the Greeks, a keen esthetic curiosity which showed itself in acute noting of all the traits of given objects. In fact, the whole conception of knowledge as beholding and noting is fundamentally an idea connected with esthetic enjoyment and appreciation where the environment is beautiful and life is serene, and with esthetic repulsion and depreciation where life is troubled, nature morose and hard. But in the degree in which the active conception of knowledge prevails, and the environment is regarded as something that has to be changed in order to be truly known, men are imbued with courage, with what may almost be termed an aggressive attitude toward nature. The latter becomes plastic, something to be subjected to human uses. The moral disposition toward change is deeply modified. This loses its pathos, it ceases to be haunted with melancholy through suggesting only decay and loss. Change becomes significant of new possibilities and ends to be attained; it becomes prophetic of a better future. Change is associated with progress rather than with lapse and fall. Since changes are going on anyway, the great thing is to learn enough about them so that we be able to lay hold of them and turn them in the direction of our desires. Conditions and events are neither to be fled from nor passively acquiesced in; they are to be utilized and directed. They are either obstacles to our ends or else means for their accomplishment. In a profound sense knowing ceases to be contemplative and becomes practical.

Unfortunately men, educated men, cultivated men in particular, are still so dominated by the older conception of an aloof and self-sufficing reason and knowledge that they refuse to perceive the import of this doctrine. They think they are sustaining the cause of impartial, thorough-going and disinterested reflection when they maintain the traditional philosophy of intellectualism—that is, of knowing as something self-sufficing and self-enclosed. But in truth, historic intellectualism, the spectator view of knowledge, is a purely compensatory doctrine which men of an intellectual turn have built up to console themselves for the actual and social impotency of the calling of thought to which they are devoted. Forbidden by conditions and held back by lack of courage from making their knowledge a factor in the determination of the course of events, they have sought a refuge of complacency in the notion that knowing is something too sublime to be contaminated by contact with things of change and practice. They have transformed knowing into a morally irresponsible estheticism. The true import of the doctrine of the operative or practical character of knowing, of intelligence, is objective. It means that the structures and objects which science and philosophy set up in contrast to the things and events of concrete daily experience do not constitute a realm apart in which rational contemplation may rest satisfied; it means that they represent the selected obstacles, material means and ideal methods of giving direction to that change which is bound to occur anyway.

This change of human disposition toward the world does not mean that man ceases to have ideals, or ceases to be primarily a creature of the imagination. But it does signify a radical change in the character and function of the ideal realm which man shapes for himself. In the classic philosophy, the ideal world is essentially a haven in which man finds rest from the storms of life; it is an asylum in which he takes refuge from the troubles of existence with the calm assurance that it alone is supremely real. When the belief that knowledge is active and operative takes hold of men, the ideal realm is no longer something aloof and separate; it is rather that collection of imagined possibilities that stimulates men to new efforts and realizations. It still remains true that the troubles which men undergo are the forces that lead them to project pictures of a better state of things. But the picture of the better is shaped so that it may become an instrumentality of action, while in the classic view the Idea belongs ready-made in a noumenal world. Hence, it is only an object of personal aspiration or consolation, while to the modern, an idea is a suggestion of something to be done or of a way of doing.

An illustration will, perhaps, make the difference clear. Distance is an obstacle, a source of trouble. It separates friends and prevents intercourse. It isolates, and makes contact and mutual understanding difficult. This state of affairs provokes discontent and restlessness; it excites the imagination to construct pictures of a state of things where human intercourse is not injuriously affected by space. Now there are two ways out. One way is to pass from a mere dream of some heavenly realm in which distance is abolished and by some magic all friends are in perpetual transparent communication, to pass, I say, from some idle castle-building to philosophic reflection. Space, distance, it will then be argued, is merely phenomenal; or, in a more modern version, subjective. It is not, metaphysically speaking, real. Hence the obstruction and trouble it gives is not after all "real" in the metaphysical sense of reality. Pure minds, pure spirits, do not live in a space world; for them distance is not. Their relationships in the true world are not in any way affected by special considerations. Their intercommunication is direct, fluent, unobstructed.

Does the illustration involve a caricature of ways of philosophizing with which we are all familiar? But if it is not an absurd caricature, does it not suggest that much of what philosophies have taught about the ideal and noumenal or superiorly real world, is after all, only casting a dream into an elaborate dialectic form through the use of a speciously scientific terminology? Practically, the difficulty, the trouble, remains. Practically, however it may be "metaphysically," space is still real:—it acts in a definite objectionable way. Again, man dreams of some better state of things. From troublesome fact he takes refuge in fantasy. But this time, the refuge does not remain a permanent and remote asylum.

The idea becomes a standpoint from which to examine existing occurrences and to see if there is not among them something which gives a hint of how communication at a distance can be effected, something to be utilized as a medium of speech at long range. The suggestion or fancy though still ideal is treated as a possibility capable of realization *in* the concrete natural world, not as a superior reality apart from that world. As such, it becomes a platform from which to scrutinize natural events. Observed from the point of view of this possibility, things disclose properties hitherto undetected. In the light of these ascertainments, the idea of some agency for speech at a distance becomes less vague and floating: it takes on positive form. This action and reaction goes on. The possibility or idea is employed as a method for observing actual existence; and in the light of what is discovered the possibility takes on concrete existence. It becomes less of a mere idea, a fancy, a wished-for possibility, and more of an actual fact. Invention proceeds, and at last we have the telegraph, the telephone, first through wires, and then with no artificial medium. The concrete environment is transformed in the desired direction; it is idealized in fact and not merely in fancy. The ideal is realized through its own use as a tool or method of inspection, experimentation, selection and combination of concrete natural operations.

Let us pause to take stock of results. The division of the world into two kinds of Being, one superior, accessible only to reason and ideal in nature, the other inferior, material, changeable, empirical, accessible to sense-observation, turns inevitably into the idea that knowledge is contemplative in nature. It assumes a contrast between theory and practice which was all to the disadvantage of the latter. But in the actual course of the development of science, a tremendous change has come about. When the practice of knowledge ceased to be dialectical and became experimental, knowing became preoccupied with changes and the test of knowledge became the ability to bring about certain changes. Knowing, for the experimental sciences, means a certain kind of intelligently conducted doing; it ceases to be contemplative and becomes in a true sense practical. Now this implies that philosophy, unless it is to undergo a complete break with the authorized spirit of science, must also alter its nature. It must assume a practical nature; it must become operative and experimental. And we have pointed out what an enormous change this transformation of philosophy entails in the two conceptions which have played the greatest rôle in historic philosophizing—the conceptions of the "real" and "ideal" respectively. The former ceases to be something ready-made and final; it becomes that which has to be accepted as the material of change, as the obstructions and the means of certain specific desired changes. The ideal and rational also ceased to be a separate ready-made world incapable of being used as a lever to transform the actual empirical world, a mere asylum from empirical deficiencies. They represent intelligently thought-out possibilities *of* the existent world which may be used as methods for making over and improving it.

Philosophically speaking, this is the great difference involved in the change from knowledge and philosophy as contemplative to operative. The change does not mean the lowering in dignity of philosophy from a lofty plane to one of gross utilitarianism. It signifies that the prime function of philosophy is that of rationalizing the *possibilities* of experience, especially collective human experience. The scope of this change may be realized by considering how far we are from accomplishing it. In spite of inventions which enable men to use the energies of nature for their purposes, we are still far from habitually treating knowledge as the method of active control of nature and of experience. We tend to think of it after the model of a spectator viewing a finished picture rather than after that of the artist producing the painting. Thus there arise all the questions of epistemology with which the technical student of philosophy is so familiar, and which have made modern philosophy in especial so remote from the understanding of the everyday person and from the results and processes of science. For these questions all spring from the assumption of a merely beholding mind on one side and a foreign and remote object to be viewed and noted on the other. They ask how a mind and world, subject and object, so separate and independent can by any possibility come into such relationship to each other as to make true knowledge possible. If knowing were habitually conceived of as active and operative, after the analogy of experiment guided by hypothesis, or of invention guided by the imagination of some possibility, it is not too much to say that the first effect would be to emancipate philosophy from all the epistemological puzzles which now perplex it. For these all arise from a conception of the relation of mind and world, subject and object, in knowing, which assumes that to know is to seize upon what is already in existence.

Modern philosophic thought has been so preoccupied with these puzzles of epistemology and the disputes between realist and idealist, between phenomenalist and absolutist, that many students are at a loss to know what would be left for philosophy if there were removed both the metaphysical task of distinguishing between the noumenal and phenomenal worlds and the epistemological task of telling how a separate subject can know an independent object. But would not the elimination of these traditional problems permit philosophy to devote itself to a more fruitful and more needed task? Would it not encourage philosophy to face the great social and moral defects and troubles from which humanity suffers, to concentrate its attention upon clearing up the causes and exact nature of these evils and upon developing a clear idea of better social possibilities; in short upon projecting an idea or ideal which, instead of expressing the notion of another world or some far-away unrealizable goal, would be used as a method of understanding and rectifying specific social ills?

This is a vague statement. But note in the first place that such a conception of the proper province of philosophy where it is released from vain metaphysics and idle epistemology is in line with the origin of philosophy sketched in the first hour. And in the second place, note how contemporary society, the world over, is in need of more general and fundamental enlightenment and guidance than it now possesses. I have tried to show that a radical change of the conception of knowledge from contemplative to active is the inevitable result of the way in which inquiry and invention are now conducted. But in claiming this, it must also be conceded, or rather asserted, that so far the change has influenced for the most part only the more technical side of human life. The sciences have created new industrial arts. Man's physical command of natural energies has been indefinitely multiplied. There is control of the sources of material wealth and prosperity. What would once have been miracles are now daily performed with steam and coal and electricity and air, and with the human body. But there are few persons optimistic enough to declare that any similar command of the forces which control man's social and moral welfare has been achieved.

Where is the moral progress that corresponds to our economic accomplishments? The latter is the direct fruit of the revolution that has been wrought in physical science. But where is there a corresponding human science and art? Not only has the improvement in the method of knowing remained so far mainly limited to technical and economic matters but this progress has brought with it serious new moral disturbances. I need only cite the late war, the problem of capital and labor, the relation of economic classes, the fact that while the new science has achieved wonders in medicine and surgery, it has also produced and spread occasions for diseases and weaknesses. These considerations indicate to us how undeveloped are our politics, how crude and primitive our education, how passive and inert our morals. The causes remain which brought philosophy into existence as an attempt to find an intelligent substitute for blind custom and blind impulse as guides to life and conduct. The attempt has not been successfully accomplished. Is there not reason for believing that the release of philosophy from its burden of sterile metaphysics and sterile epistemology instead of depriving philosophy of problems and subject-matter would open a way to questions of the most perplexing and the most significant sort?

Let me specify one problem quite directly suggested by certain points in this lecture. It has been pointed out that the really fruitful application of the contemplative idea was not in science but in the esthetic field. It is difficult to imagine any high development of the fine arts except where there is curious and loving interest in forms and motions of the world quite irrespective of any use to which they may be put. And it is not too much to say that every people that has attained a high esthetic development has been a people in which the contemplative attitude has flourished—as the Greek, the Hindoo, the medieval Christian. On the other hand, the scientific attitude that has actually proved itself in scientific progress is, as has been pointed out, a practical attitude. It takes forms as disguises for hidden processes. Its interest in change is in what it leads to, what can be done with it, to what use it can be put. While it has brought nature under control, there is something hard and aggressive in its attitude toward nature unfavorable to the esthetic enjoyment of the world. Surely there is no more significant question before the world than this question of the possibility and method of reconciliation of the attitudes of practical science and contemplative esthetic appreciation. Without the former, man will be the sport and victim of natural forces which he cannot use or control. Without the latter, mankind might become a race of economic monsters, restlessly driving hard bargains with nature and with one another, bored with leisure or capable of putting it to use only in ostentatious display and extravagant dissipation.

Like other moral questions, this matter is social and even political. The western peoples advanced earlier on the path of experimental science and its applications in control of nature than the oriental. It is not, I suppose wholly fanciful, to believe that the latter have embodied in their habits of life more of the contemplative, esthetic and speculatively religious temper, and the former more of the scientific, industrial and practical. This difference and others which have grown up around it is one barrier to easy mutual understanding, and one source of misunderstanding. The philosophy which, then, makes a serious effort to comprehend these respective attitudes in their relation and due balance, could hardly fail to promote the capacity of peoples to profit by one another's experience and to co-operate more effectually with one another in the tasks of fruitful culture.

Indeed, it is incredible that the question of the relation of the "real" and the "ideal" should ever have been thought to be a problem belonging distinctively to philosophy. The very fact that this most serious of all human issues has been taken possession of by philosophy is only another proof of the disasters that follow in the wake of regarding knowledge and intellect as something self-sufficient. Never have the "real" and the "ideal" been so clamorous, so self-assertive, as at the present time. And never in the history of the world have they been so far apart. The world war was carried on for purely ideal ends:—for humanity, justice and equal liberty for strong and weak alike. And it was carried on by realistic means of applied science, by high explosives, and bombing airplanes and blockading marvels of mechanism that reduced the world well nigh to ruin, so that the serious-minded are concerned for the perpetuity of those choice values we call civilization. The peace settlement is loudly proclaimed in the name of the ideals that stir man's deepest emotions, but with the most realistic attention to details of economic advantage distributed in proportion to physical power to create future disturbances.

It is not surprising that some men are brought to regard all idealism as a mere smoke-screen behind which the search for material profit may be more effectually carried on, and are converted to the materialistic interpretation of history. "Reality" is then conceived as physical force and as sensations of power, profit and enjoyment; any politics that takes account of other factors, save as elements of clever propaganda and for control of those human beings who have not become realistically enlightened, is based on illusions. But others are equally sure that the real lesson of the war is that humanity took its first great wrong step when it entered upon a cultivation of physical science and an application of the fruits of science to the improvement of the instruments of life—industry and commerce. They will sigh for the return of the day when, while the great mass died as they were born in animal fashion, the few elect devoted themselves not to science and the material decencies and comforts of existence but to "ideal" things, the things of the spirit.

Yet the most obvious conclusion would seem to be the impotency and the harmfulness of any and every ideal that is proclaimed wholesale and in the abstract, that is, as something in itself apart from the detailed concrete existences whose moving possibilities it embodies. The true moral would seem to lie in enforcing the tragedy of that idealism which believes in a spiritual world which exists in and by itself, and the tragic need for the most realistic study of forces and consequences, a study conducted in a more scientifically accurate and complete manner than that of the professed *Real-politik*. For it is not truly realistic or scientific to take short views, to sacrifice the future to immediate pressure, to ignore facts and forces that are disagreeable and to magnify the enduring quality of whatever falls in with immediate desire. It is false that the evils of the situation arise from absence of ideals; they spring from wrong ideals. And these wrong ideals have in turn their foundation in the absence in social matters of that methodic, systematic, impartial, critical, searching inquiry into "real" and operative conditions which we call science and which has brought man in the technical realm to the command of physical energies.

Philosophy, let it be repeated, cannot "solve" the problem of the relation of the ideal and the real. That is the standing problem of life. But it can at least lighten the burden of humanity in dealing with the problem by emancipating mankind from the errors which philosophy has itself fostered—the existence of conditions which are real apart from their movement into something new and different, and the existence of ideals, spirit and reason independent of the possibilities of the material and physical. For as long as humanity is committed to this radically false bias, it will walk forward with blinded eyes and bound limbs. And philosophy can effect, if it will, something more than this negative task. It can make it easier for mankind to take the right steps in action by making it clear that a sympathetic and integral intelligence brought to bear upon the observation and understanding of concrete social events and forces, can form ideals, that is aims, which shall not be either illusions or mere emotional compensations.